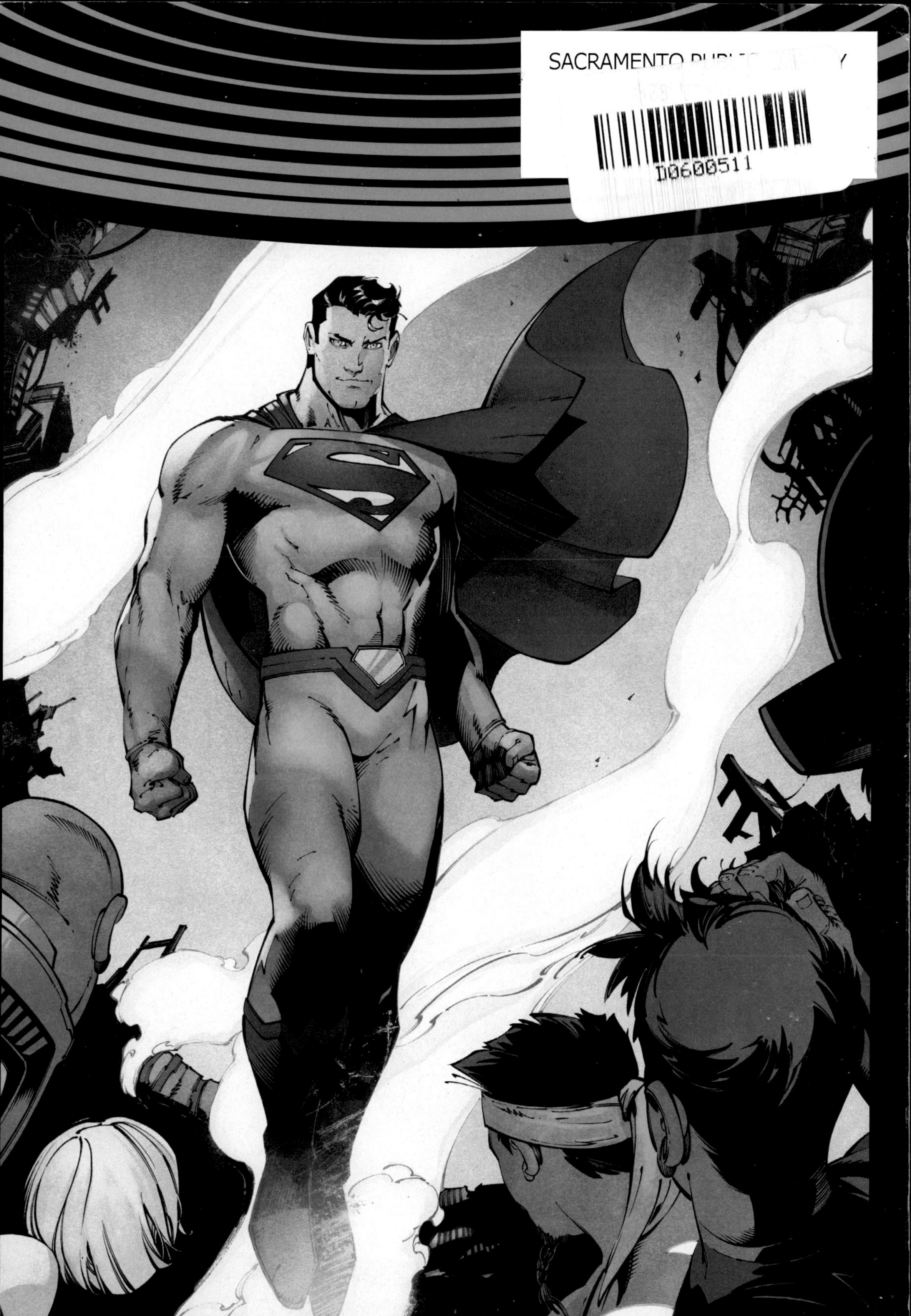

NEW SUPER-MAN

VOL.2 COMING TO AMERICA

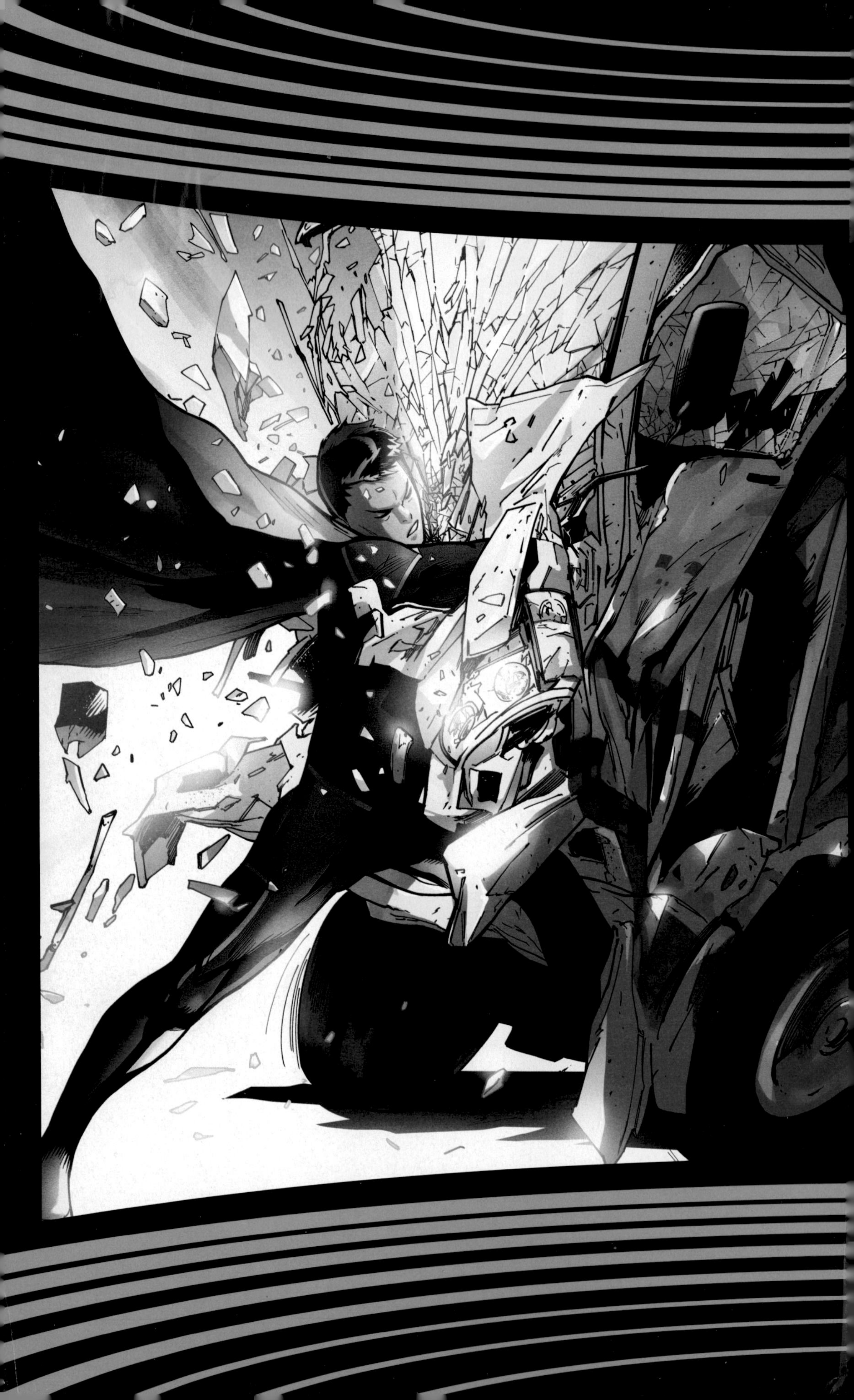

NEW SUPER-MAN

VOL.2 COMING TO AMERICA

GENE LUEN YANG
writer

BILLY TAN
VIKTOR BOGDANOVIC
pencillers

YANQIU LI
HAINING
JONATHAN GLAPION
VIKTOR BOGDANOVIC
TAKO ZHANG
inkers

YANFENG GUO
MIKE SPICER
YING ZHAN
GADSON
colorists

DAVE SHARPE
letterer

VIKTOR BOGDANOVIC and MIKE SPICER
collection cover artists

SUPERMAN created by **JERRY SIEGEL** and **JOE SHUSTER**
By special arrangement with the Jerry Siegel family

PAUL KAMINSKI Editor – Original Series
JEB WOODARD Group Editor – Collected Editions ＊ **ERIKA ROTHBERG** Editor – Collected Edition
STEVE COOK Design Director – Books ＊ **SHANNON STEWART** Publication Design

BOB HARRAS Senior VP – Editor-in-Chief, DC Comics
PAT McCULLUM Executive Editor, DC Comics

DIANE NELSON President ＊ **DAN DiDIO** Publisher ＊ **JIM LEE** Publisher ＊ **GEOFF JOHNS** President & Chief Creative Officer
AMIT DESAI Executive VP – Business & Marketing Strategy, Direct to Consumer & Global Franchise Management
SAM ADES Senior VP & General Manager, Digital Services ＊ **BOBBIE CHASE** VP & Executive Editor, Young Reader & Talent Development
MARK CHIARELLO Senior VP – Art, Design & Collected Editions ＊ **JOHN CUNNINGHAM** Senior VP – Sales & Trade Marketing
ANNE DePIES Senior VP – Business Strategy, Finance & Administration ＊ **DON FALLETTI** VP – Manufacturing Operations
LAWRENCE GANEM VP – Editorial Administration & Talent Relations ＊ **ALISON GILL** Senior VP – Manufacturing & Operations
HANK KANALZ Senior VP – Editorial Strategy & Administration ＊ **JAY KOGAN** VP – Legal Affairs
THOMAS LOFTUS VP – Business Affairs ＊ **JACK MAHAN** VP – Business Affairs
NICK J. NAPOLITANO VP – Manufacturing Administration ＊ **EDDIE SCANNELL** VP – Consumer Marketing
COURTNEY SIMMONS Senior VP – Publicity & Communications ＊ **JIM (SKI) SOKOLOWSKI** VP – Comic Book Specialty Sales & Trade Marketing
NANCY SPEARS VP – Mass, Book, Digital Sales & Trade Marketing ＊ **MICHELE R. WELLS** VP – Content Strategy

NEW SUPER-MAN VOL. 2: COMING TO AMERICA

Published by DC Comics. Compilation and all new material Copyright © 2017 DC Comics. All Rights Reserved.
Originally published in single magazine form in NEW SUPER-MAN 7-12. Copyright © 2017 DC Comics.
All Rights Reserved. All characters, their distinctive likenesses and related elements featured in this publication
are trademarks of DC Comics. The stories, characters and incidents featured in this publication are entirely fictional.
DC Comics does not read or accept unsolicited submissions of ideas, stories or artwork.

DC Comics, 2900 West Alameda Ave., Burbank, CA 91505.
Printed by LSC Communications, Kendallville, IN, USA. 9/1/17. First Printing.
ISBN: 978-1-4012-7390-3

Library of Congress Cataloging-in-Publication Data is available.

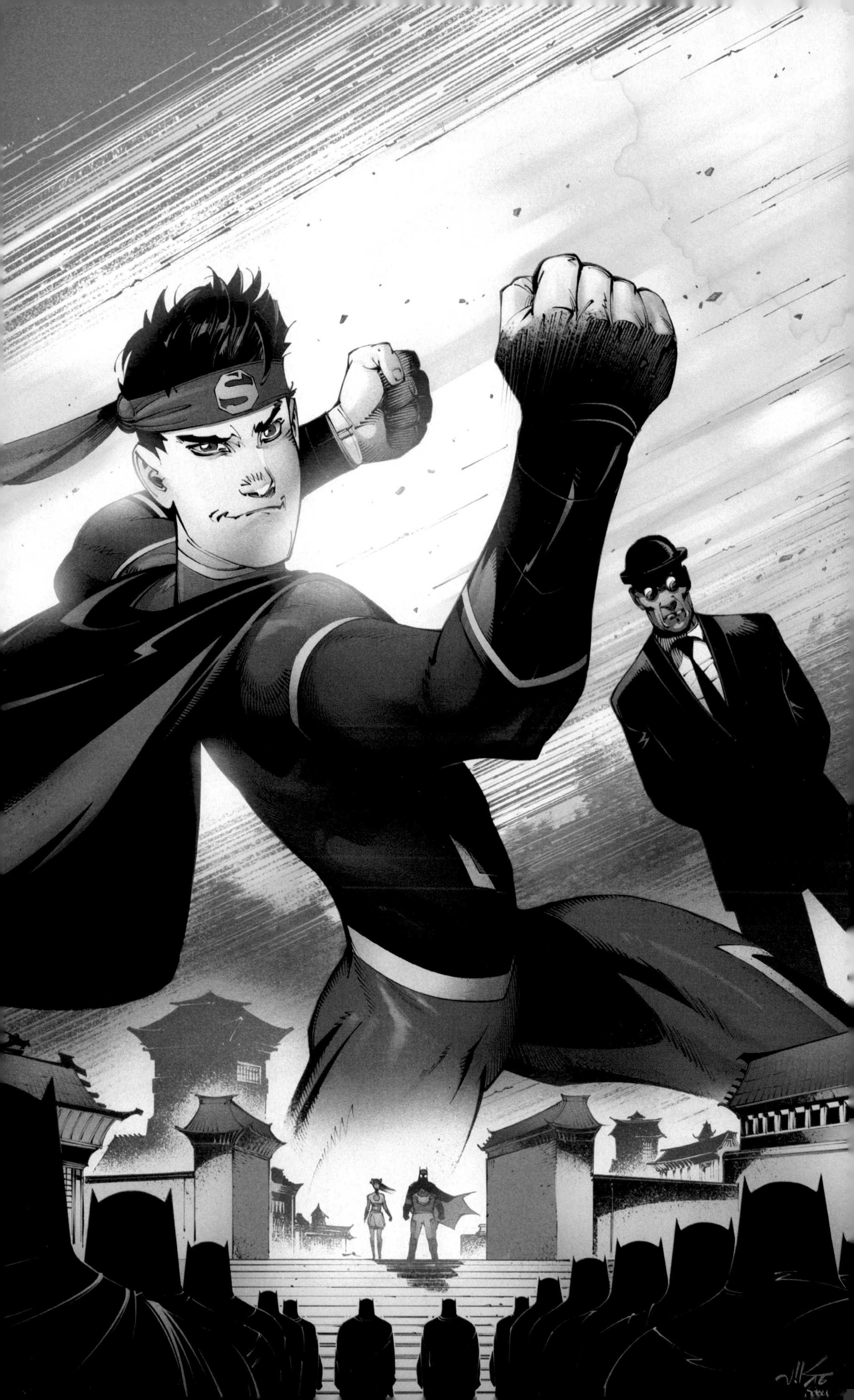

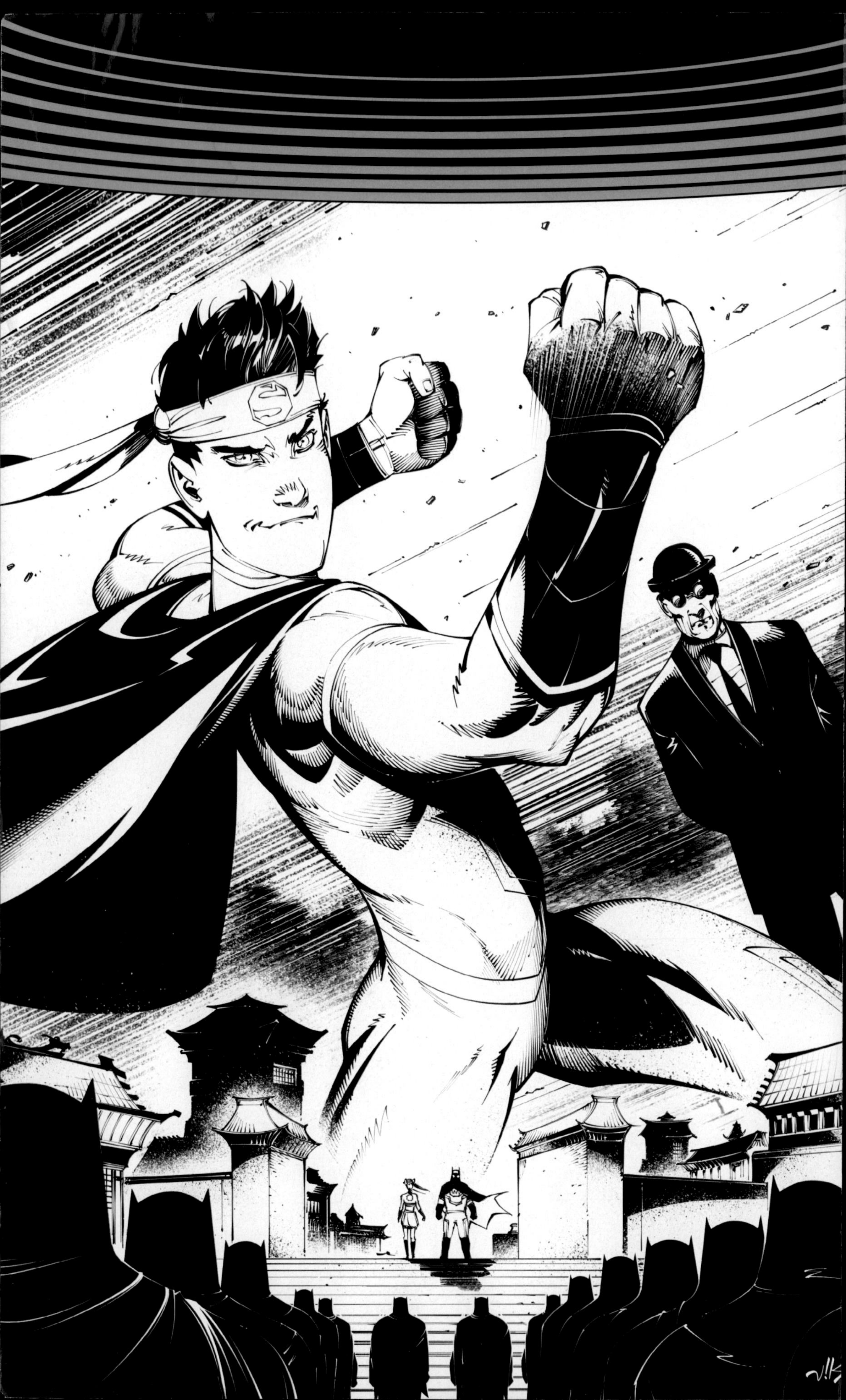

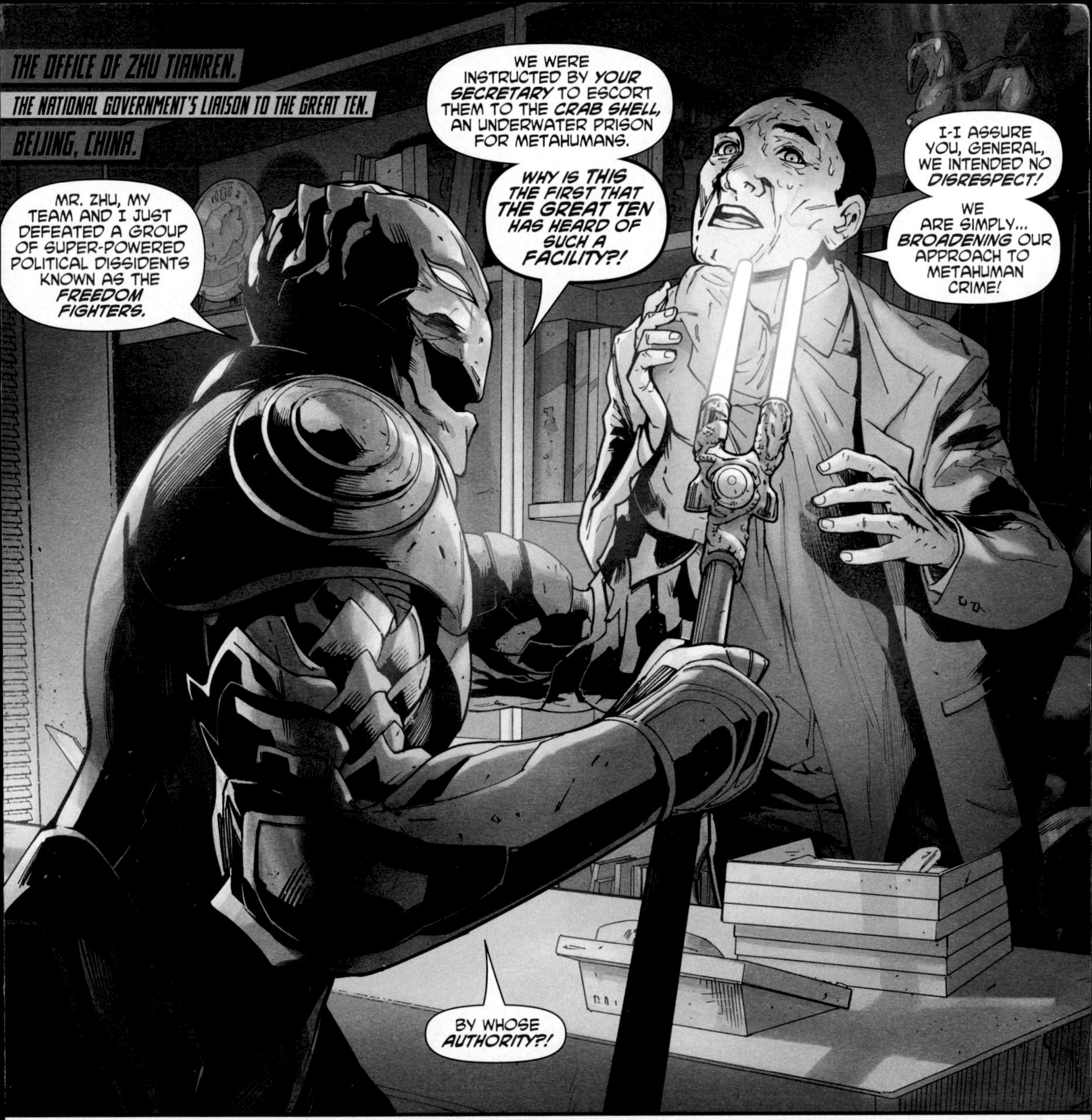
THE OFFICE OF ZHU TIANREN.
THE NATIONAL GOVERNMENT'S LIAISON TO THE GREAT TEN.
BEIJING, CHINA.
MR. ZHU, MY TEAM AND I JUST DEFEATED A GROUP OF SUPER-POWERED POLITICAL DISSIDENTS KNOWN AS THE FREEDOM FIGHTERS.
WE WERE INSTRUCTED BY YOUR SECRETARY TO ESCORT THEM TO THE CRAB SHELL, AN UNDERWATER PRISON FOR METAHUMANS.
WHY IS THIS THE FIRST THAT THE GREAT TEN HAS HEARD OF SUCH A FACILITY?!
I-I ASSURE YOU, GENERAL, WE INTENDED NO DISRESPECT!
WE ARE SIMPLY... BROADENING OUR APPROACH TO METAHUMAN CRIME!
BY WHOSE AUTHORITY?!

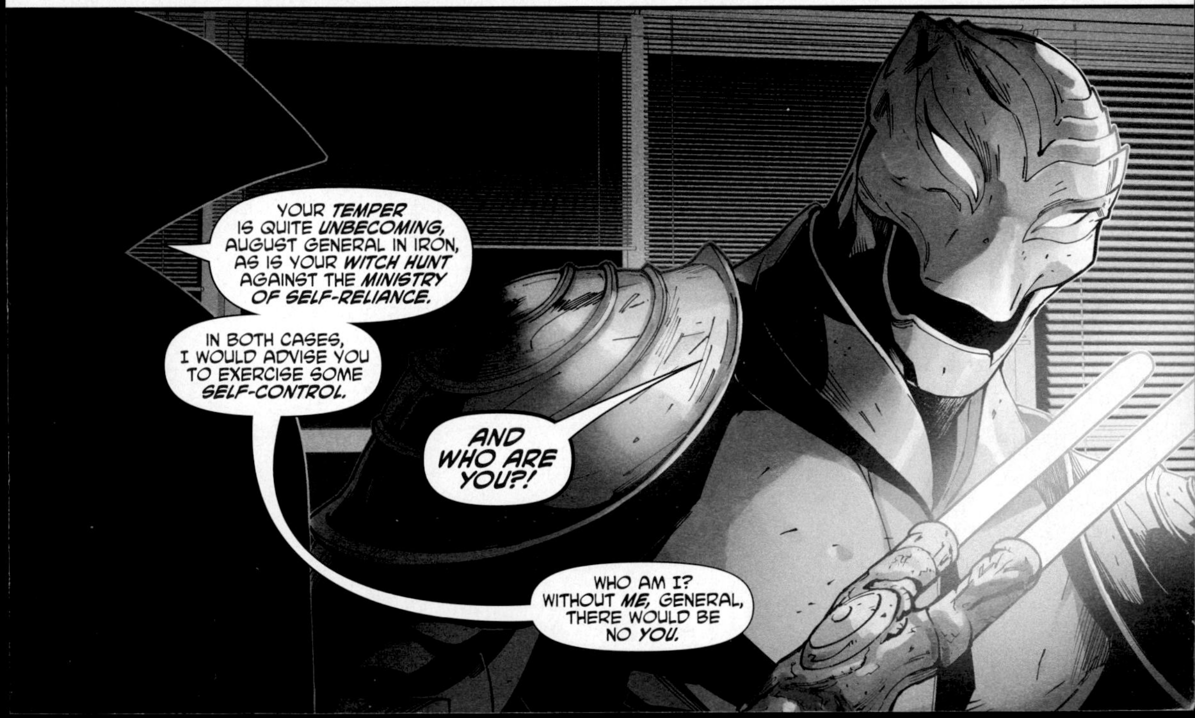
YOUR TEMPER IS QUITE UNBECOMING, AUGUST GENERAL IN IRON, AS IS YOUR WITCH HUNT AGAINST THE MINISTRY OF SELF-RELIANCE.
IN BOTH CASES, I WOULD ADVISE YOU TO EXERCISE SOME SELF-CONTROL.
AND WHO ARE YOU?!
WHO AM I? WITHOUT ME, GENERAL, THERE WOULD BE NO YOU.

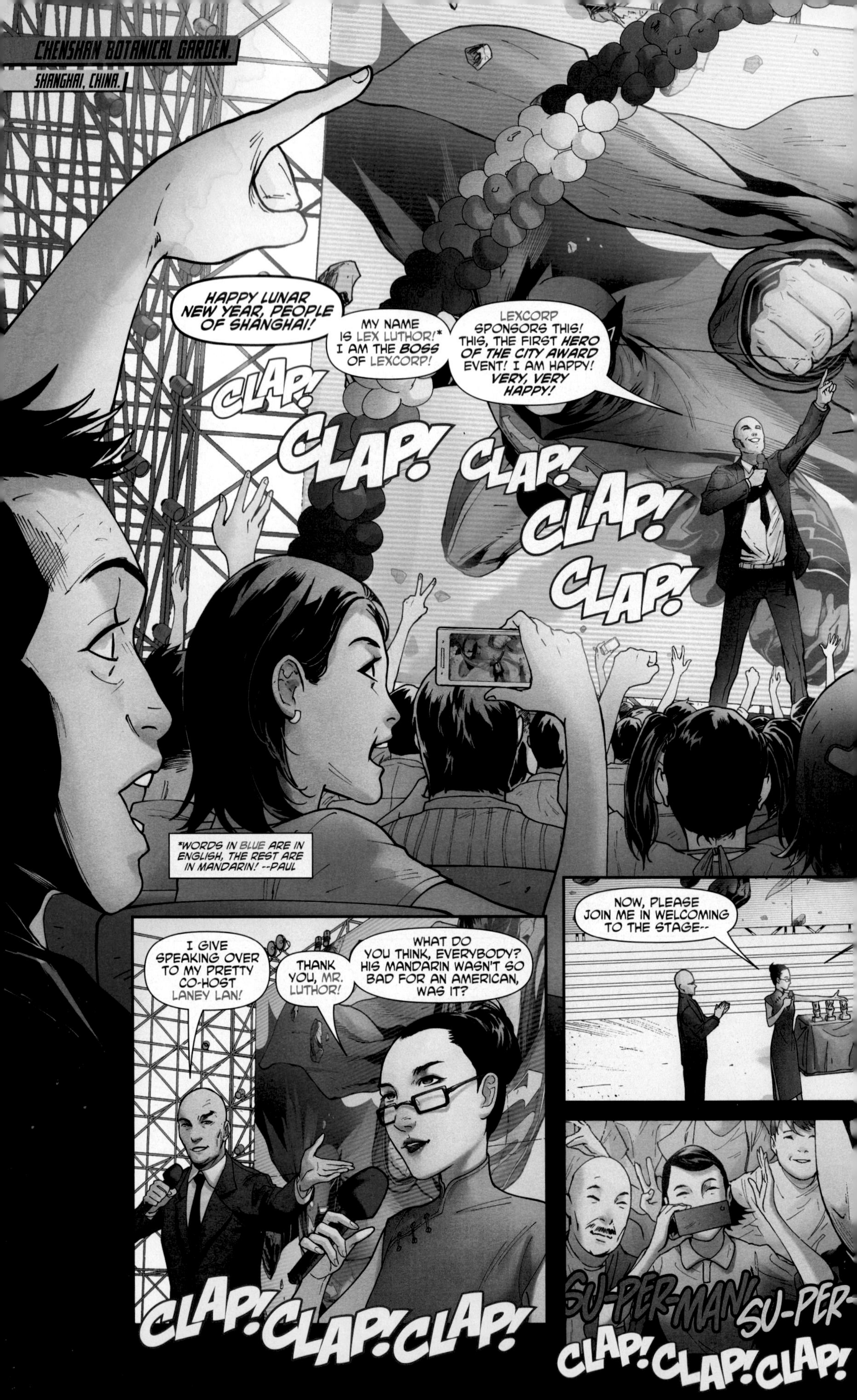
CHENSHAN BOTANICAL GARDEN.
SHANGHAI, CHINA.
HAPPY LUNAR NEW YEAR, PEOPLE OF SHANGHAI!
MY NAME IS LEX LUTHOR!* I AM THE BOSS OF LEXCORP!
LEXCORP SPONSORS THIS! THIS, THE FIRST HERO OF THE CITY AWARD EVENT! I AM HAPPY! VERY, VERY HAPPY!
CLAP!
CLAP!
CLAP!
CLAP!
CLAP!
*WORDS IN BLUE ARE IN ENGLISH, THE REST ARE IN MANDARIN! --PAUL
I GIVE SPEAKING OVER TO MY PRETTY CO-HOST LANEY LAN!
THANK YOU, MR. LUTHOR!
WHAT DO YOU THINK, EVERYBODY? HIS MANDARIN WASN'T SO BAD FOR AN AMERICAN, WAS IT?
CLAP! CLAP! CLAP!
NOW, PLEASE JOIN ME IN WELCOMING TO THE STAGE--
SU-PER-MAN! SU-PER-
CLAP! CLAP! CLAP!

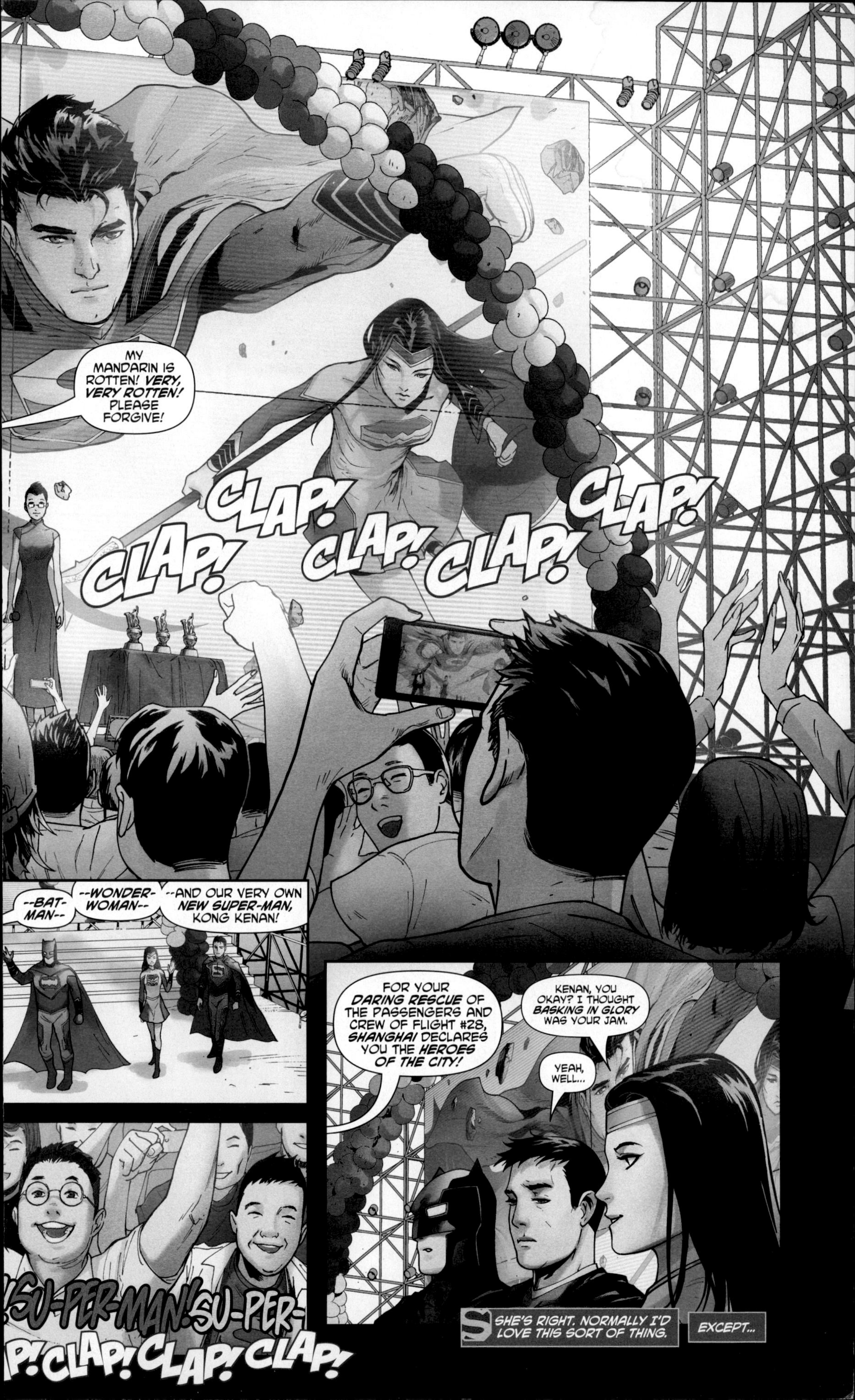
MY MANDARIN IS ROTTEN! VERY, VERY ROTTEN! PLEASE FORGIVE!
CLAP! CLAP! CLAP! CLAP! CLAP!
--BAT-MAN--
--WONDER-WOMAN--
--AND OUR VERY OWN NEW SUPER-MAN, KONG KENAN!
SU-PER-MAN! SU-PER-
P! CLAP! CLAP! CLAP!
FOR YOUR DARING RESCUE OF THE PASSENGERS AND CREW OF FLIGHT #28, SHANGHAI DECLARES YOU THE HEROES OF THE CITY!
KENAN, YOU OKAY? I THOUGHT BASKING IN GLORY WAS YOUR JAM.
YEAH, WELL...
SHE'S RIGHT. NORMALLY I'D LOVE THIS SORT OF THING.
EXCEPT...

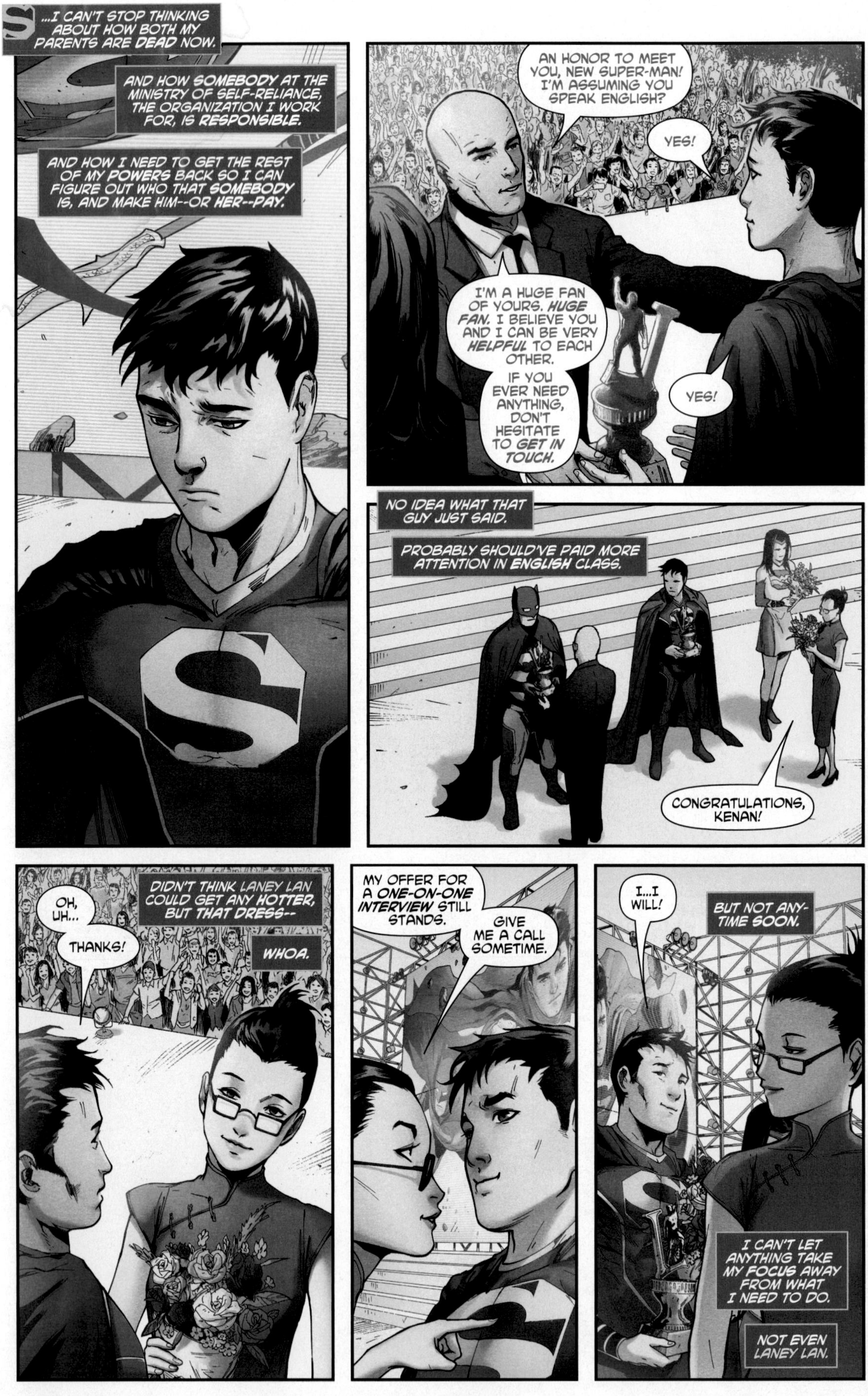
...I CAN'T STOP THINKING ABOUT HOW BOTH MY PARENTS ARE DEAD NOW.
AND HOW SOMEBODY AT THE MINISTRY OF SELF-RELIANCE, THE ORGANIZATION I WORK FOR, IS RESPONSIBLE.
AND HOW I NEED TO GET THE REST OF MY POWERS BACK SO I CAN FIGURE OUT WHO THAT SOMEBODY IS, AND MAKE HIM--OR HER--PAY.
AN HONOR TO MEET YOU, NEW SUPER-MAN! I'M ASSUMING YOU SPEAK ENGLISH?
YES!
I'M A HUGE FAN OF YOURS. HUGE FAN. I BELIEVE YOU AND I CAN BE VERY HELPFUL TO EACH OTHER.
IF YOU EVER NEED ANYTHING, DON'T HESITATE TO GET IN TOUCH.
YES!
NO IDEA WHAT THAT GUY JUST SAID.
PROBABLY SHOULD'VE PAID MORE ATTENTION IN ENGLISH CLASS.
CONGRATULATIONS, KENAN!
DIDN'T THINK LANEY LAN COULD GET ANY HOTTER, BUT THAT DRESS--
OH, UH...
THANKS!
WHOA.
MY OFFER FOR A ONE-ON-ONE INTERVIEW STILL STANDS.
GIVE ME A CALL SOMETIME.
I...I WILL!
BUT NOT ANY-TIME SOON.
I CAN'T LET ANYTHING TAKE MY FOCUS AWAY FROM WHAT I NEED TO DO.
NOT EVEN LANEY LAN.

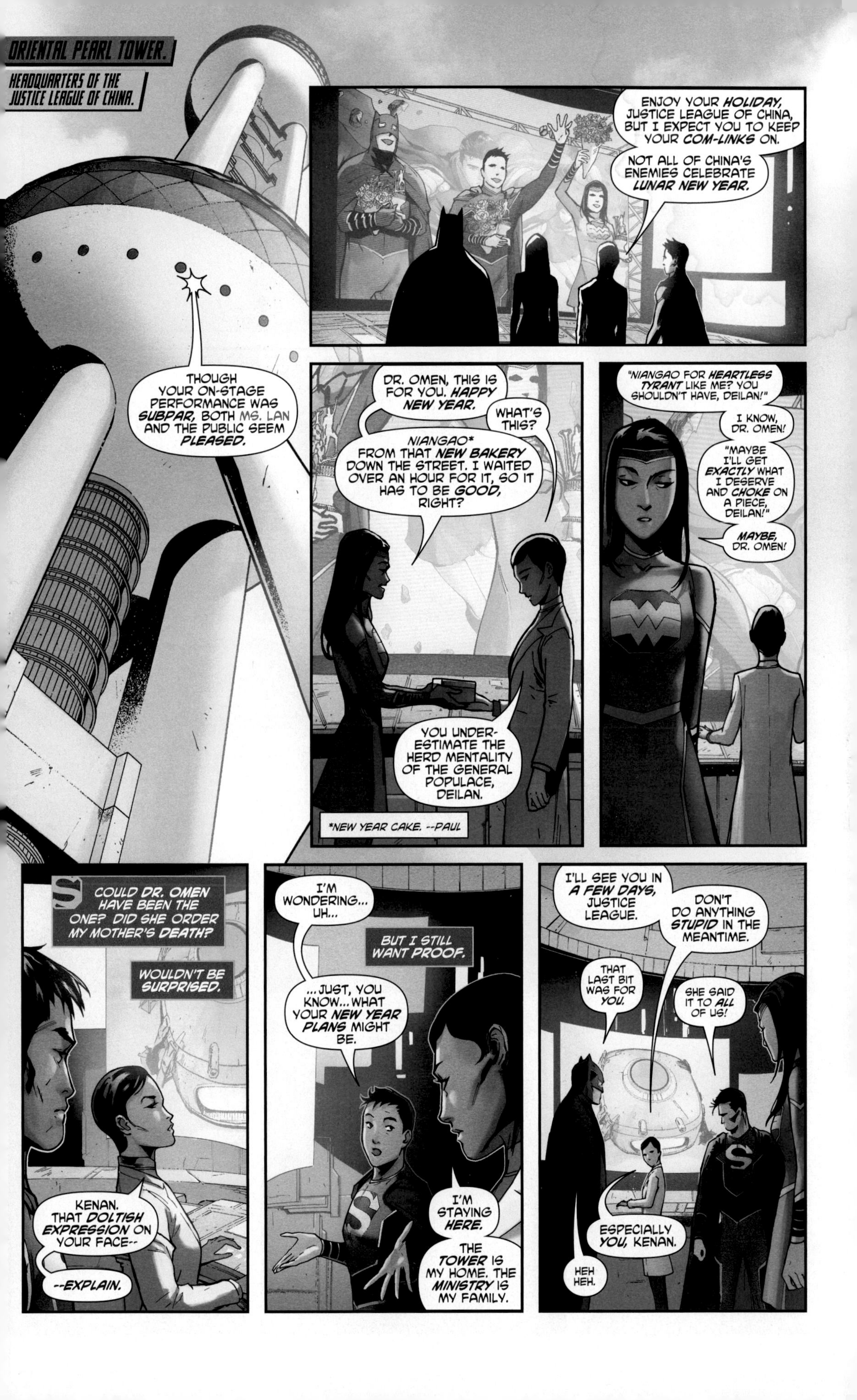
ORIENTAL PEARL TOWER.
HEADQUARTERS OF THE JUSTICE LEAGUE OF CHINA.
ENJOY YOUR HOLIDAY, JUSTICE LEAGUE OF CHINA, BUT I EXPECT YOU TO KEEP YOUR COM-LINKS ON.
NOT ALL OF CHINA'S ENEMIES CELEBRATE LUNAR NEW YEAR.
THOUGH YOUR ON-STAGE PERFORMANCE WAS SUBPAR, BOTH MS. LAN AND THE PUBLIC SEEM PLEASED.
DR. OMEN, THIS IS FOR YOU. HAPPY NEW YEAR.
WHAT'S THIS?
NIANGAO* FROM THAT NEW BAKERY DOWN THE STREET. I WAITED OVER AN HOUR FOR IT, SO IT HAS TO BE GOOD, RIGHT?
YOU UNDER-ESTIMATE THE HERD MENTALITY OF THE GENERAL POPULACE, DEILAN.
*NEW YEAR CAKE. --PAUL
"NIANGAO FOR HEARTLESS TYRANT LIKE ME? YOU SHOULDN'T HAVE, DEILAN!"
I KNOW, DR. OMEN!
"MAYBE I'LL GET EXACTLY WHAT I DESERVE AND CHOKE ON A PIECE, DEILAN!"
MAYBE, DR. OMEN!
COULD DR. OMEN HAVE BEEN THE ONE? DID SHE ORDER MY MOTHER'S DEATH?
WOULDN'T BE SURPRISED.
KENAN. THAT DOLTISH EXPRESSION ON YOUR FACE--
--EXPLAIN.
I'M WONDERING... UH...
BUT I STILL WANT PROOF.
...JUST, YOU KNOW...WHAT YOUR NEW YEAR PLANS MIGHT BE.
I'M STAYING HERE.
THE TOWER IS MY HOME. THE MINISTRY IS MY FAMILY.
I'LL SEE YOU IN A FEW DAYS, JUSTICE LEAGUE.
DON'T DO ANYTHING STUPID IN THE MEANTIME.
THAT LAST BIT WAS FOR YOU.
SHE SAID IT TO ALL OF US!
ESPECIALLY YOU, KENAN.
HEH HEH.

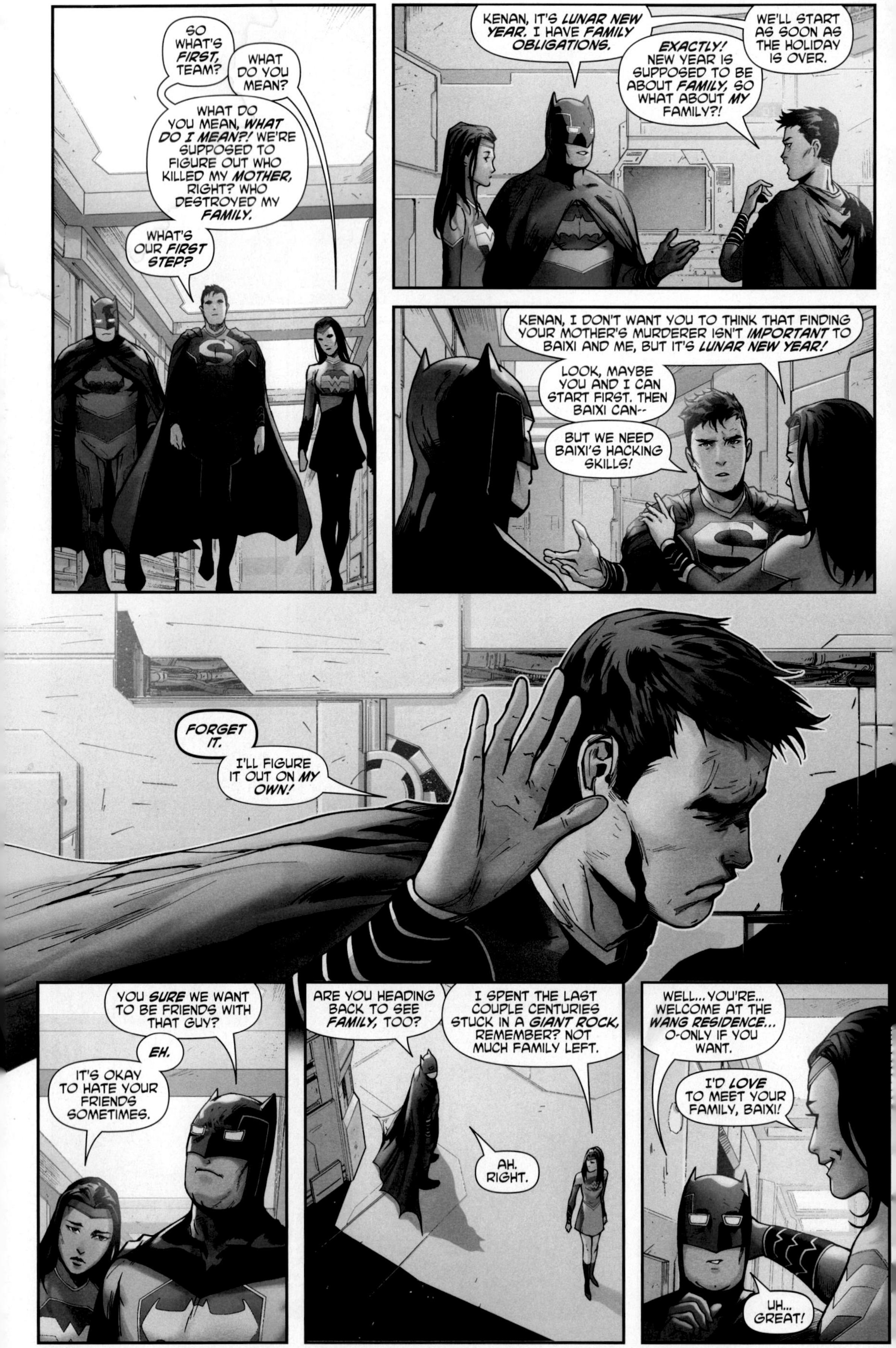
SO WHAT'S FIRST, TEAM?
WHAT DO YOU MEAN?
WHAT DO YOU MEAN, WHAT DO I MEAN?! WE'RE SUPPOSED TO FIGURE OUT WHO KILLED MY MOTHER, RIGHT? WHO DESTROYED MY FAMILY.
WHAT'S OUR FIRST STEP?
KENAN, IT'S LUNAR NEW YEAR. I HAVE FAMILY OBLIGATIONS.
WE'LL START AS SOON AS THE HOLIDAY IS OVER.
EXACTLY! NEW YEAR IS SUPPOSED TO BE ABOUT FAMILY, SO WHAT ABOUT MY FAMILY?!
KENAN, I DON'T WANT YOU TO THINK THAT FINDING YOUR MOTHER'S MURDERER ISN'T IMPORTANT TO BAIXI AND ME, BUT IT'S LUNAR NEW YEAR!
LOOK, MAYBE YOU AND I CAN START FIRST. THEN BAIXI CAN--
BUT WE NEED BAIXI'S HACKING SKILLS!
FORGET IT.
I'LL FIGURE IT OUT ON MY OWN!
YOU SURE WE WANT TO BE FRIENDS WITH THAT GUY?
EH.
IT'S OKAY TO HATE YOUR FRIENDS SOMETIMES.
ARE YOU HEADING BACK TO SEE FAMILY, TOO?
I SPENT THE LAST COUPLE CENTURIES STUCK IN A GIANT ROCK, REMEMBER? NOT MUCH FAMILY LEFT.
AH. RIGHT.
WELL...YOU'RE... WELCOME AT THE WANG RESIDENCE... O-ONLY IF YOU WANT.
I'D LOVE TO MEET YOUR FAMILY, BAIXI!
UH... GREAT!

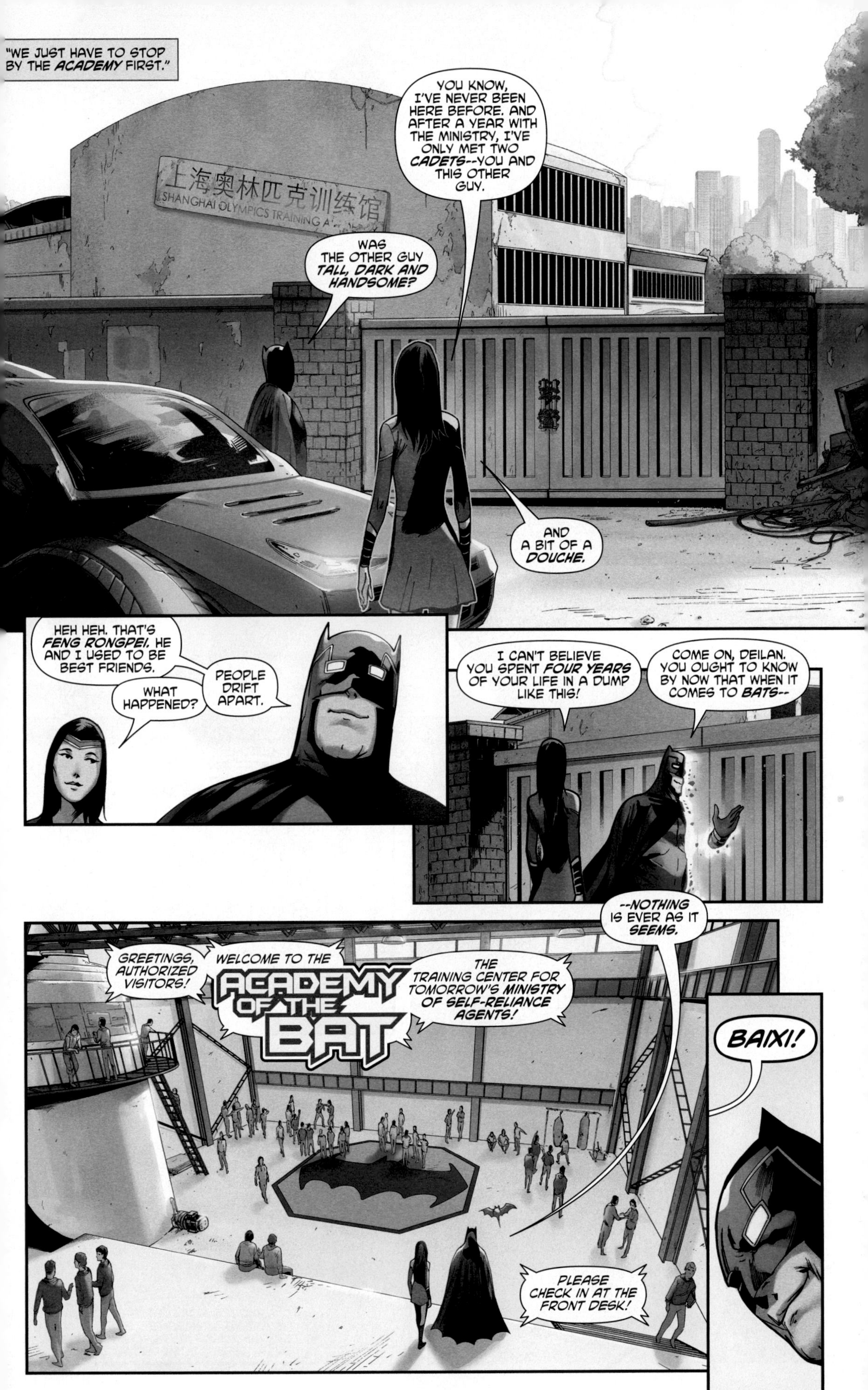
"WE JUST HAVE TO STOP BY THE *ACADEMY* FIRST."
上海奥林匹克训练馆
SHANGHAI OLYMPICS TRAINING
YOU KNOW, I'VE NEVER BEEN HERE BEFORE. AND AFTER A YEAR WITH THE MINISTRY, I'VE ONLY MET TWO *CADETS*--YOU AND THIS OTHER GUY.
WAS THE OTHER GUY *TALL, DARK AND HANDSOME?*
AND A BIT OF A *DOUCHE.*
HEH HEH. THAT'S *FENG RONGPEI.* HE AND I USED TO BE BEST FRIENDS.
WHAT HAPPENED?
PEOPLE DRIFT APART.
I CAN'T BELIEVE YOU SPENT *FOUR YEARS* OF YOUR LIFE IN A DUMP LIKE THIS!
COME ON, DEILAN. YOU OUGHT TO KNOW BY NOW THAT WHEN IT COMES TO *BATS*--
--*NOTHING* IS EVER AS IT *SEEMS.*
GREETINGS, AUTHORIZED VISITORS!
WELCOME TO THE
ACADEMY OF THE BAT
THE TRAINING CENTER FOR TOMORROW'S *MINISTRY OF SELF-RELIANCE AGENTS!*
PLEASE CHECK IN AT THE FRONT DESK!
BAIXI!

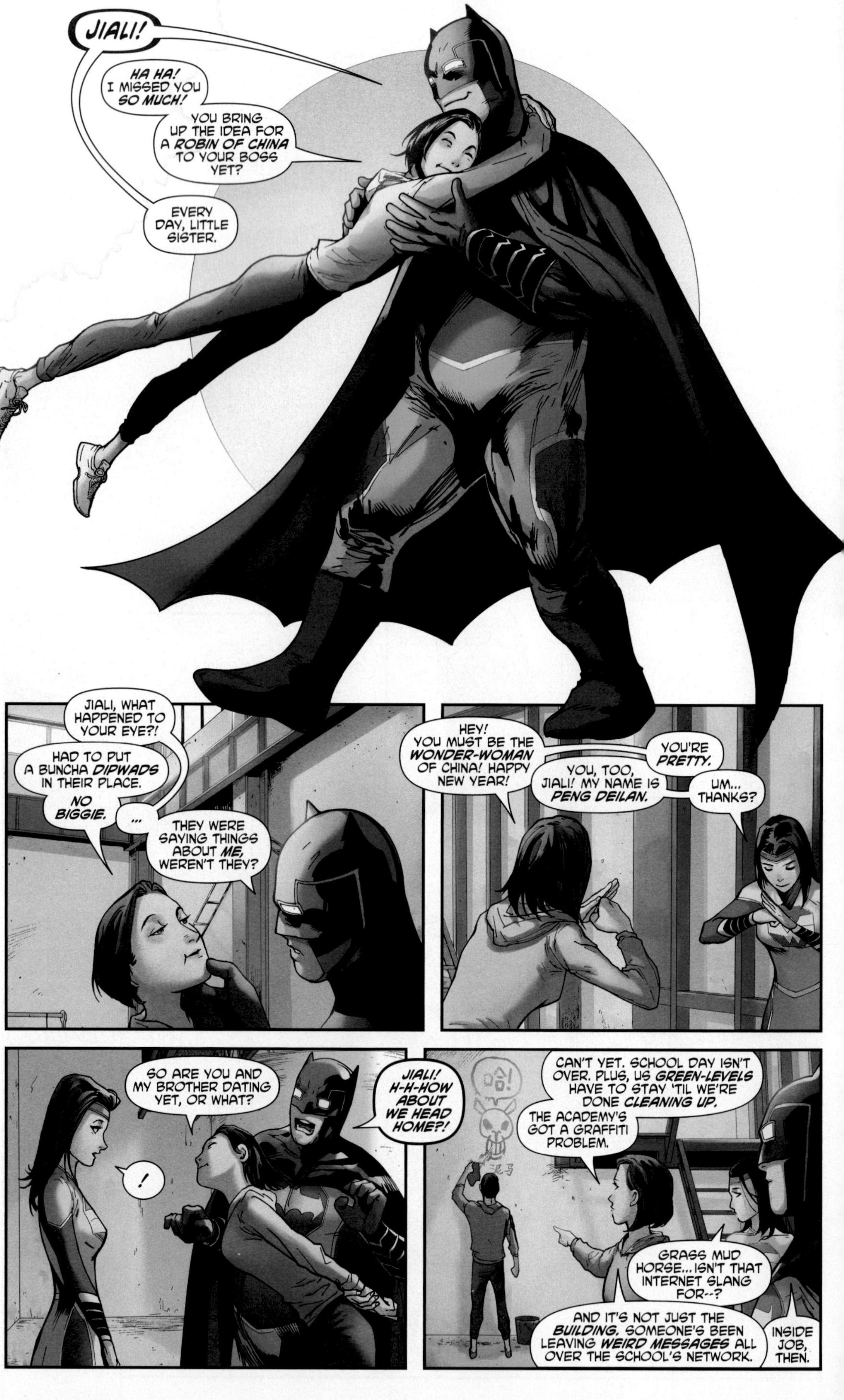

JIALI!
HA HA! I MISSED YOU SO MUCH!
YOU BRING UP THE IDEA FOR A ROBIN OF CHINA TO YOUR BOSS YET?
EVERY DAY, LITTLE SISTER.
JIALI, WHAT HAPPENED TO YOUR EYE?!
HAD TO PUT A BUNCHA DIPWADS IN THEIR PLACE.
NO BIGGIE.
...
THEY WERE SAYING THINGS ABOUT ME, WEREN'T THEY?
HEY! YOU MUST BE THE WONDER-WOMAN OF CHINA! HAPPY NEW YEAR!
YOU'RE PRETTY.
YOU, TOO, JIALI! MY NAME IS PENG DEILAN.
UM... THANKS?
SO ARE YOU AND MY BROTHER DATING YET, OR WHAT?
!
JIALI! H-H-HOW ABOUT WE HEAD HOME?!
CAN'T YET. SCHOOL DAY ISN'T OVER. PLUS, US GREEN-LEVELS HAVE TO STAY 'TIL WE'RE DONE CLEANING UP.
THE ACADEMY'S GOT A GRAFFITI PROBLEM.
GRASS MUD HORSE...ISN'T THAT INTERNET SLANG FOR--?
AND IT'S NOT JUST THE BUILDING. SOMEONE'S BEEN LEAVING WEIRD MESSAGES ALL OVER THE SCHOOL'S NETWORK.
INSIDE JOB, THEN.

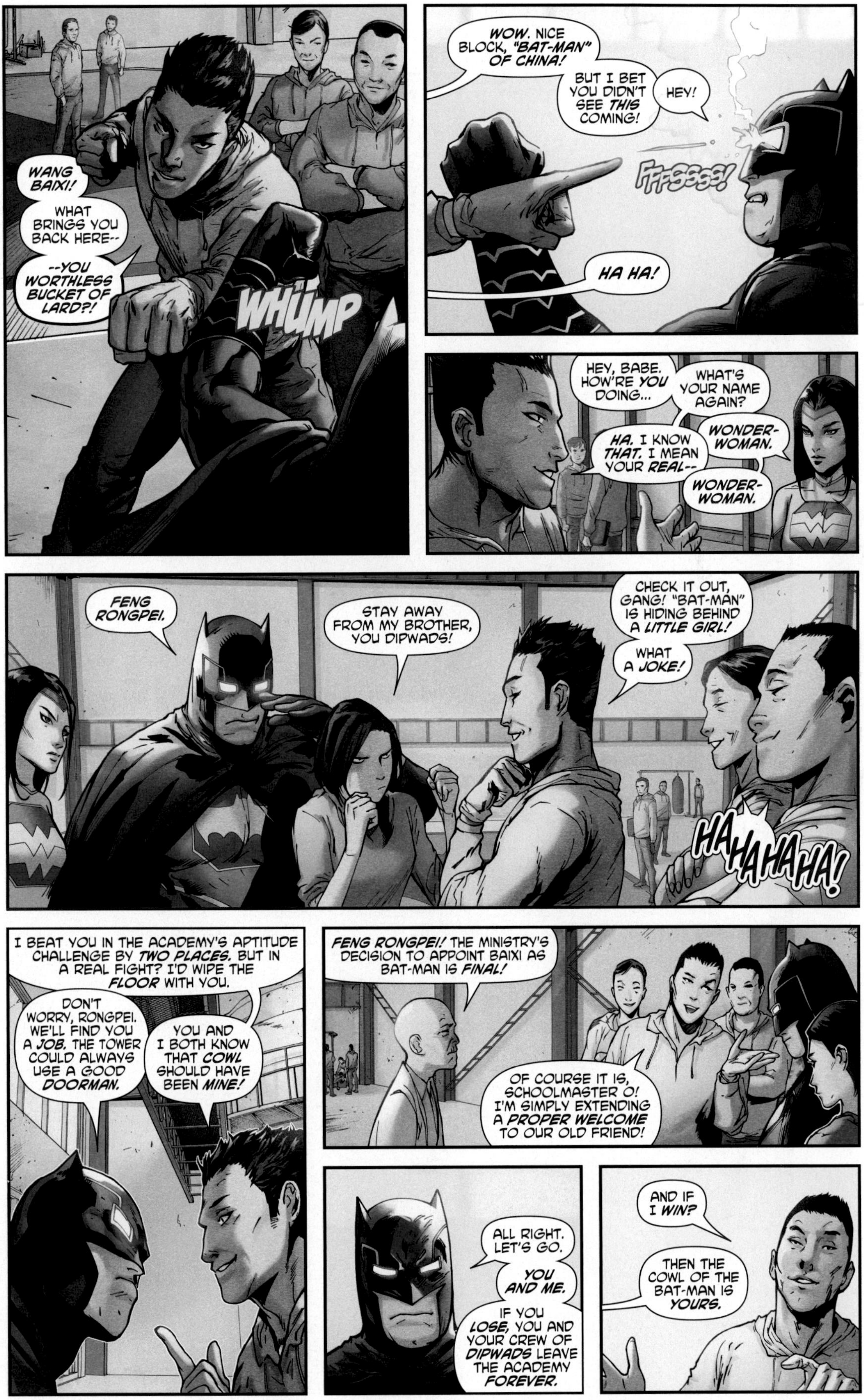
WANG BAIXI!
WHAT BRINGS YOU BACK HERE--
--YOU WORTHLESS BUCKET OF LARD?!
WHUMP
WOW. NICE BLOCK, "BAT-MAN" OF CHINA!
BUT I BET YOU DIDN'T SEE THIS COMING!
HEY!
FFFSSSS!
HA HA!
HEY, BABE. HOW'RE YOU DOING...
WHAT'S YOUR NAME AGAIN?
WONDER-WOMAN.
HA. I KNOW THAT. I MEAN YOUR REAL--
WONDER-WOMAN.
FENG RONGPEI.
STAY AWAY FROM MY BROTHER, YOU DIPWADS!
CHECK IT OUT, GANG! "BAT-MAN" IS HIDING BEHIND A LITTLE GIRL!
WHAT A JOKE!
HAHAHAHA!
I BEAT YOU IN THE ACADEMY'S APTITUDE CHALLENGE BY TWO PLACES. BUT IN A REAL FIGHT? I'D WIPE THE FLOOR WITH YOU.
DON'T WORRY, RONGPEI. WE'LL FIND YOU A JOB. THE TOWER COULD ALWAYS USE A GOOD DOORMAN.
YOU AND I BOTH KNOW THAT COWL SHOULD HAVE BEEN MINE!
FENG RONGPEI! THE MINISTRY'S DECISION TO APPOINT BAIXI AS BAT-MAN IS FINAL!
OF COURSE IT IS, SCHOOLMASTER O! I'M SIMPLY EXTENDING A PROPER WELCOME TO OUR OLD FRIEND!
ALL RIGHT. LET'S GO.
YOU AND ME.
IF YOU LOSE, YOU AND YOUR CREW OF DIPWADS LEAVE THE ACADEMY FOREVER.
AND IF I WIN?
THEN THE COWL OF THE BAT-MAN IS YOURS.

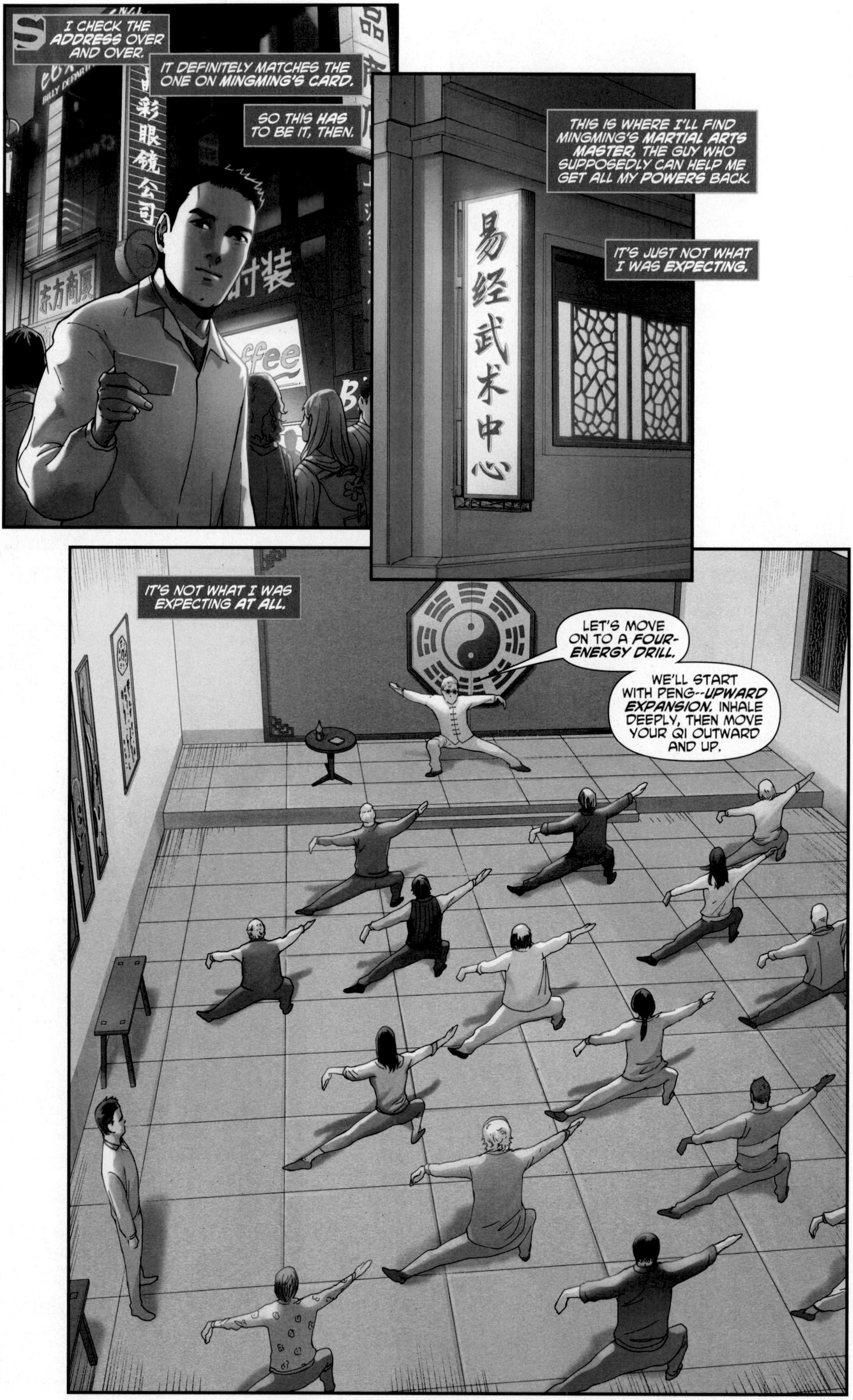

I CHECK THE ADDRESS OVER AND OVER.
IT DEFINITELY MATCHES THE ONE ON MINGMING'S CARD.
SO THIS HAS TO BE IT, THEN.
东方商厦
THIS IS WHERE I'LL FIND MINGMING'S MARTIAL ARTS MASTER, THE GUY WHO SUPPOSEDLY CAN HELP ME GET ALL MY POWERS BACK.
IT'S JUST NOT WHAT I WAS EXPECTING.
易经武术中心
IT'S NOT WHAT I WAS EXPECTING AT ALL.
LET'S MOVE ON TO A FOUR-ENERGY DRILL.
WE'LL START WITH PENG--UPWARD EXPANSION. INHALE DEEPLY, THEN MOVE YOUR QI OUTWARD AND UP.

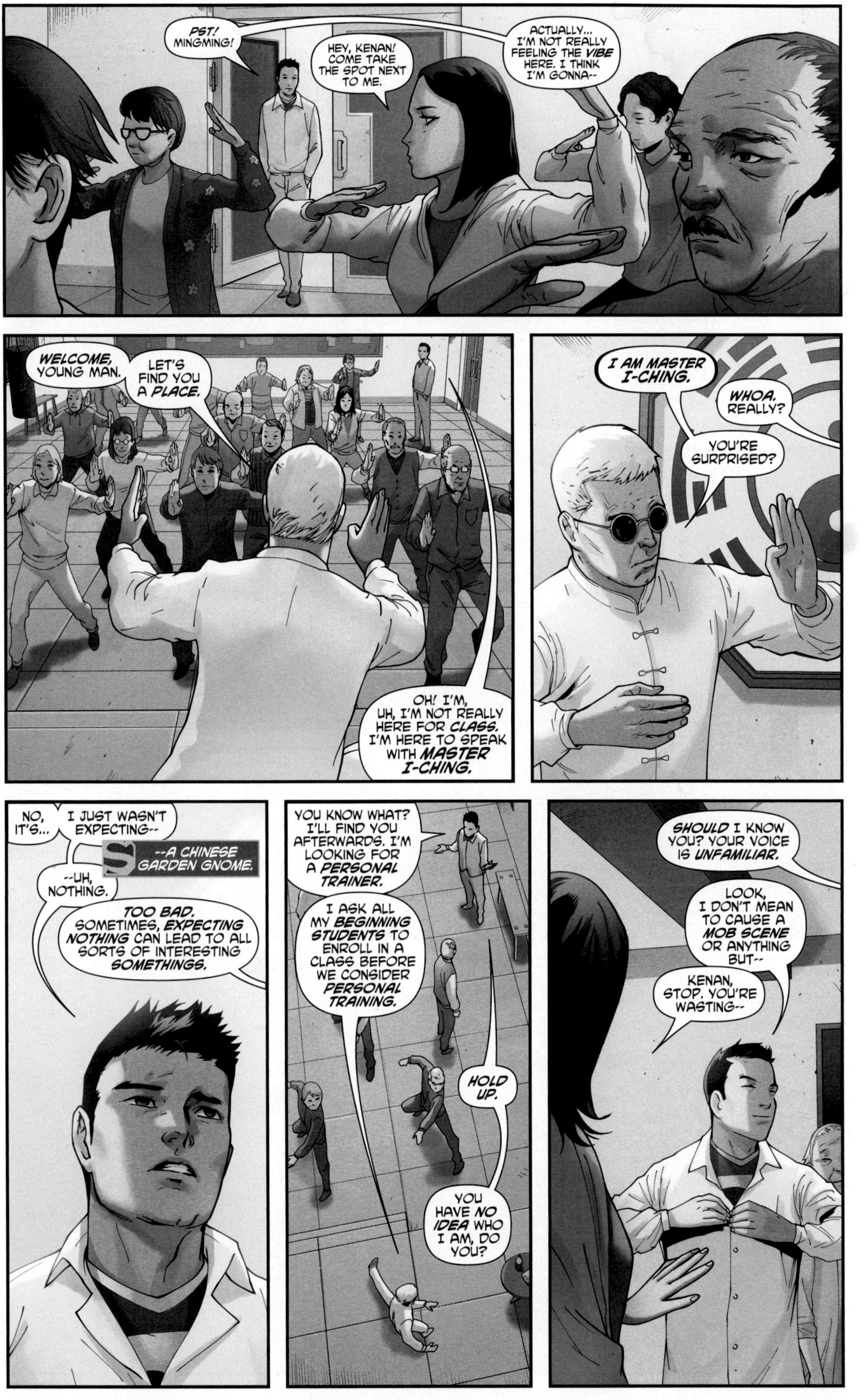
PST! MINGMING!
HEY, KENAN! COME TAKE THE SPOT NEXT TO ME.
ACTUALLY... I'M NOT REALLY FEELING THE VIBE HERE. I THINK I'M GONNA--
WELCOME, YOUNG MAN.
LET'S FIND YOU A PLACE.
OH! I'M, UH, I'M NOT REALLY HERE FOR CLASS. I'M HERE TO SPEAK WITH MASTER I-CHING.
I AM MASTER I-CHING.
WHOA. REALLY?
YOU'RE SURPRISED?
NO, IT'S...
I JUST WASN'T EXPECTING--
--A CHINESE GARDEN GNOME.
--UH, NOTHING.
TOO BAD. SOMETIMES, EXPECTING NOTHING CAN LEAD TO ALL SORTS OF INTERESTING SOMETHINGS.
YOU KNOW WHAT? I'LL FIND YOU AFTERWARDS. I'M LOOKING FOR A PERSONAL TRAINER.
I ASK ALL MY BEGINNING STUDENTS TO ENROLL IN A CLASS BEFORE WE CONSIDER PERSONAL TRAINING.
HOLD UP.
YOU HAVE NO IDEA WHO I AM, DO YOU?
SHOULD I KNOW YOU? YOUR VOICE IS UNFAMILIAR.
LOOK, I DON'T MEAN TO CAUSE A MOB SCENE OR ANYTHING BUT--
KENAN, STOP. YOU'RE WASTING--

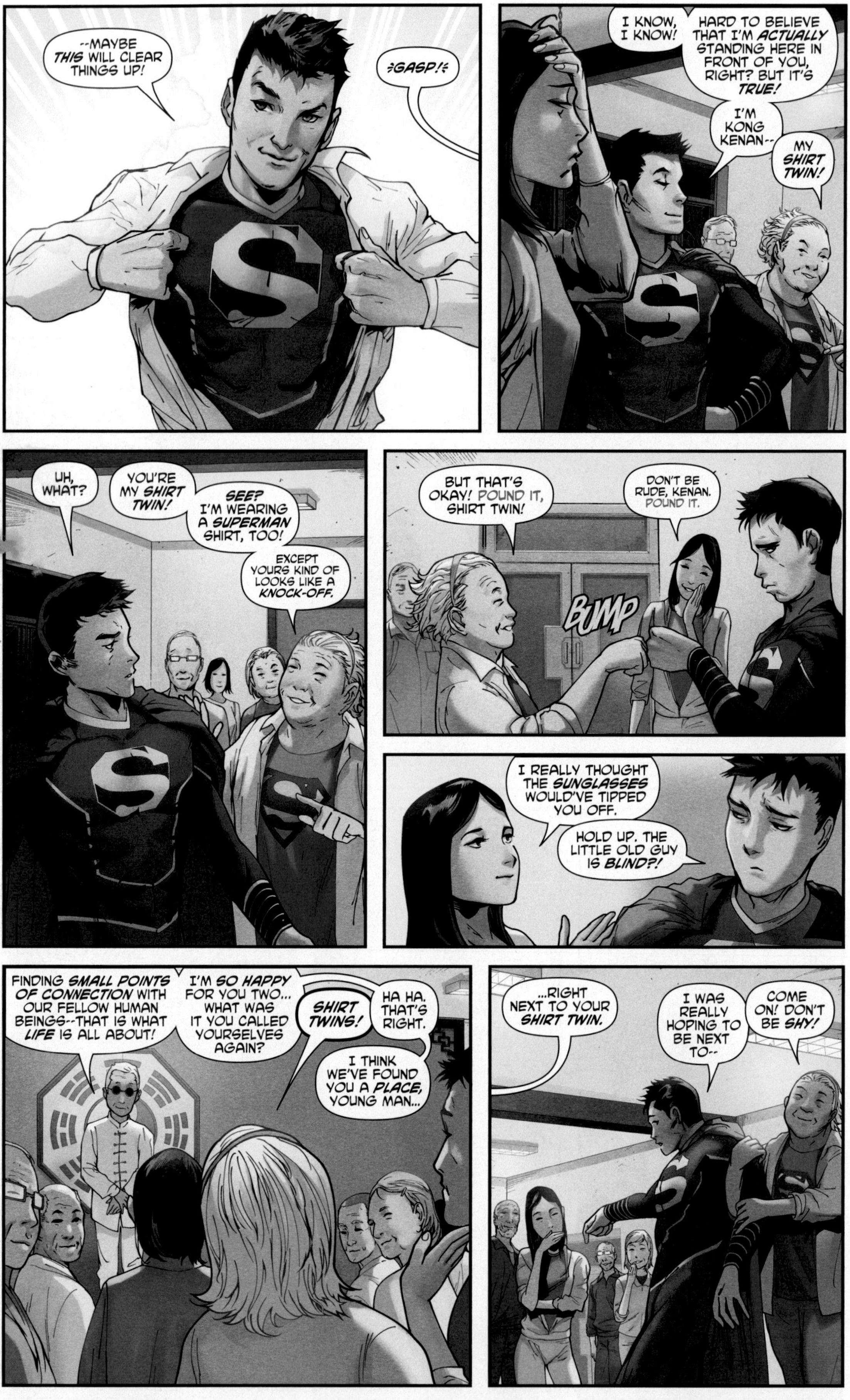
--MAYBE THIS WILL CLEAR THINGS UP!
GASP!
I KNOW, I KNOW!
HARD TO BELIEVE THAT I'M ACTUALLY STANDING HERE IN FRONT OF YOU, RIGHT? BUT IT'S TRUE!
I'M KONG KENAN--
MY SHIRT TWIN!
UH, WHAT?
YOU'RE MY SHIRT TWIN!
SEE? I'M WEARING A SUPERMAN SHIRT, TOO!
EXCEPT YOURS KIND OF LOOKS LIKE A KNOCK-OFF.
BUT THAT'S OKAY! POUND IT, SHIRT TWIN!
DON'T BE RUDE, KENAN. POUND IT.
BUMP
I REALLY THOUGHT THE SUNGLASSES WOULD'VE TIPPED YOU OFF.
HOLD UP. THE LITTLE OLD GUY IS BLIND?!
FINDING SMALL POINTS OF CONNECTION WITH OUR FELLOW HUMAN BEINGS--THAT IS WHAT LIFE IS ALL ABOUT!
I'M SO HAPPY FOR YOU TWO... WHAT WAS IT YOU CALLED YOURSELVES AGAIN?
SHIRT TWINS!
HA HA. THAT'S RIGHT.
I THINK WE'VE FOUND YOU A PLACE, YOUNG MAN...
...RIGHT NEXT TO YOUR SHIRT TWIN.
I WAS REALLY HOPING TO BE NEXT TO--
COME ON! DON'T BE SHY!

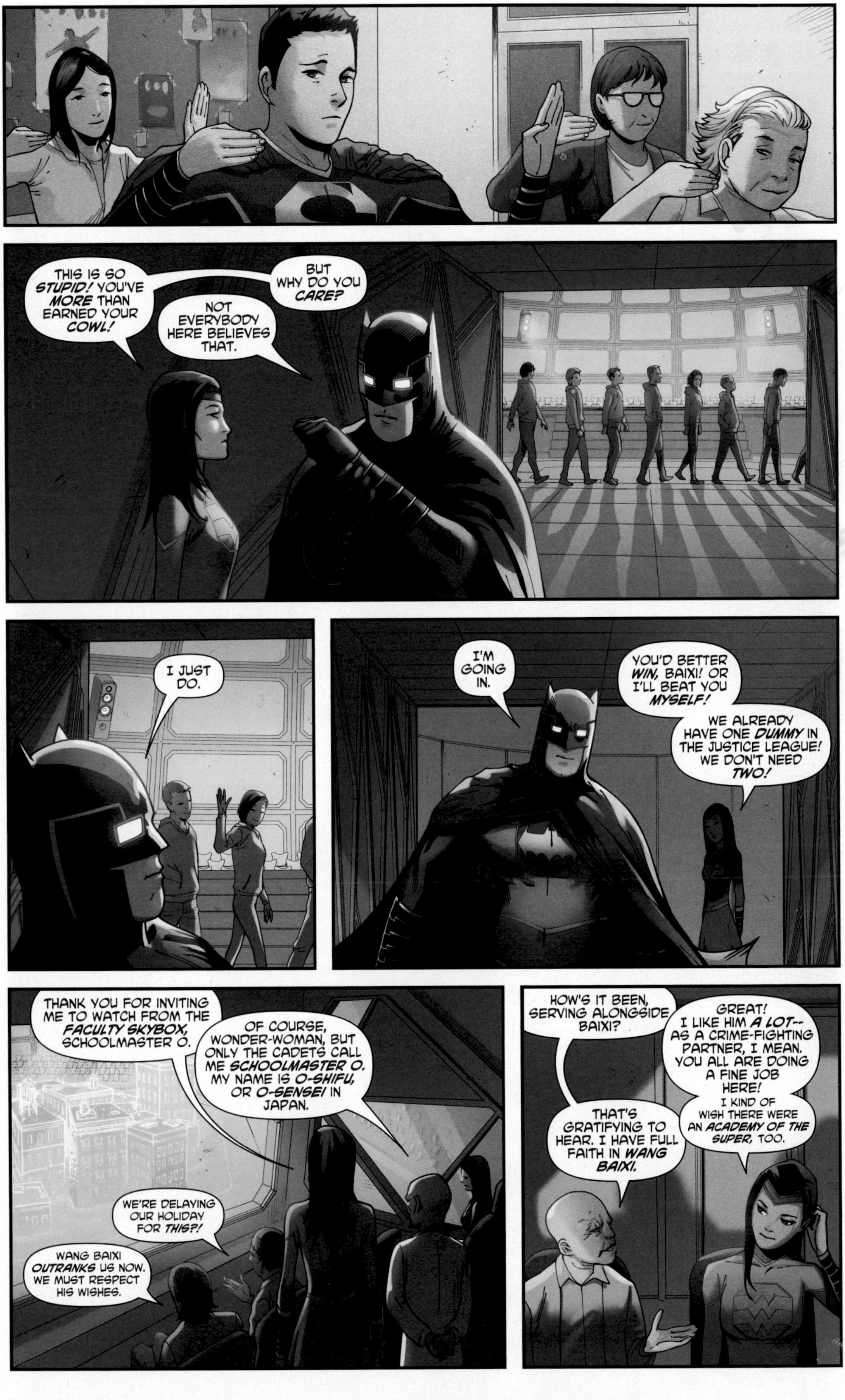
THIS IS SO STUPID! YOU'VE MORE THAN EARNED YOUR COWL!
NOT EVERYBODY HERE BELIEVES THAT.
BUT WHY DO YOU CARE?
I JUST DO.
I'M GOING IN.
YOU'D BETTER WIN, BAIXI! OR I'LL BEAT YOU MYSELF!
WE ALREADY HAVE ONE DUMMY IN THE JUSTICE LEAGUE! WE DON'T NEED TWO!
THANK YOU FOR INVITING ME TO WATCH FROM THE FACULTY SKYBOX, SCHOOLMASTER O.
OF COURSE, WONDER-WOMAN, BUT ONLY THE CADETS CALL ME SCHOOLMASTER O. MY NAME IS O-SHIFU, OR O-SENSEI IN JAPAN.
WE'RE DELAYING OUR HOLIDAY FOR THIS?!
WANG BAIXI OUTRANKS US NOW. WE MUST RESPECT HIS WISHES.
HOW'S IT BEEN, SERVING ALONGSIDE BAIXI?
GREAT! I LIKE HIM A LOT--AS A CRIME-FIGHTING PARTNER, I MEAN. YOU ALL ARE DOING A FINE JOB HERE!
I KIND OF WISH THERE WERE AN ACADEMY OF THE SUPER, TOO.
THAT'S GRATIFYING TO HEAR. I HAVE FULL FAITH IN WANG BAIXI.

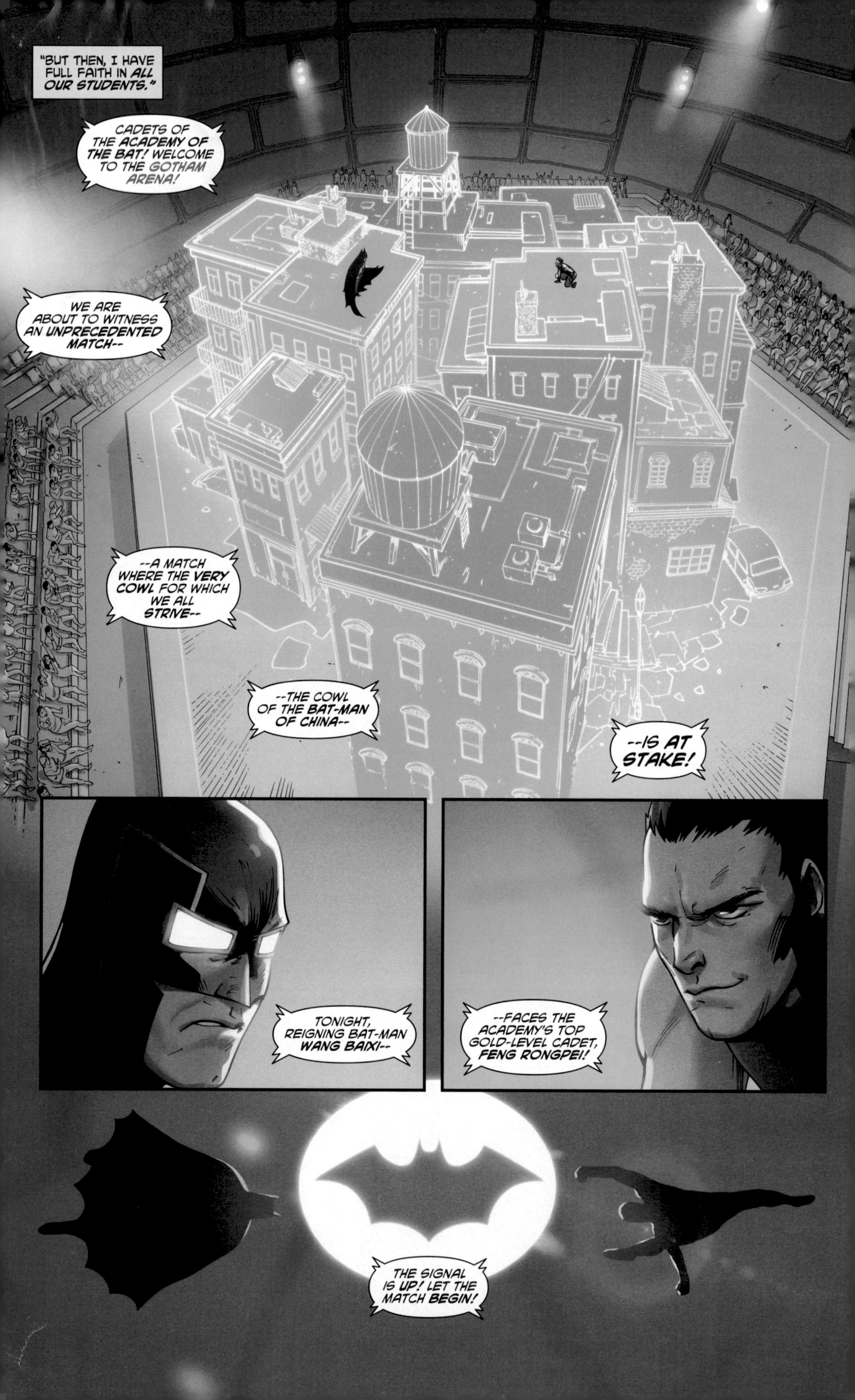
"BUT THEN, I HAVE FULL FAITH IN ALL OUR STUDENTS."
CADETS OF THE ACADEMY OF THE BAT! WELCOME TO THE GOTHAM ARENA!
WE ARE ABOUT TO WITNESS AN UNPRECEDENTED MATCH--
--A MATCH WHERE THE VERY COWL FOR WHICH WE ALL STRIVE--
--THE COWL OF THE BAT-MAN OF CHINA--
--IS AT STAKE!
TONIGHT, REIGNING BAT-MAN WANG BAIXI--
--FACES THE ACADEMY'S TOP GOLD-LEVEL CADET, FENG RONGPEI!
THE SIGNAL IS UP! LET THE MATCH BEGIN!

SShhKRRBUREEEEEEEEE!!

WHAT--?!

SHINNG!

SHINNG!

HAHAHA! WHAT'S YOUR GUESS, LARD BUCKET? THIS GONNA BE A COMEDY OR A TRAGEDY?

HAHAHA!

PROBABLY BOTH!

KRAKK!

COME ON, BAIXI!

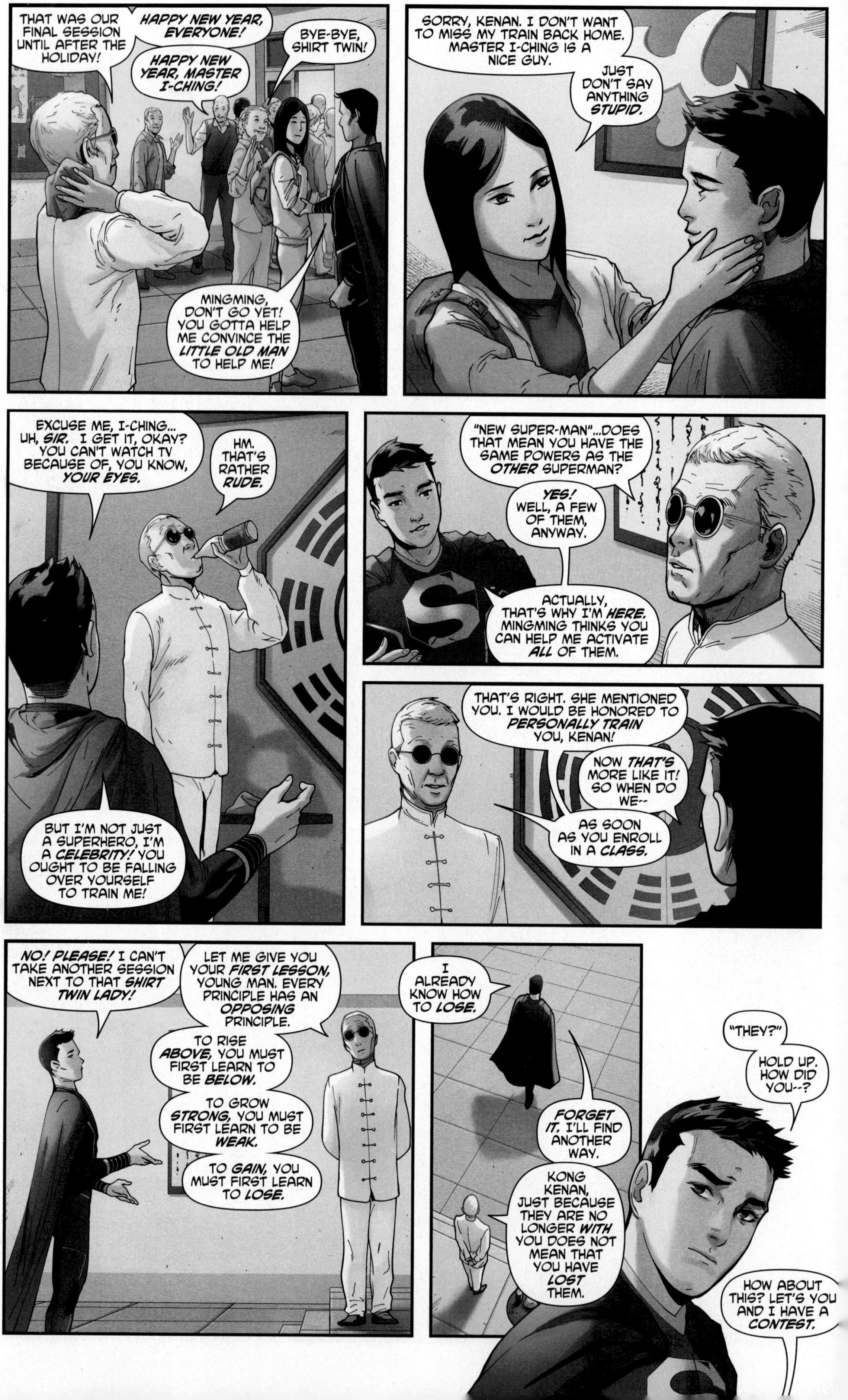
THAT WAS OUR FINAL SESSION UNTIL AFTER THE HOLIDAY!
HAPPY NEW YEAR, EVERYONE!
HAPPY NEW YEAR, MASTER I-CHING!
BYE-BYE, SHIRT TWIN!
MINGMING, DON'T GO YET! YOU GOTTA HELP ME CONVINCE THE LITTLE OLD MAN TO HELP ME!
SORRY, KENAN. I DON'T WANT TO MISS MY TRAIN BACK HOME. MASTER I-CHING IS A NICE GUY.
JUST DON'T SAY ANYTHING STUPID.
EXCUSE ME, I-CHING... UH, SIR. I GET IT, OKAY? YOU CAN'T WATCH TV BECAUSE OF, YOU KNOW, YOUR EYES.
HM. THAT'S RATHER RUDE.
BUT I'M NOT JUST A SUPERHERO, I'M A CELEBRITY! YOU OUGHT TO BE FALLING OVER YOURSELF TO TRAIN ME!
"NEW SUPER-MAN"...DOES THAT MEAN YOU HAVE THE SAME POWERS AS THE OTHER SUPERMAN?
YES! WELL, A FEW OF THEM, ANYWAY.
ACTUALLY, THAT'S WHY I'M HERE. MINGMING THINKS YOU CAN HELP ME ACTIVATE ALL OF THEM.
THAT'S RIGHT. SHE MENTIONED YOU. I WOULD BE HONORED TO PERSONALLY TRAIN YOU, KENAN!
NOW THAT'S MORE LIKE IT! SO WHEN DO WE--
AS SOON AS YOU ENROLL IN A CLASS.
NO! PLEASE! I CAN'T TAKE ANOTHER SESSION NEXT TO THAT SHIRT TWIN LADY!
LET ME GIVE YOU YOUR FIRST LESSON, YOUNG MAN. EVERY PRINCIPLE HAS AN OPPOSING PRINCIPLE.
TO RISE ABOVE, YOU MUST FIRST LEARN TO BE BELOW.
TO GROW STRONG, YOU MUST FIRST LEARN TO BE WEAK.
TO GAIN, YOU MUST FIRST LEARN TO LOSE.
I ALREADY KNOW HOW TO LOSE.
FORGET IT. I'LL FIND ANOTHER WAY.
KONG KENAN, JUST BECAUSE THEY ARE NO LONGER WITH YOU DOES NOT MEAN THAT YOU HAVE LOST THEM.
"THEY?"
HOLD UP. HOW DID YOU--?
HOW ABOUT THIS? LET'S YOU AND I HAVE A CONTEST.

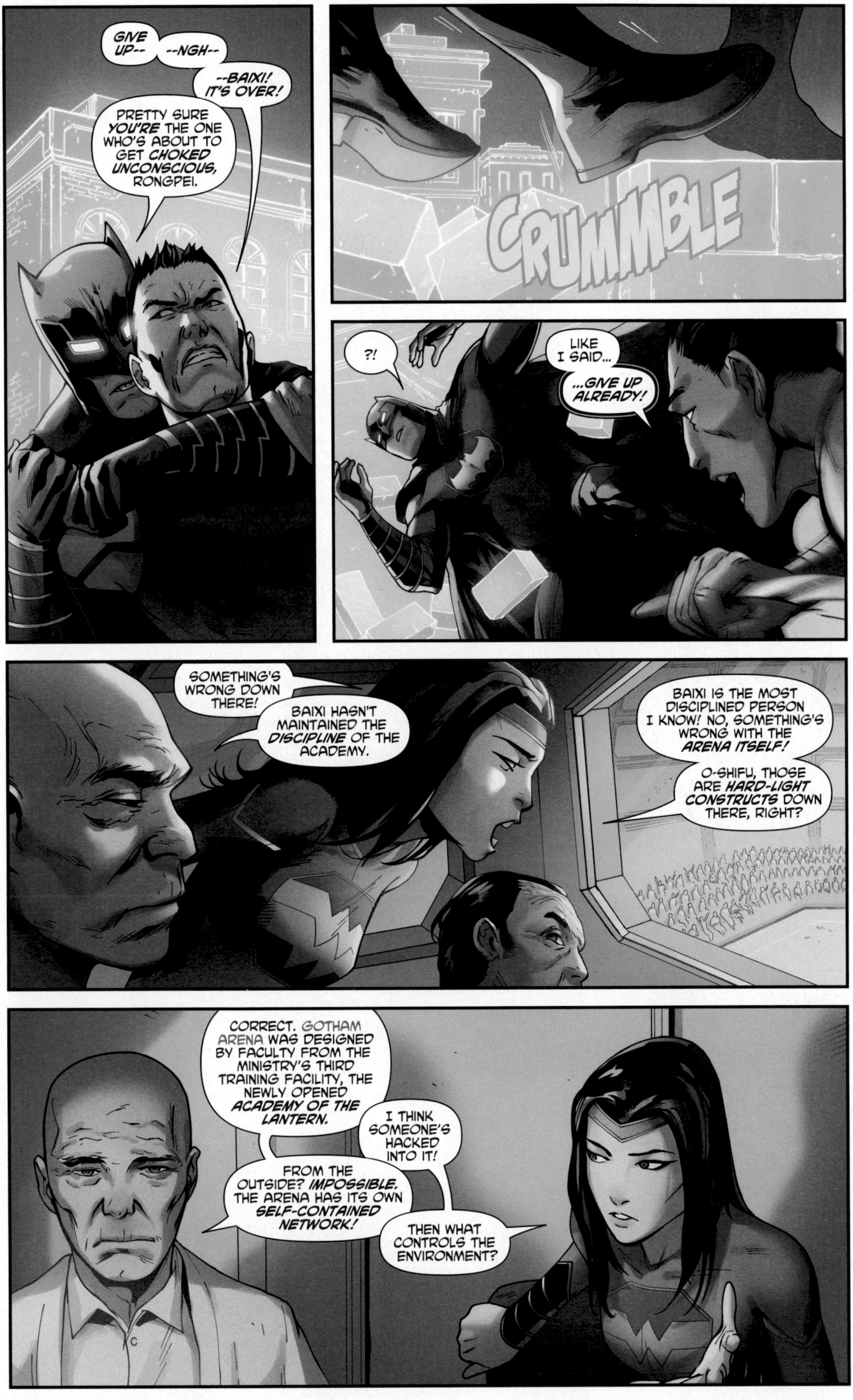
GIVE UP--
--NGH--
--BAIXI! IT'S OVER!
PRETTY SURE YOU'RE THE ONE WHO'S ABOUT TO GET CHOKED UNCONSCIOUS, RONGPEI.
CRUMMBLE
?!
LIKE I SAID...
...GIVE UP ALREADY!
SOMETHING'S WRONG DOWN THERE!
BAIXI HASN'T MAINTAINED THE DISCIPLINE OF THE ACADEMY.
BAIXI IS THE MOST DISCIPLINED PERSON I KNOW! NO, SOMETHING'S WRONG WITH THE ARENA ITSELF!
O-SHIFU, THOSE ARE HARD-LIGHT CONSTRUCTS DOWN THERE, RIGHT?
CORRECT. GOTHAM ARENA WAS DESIGNED BY FACULTY FROM THE MINISTRY'S THIRD TRAINING FACILITY, THE NEWLY OPENED ACADEMY OF THE LANTERN.
I THINK SOMEONE'S HACKED INTO IT!
FROM THE OUTSIDE? IMPOSSIBLE. THE ARENA HAS ITS OWN SELF-CONTAINED NETWORK!
THEN WHAT CONTROLS THE ENVIRONMENT?

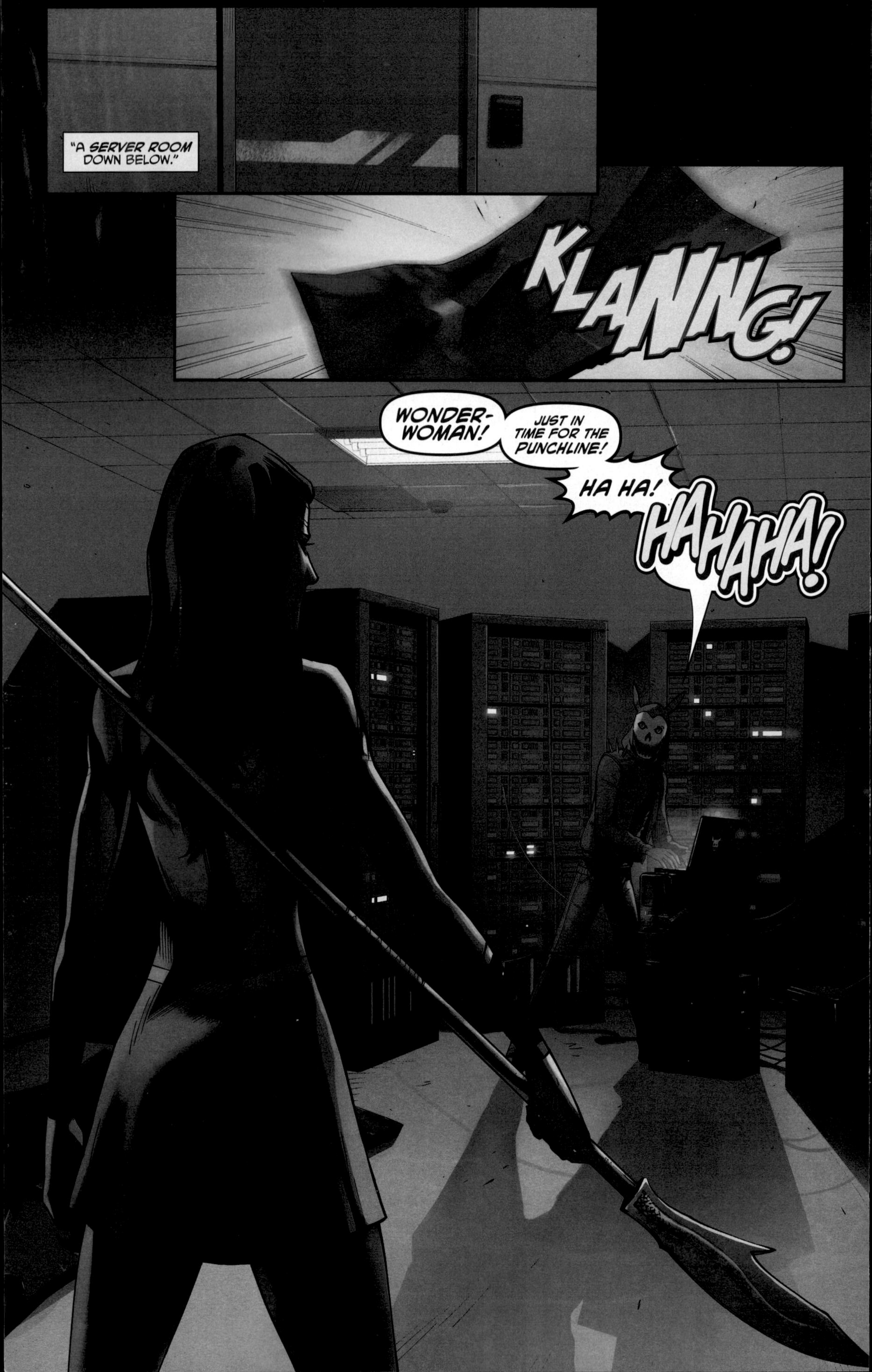
"A SERVER ROOM DOWN BELOW."
KLANNNG!
WONDER-WOMAN!
JUST IN TIME FOR THE PUNCHLINE!
HA HA!
HAHAHA!

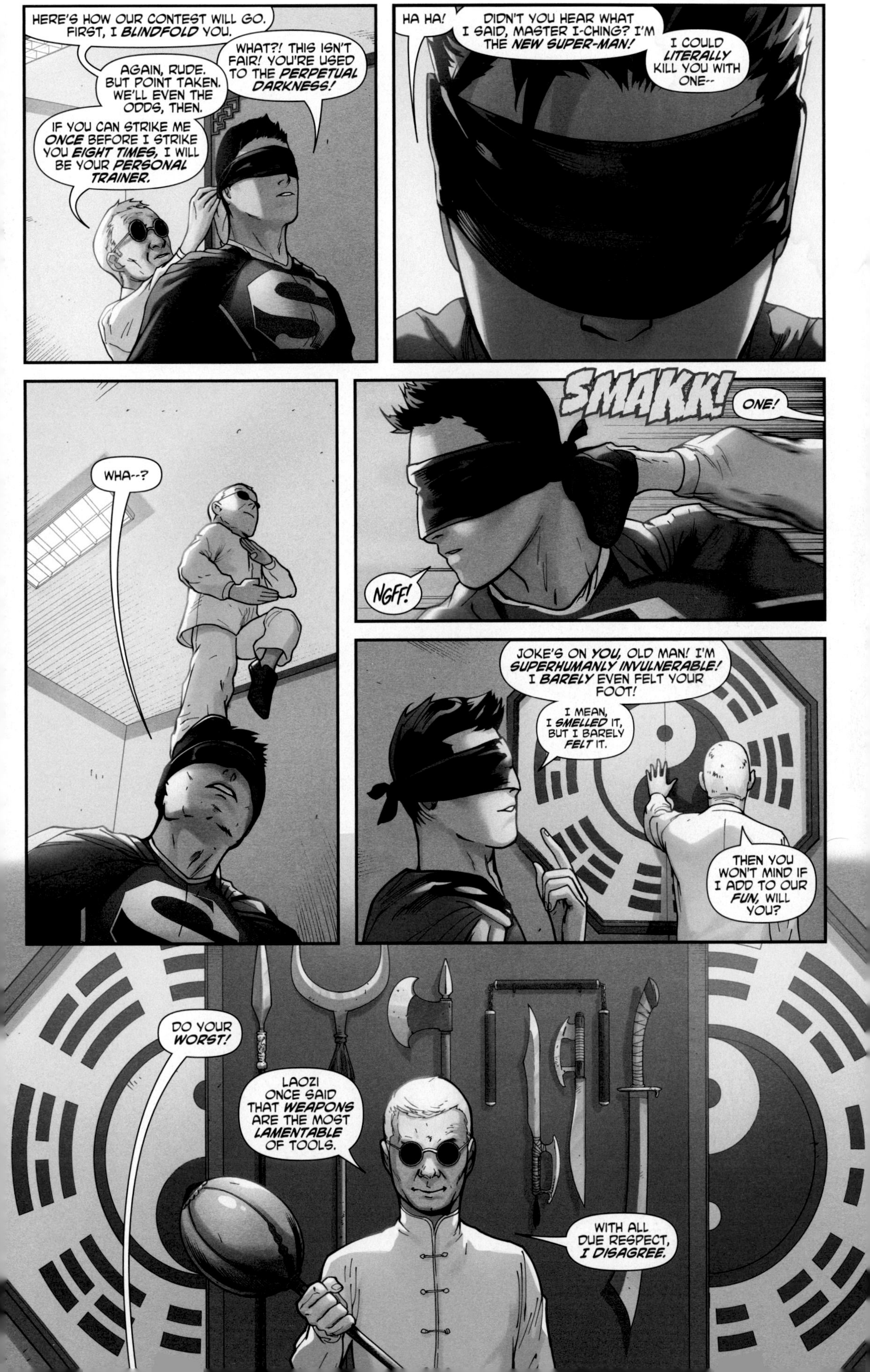
HERE'S HOW OUR CONTEST WILL GO. FIRST, I BLINDFOLD YOU.
WHAT?! THIS ISN'T FAIR! YOU'RE USED TO THE PERPETUAL DARKNESS!
AGAIN, RUDE. BUT POINT TAKEN. WE'LL EVEN THE ODDS, THEN.
IF YOU CAN STRIKE ME ONCE BEFORE I STRIKE YOU EIGHT TIMES, I WILL BE YOUR PERSONAL TRAINER.
HA HA!
DIDN'T YOU HEAR WHAT I SAID, MASTER I-CHING? I'M THE NEW SUPER-MAN!
I COULD LITERALLY KILL YOU WITH ONE--
WHA--?
SMAKK!
ONE!
NGFF!
JOKE'S ON YOU, OLD MAN! I'M SUPERHUMANLY INVULNERABLE! I BARELY EVEN FELT YOUR FOOT!
I MEAN, I SMELLED IT, BUT I BARELY FELT IT.
THEN YOU WON'T MIND IF I ADD TO OUR FUN, WILL YOU?
DO YOUR WORST!
LAOZI ONCE SAID THAT WEAPONS ARE THE MOST LAMENTABLE OF TOOLS.
WITH ALL DUE RESPECT, I DISAGREE.

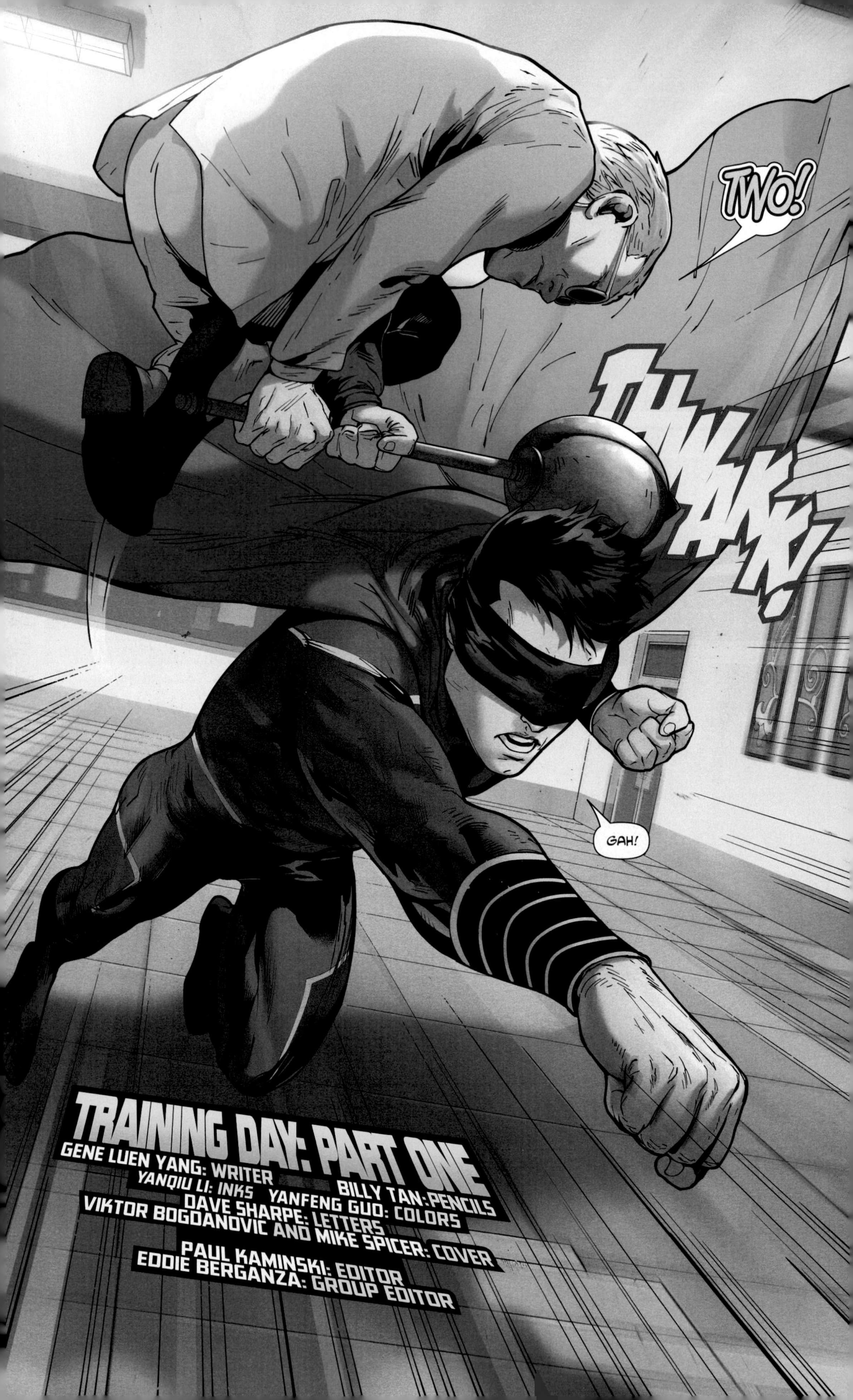
TWO!
THWAK!
GAH!
TRAINING DAY: PART ONE
GENE LUEN YANG: WRITER
BILLY TAN: PENCILS
YANQIU LI: INKS
YANFENG GUO: COLORS
DAVE SHARPE: LETTERS
VIKTOR BOGDANOVIC AND MIKE SPICER: COVER
PAUL KAMINSKI: EDITOR
EDDIE BERGANZA: GROUP EDITOR

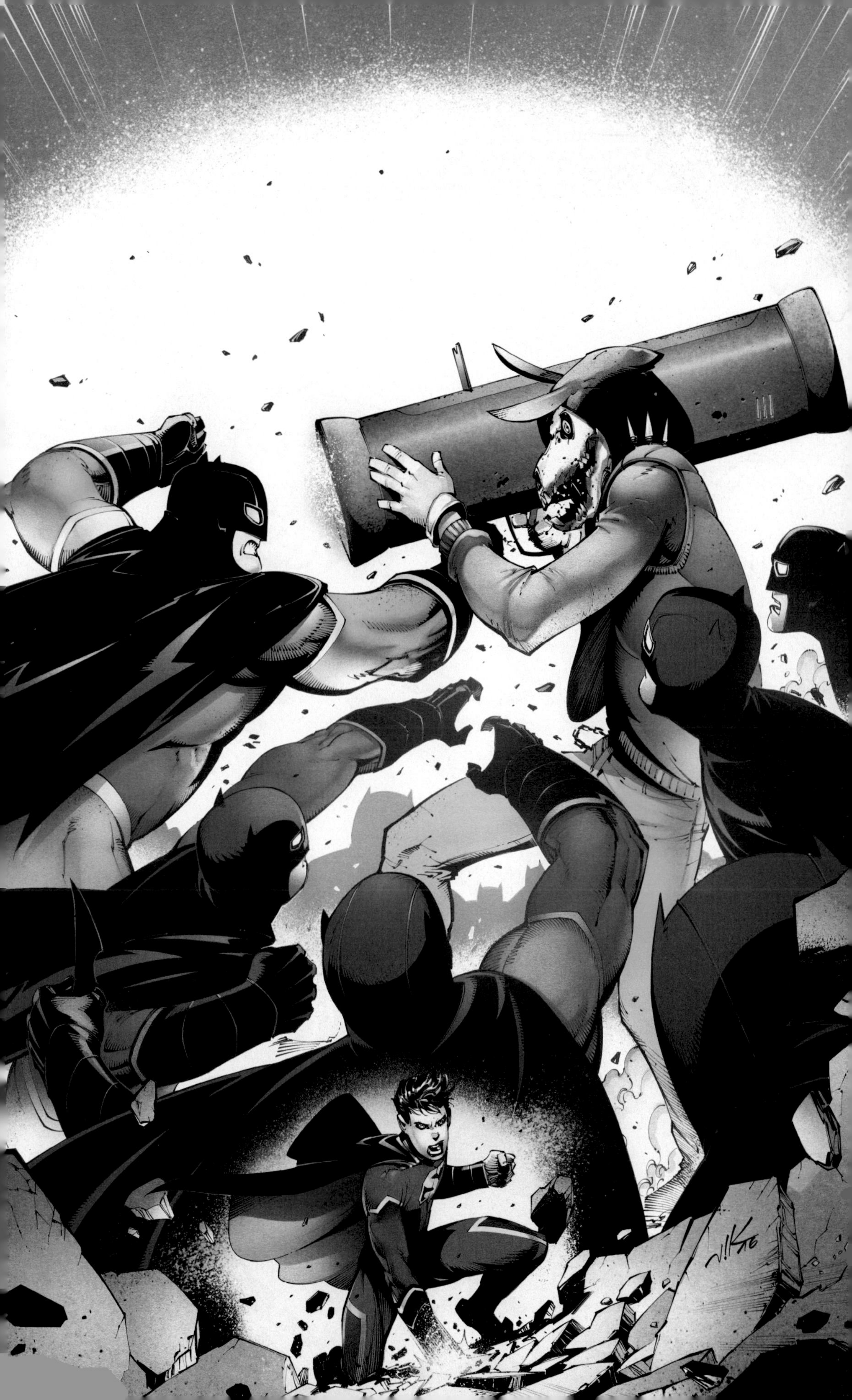

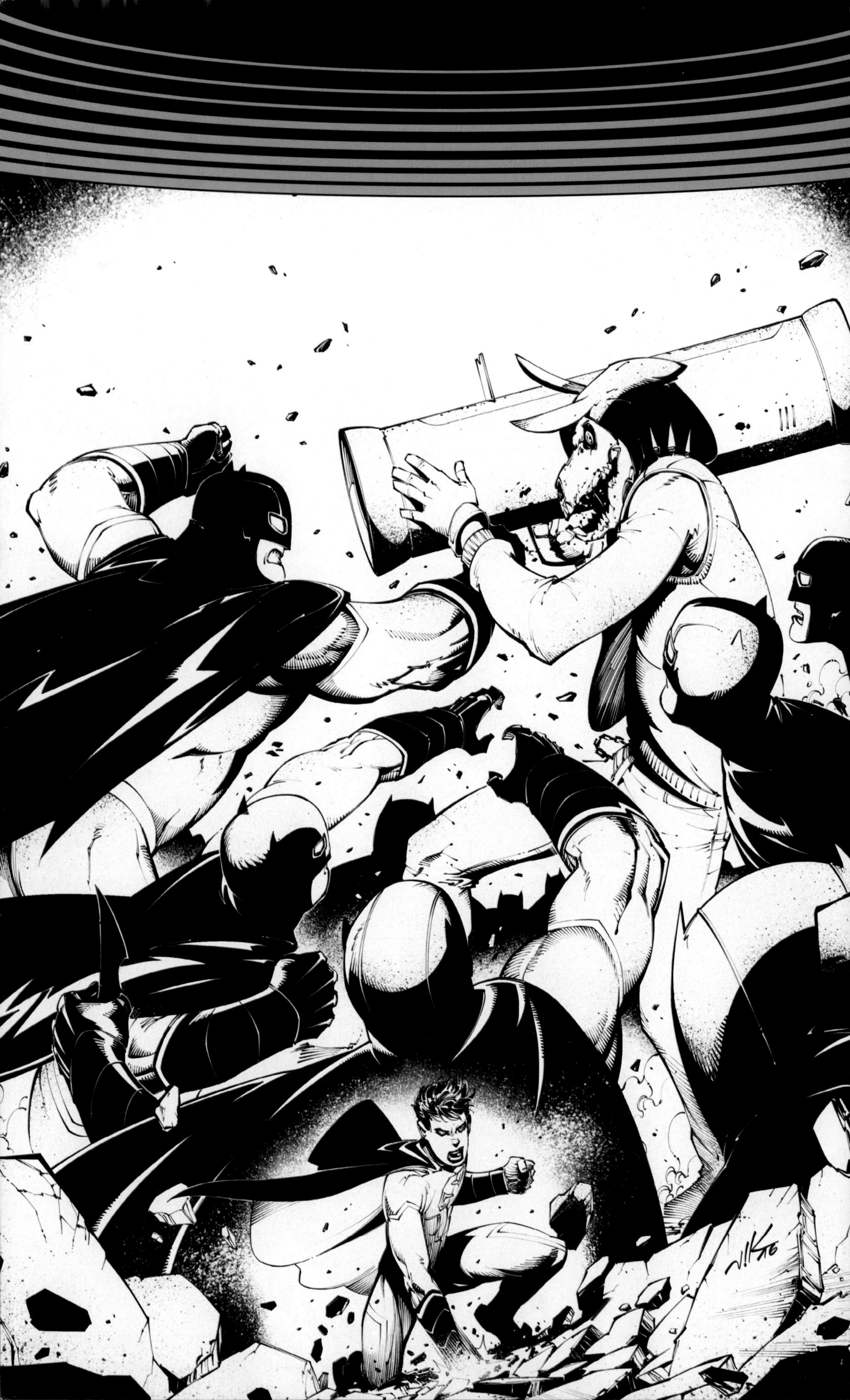

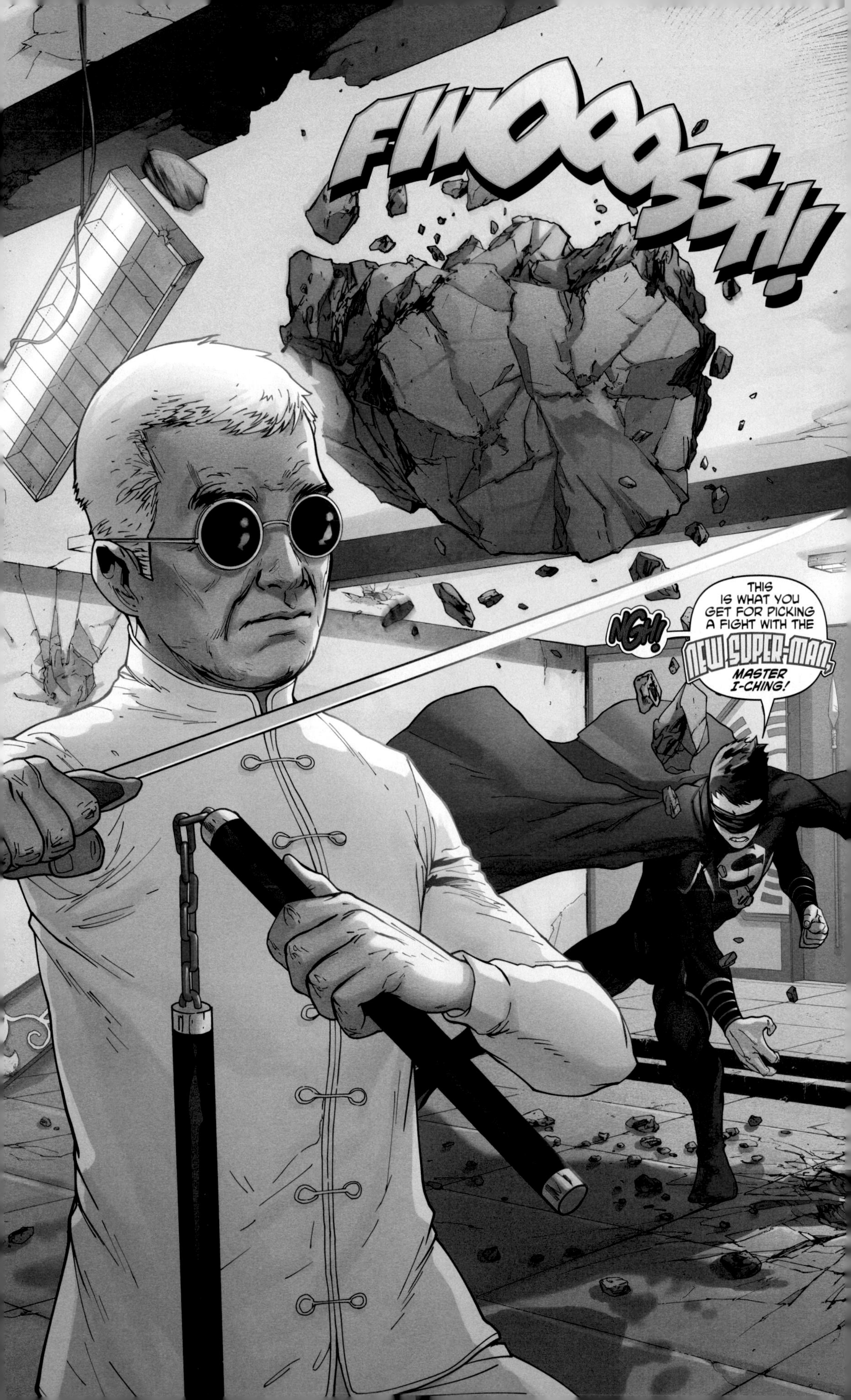
FWOOOSSH!
NGH!
THIS IS WHAT YOU GET FOR PICKING A FIGHT WITH THE NEW SUPER-MAN, MASTER I-CHING!

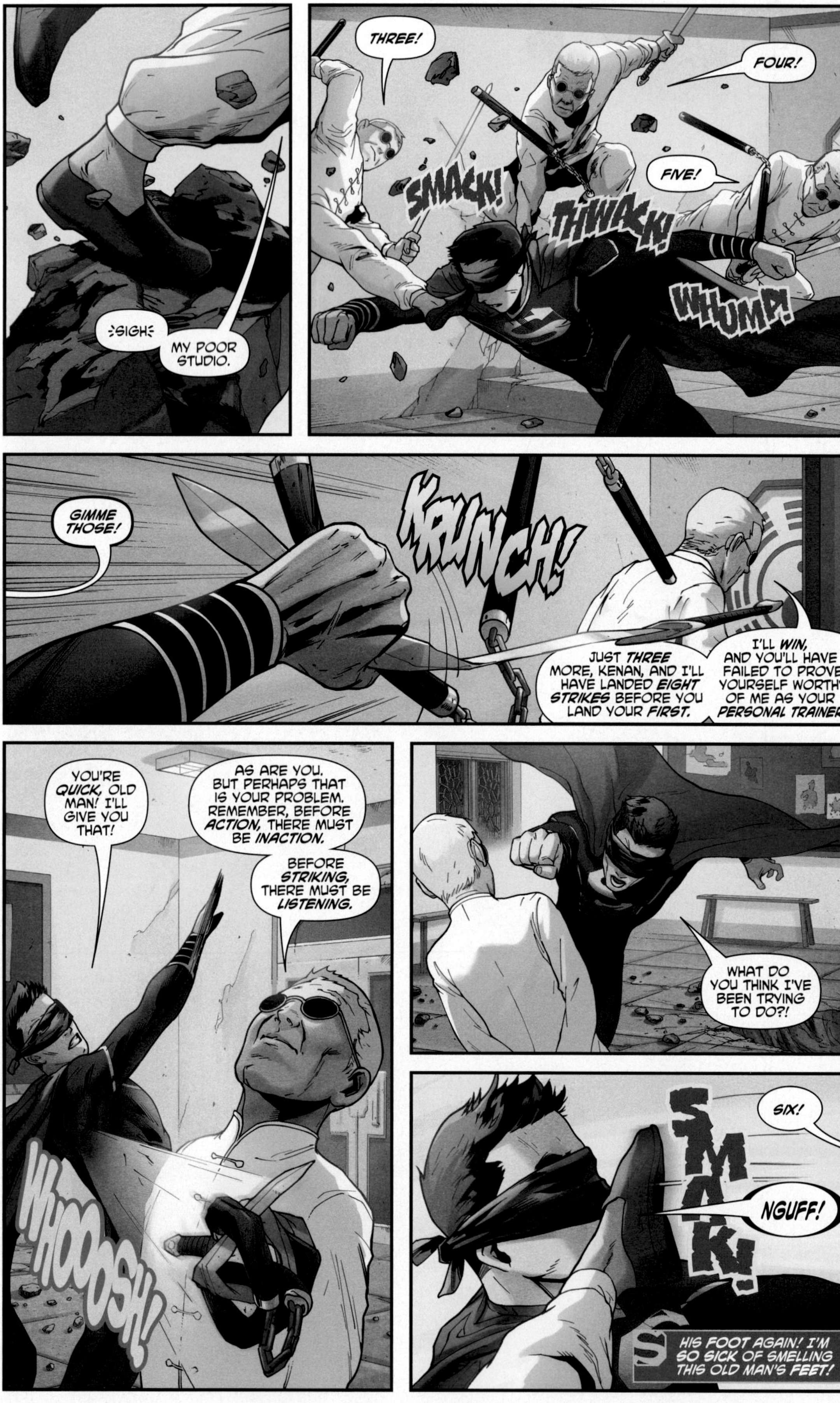

:SIGH:
MY POOR STUDIO.
THREE!
FOUR!
SMACK!
FIVE!
THWACK!
WHUMP!
GIMME THOSE!
KRUNCH!
JUST THREE MORE, KENAN, AND I'LL HAVE LANDED EIGHT STRIKES BEFORE YOU LAND YOUR FIRST.
I'LL WIN, AND YOU'LL HAVE FAILED TO PROVE YOURSELF WORTHY OF ME AS YOUR PERSONAL TRAINER.
YOU'RE QUICK, OLD MAN! I'LL GIVE YOU THAT!
AS ARE YOU. BUT PERHAPS THAT IS YOUR PROBLEM. REMEMBER, BEFORE ACTION, THERE MUST BE INACTION.
BEFORE STRIKING, THERE MUST BE LISTENING.
WHOOOSH!
WHAT DO YOU THINK I'VE BEEN TRYING TO DO?!
SMAK!
SIX!
NGUFF!
HIS FOOT AGAIN! I'M SO SICK OF SMELLING THIS OLD MAN'S FEET!

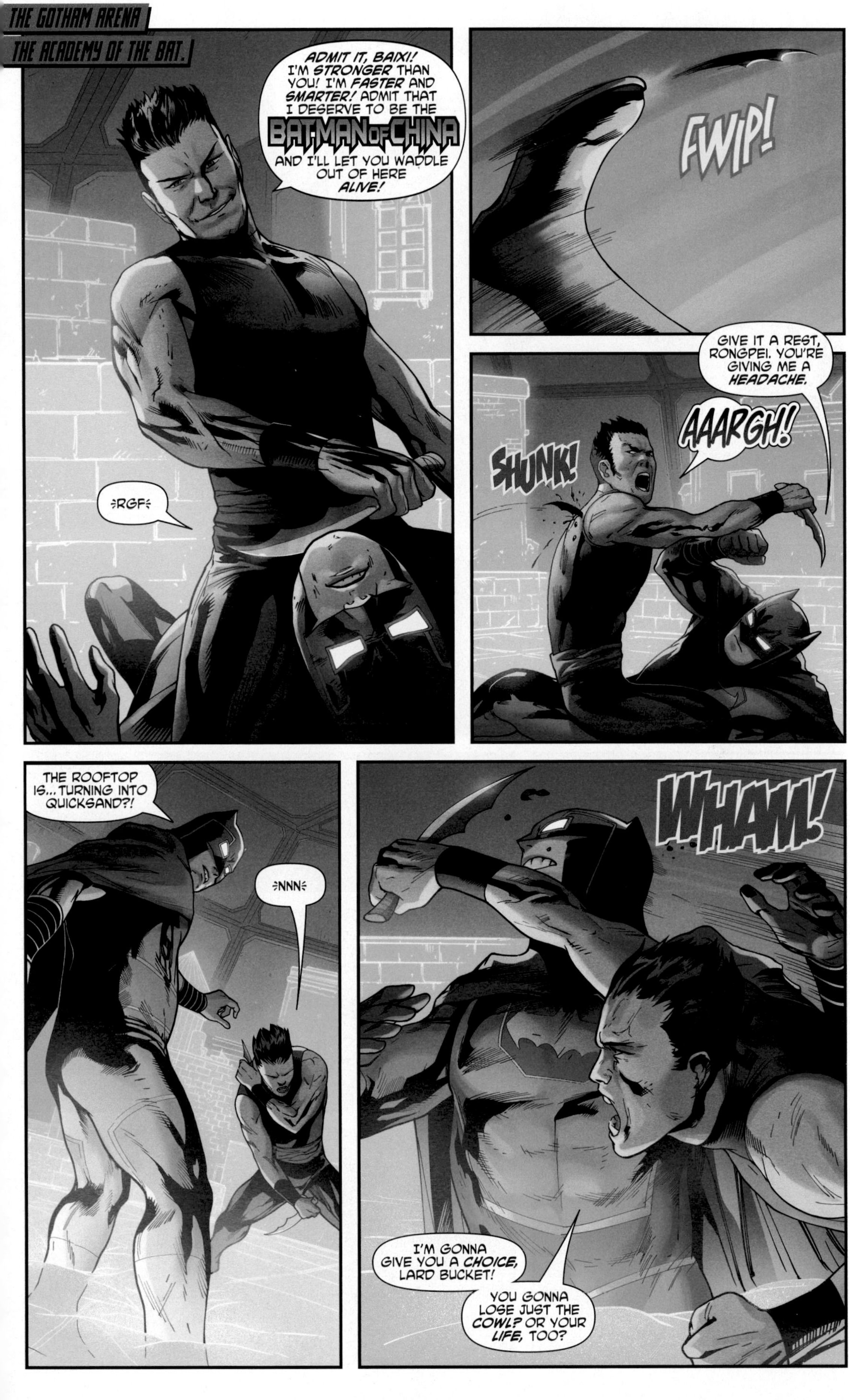
THE GOTHAM ARENA
THE ACADEMY OF THE BAT.
ADMIT IT, BAIXI! I'M STRONGER THAN YOU! I'M FASTER AND SMARTER! ADMIT THAT I DESERVE TO BE THE BATMAN OF CHINA AND I'LL LET YOU WADDLE OUT OF HERE ALIVE!
RGF
FWIP!
GIVE IT A REST, RONGPEI. YOU'RE GIVING ME A HEADACHE.
AAARGH!
SHUNK!
THE ROOFTOP IS...TURNING INTO QUICKSAND?!
NNN
WHAM!
I'M GONNA GIVE YOU A CHOICE, LARD BUCKET!
YOU GONNA LOSE JUST THE COWL? OR YOUR LIFE, TOO?

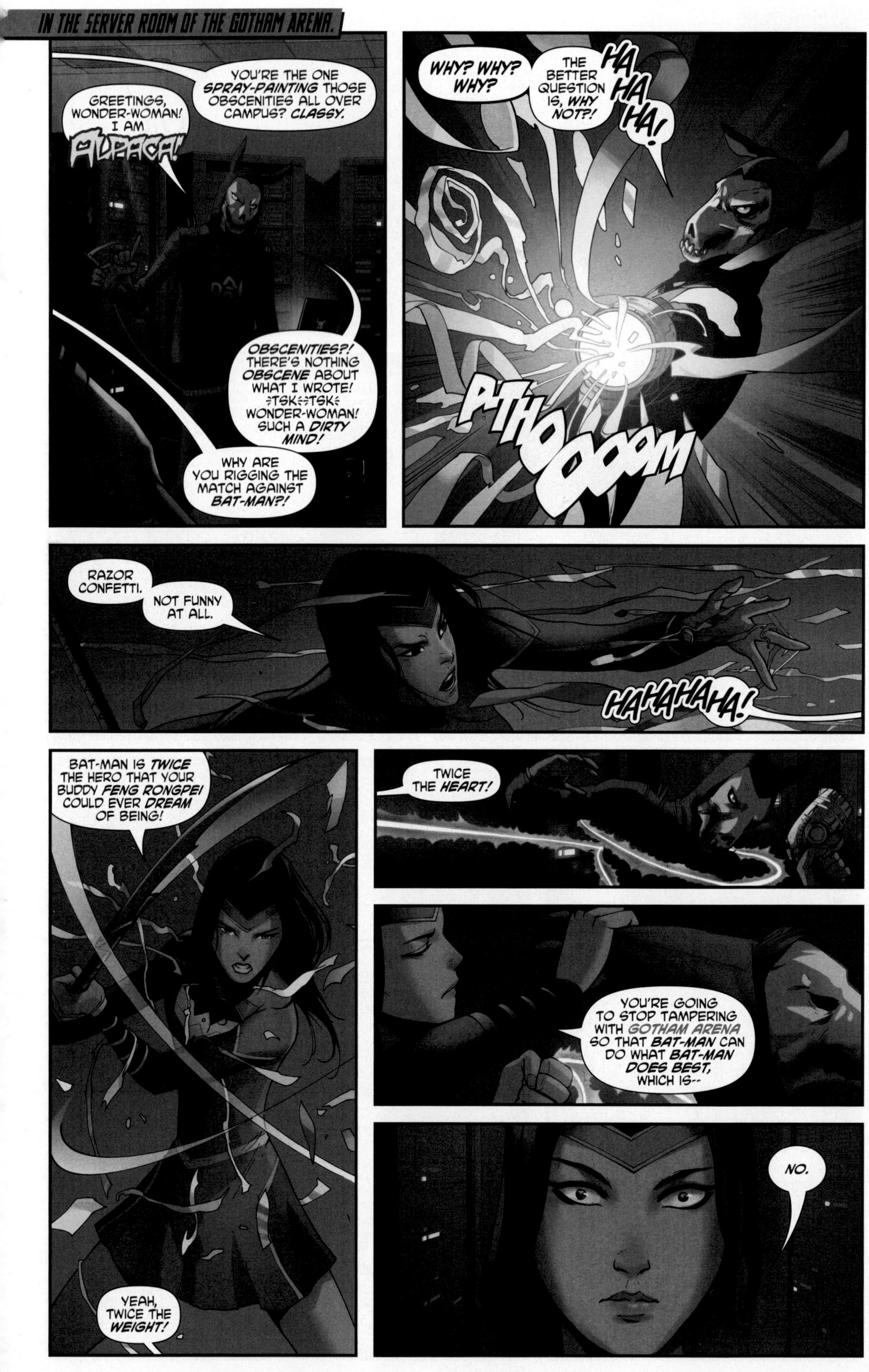
IN THE SERVER ROOM OF THE GOTHAM ARENA.
GREETINGS, WONDER-WOMAN! I AM ALPACA!
YOU'RE THE ONE SPRAY-PAINTING THOSE OBSCENITIES ALL OVER CAMPUS? CLASSY.
OBSCENITIES?! THERE'S NOTHING OBSCENE ABOUT WHAT I WROTE! TSK TSK WONDER-WOMAN! SUCH A DIRTY MIND!
WHY ARE YOU RIGGING THE MATCH AGAINST BAT-MAN?!
WHY? WHY? WHY?
THE BETTER QUESTION IS, WHY NOT?!
HA HA HA HA!
PTHOOOOOM
RAZOR CONFETTI.
NOT FUNNY AT ALL.
HAHAHAHA!
BAT-MAN IS TWICE THE HERO THAT YOUR BUDDY FENG RONGPEI COULD EVER DREAM OF BEING!
YEAH, TWICE THE WEIGHT!
TWICE THE HEART!
YOU'RE GOING TO STOP TAMPERING WITH GOTHAM ARENA SO THAT BAT-MAN CAN DO WHAT BAT-MAN DOES BEST, WHICH IS--
NO.

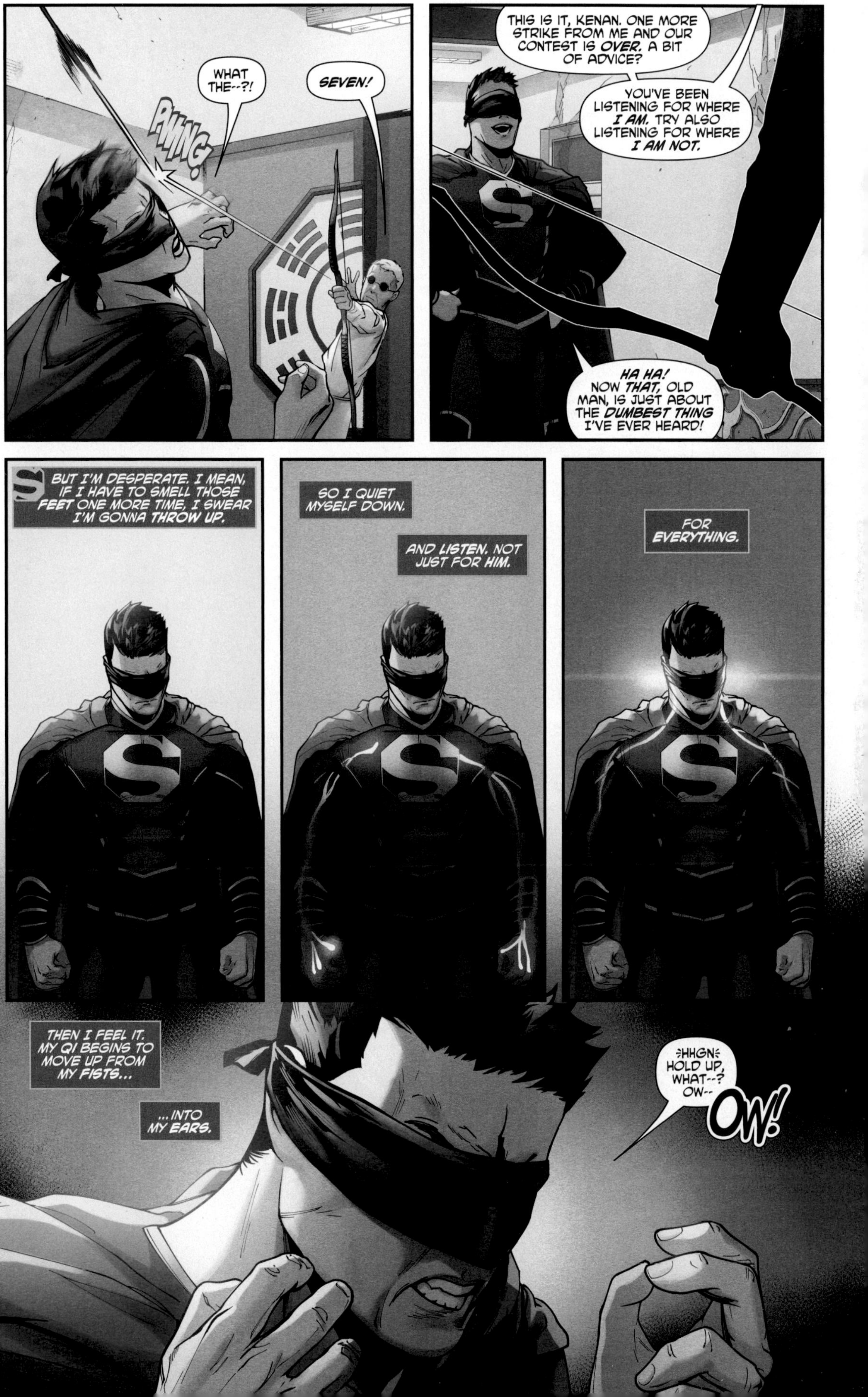
PWING!
WHAT THE--?!
SEVEN!
THIS IS IT, KENAN. ONE MORE STRIKE FROM ME AND OUR CONTEST IS OVER. A BIT OF ADVICE?
YOU'VE BEEN LISTENING FOR WHERE I AM. TRY ALSO LISTENING FOR WHERE I AM NOT.
HA HA! NOW THAT, OLD MAN, IS JUST ABOUT THE DUMBEST THING I'VE EVER HEARD!
BUT I'M DESPERATE. I MEAN, IF I HAVE TO SMELL THOSE FEET ONE MORE TIME, I SWEAR I'M GONNA THROW UP.
SO I QUIET MYSELF DOWN.
AND LISTEN. NOT JUST FOR HIM.
FOR EVERYTHING.
THEN I FEEL IT. MY QI BEGINS TO MOVE UP FROM MY FISTS...
...INTO MY EARS.
HHGN HOLD UP, WHAT--? OW--
OW!

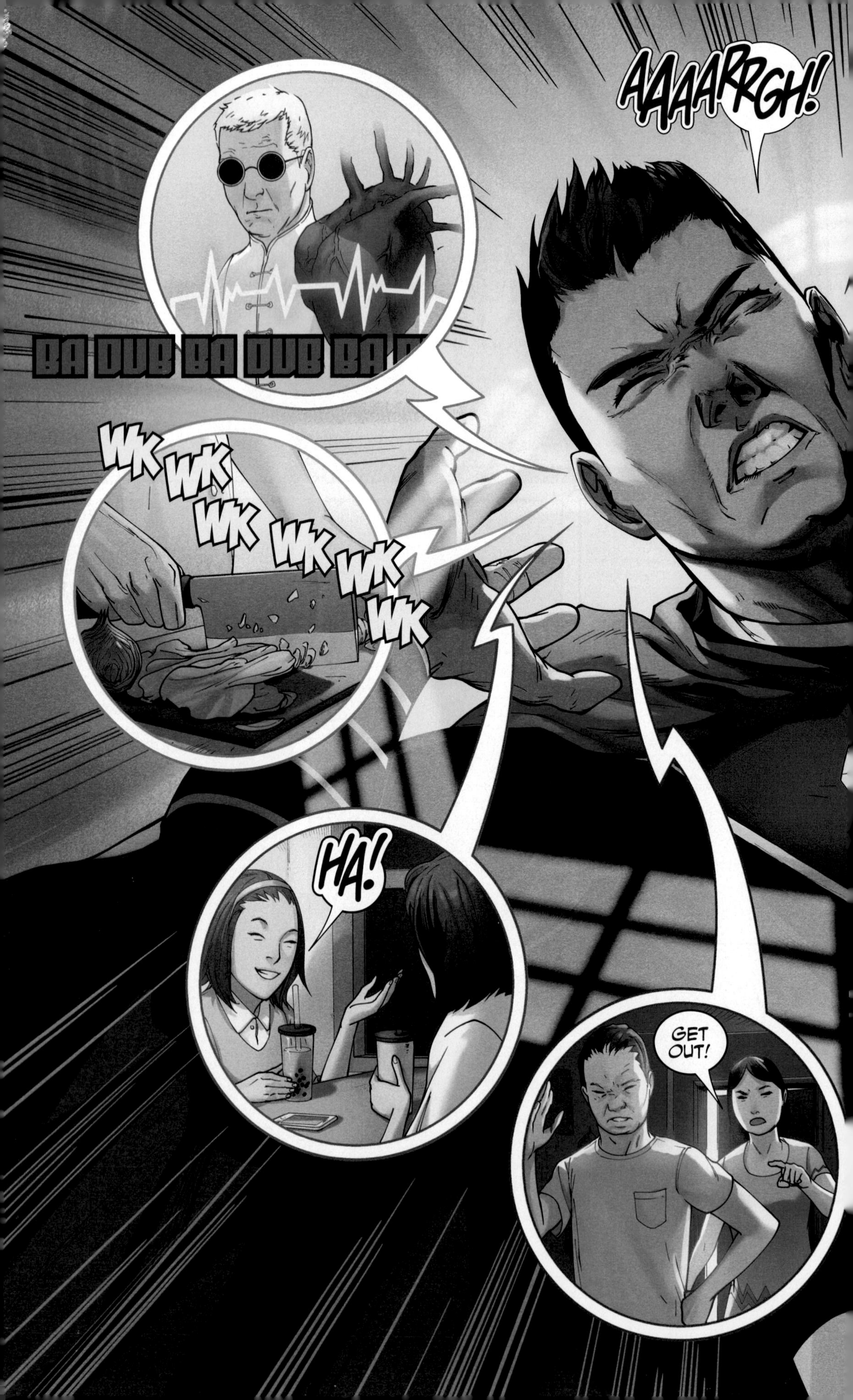
AAAARRGH!
BA DUB BA DUB BA
WK WK WK WK WK WK
HA!
GET OUT!

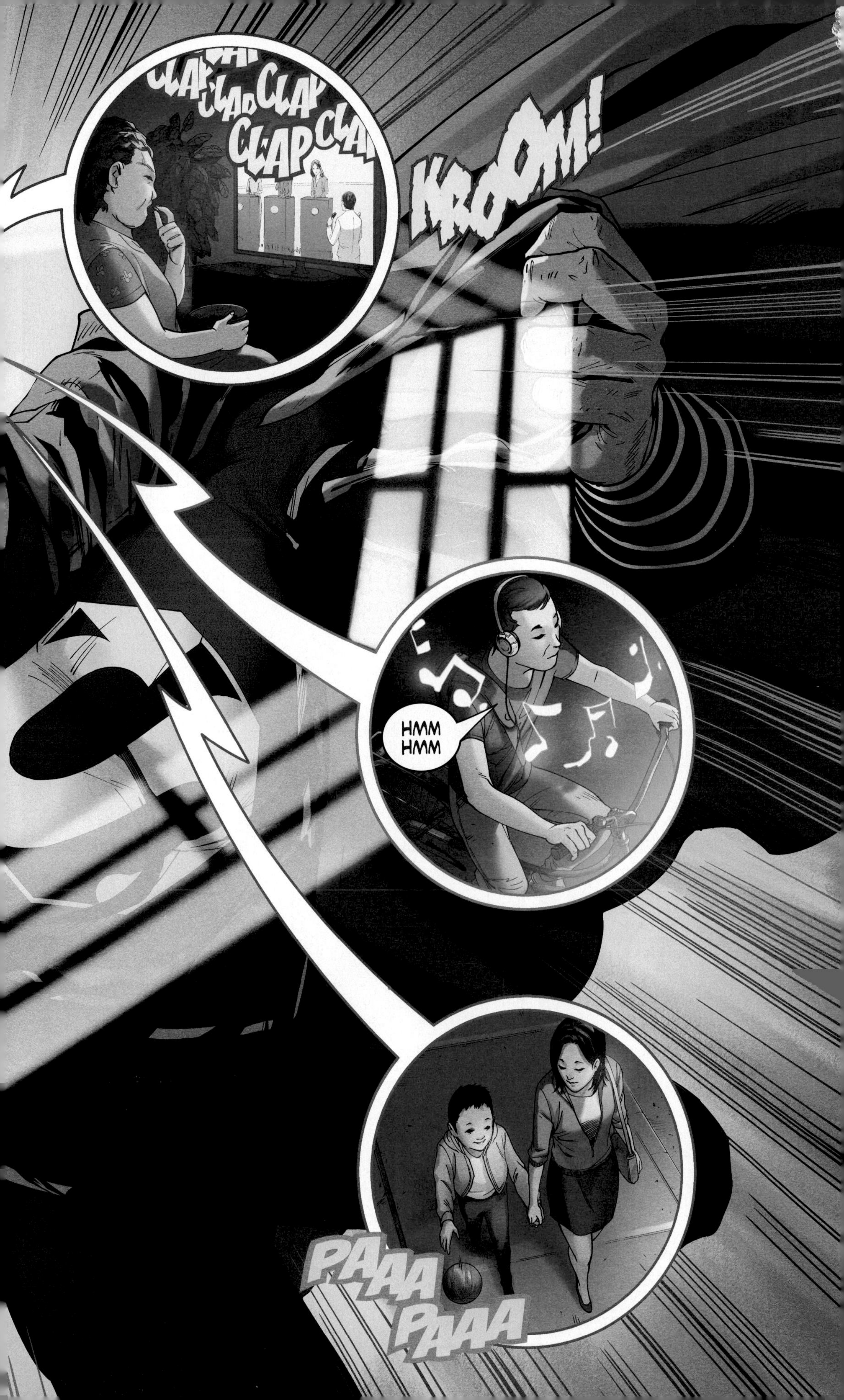
CLAP CLAP CLAP
CLAP CLAP
KROOM!
HMM HMM
PAAAA PAAAA

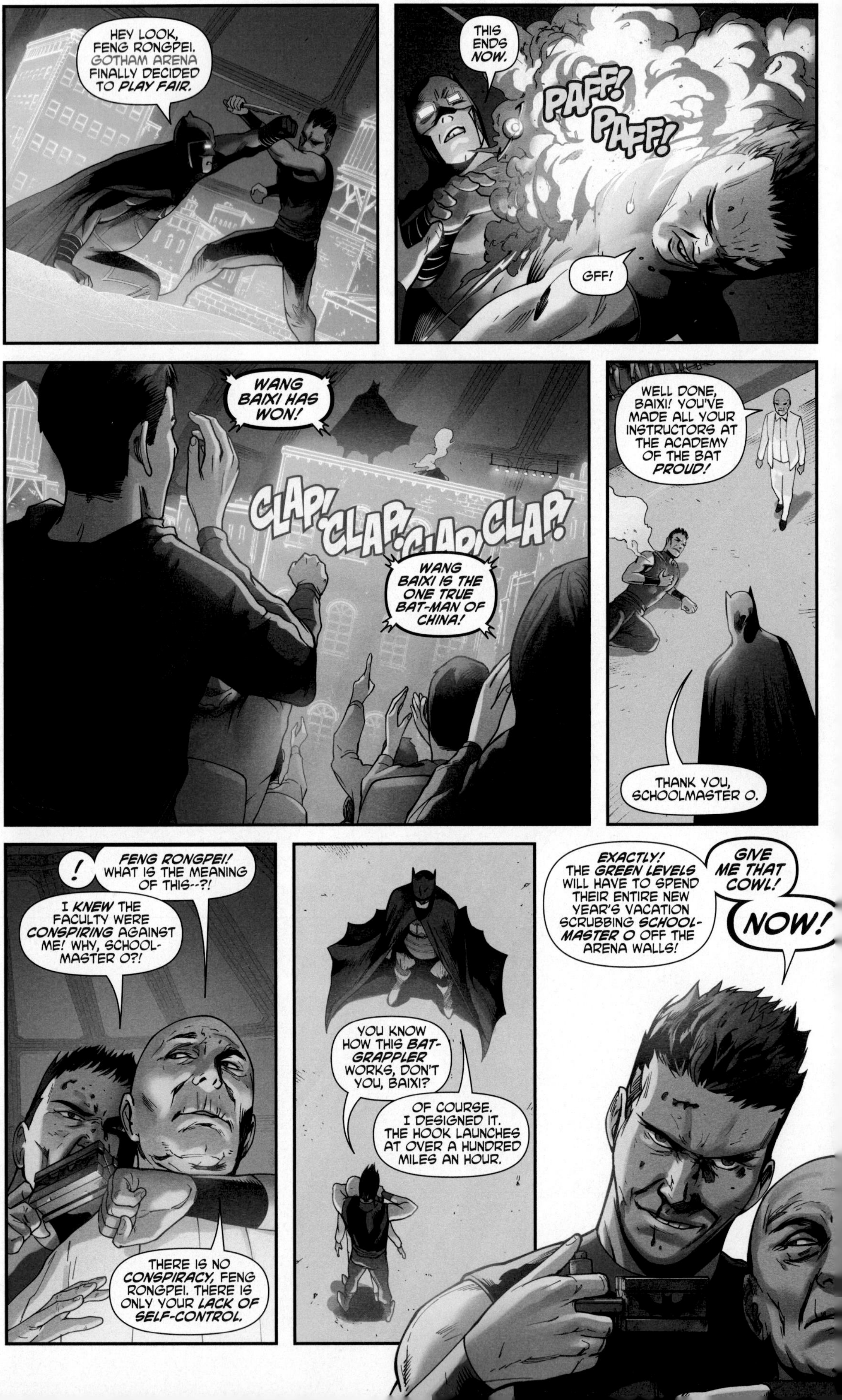
HEY LOOK, FENG RONGPEI. GOTHAM ARENA FINALLY DECIDED TO PLAY FAIR.
THIS ENDS NOW.
PAFF! PAFF!
GFF!
WANG BAIXI HAS WON!
CLAP! CLAP! CLAP! CLAP!
WANG BAIXI IS THE ONE TRUE BAT-MAN OF CHINA!
WELL DONE, BAIXI! YOU'VE MADE ALL YOUR INSTRUCTORS AT THE ACADEMY OF THE BAT PROUD!
THANK YOU, SCHOOLMASTER O.
!
FENG RONGPEI! WHAT IS THE MEANING OF THIS--?!
I KNEW THE FACULTY WERE CONSPIRING AGAINST ME! WHY, SCHOOL-MASTER O?!
THERE IS NO CONSPIRACY, FENG RONGPEI. THERE IS ONLY YOUR LACK OF SELF-CONTROL.
YOU KNOW HOW THIS BAT-GRAPPLER WORKS, DON'T YOU, BAIXI?
OF COURSE. I DESIGNED IT. THE HOOK LAUNCHES AT OVER A HUNDRED MILES AN HOUR.
EXACTLY! THE GREEN LEVELS WILL HAVE TO SPEND THEIR ENTIRE NEW YEAR'S VACATION SCRUBBING SCHOOL-MASTER O OFF THE ARENA WALLS!
GIVE ME THAT COWL!
NOW!

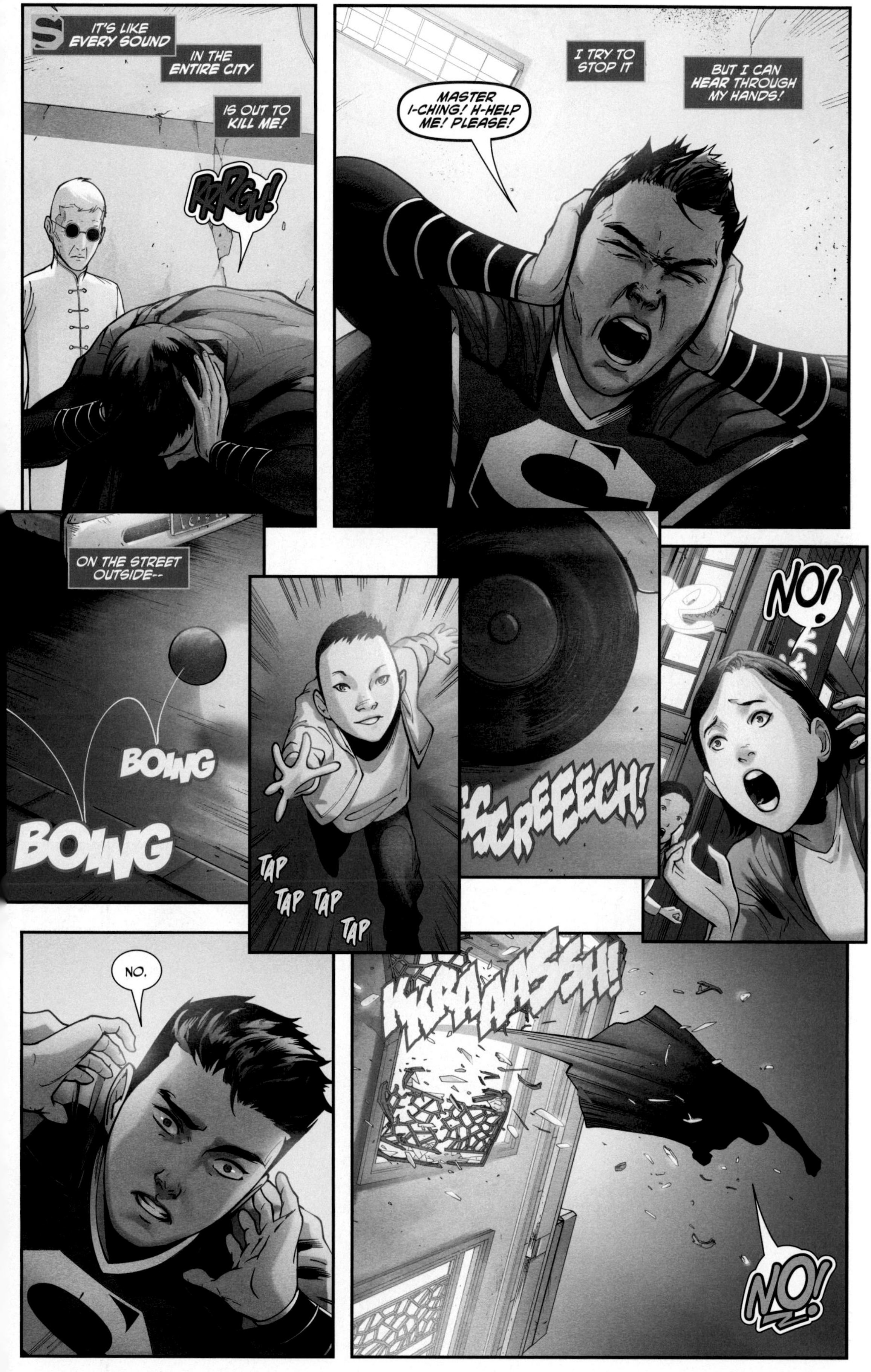
IT'S LIKE EVERY SOUND
IN THE ENTIRE CITY
IS OUT TO KILL ME!
RARGH!
MASTER I-CHING! H-HELP ME! PLEASE!
I TRY TO STOP IT
BUT I CAN HEAR THROUGH MY HANDS!
ON THE STREET OUTSIDE--
BOING
BOING
TAP
TAP TAP
TAP
SCREEECH!
NO!
NO.
KRRAAASSH!
NO!

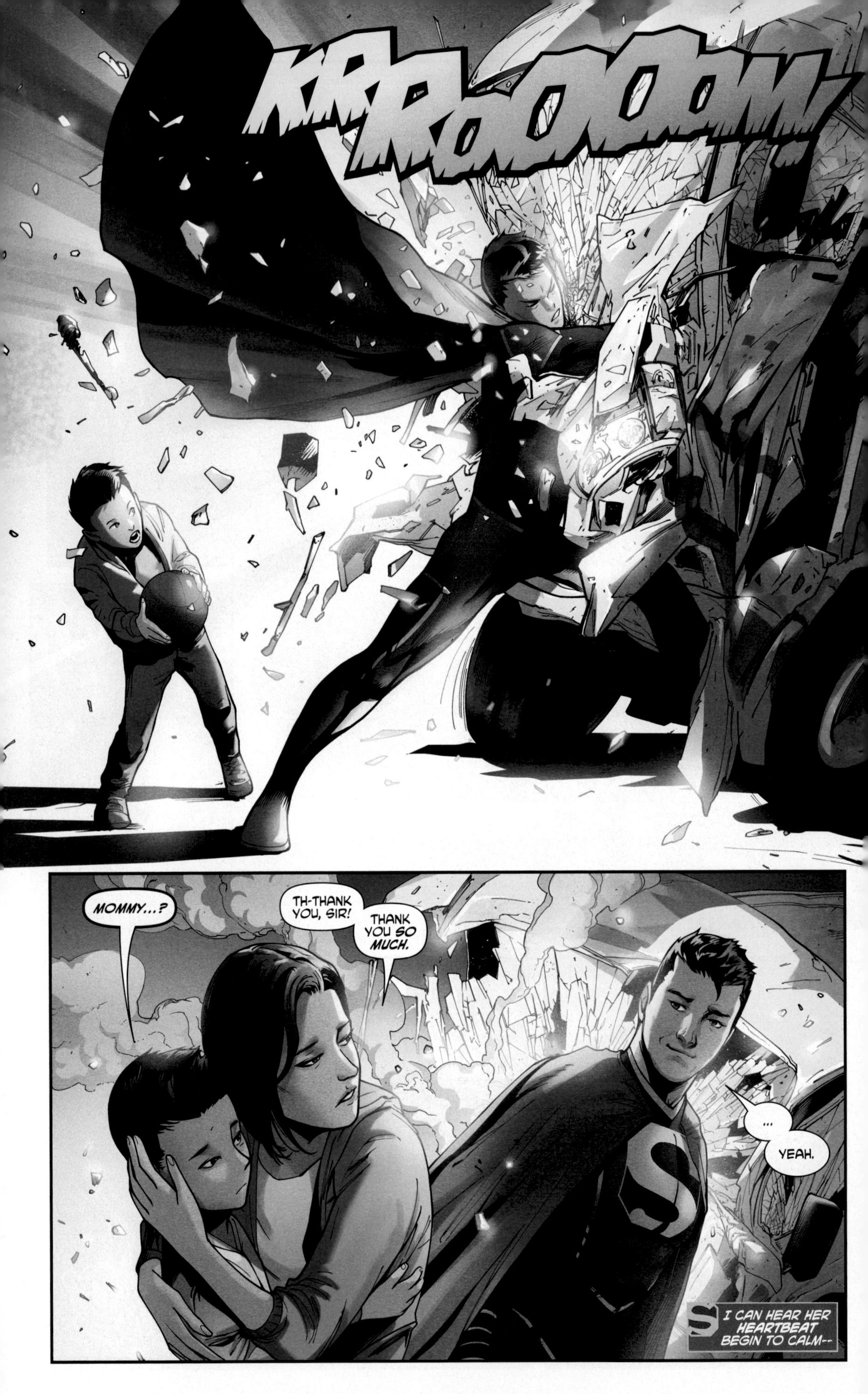
MOMMY...?
TH-THANK YOU, SIR!
THANK YOU SO MUCH.
...
YEAH.
I CAN HEAR HER HEARTBEAT BEGIN TO CALM--

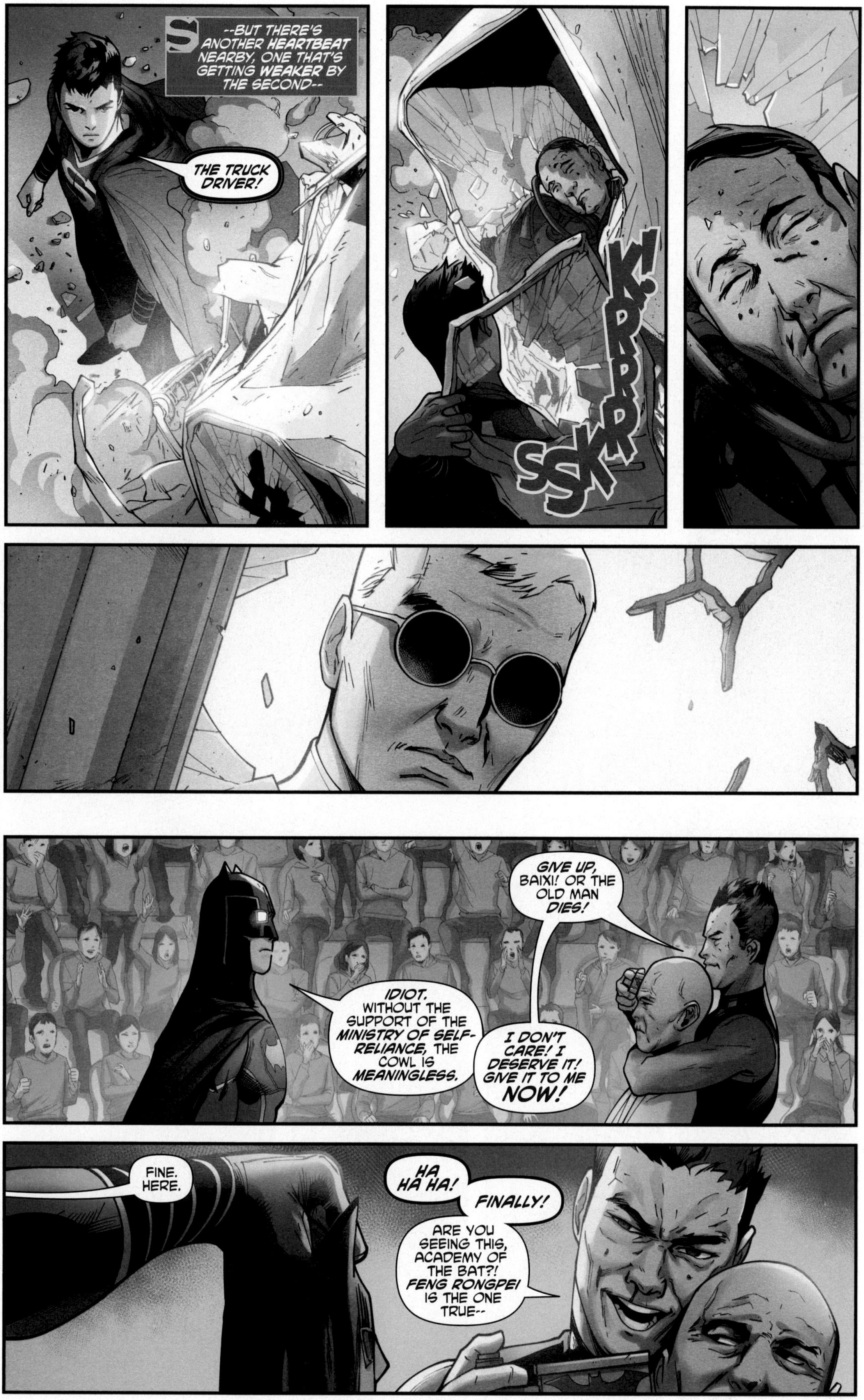
--BUT THERE'S ANOTHER HEARTBEAT NEARBY, ONE THAT'S GETTING WEAKER BY THE SECOND--
THE TRUCK DRIVER!
SSKRRRRRK!
GIVE UP, BAIXI! OR THE OLD MAN DIES!
IDIOT. WITHOUT THE SUPPORT OF THE MINISTRY OF SELF-RELIANCE, THE COWL IS MEANINGLESS.
I DON'T CARE! I DESERVE IT! GIVE IT TO ME NOW!
FINE. HERE.
HA HA HA!
FINALLY!
ARE YOU SEEING THIS, ACADEMY OF THE BAT?! FENG RONGPEI IS THE ONE TRUE--

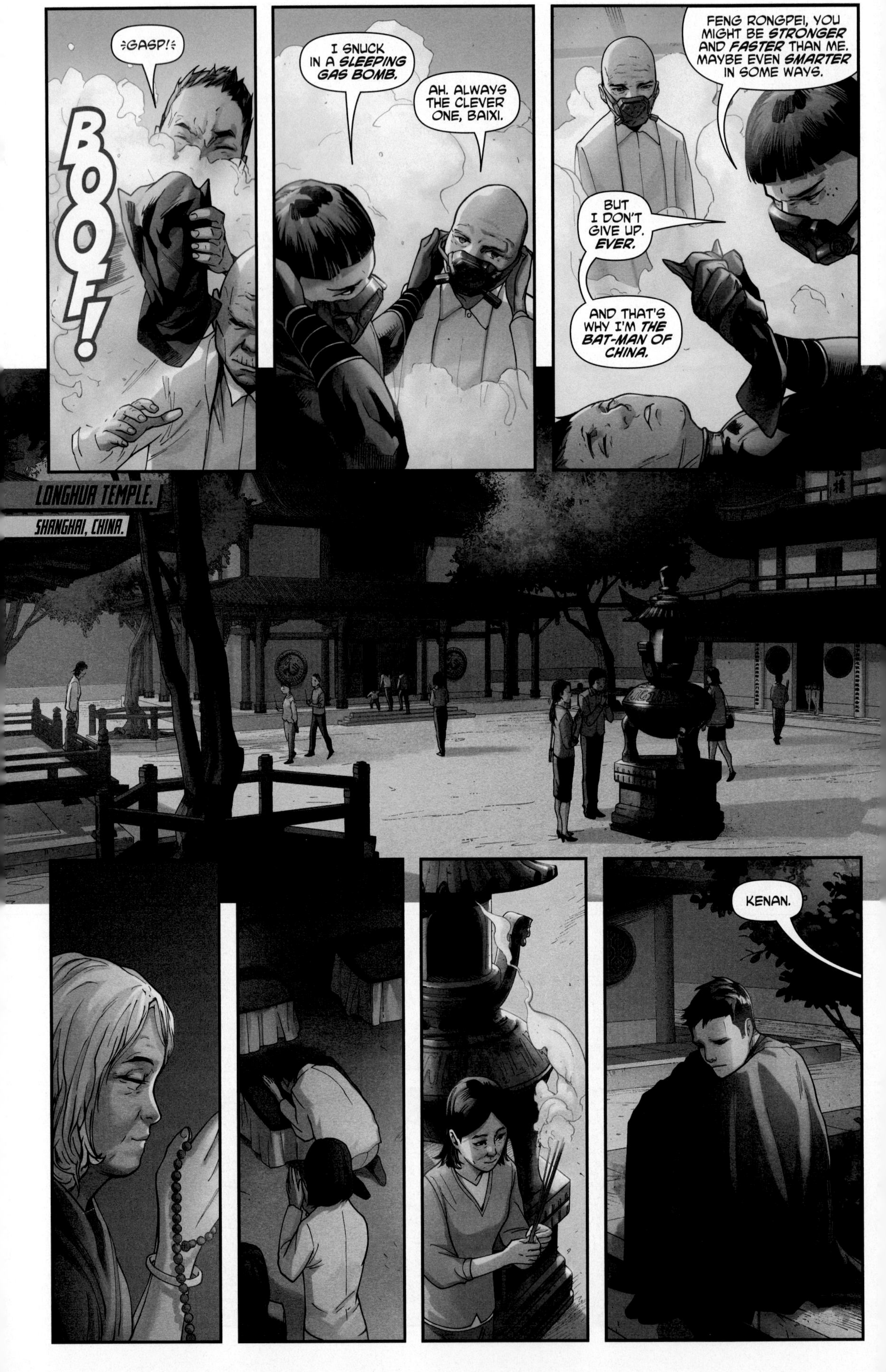
GASP!
BOOF!
I SNUCK IN A SLEEPING GAS BOMB.
AH. ALWAYS THE CLEVER ONE, BAIXI.
FENG RONGPEI, YOU MIGHT BE STRONGER AND FASTER THAN ME. MAYBE EVEN SMARTER IN SOME WAYS.
BUT I DON'T GIVE UP. EVER.
AND THAT'S WHY I'M THE BAT-MAN OF CHINA.
LONGHUA TEMPLE.
SHANGHAI, CHINA.
KENAN.

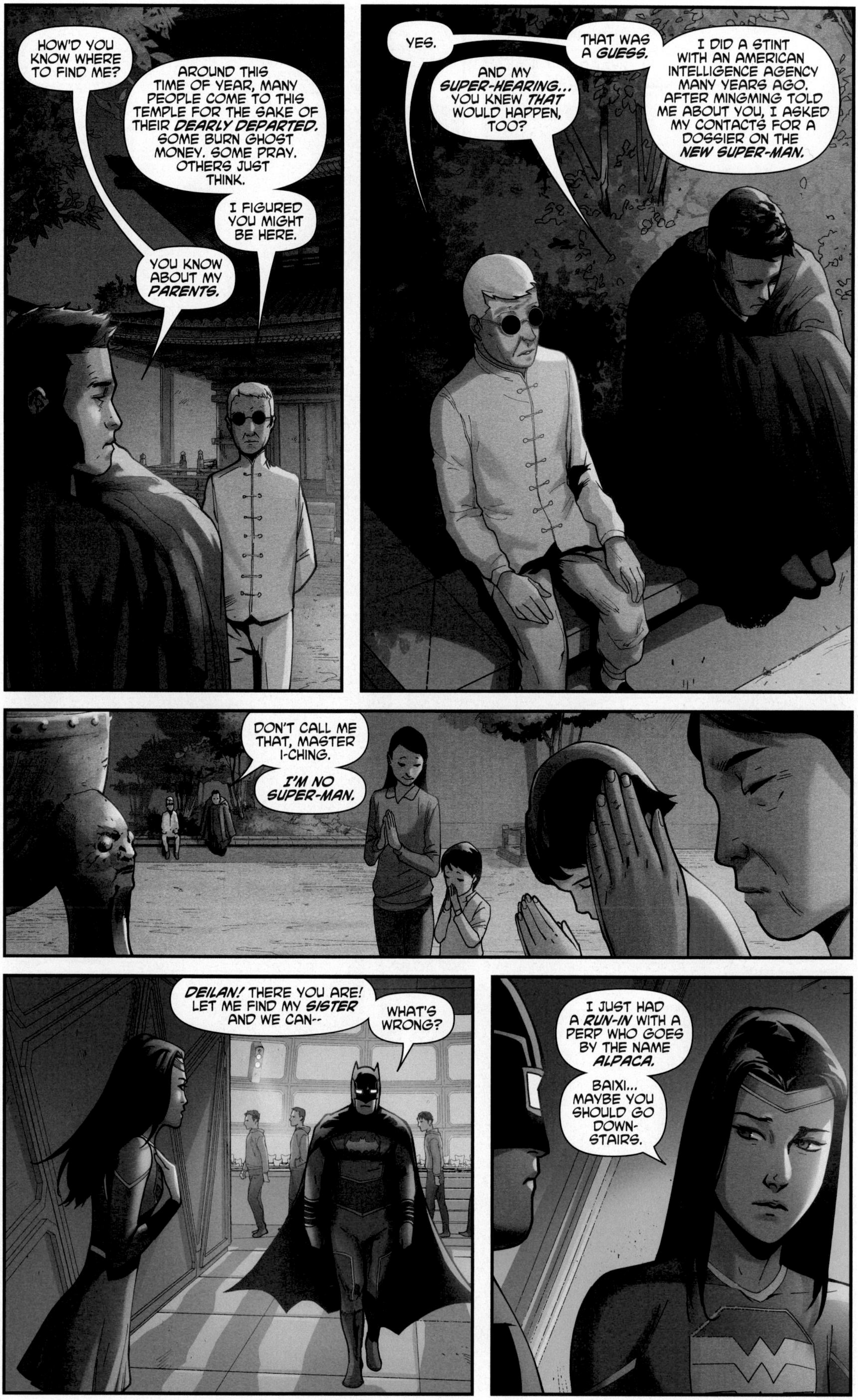
HOW'D YOU KNOW WHERE TO FIND ME?
AROUND THIS TIME OF YEAR, MANY PEOPLE COME TO THIS TEMPLE FOR THE SAKE OF THEIR DEARLY DEPARTED. SOME BURN GHOST MONEY. SOME PRAY. OTHERS JUST THINK.
I FIGURED YOU MIGHT BE HERE.
YOU KNOW ABOUT MY PARENTS.
YES.
THAT WAS A GUESS.
I DID A STINT WITH AN AMERICAN INTELLIGENCE AGENCY MANY YEARS AGO. AFTER MINGMING TOLD ME ABOUT YOU, I ASKED MY CONTACTS FOR A DOSSIER ON THE NEW SUPER-MAN.
AND MY SUPER-HEARING... YOU KNEW THAT WOULD HAPPEN, TOO?
DON'T CALL ME THAT, MASTER I-CHING.
I'M NO SUPER-MAN.
DEILAN! THERE YOU ARE! LET ME FIND MY SISTER AND WE CAN--
WHAT'S WRONG?
I JUST HAD A RUN-IN WITH A PERP WHO GOES BY THE NAME ALPACA.
BAIXI... MAYBE YOU SHOULD GO DOWN-STAIRS.

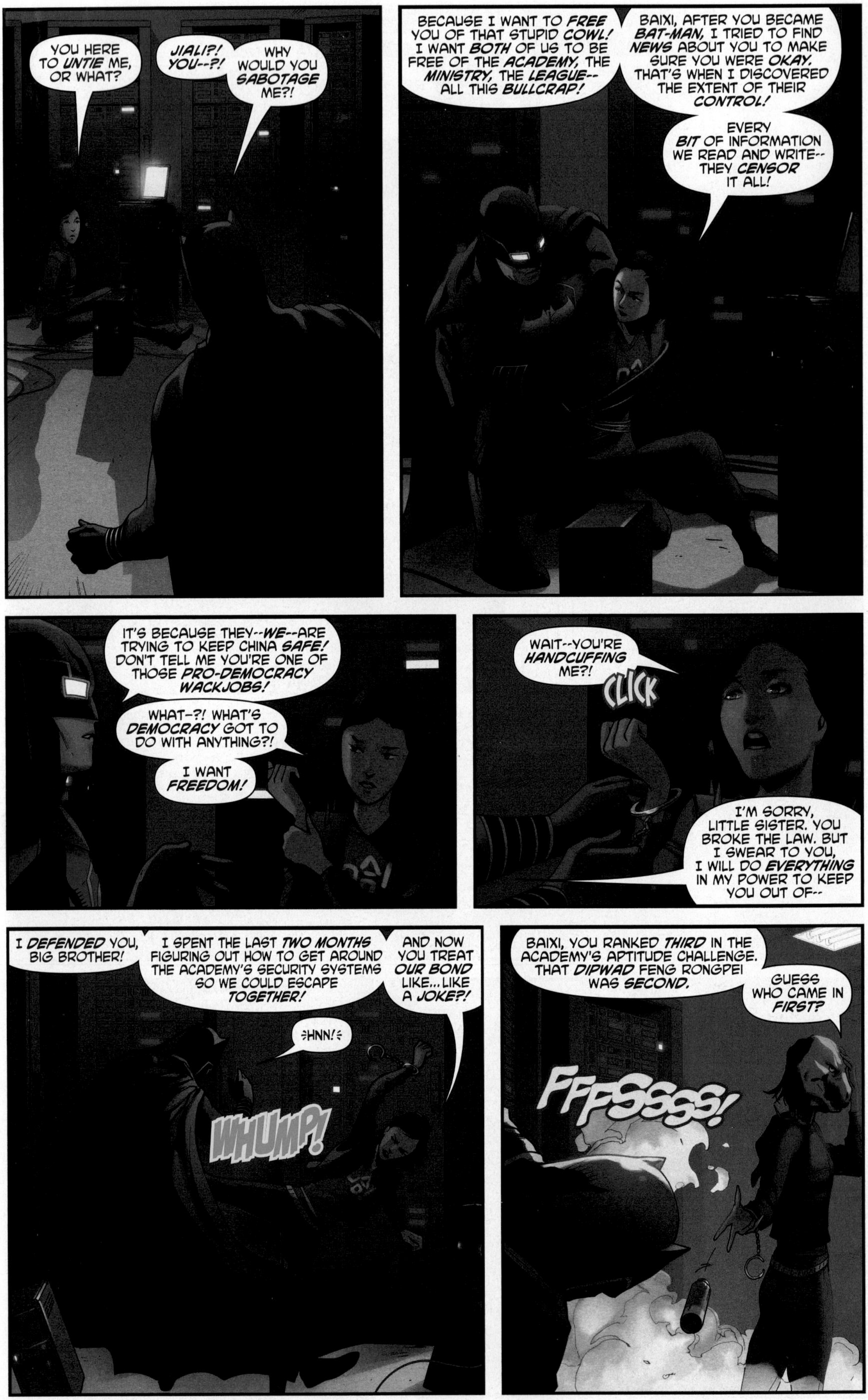
YOU HERE TO UNTIE ME, OR WHAT?
JIALI?! YOU--?!
WHY WOULD YOU SABOTAGE ME?!
BECAUSE I WANT TO FREE YOU OF THAT STUPID COWL! I WANT BOTH OF US TO BE FREE OF THE ACADEMY, THE MINISTRY, THE LEAGUE-- ALL THIS BULLCRAP!
BAIXI, AFTER YOU BECAME BAT-MAN, I TRIED TO FIND NEWS ABOUT YOU TO MAKE SURE YOU WERE OKAY. THAT'S WHEN I DISCOVERED THE EXTENT OF THEIR CONTROL!
EVERY BIT OF INFORMATION WE READ AND WRITE-- THEY CENSOR IT ALL!
IT'S BECAUSE THEY--WE--ARE TRYING TO KEEP CHINA SAFE! DON'T TELL ME YOU'RE ONE OF THOSE PRO-DEMOCRACY WACKJOBS!
WHAT-?! WHAT'S DEMOCRACY GOT TO DO WITH ANYTHING?!
I WANT FREEDOM!
WAIT--YOU'RE HANDCUFFING ME?!
CLICK
I'M SORRY, LITTLE SISTER. YOU BROKE THE LAW. BUT I SWEAR TO YOU, I WILL DO EVERYTHING IN MY POWER TO KEEP YOU OUT OF--
I DEFENDED YOU, BIG BROTHER!
I SPENT THE LAST TWO MONTHS FIGURING OUT HOW TO GET AROUND THE ACADEMY'S SECURITY SYSTEMS SO WE COULD ESCAPE TOGETHER!
AND NOW YOU TREAT OUR BOND LIKE...LIKE A JOKE?!
HNN!
WHUMP!
BAIXI, YOU RANKED THIRD IN THE ACADEMY'S APTITUDE CHALLENGE. THAT DIPWAD FENG RONGPEI WAS SECOND.
GUESS WHO CAME IN FIRST?
FFFSSSS!

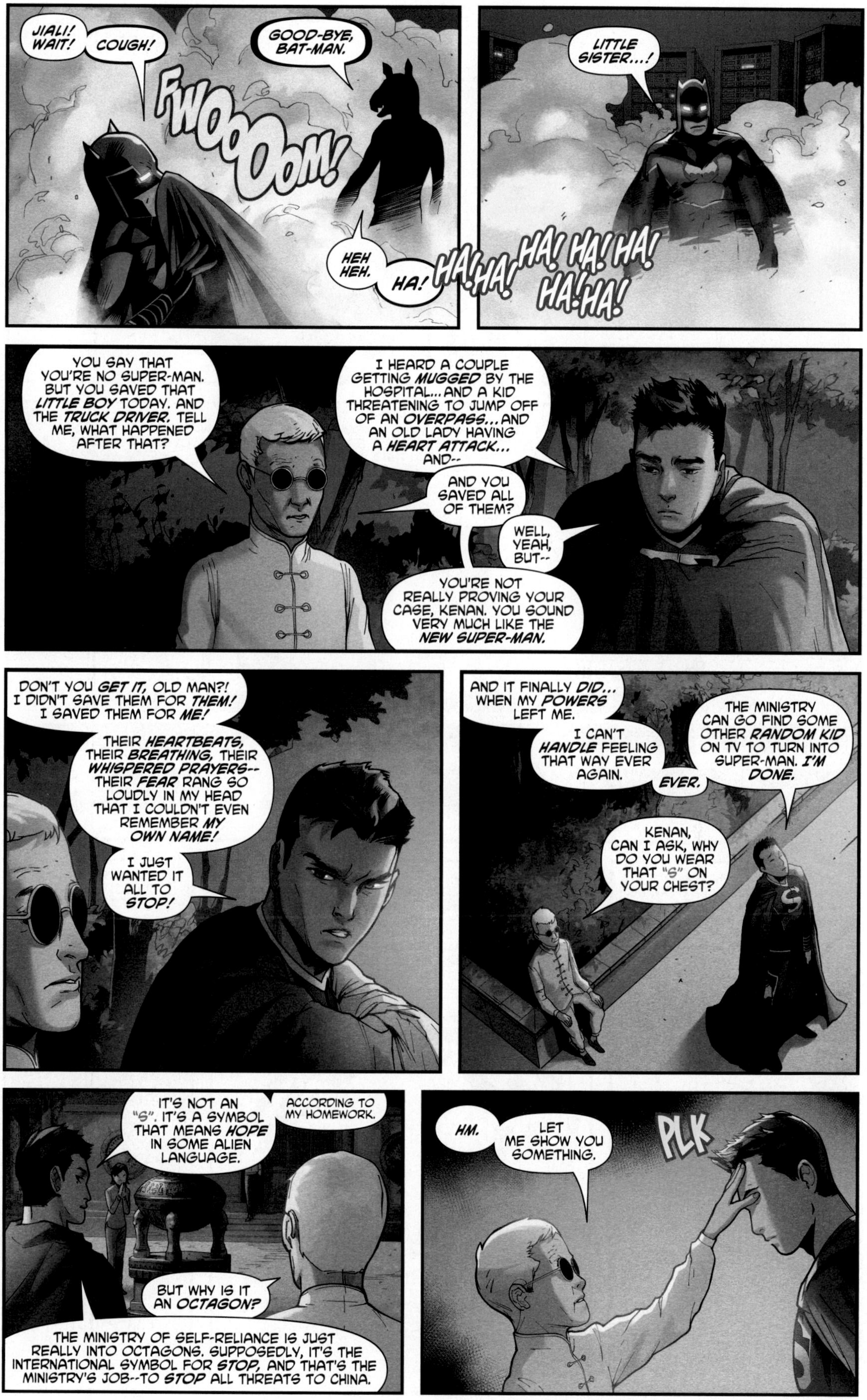
JIALI! WAIT!
COUGH!
GOOD-BYE, BAT-MAN.
FWOOOOOM!
HEH HEH.
HA!
HA! HA! HA! HA! HA! HA! HA!
LITTLE SISTER...!
YOU SAY THAT YOU'RE NO SUPER-MAN. BUT YOU SAVED THAT LITTLE BOY TODAY. AND THE TRUCK DRIVER. TELL ME, WHAT HAPPENED AFTER THAT?
I HEARD A COUPLE GETTING MUGGED BY THE HOSPITAL... AND A KID THREATENING TO JUMP OFF OF AN OVERPASS... AND AN OLD LADY HAVING A HEART ATTACK... AND--
AND YOU SAVED ALL OF THEM?
WELL, YEAH, BUT--
YOU'RE NOT REALLY PROVING YOUR CASE, KENAN. YOU SOUND VERY MUCH LIKE THE NEW SUPER-MAN.
DON'T YOU GET IT, OLD MAN?! I DIDN'T SAVE THEM FOR THEM! I SAVED THEM FOR ME!
THEIR HEARTBEATS, THEIR BREATHING, THEIR WHISPERED PRAYERS-- THEIR FEAR RANG SO LOUDLY IN MY HEAD THAT I COULDN'T EVEN REMEMBER MY OWN NAME!
I JUST WANTED IT ALL TO STOP!
AND IT FINALLY DID... WHEN MY POWERS LEFT ME.
I CAN'T HANDLE FEELING THAT WAY EVER AGAIN.
EVER.
THE MINISTRY CAN GO FIND SOME OTHER RANDOM KID ON TV TO TURN INTO SUPER-MAN. I'M DONE.
KENAN, CAN I ASK, WHY DO YOU WEAR THAT "S" ON YOUR CHEST?
IT'S NOT AN "S". IT'S A SYMBOL THAT MEANS HOPE IN SOME ALIEN LANGUAGE.
ACCORDING TO MY HOMEWORK.
BUT WHY IS IT AN OCTAGON?
THE MINISTRY OF SELF-RELIANCE IS JUST REALLY INTO OCTAGONS. SUPPOSEDLY, IT'S THE INTERNATIONAL SYMBOL FOR STOP, AND THAT'S THE MINISTRY'S JOB--TO STOP ALL THREATS TO CHINA.
HM.
LET ME SHOW YOU SOMETHING.
PLK

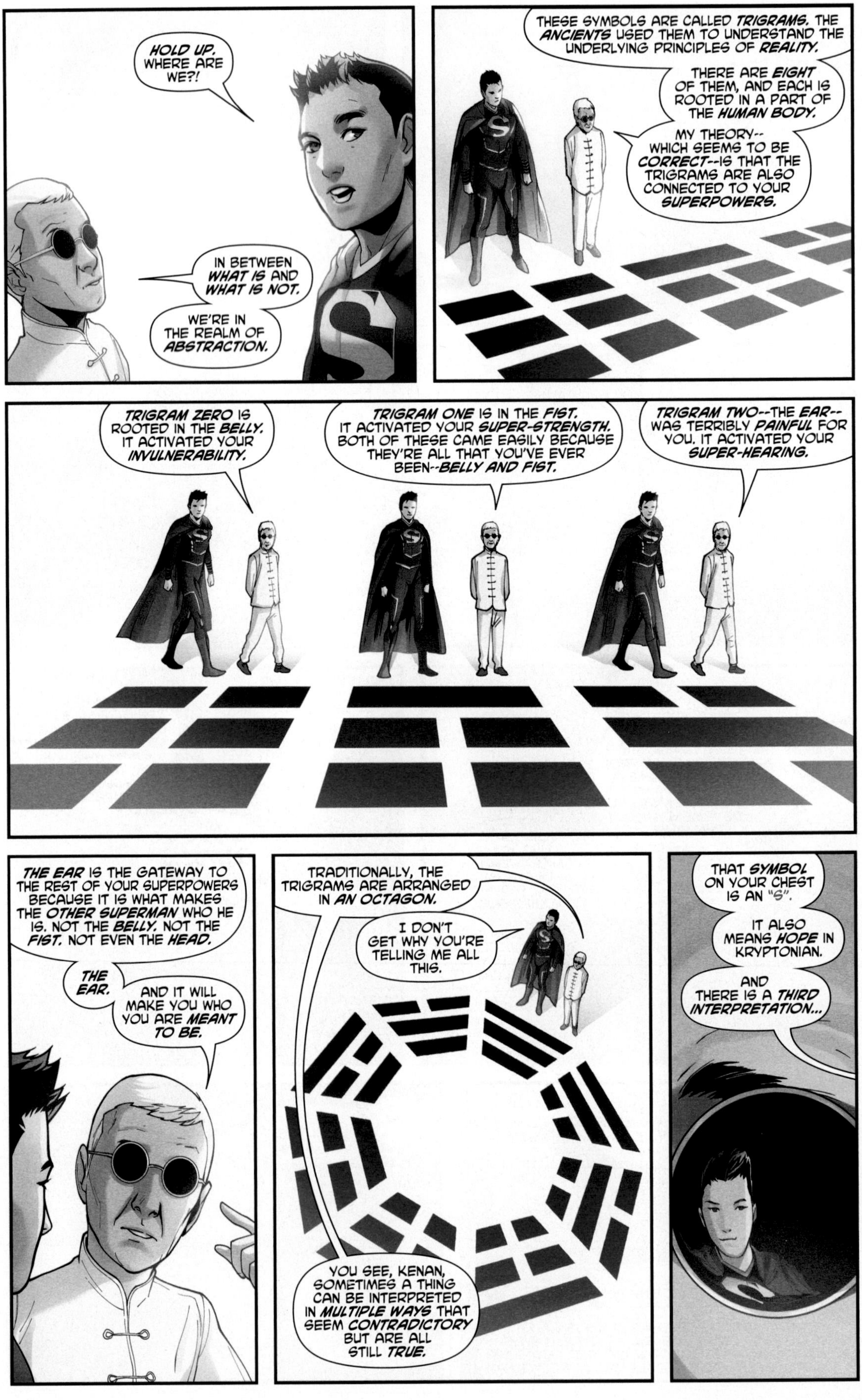
HOLD UP. WHERE ARE WE?!
IN BETWEEN WHAT IS AND WHAT IS NOT.
WE'RE IN THE REALM OF ABSTRACTION.
THESE SYMBOLS ARE CALLED TRIGRAMS. THE ANCIENTS USED THEM TO UNDERSTAND THE UNDERLYING PRINCIPLES OF REALITY.
THERE ARE EIGHT OF THEM, AND EACH IS ROOTED IN A PART OF THE HUMAN BODY.
MY THEORY-- WHICH SEEMS TO BE CORRECT--IS THAT THE TRIGRAMS ARE ALSO CONNECTED TO YOUR SUPERPOWERS.
TRIGRAM ZERO IS ROOTED IN THE BELLY. IT ACTIVATED YOUR INVULNERABILITY.
TRIGRAM ONE IS IN THE FIST. IT ACTIVATED YOUR SUPER-STRENGTH. BOTH OF THESE CAME EASILY BECAUSE THEY'RE ALL THAT YOU'VE EVER BEEN--BELLY AND FIST.
TRIGRAM TWO--THE EAR--WAS TERRIBLY PAINFUL FOR YOU. IT ACTIVATED YOUR SUPER-HEARING.
THE EAR IS THE GATEWAY TO THE REST OF YOUR SUPERPOWERS BECAUSE IT IS WHAT MAKES THE OTHER SUPERMAN WHO HE IS. NOT THE BELLY. NOT THE FIST. NOT EVEN THE HEAD.
THE EAR.
AND IT WILL MAKE YOU WHO YOU ARE MEANT TO BE.
TRADITIONALLY, THE TRIGRAMS ARE ARRANGED IN AN OCTAGON.
I DON'T GET WHY YOU'RE TELLING ME ALL THIS.
YOU SEE, KENAN, SOMETIMES A THING CAN BE INTERPRETED IN MULTIPLE WAYS THAT SEEM CONTRADICTORY BUT ARE ALL STILL TRUE.
THAT SYMBOL ON YOUR CHEST IS AN "S".
IT ALSO MEANS HOPE IN KRYPTONIAN.
AND THERE IS A THIRD INTERPRETATION...

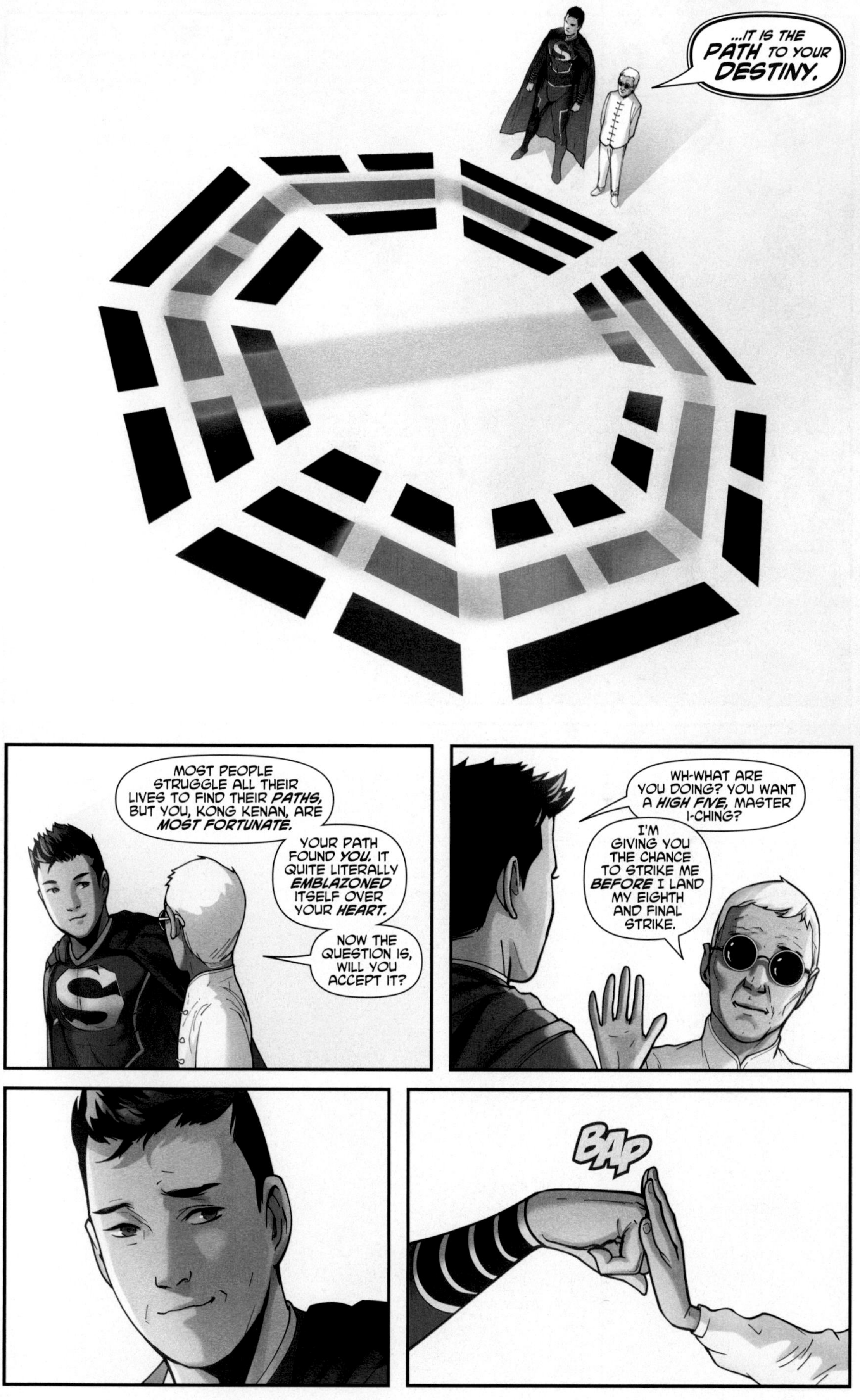
...IT IS THE PATH TO YOUR DESTINY.
MOST PEOPLE STRUGGLE ALL THEIR LIVES TO FIND THEIR PATHS, BUT YOU, KONG KENAN, ARE MOST FORTUNATE.
YOUR PATH FOUND YOU. IT QUITE LITERALLY EMBLAZONED ITSELF OVER YOUR HEART.
NOW THE QUESTION IS, WILL YOU ACCEPT IT?
WH-WHAT ARE YOU DOING? YOU WANT A HIGH FIVE, MASTER I-CHING?
I'M GIVING YOU THE CHANCE TO STRIKE ME BEFORE I LAND MY EIGHTH AND FINAL STRIKE.
BAP

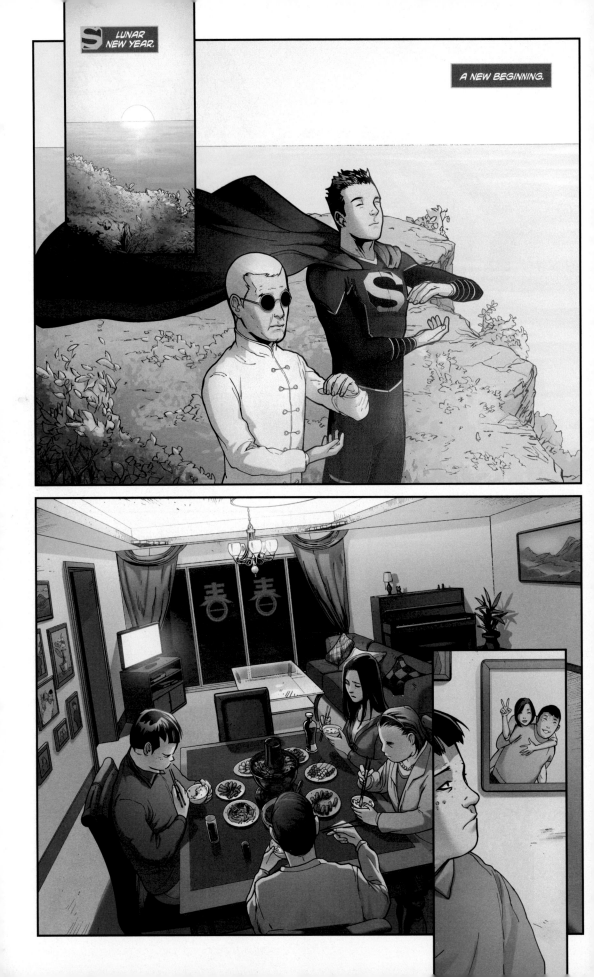

LUNAR
NEW YEAR.

A NEW BEGINNING.

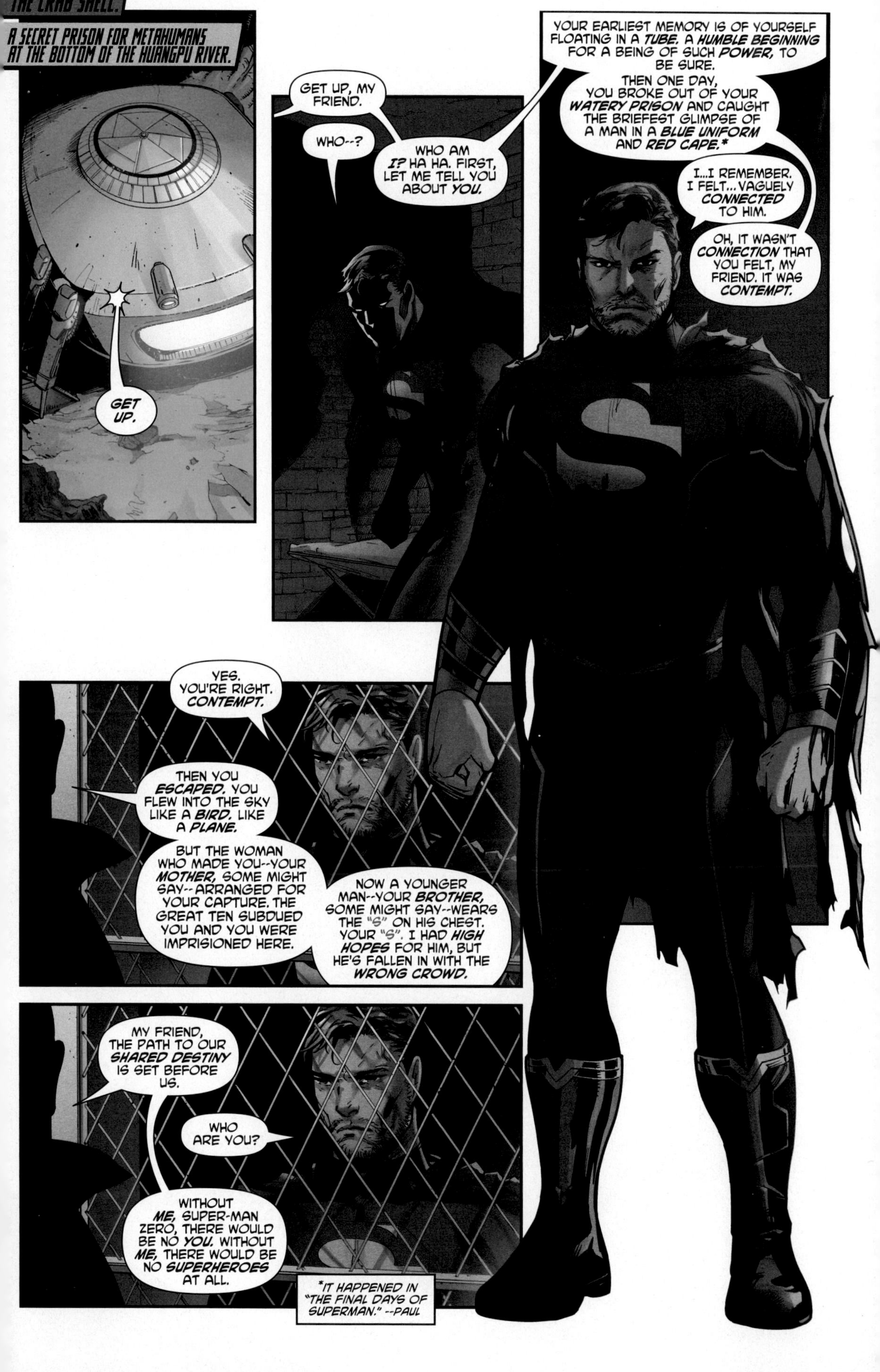

THE CRAB SHELL.
A SECRET PRISON FOR METAHUMANS AT THE BOTTOM OF THE HUANGPU RIVER.
GET UP.
GET UP, MY FRIEND.
WHO--?
WHO AM I? HA HA. FIRST, LET ME TELL YOU ABOUT YOU.
YOUR EARLIEST MEMORY IS OF YOURSELF FLOATING IN A TUBE. A HUMBLE BEGINNING FOR A BEING OF SUCH POWER, TO BE SURE.
THEN ONE DAY, YOU BROKE OUT OF YOUR WATERY PRISON AND CAUGHT THE BRIEFEST GLIMPSE OF A MAN IN A BLUE UNIFORM AND RED CAPE.*
I...I REMEMBER. I FELT...VAGUELY CONNECTED TO HIM.
OH, IT WASN'T CONNECTION THAT YOU FELT, MY FRIEND. IT WAS CONTEMPT.
YES. YOU'RE RIGHT. CONTEMPT.
THEN YOU ESCAPED. YOU FLEW INTO THE SKY LIKE A BIRD. LIKE A PLANE.
BUT THE WOMAN WHO MADE YOU--YOUR MOTHER, SOME MIGHT SAY--ARRANGED FOR YOUR CAPTURE. THE GREAT TEN SUBDUED YOU AND YOU WERE IMPRISIONED HERE.
NOW A YOUNGER MAN--YOUR BROTHER, SOME MIGHT SAY--WEARS THE "S" ON HIS CHEST. YOUR "S". I HAD HIGH HOPES FOR HIM, BUT HE'S FALLEN IN WITH THE WRONG CROWD.
MY FRIEND, THE PATH TO OUR SHARED DESTINY IS SET BEFORE US.
WHO ARE YOU?
WITHOUT ME, SUPER-MAN ZERO, THERE WOULD BE NO YOU. WITHOUT ME, THERE WOULD BE NO SUPERHEROES AT ALL.
*IT HAPPENED IN "THE FINAL DAYS OF SUPERMAN." --PAUL

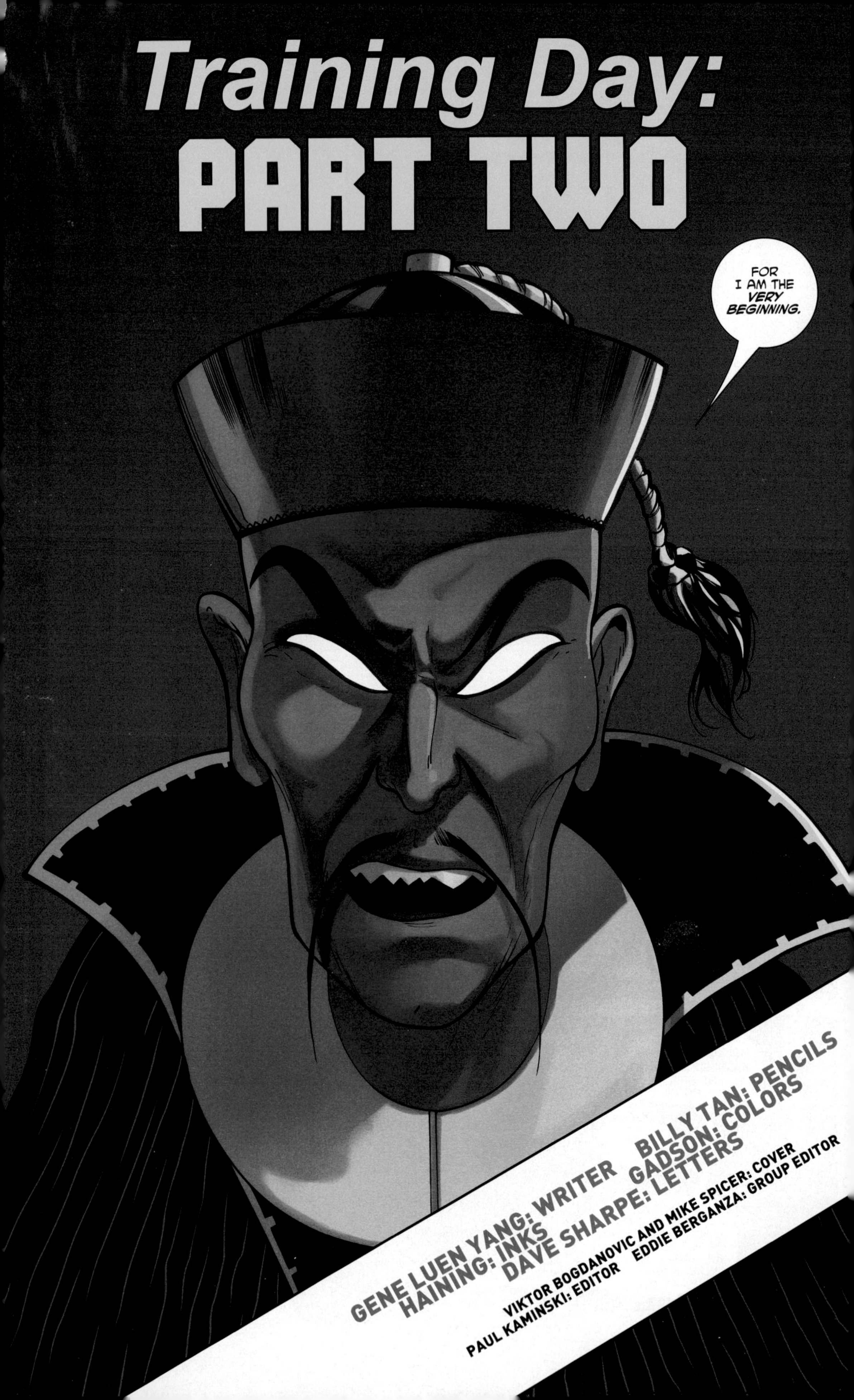
Training Day:
PART TWO
FOR I AM THE VERY BEGINNING.
GENE LUEN YANG: WRITER BILLY TAN: PENCILS
HAINING: INKS GADSON: COLORS
DAVE SHARPE: LETTERS
VIKTOR BOGDANOVIC AND MIKE SPICER: COVER
PAUL KAMINSKI: EDITOR EDDIE BERGANZA: GROUP EDITOR

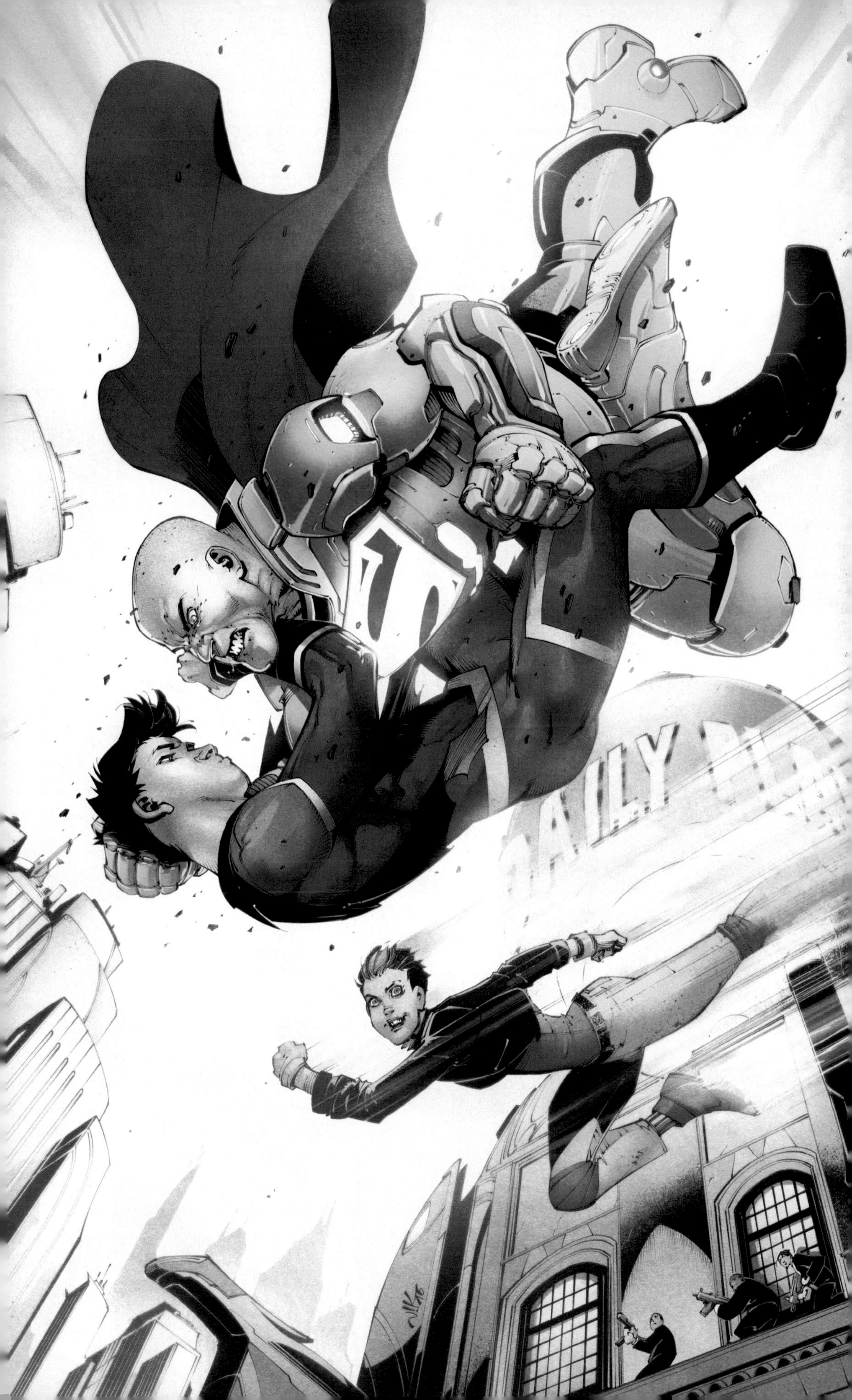

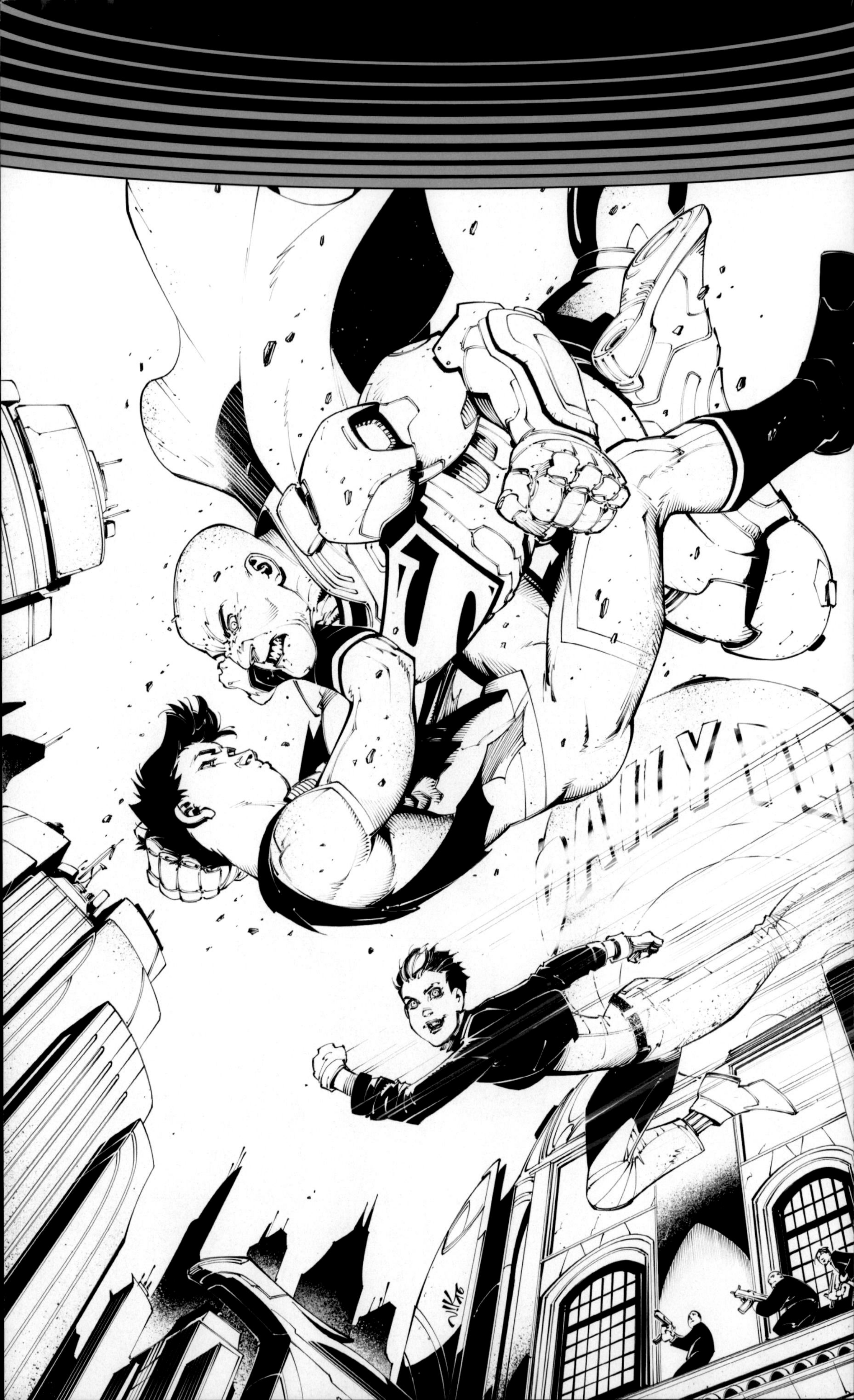
DAILY

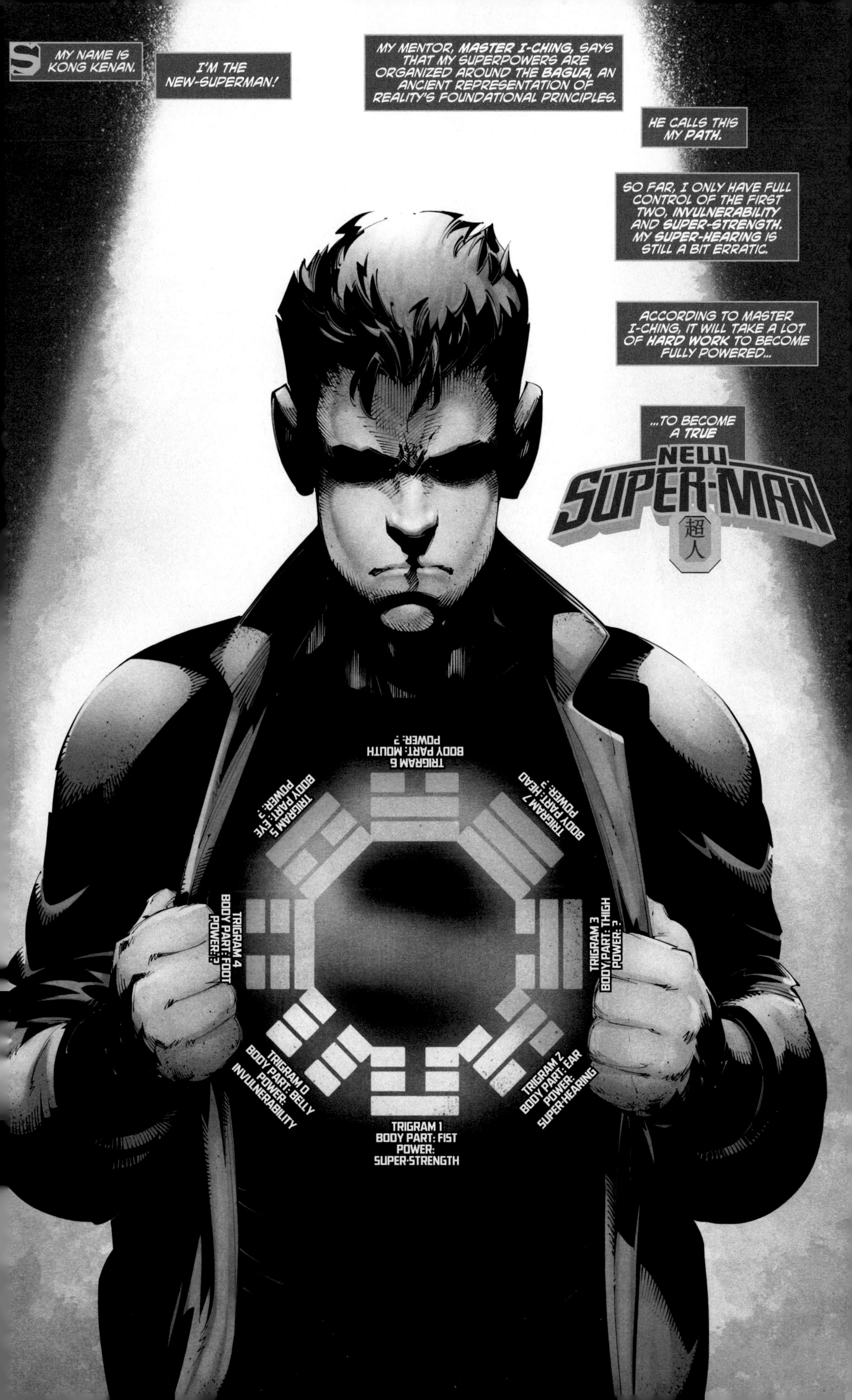
MY NAME IS KONG KENAN.
I'M THE NEW-SUPERMAN!
MY MENTOR, MASTER I-CHING, SAYS THAT MY SUPERPOWERS ARE ORGANIZED AROUND THE BAGUA, AN ANCIENT REPRESENTATION OF REALITY'S FOUNDATIONAL PRINCIPLES.
HE CALLS THIS MY PATH.
SO FAR, I ONLY HAVE FULL CONTROL OF THE FIRST TWO, INVULNERABILITY AND SUPER-STRENGTH. MY SUPER-HEARING IS STILL A BIT ERRATIC.
ACCORDING TO MASTER I-CHING, IT WILL TAKE A LOT OF HARD WORK TO BECOME FULLY POWERED...
...TO BECOME A TRUE
NEW SUPER-MAN
超人
TRIGRAM 6 BODY PART: MOUTH POWER: ?
TRIGRAM 7 BODY PART: HEAD POWER: ?
TRIGRAM 5 BODY PART: EYE POWER: ?
TRIGRAM 4 BODY PART: FOOT POWER: ?
TRIGRAM 3 BODY PART: THIGH POWER: ?
TRIGRAM 0 BODY PART: BELLY POWER: INVULNERABILITY
TRIGRAM 2 BODY PART: EAR POWER: SUPER-HEARING
TRIGRAM 1 BODY PART: FIST POWER: SUPER-STRENGTH

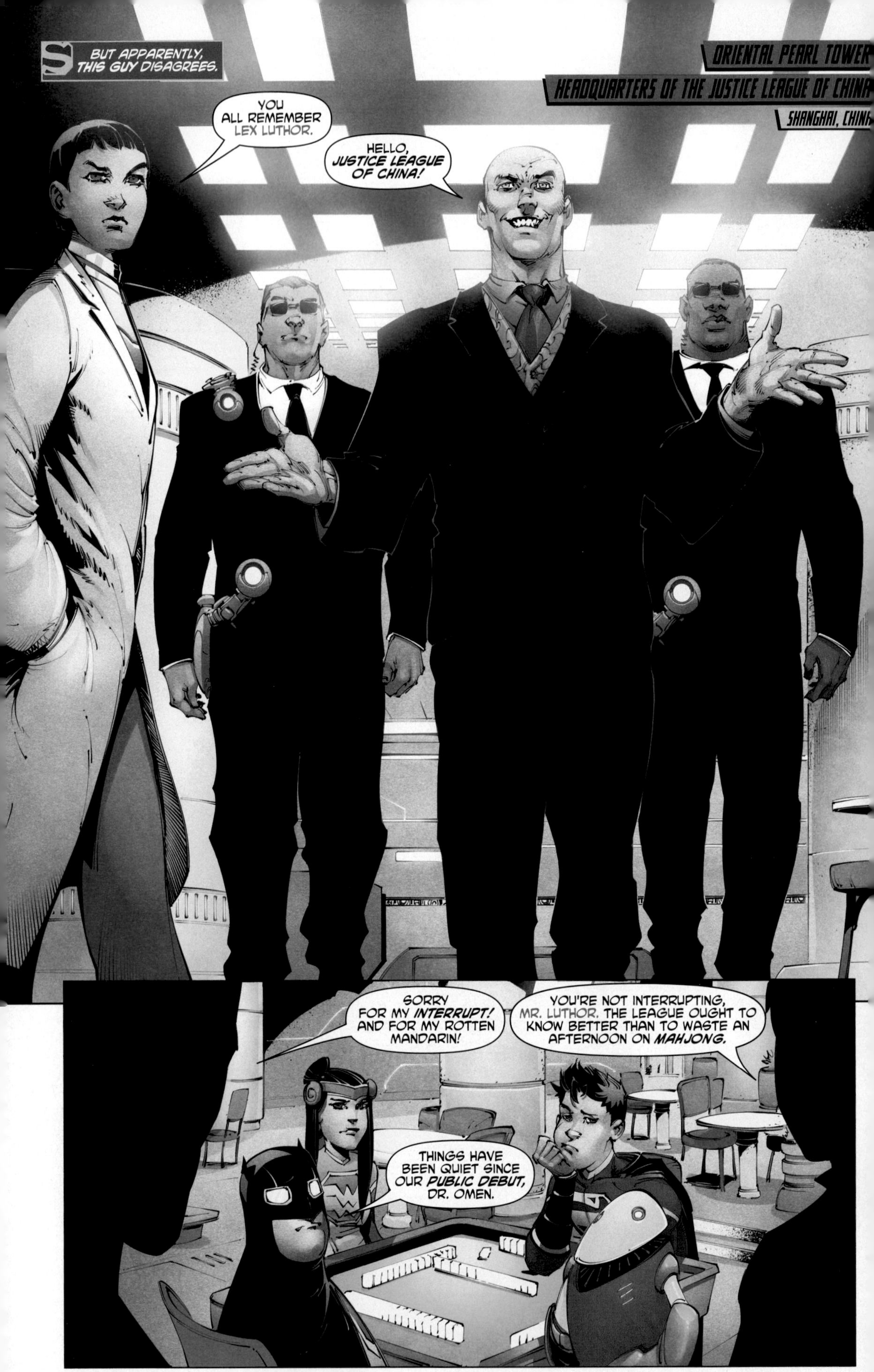
BUT APPARENTLY, THIS GUY DISAGREES.
ORIENTAL PEARL TOWER
HEADQUARTERS OF THE JUSTICE LEAGUE OF CHINA
SHANGHAI, CHINA
YOU ALL REMEMBER LEX LUTHOR.
HELLO, JUSTICE LEAGUE OF CHINA!
SORRY FOR MY INTERRUPT! AND FOR MY ROTTEN MANDARIN!
YOU'RE NOT INTERRUPTING, MR. LUTHOR. THE LEAGUE OUGHT TO KNOW BETTER THAN TO WASTE AN AFTERNOON ON MAHJONG.
THINGS HAVE BEEN QUIET SINCE OUR PUBLIC DEBUT, DR. OMEN.

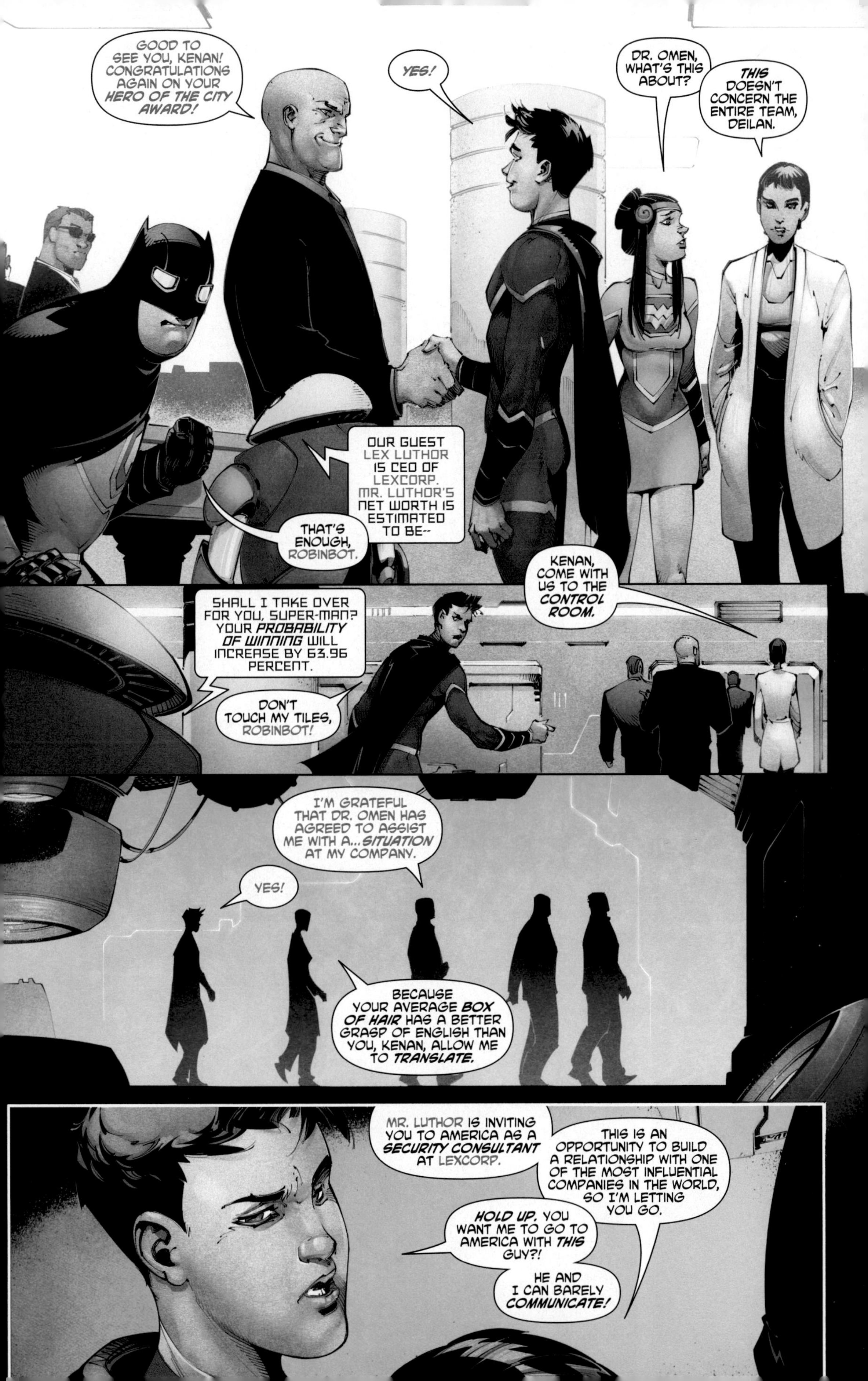
GOOD TO SEE YOU, KENAN! CONGRATULATIONS AGAIN ON YOUR HERO OF THE CITY AWARD!
YES!
DR. OMEN, WHAT'S THIS ABOUT?
THIS DOESN'T CONCERN THE ENTIRE TEAM, DEILAN.
OUR GUEST LEX LUTHOR IS CEO OF LEXCORP. MR. LUTHOR'S NET WORTH IS ESTIMATED TO BE--
THAT'S ENOUGH, ROBINBOT.
KENAN, COME WITH US TO THE CONTROL ROOM.
SHALL I TAKE OVER FOR YOU, SUPER-MAN? YOUR PROBABILITY OF WINNING WILL INCREASE BY 63.96 PERCENT.
DON'T TOUCH MY TILES, ROBINBOT!
I'M GRATEFUL THAT DR. OMEN HAS AGREED TO ASSIST ME WITH A... SITUATION AT MY COMPANY.
YES!
BECAUSE YOUR AVERAGE BOX OF HAIR HAS A BETTER GRASP OF ENGLISH THAN YOU, KENAN, ALLOW ME TO TRANSLATE.
MR. LUTHOR IS INVITING YOU TO AMERICA AS A SECURITY CONSULTANT AT LEXCORP.
THIS IS AN OPPORTUNITY TO BUILD A RELATIONSHIP WITH ONE OF THE MOST INFLUENTIAL COMPANIES IN THE WORLD, SO I'M LETTING YOU GO.
HOLD UP. YOU WANT ME TO GO TO AMERICA WITH THIS GUY?!
HE AND I CAN BARELY COMMUNICATE!

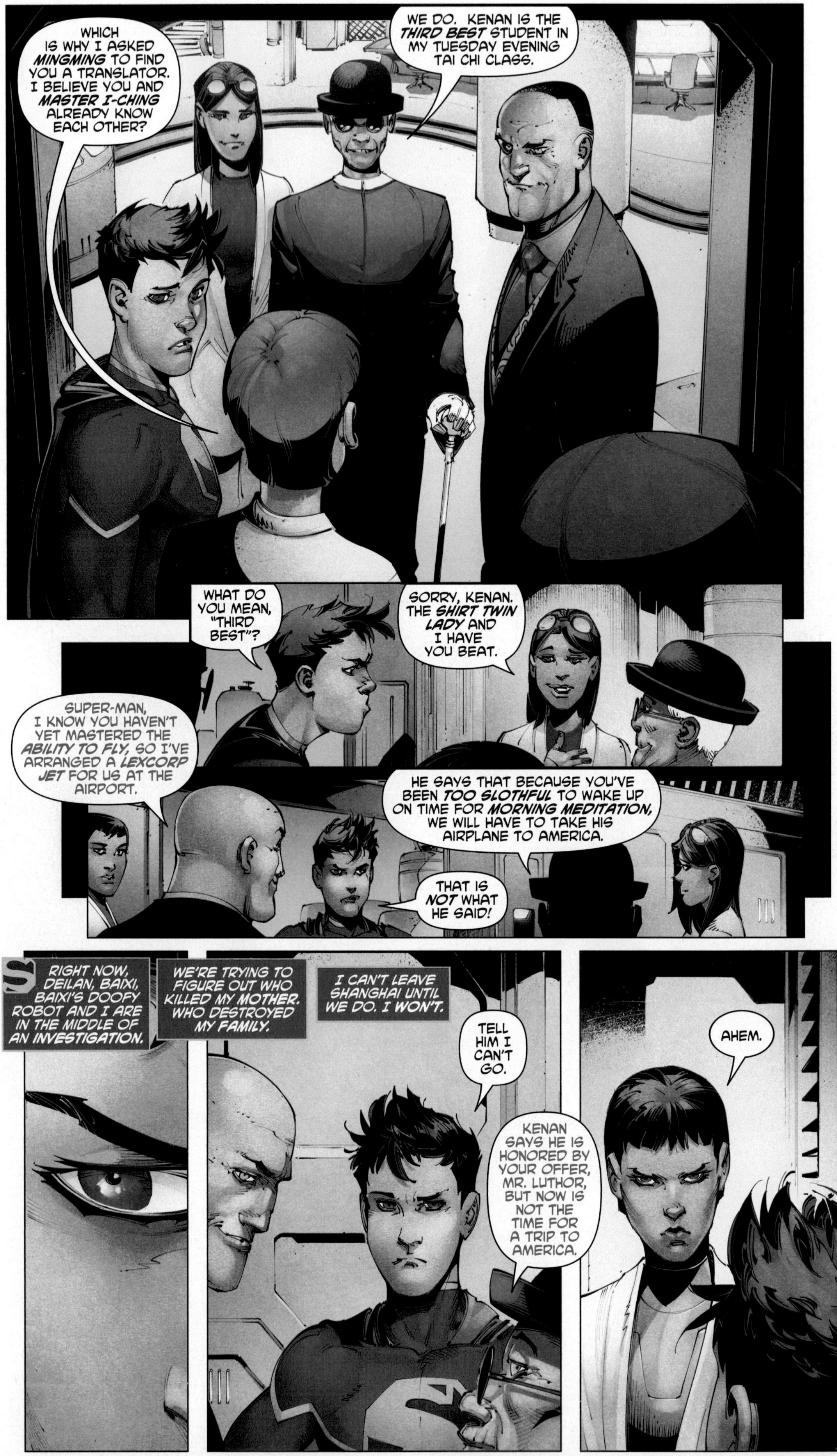
WHICH IS WHY I ASKED MINGMING TO FIND YOU A TRANSLATOR. I BELIEVE YOU AND MASTER I-CHING ALREADY KNOW EACH OTHER?
WE DO. KENAN IS THE THIRD BEST STUDENT IN MY TUESDAY EVENING TAI CHI CLASS.
WHAT DO YOU MEAN, "THIRD BEST"?
SORRY, KENAN. THE SHIRT TWIN LADY AND I HAVE YOU BEAT.
SUPER-MAN, I KNOW YOU HAVEN'T YET MASTERED THE ABILITY TO FLY, SO I'VE ARRANGED A LEXCORP JET FOR US AT THE AIRPORT.
HE SAYS THAT BECAUSE YOU'VE BEEN TOO SLOTHFUL TO WAKE UP ON TIME FOR MORNING MEDITATION, WE WILL HAVE TO TAKE HIS AIRPLANE TO AMERICA.
THAT IS NOT WHAT HE SAID!
RIGHT NOW, DEILAN, BAIXI, BAIXI'S DOOFY ROBOT AND I ARE IN THE MIDDLE OF AN INVESTIGATION.
WE'RE TRYING TO FIGURE OUT WHO KILLED MY MOTHER. WHO DESTROYED MY FAMILY.
I CAN'T LEAVE SHANGHAI UNTIL WE DO. I WON'T.
TELL HIM I CAN'T GO.
KENAN SAYS HE IS HONORED BY YOUR OFFER, MR. LUTHOR, BUT NOW IS NOT THE TIME FOR A TRIP TO AMERICA.
AHEM.

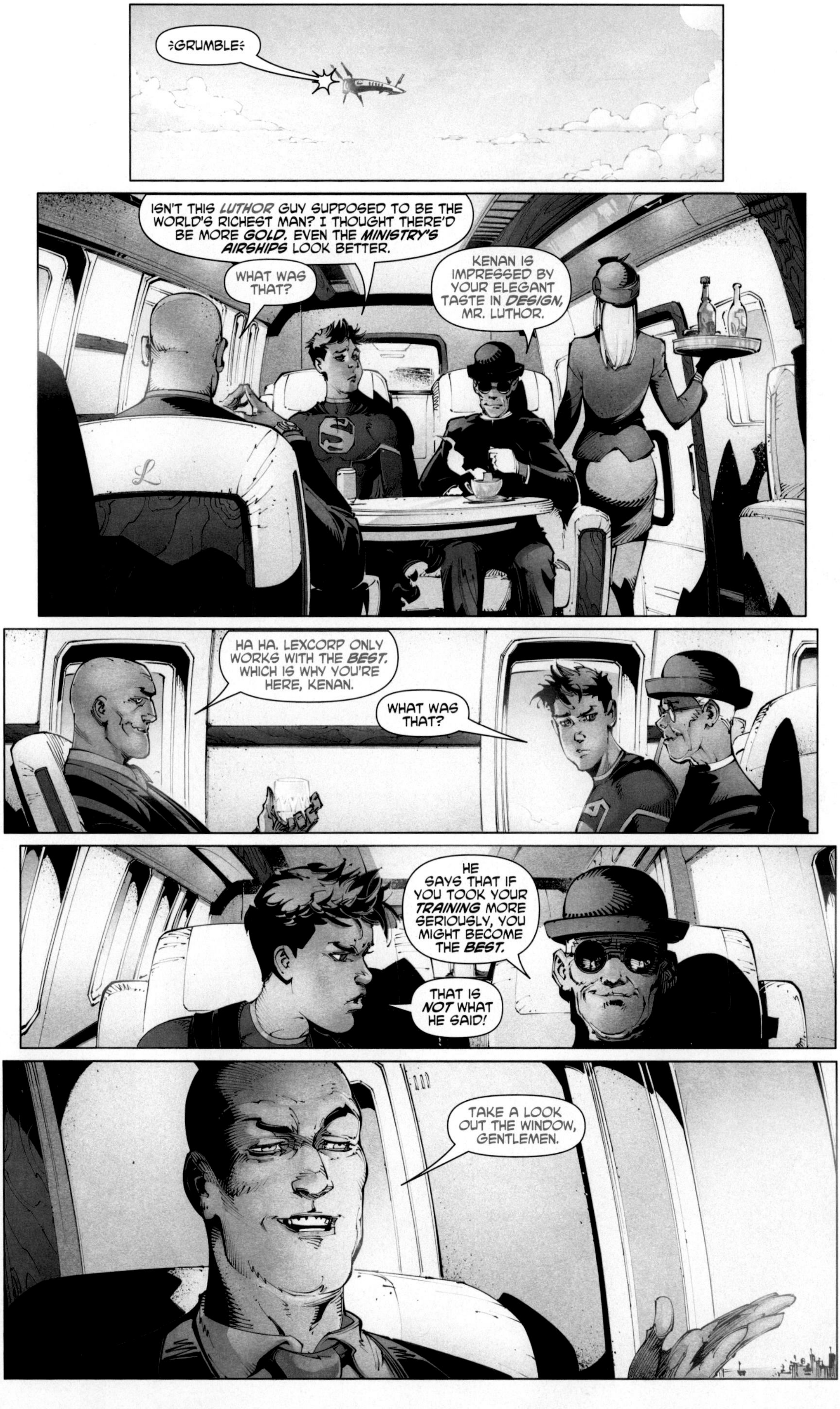
GRUMBLE
ISN'T THIS LUTHOR GUY SUPPOSED TO BE THE WORLD'S RICHEST MAN? I THOUGHT THERE'D BE MORE GOLD. EVEN THE MINISTRY'S AIRSHIPS LOOK BETTER.
WHAT WAS THAT?
KENAN IS IMPRESSED BY YOUR ELEGANT TASTE IN DESIGN, MR. LUTHOR.
HA HA. LEXCORP ONLY WORKS WITH THE BEST. WHICH IS WHY YOU'RE HERE, KENAN.
WHAT WAS THAT?
HE SAYS THAT IF YOU TOOK YOUR TRAINING MORE SERIOUSLY, YOU MIGHT BECOME THE BEST.
THAT IS NOT WHAT HE SAID!
TAKE A LOOK OUT THE WINDOW, GENTLEMEN.

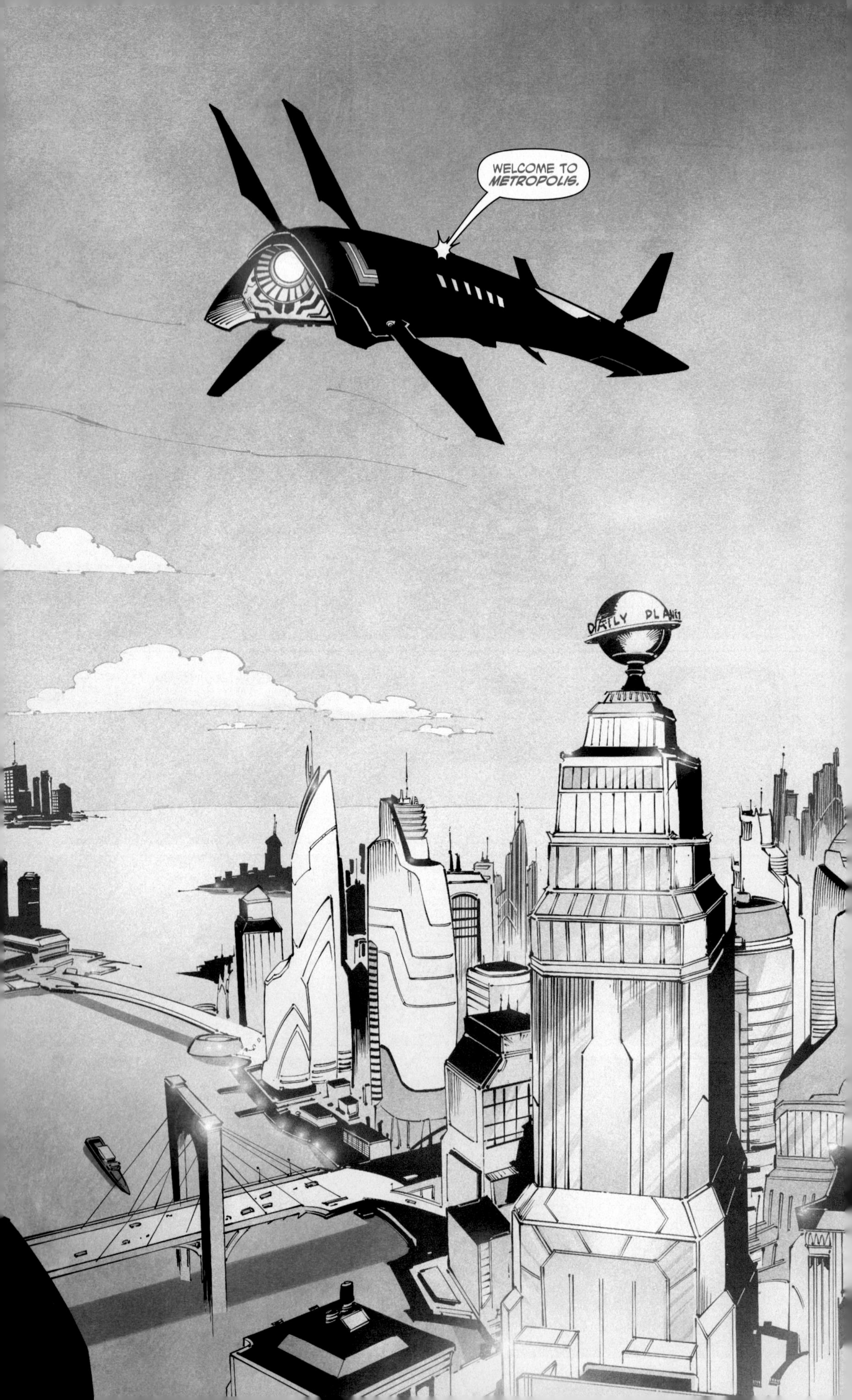
WELCOME TO METROPOLIS.

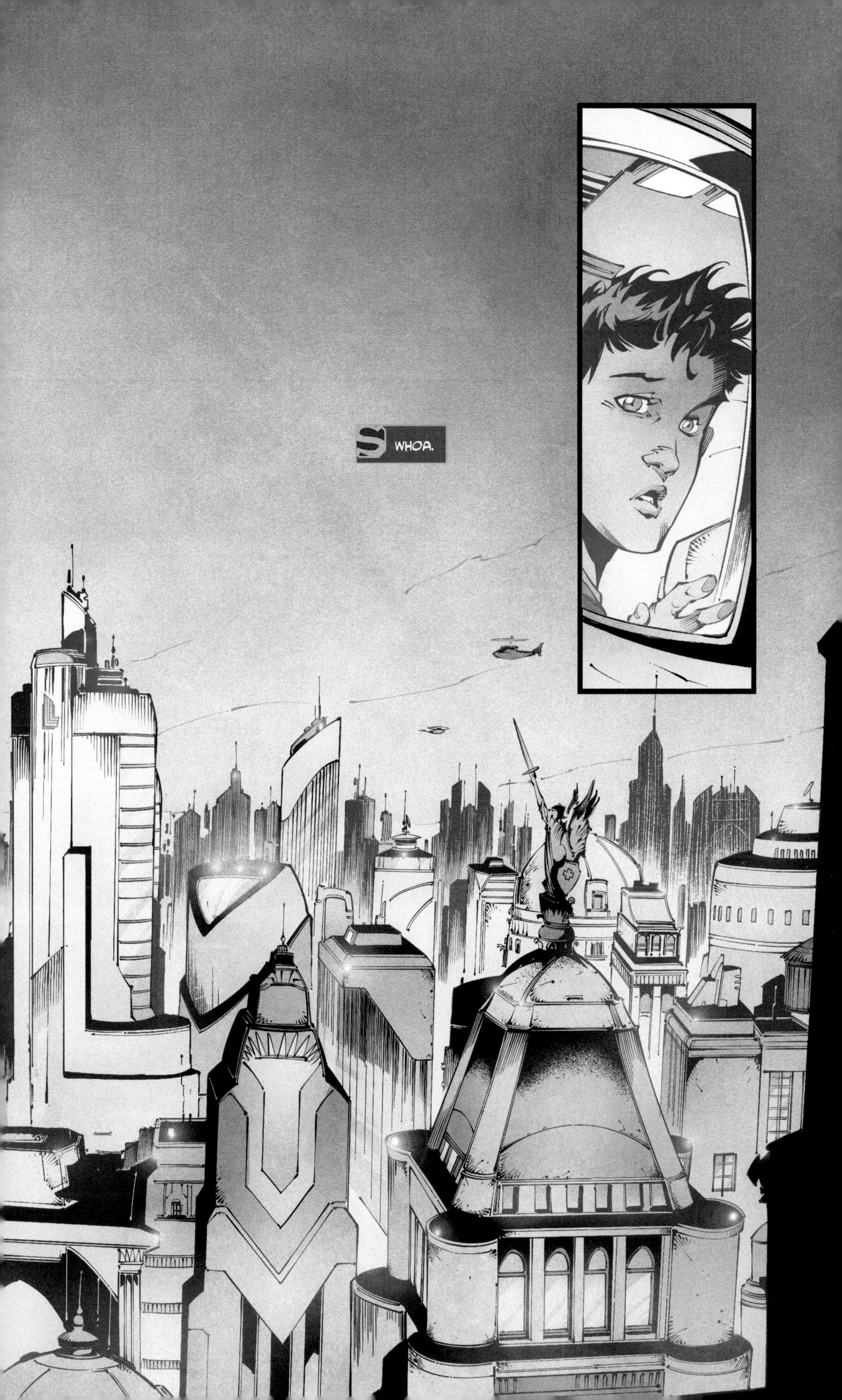
WHOA.

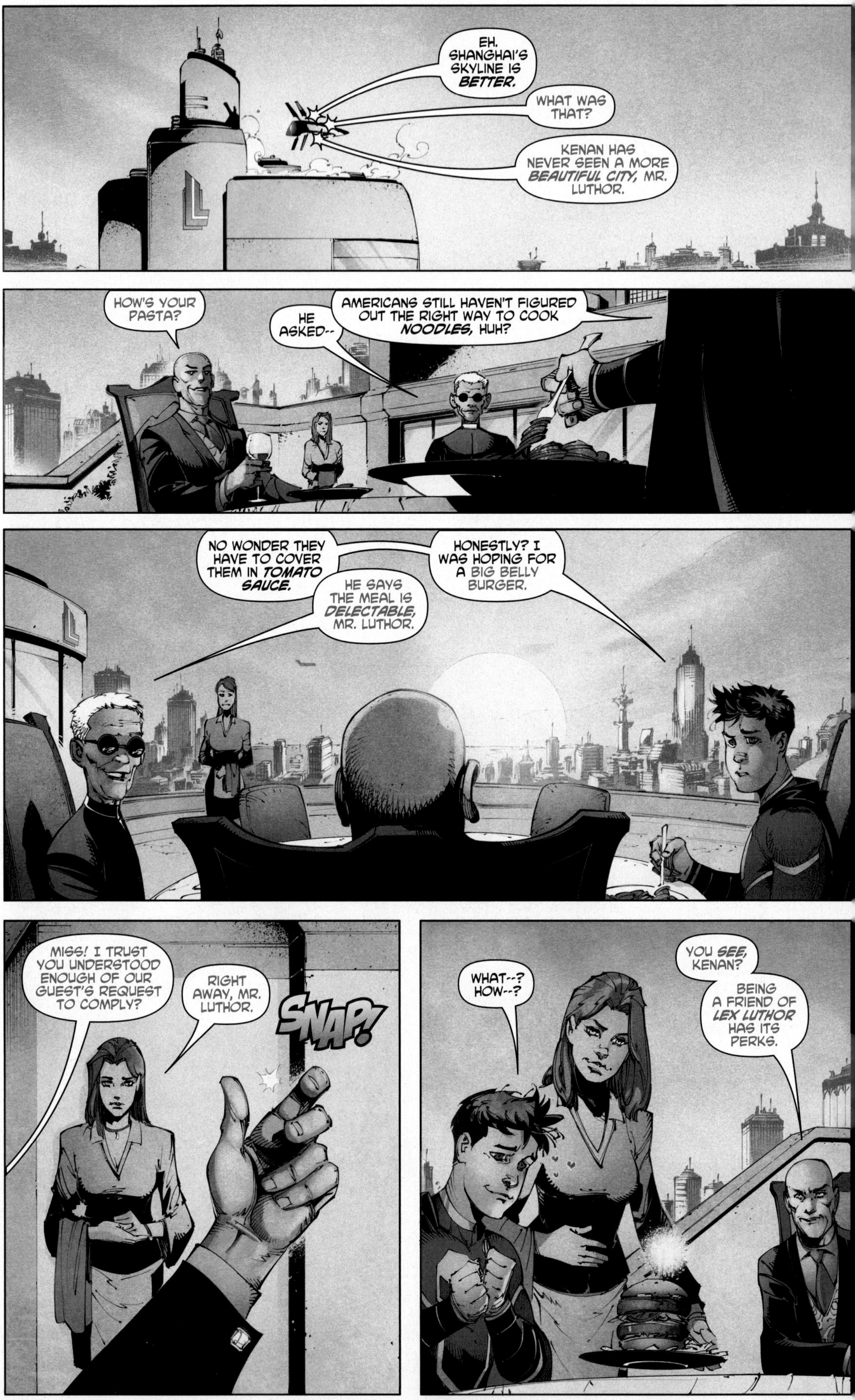
EH. SHANGHAI'S SKYLINE IS BETTER.
WHAT WAS THAT?
KENAN HAS NEVER SEEN A MORE BEAUTIFUL CITY, MR. LUTHOR.
HOW'S YOUR PASTA?
HE ASKED--
AMERICANS STILL HAVEN'T FIGURED OUT THE RIGHT WAY TO COOK NOODLES, HUH?
NO WONDER THEY HAVE TO COVER THEM IN TOMATO SAUCE.
HE SAYS THE MEAL IS DELECTABLE, MR. LUTHOR.
HONESTLY? I WAS HOPING FOR A BIG BELLY BURGER.
MISS! I TRUST YOU UNDERSTOOD ENOUGH OF OUR GUEST'S REQUEST TO COMPLY?
RIGHT AWAY, MR. LUTHOR.
SNAP!
WHAT--? HOW--?
YOU SEE, KENAN?
BEING A FRIEND OF LEX LUTHOR HAS ITS PERKS.

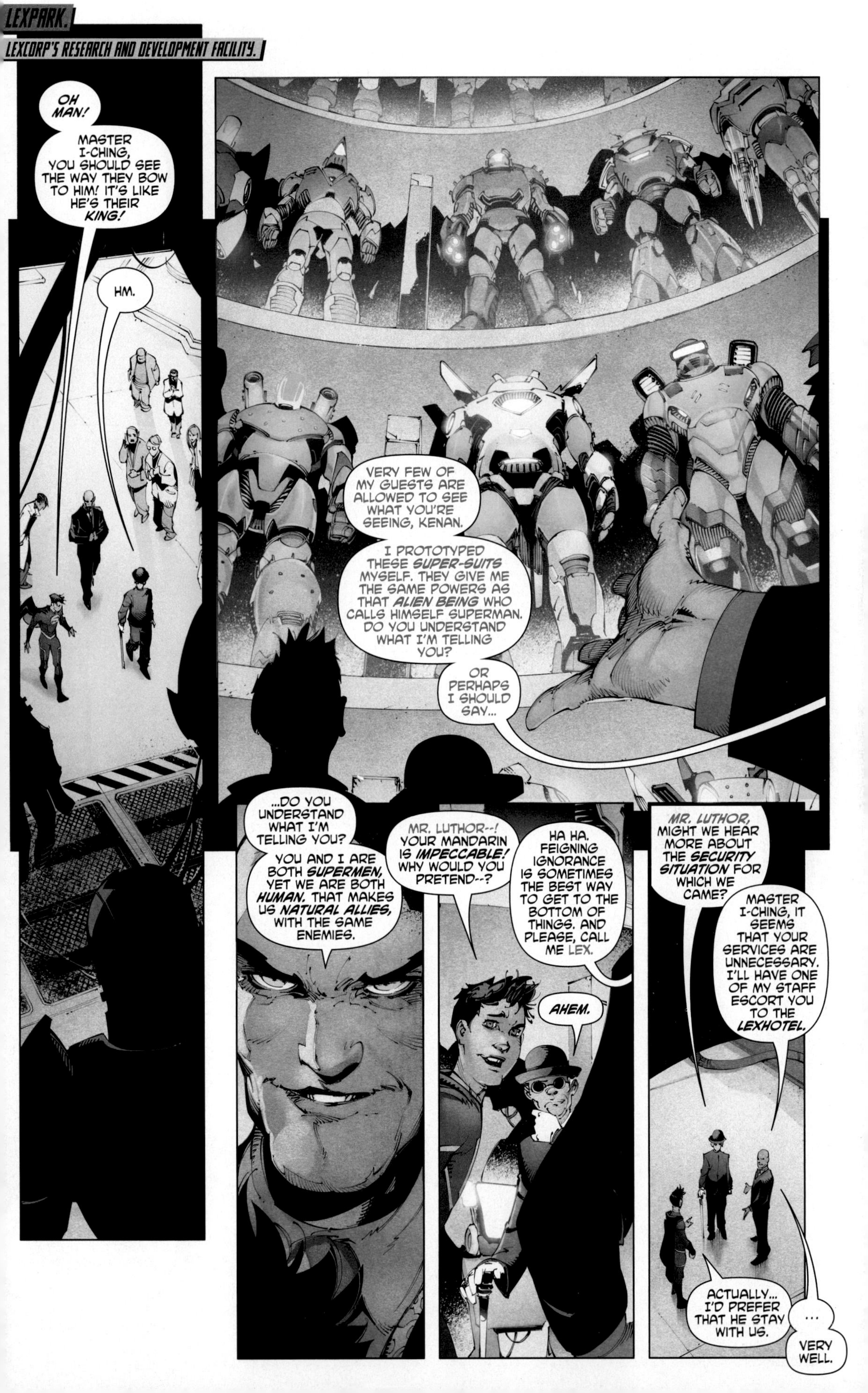
LEXPARK.
LEXCORP'S RESEARCH AND DEVELOPMENT FACILITY.
OH MAN!
MASTER I-CHING, YOU SHOULD SEE THE WAY THEY BOW TO HIM! IT'S LIKE HE'S THEIR KING!
HM.
VERY FEW OF MY GUESTS ARE ALLOWED TO SEE WHAT YOU'RE SEEING, KENAN.
I PROTOTYPED THESE SUPER-SUITS MYSELF. THEY GIVE ME THE SAME POWERS AS THAT ALIEN BEING WHO CALLS HIMSELF SUPERMAN. DO YOU UNDERSTAND WHAT I'M TELLING YOU?
OR PERHAPS I SHOULD SAY...
...DO YOU UNDERSTAND WHAT I'M TELLING YOU?
YOU AND I ARE BOTH SUPERMEN, YET WE ARE BOTH HUMAN. THAT MAKES US NATURAL ALLIES, WITH THE SAME ENEMIES.
MR. LUTHOR--! YOUR MANDARIN IS IMPECCABLE! WHY WOULD YOU PRETEND--?
HA HA. FEIGNING IGNORANCE IS SOMETIMES THE BEST WAY TO GET TO THE BOTTOM OF THINGS. AND PLEASE, CALL ME LEX.
AHEM.
MR. LUTHOR, MIGHT WE HEAR MORE ABOUT THE SECURITY SITUATION FOR WHICH WE CAME?
MASTER I-CHING, IT SEEMS THAT YOUR SERVICES ARE UNNECESSARY. I'LL HAVE ONE OF MY STAFF ESCORT YOU TO THE LEXHOTEL.
ACTUALLY... I'D PREFER THAT HE STAY WITH US.
...
VERY WELL.

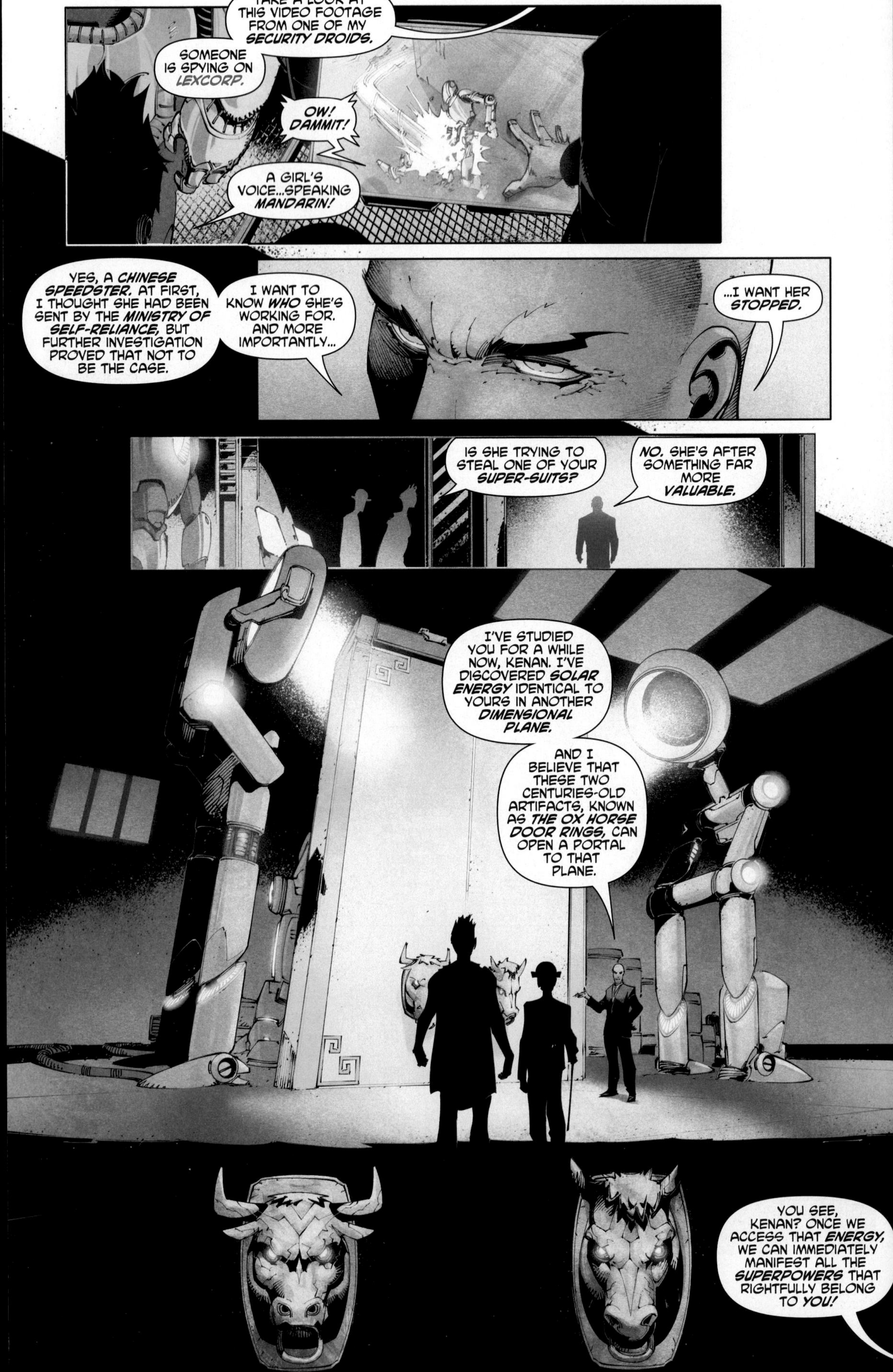
TAKE A LOOK AT THIS VIDEO FOOTAGE FROM ONE OF MY SECURITY DROIDS.
SOMEONE IS SPYING ON LEXCORP.
OW! DAMMIT!
A GIRL'S VOICE...SPEAKING MANDARIN!
YES, A CHINESE SPEEDSTER. AT FIRST, I THOUGHT SHE HAD BEEN SENT BY THE MINISTRY OF SELF-RELIANCE, BUT FURTHER INVESTIGATION PROVED THAT NOT TO BE THE CASE.
I WANT TO KNOW WHO SHE'S WORKING FOR. AND MORE IMPORTANTLY...
...I WANT HER STOPPED.
IS SHE TRYING TO STEAL ONE OF YOUR SUPER-SUITS?
NO. SHE'S AFTER SOMETHING FAR MORE VALUABLE.
I'VE STUDIED YOU FOR A WHILE NOW, KENAN. I'VE DISCOVERED SOLAR ENERGY IDENTICAL TO YOURS IN ANOTHER DIMENSIONAL PLANE.
AND I BELIEVE THAT THESE TWO CENTURIES-OLD ARTIFACTS, KNOWN AS THE OX HORSE DOOR RINGS, CAN OPEN A PORTAL TO THAT PLANE.
YOU SEE, KENAN? ONCE WE ACCESS THAT ENERGY, WE CAN IMMEDIATELY MANIFEST ALL THE SUPERPOWERS THAT RIGHTFULLY BELONG TO YOU!

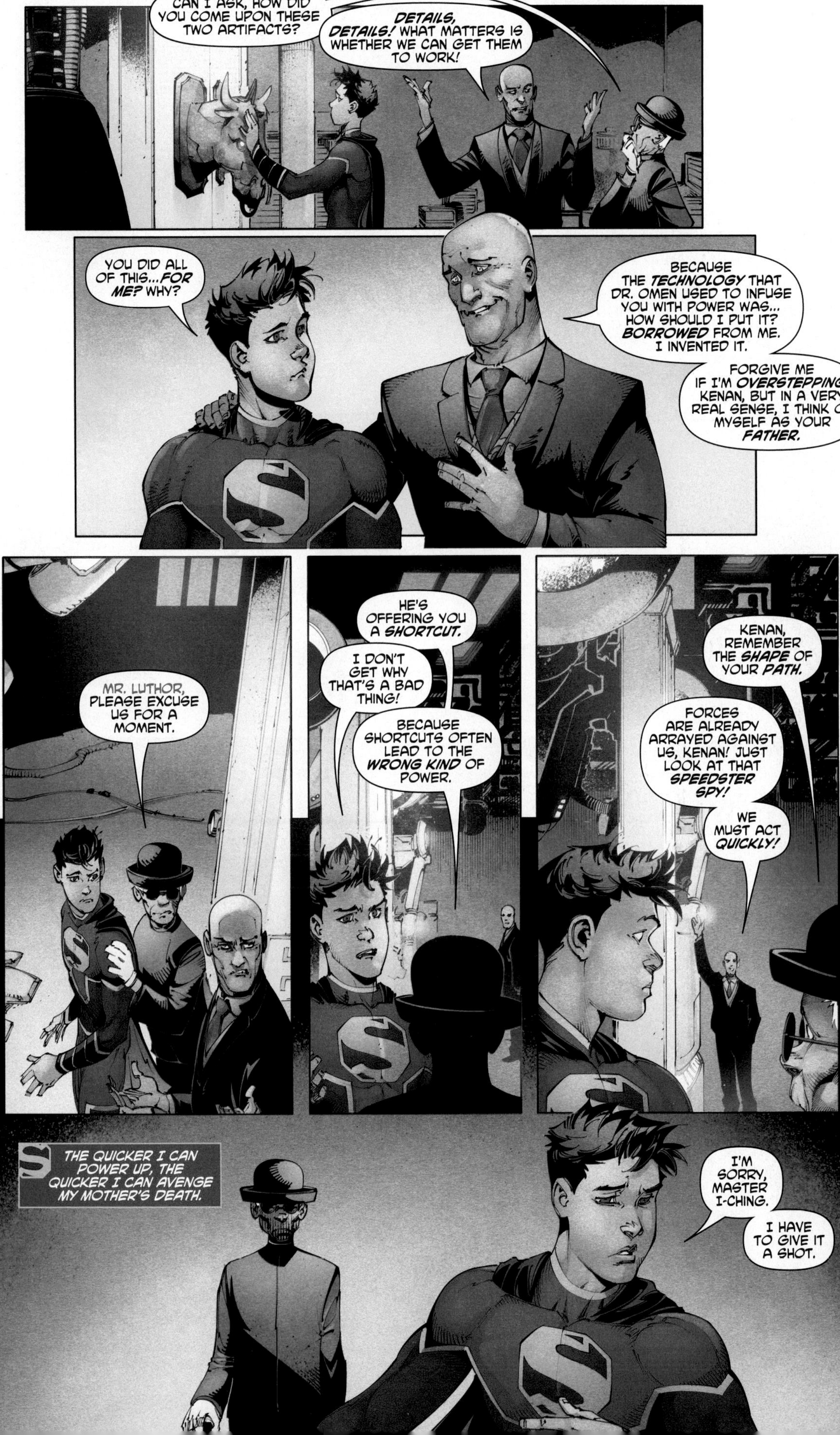
CAN I ASK, HOW DID YOU COME UPON THESE TWO ARTIFACTS?
DETAILS, DETAILS! WHAT MATTERS IS WHETHER WE CAN GET THEM TO WORK!
YOU DID ALL OF THIS...FOR ME? WHY?
BECAUSE THE TECHNOLOGY THAT DR. OMEN USED TO INFUSE YOU WITH POWER WAS... HOW SHOULD I PUT IT? BORROWED FROM ME. I INVENTED IT.
FORGIVE ME IF I'M OVERSTEPPING, KENAN, BUT IN A VERY REAL SENSE, I THINK OF MYSELF AS YOUR FATHER.
MR. LUTHOR, PLEASE EXCUSE US FOR A MOMENT.
HE'S OFFERING YOU A SHORTCUT.
I DON'T GET WHY THAT'S A BAD THING!
BECAUSE SHORTCUTS OFTEN LEAD TO THE WRONG KIND OF POWER.
KENAN, REMEMBER THE SHAPE OF YOUR PATH.
FORCES ARE ALREADY ARRAYED AGAINST US, KENAN! JUST LOOK AT THAT SPEEDSTER SPY!
WE MUST ACT QUICKLY!
THE QUICKER I CAN POWER UP, THE QUICKER I CAN AVENGE MY MOTHER'S DEATH.
I'M SORRY, MASTER I-CHING.
I HAVE TO GIVE IT A SHOT.

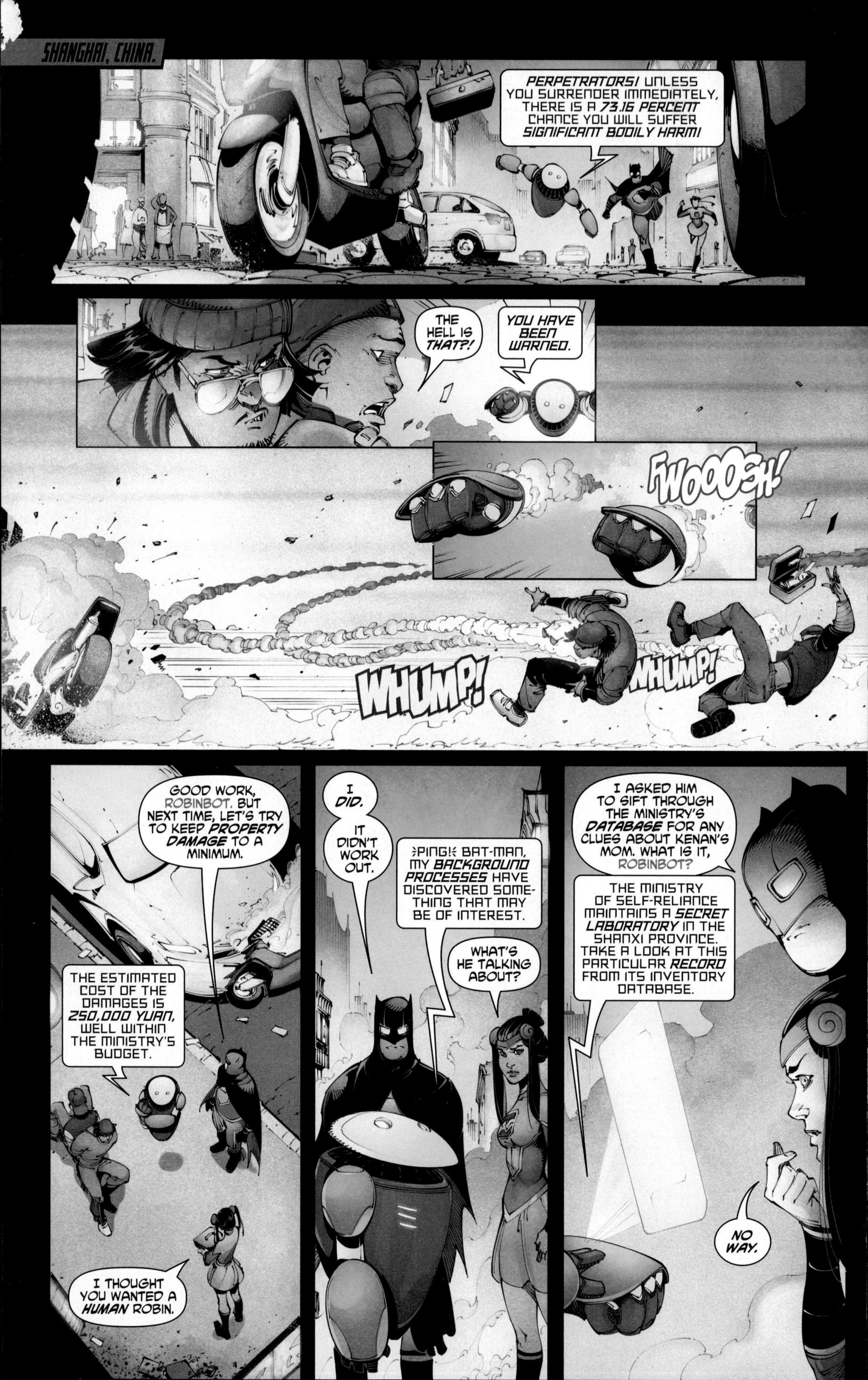
SHANGHAI, CHINA.
PERPETRATORS! UNLESS YOU SURRENDER IMMEDIATELY, THERE IS A 73.16 PERCENT CHANCE YOU WILL SUFFER SIGNIFICANT BODILY HARM!
THE HELL IS THAT?!
YOU HAVE BEEN WARNED.
FWOOOSH!
WHUMP!
WHUMP!
GOOD WORK, ROBINBOT. BUT NEXT TIME, LET'S TRY TO KEEP PROPERTY DAMAGE TO A MINIMUM.
THE ESTIMATED COST OF THE DAMAGES IS 250,000 YUAN, WELL WITHIN THE MINISTRY'S BUDGET.
I THOUGHT YOU WANTED A HUMAN ROBIN.
I DID.
IT DIDN'T WORK OUT.
›PING!‹ BAT-MAN, MY BACKGROUND PROCESSES HAVE DISCOVERED SOMETHING THAT MAY BE OF INTEREST.
WHAT'S HE TALKING ABOUT?
I ASKED HIM TO SIFT THROUGH THE MINISTRY'S DATABASE FOR ANY CLUES ABOUT KENAN'S MOM. WHAT IS IT, ROBINBOT?
THE MINISTRY OF SELF-RELIANCE MAINTAINS A SECRET LABORATORY IN THE SHANXI PROVINCE. TAKE A LOOK AT THIS PARTICULAR RECORD FROM ITS INVENTORY DATABASE.
NO WAY.

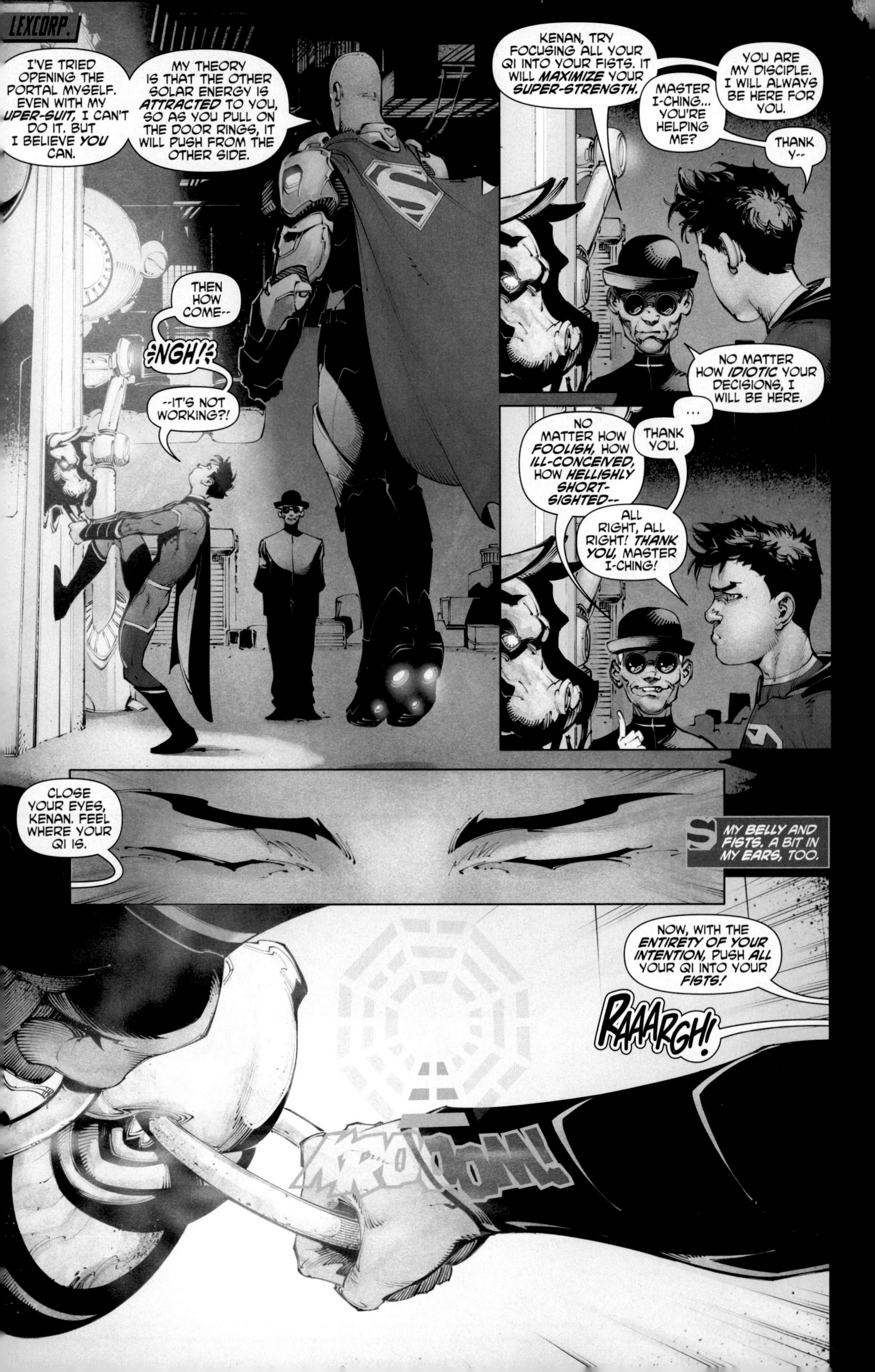
LEXCORP.
I'VE TRIED OPENING THE PORTAL MYSELF. EVEN WITH MY UPER-SUIT, I CAN'T DO IT. BUT I BELIEVE YOU CAN.
MY THEORY IS THAT THE OTHER SOLAR ENERGY IS ATTRACTED TO YOU, SO AS YOU PULL ON THE DOOR RINGS, IT WILL PUSH FROM THE OTHER SIDE.
THEN HOW COME--
NGH!
--IT'S NOT WORKING?!
KENAN, TRY FOCUSING ALL YOUR QI INTO YOUR FISTS. IT WILL MAXIMIZE YOUR SUPER-STRENGTH.
MASTER I-CHING... YOU'RE HELPING ME?
YOU ARE MY DISCIPLE. I WILL ALWAYS BE HERE FOR YOU.
THANK Y--
NO MATTER HOW IDIOTIC YOUR DECISIONS, I WILL BE HERE.
...
THANK YOU.
NO MATTER HOW FOOLISH, HOW ILL-CONCEIVED, HOW HELLISHLY SHORT-SIGHTED--
ALL RIGHT, ALL RIGHT! THANK YOU, MASTER I-CHING!
CLOSE YOUR EYES, KENAN. FEEL WHERE YOUR QI IS.
MY BELLY AND FISTS. A BIT IN MY EARS, TOO.
NOW, WITH THE ENTIRETY OF YOUR INTENTION, PUSH ALL YOUR QI INTO YOUR FISTS!
RAAARGH!
KRA-TOOOM!

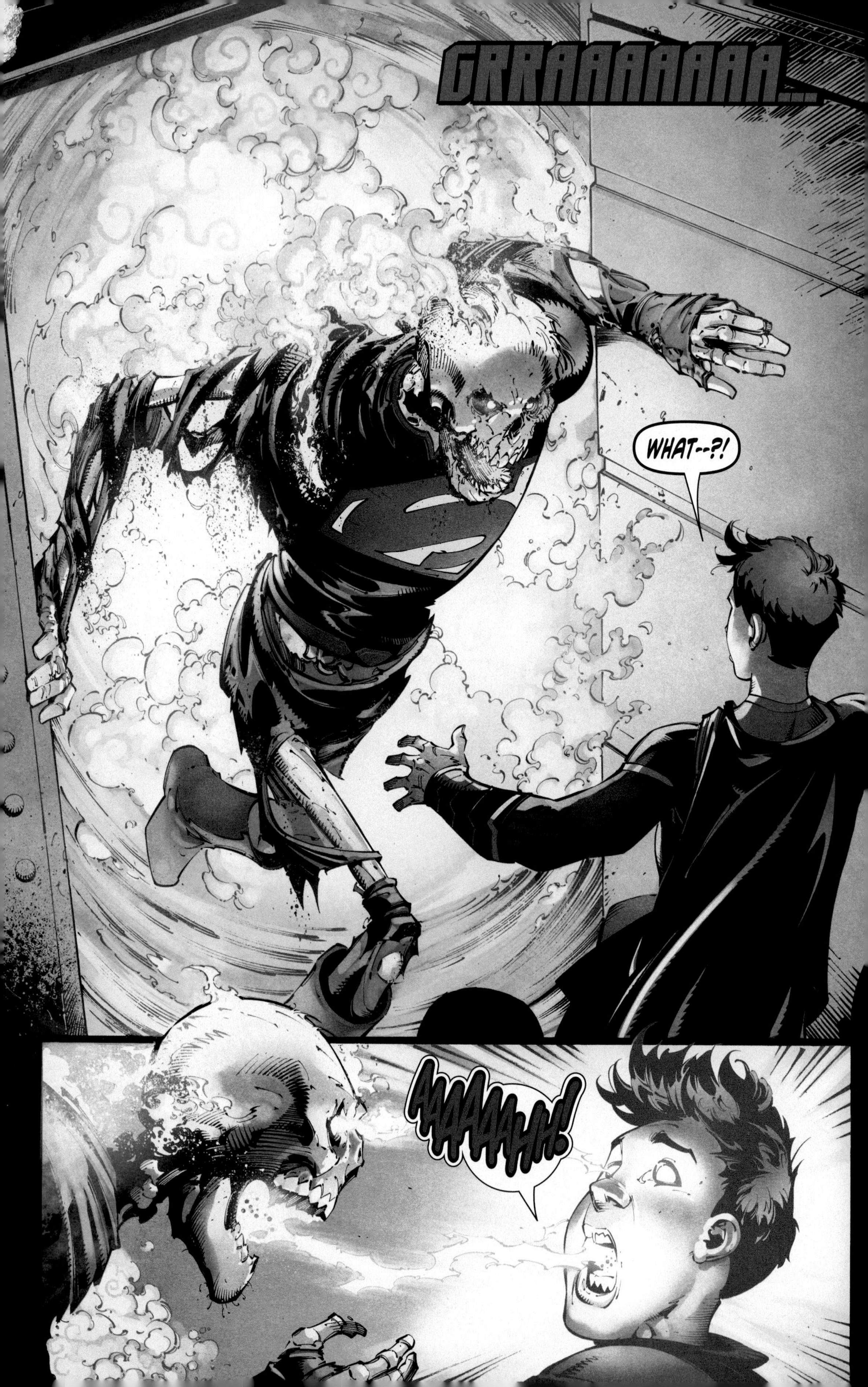
GRRAAAAAAAA...
WHAT--?!
AAAAAAHH!

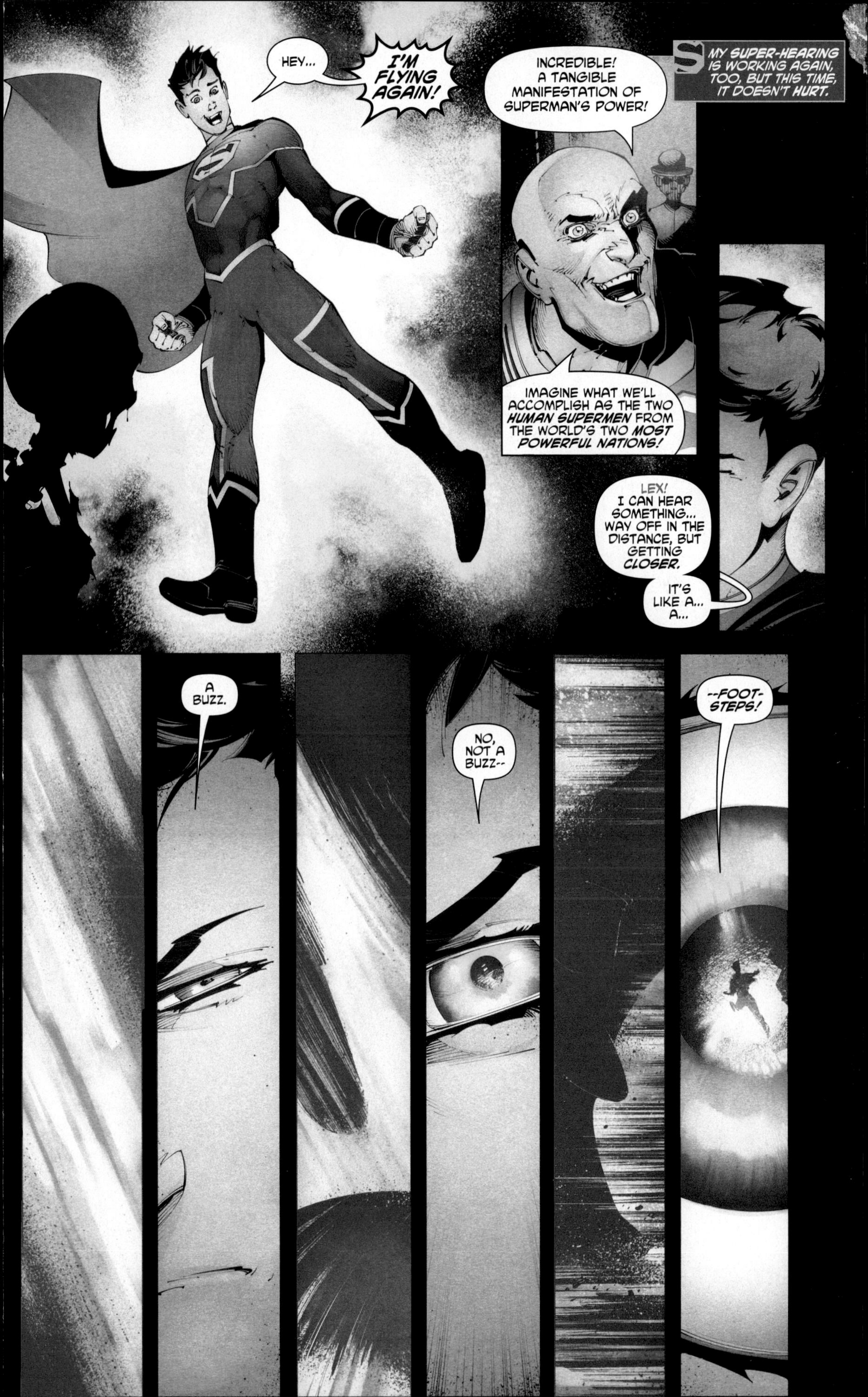
HEY...
I'M FLYING AGAIN!
INCREDIBLE! A TANGIBLE MANIFESTATION OF SUPERMAN'S POWER!
MY SUPER-HEARING IS WORKING AGAIN, TOO, BUT THIS TIME, IT DOESN'T HURT.
IMAGINE WHAT WE'LL ACCOMPLISH AS THE TWO HUMAN SUPERMEN FROM THE WORLD'S TWO MOST POWERFUL NATIONS!
LEX! I CAN HEAR SOMETHING... WAY OFF IN THE DISTANCE, BUT GETTING CLOSER.
IT'S LIKE A... A...
A BUZZ.
NO, NOT A BUZZ--
--FOOT-STEPS!

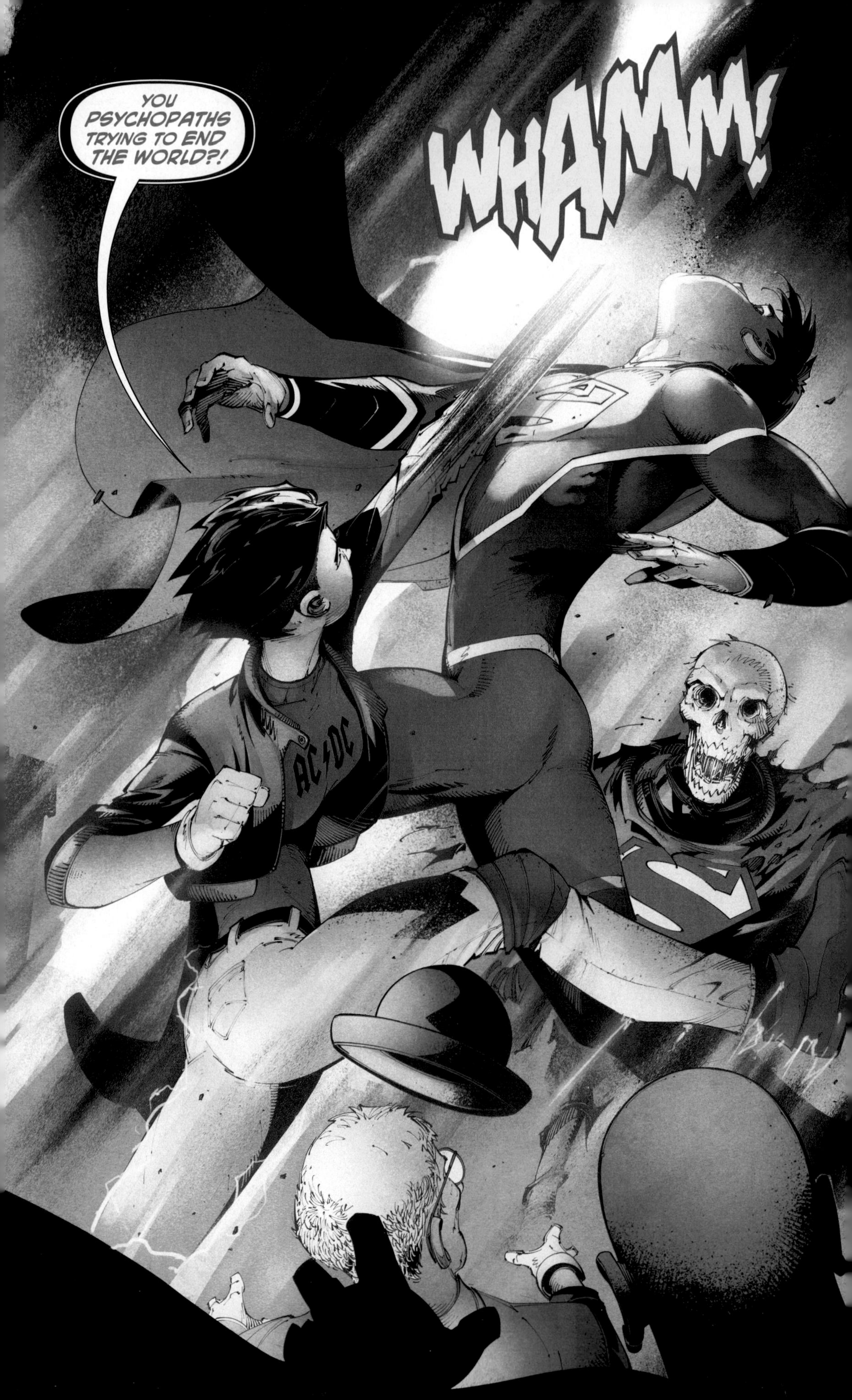
YOU PSYCHOPATHS TRYING TO END THE WORLD?!
WHAMM!
AC/DC

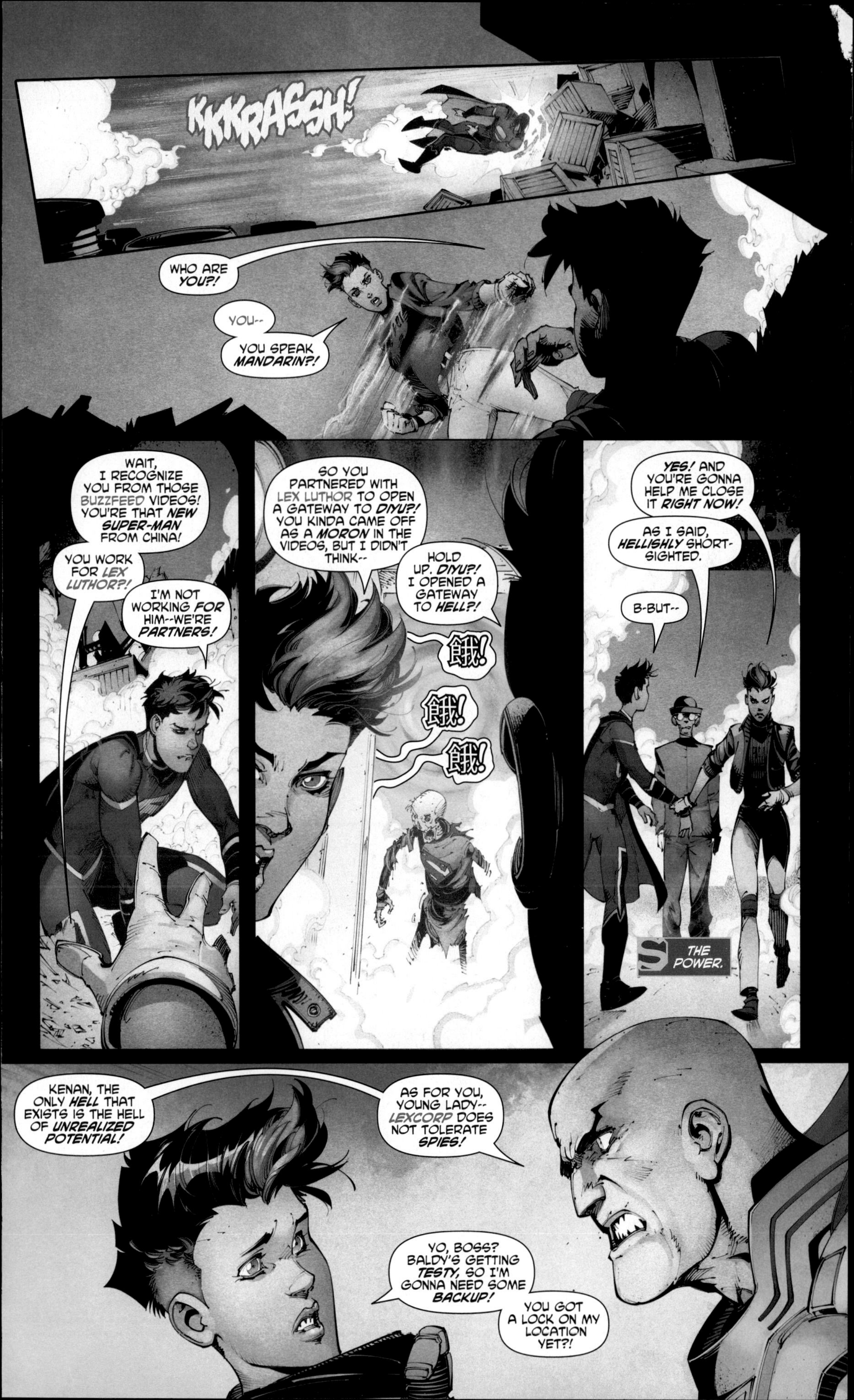
KKKRASSH!
WHO ARE YOU?!
YOU--
YOU SPEAK MANDARIN?!
WAIT, I RECOGNIZE YOU FROM THOSE BUZZFEED VIDEOS! YOU'RE THAT NEW SUPER-MAN FROM CHINA!
YOU WORK FOR LEX LUTHOR?!
I'M NOT WORKING FOR HIM--WE'RE PARTNERS!
SO YOU PARTNERED WITH LEX LUTHOR TO OPEN A GATEWAY TO DIYU?! YOU KINDA CAME OFF AS A MORON IN THE VIDEOS, BUT I DIDN'T THINK--
HOLD UP. DIYU?! I OPENED A GATEWAY TO HELL?!
餓!
餓!
餓!
YES! AND YOU'RE GONNA HELP ME CLOSE IT RIGHT NOW!
AS I SAID, HELLISHLY SHORT-SIGHTED.
B-BUT--
THE POWER.
KENAN, THE ONLY HELL THAT EXISTS IS THE HELL OF UNREALIZED POTENTIAL!
AS FOR YOU, YOUNG LADY-- LEXCORP DOES NOT TOLERATE SPIES!
YO, BOSS? BALDY'S GETTING TESTY, SO I'M GONNA NEED SOME BACKUP!
YOU GOT A LOCK ON MY LOCATION YET?!

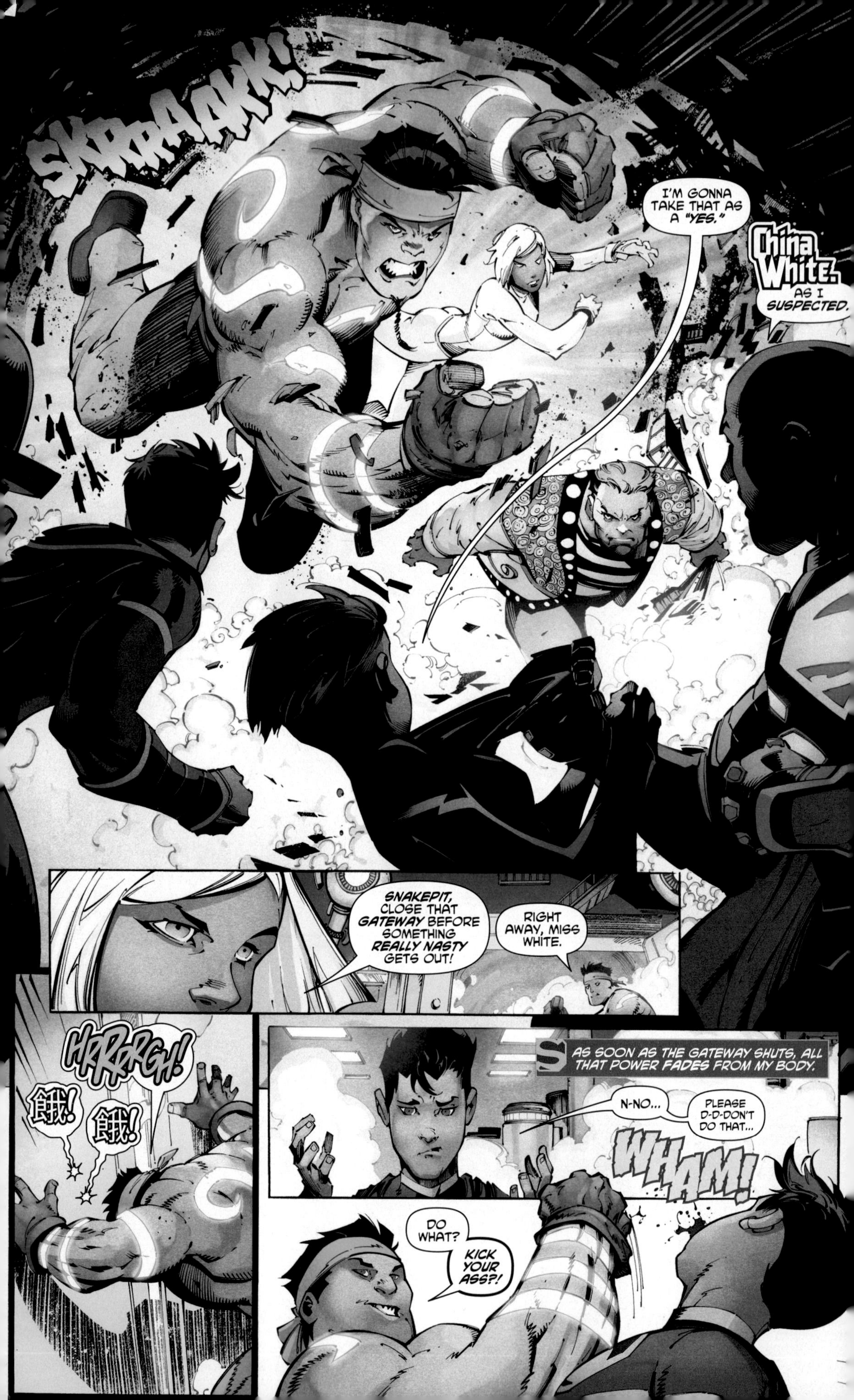
SKRRAAKK!
I'M GONNA TAKE THAT AS A "YES."
China White. AS I SUSPECTED.
SNAKEPIT, CLOSE THAT GATEWAY BEFORE SOMETHING REALLY NASTY GETS OUT!
RIGHT AWAY, MISS WHITE.
HRRRRGH!
餓!
餓!
AS SOON AS THE GATEWAY SHUTS, ALL THAT POWER FADES FROM MY BODY.
N-NO...
PLEASE D-D-DON'T DO THAT...
WHAM!
DO WHAT?
KICK YOUR ASS?!

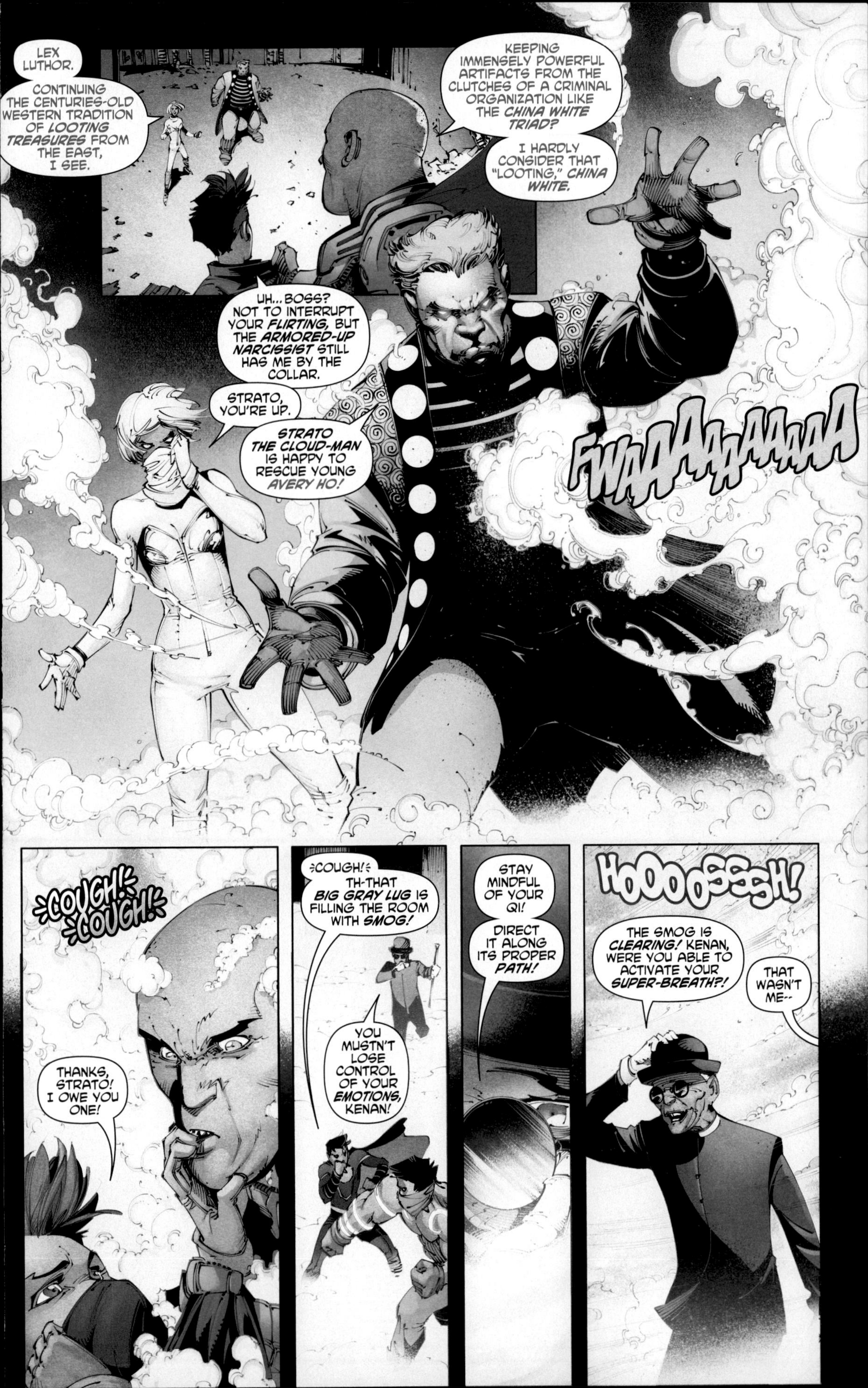
LEX LUTHOR.
CONTINUING THE CENTURIES-OLD WESTERN TRADITION OF LOOTING TREASURES FROM THE EAST, I SEE.
KEEPING IMMENSELY POWERFUL ARTIFACTS FROM THE CLUTCHES OF A CRIMINAL ORGANIZATION LIKE THE CHINA WHITE TRIAD?
I HARDLY CONSIDER THAT "LOOTING," CHINA WHITE.
UH... BOSS? NOT TO INTERRUPT YOUR FLIRTING, BUT THE ARMORED-UP NARCISSIST STILL HAS ME BY THE COLLAR.
STRATO, YOU'RE UP.
STRATO THE CLOUD-MAN IS HAPPY TO RESCUE YOUNG AVERY HO!
FWAAAAAAAAAA
COUGH! COUGH!
THANKS, STRATO! I OWE YOU ONE!
COUGH!
TH-THAT BIG GRAY LUG IS FILLING THE ROOM WITH SMOG!
YOU MUSTN'T LOSE CONTROL OF YOUR EMOTIONS, KENAN!
STAY MINDFUL OF YOUR QI!
DIRECT IT ALONG ITS PROPER PATH!
HOOOOSSSH!
THE SMOG IS CLEARING! KENAN, WERE YOU ABLE TO ACTIVATE YOUR SUPER-BREATH?!
THAT WASN'T ME--

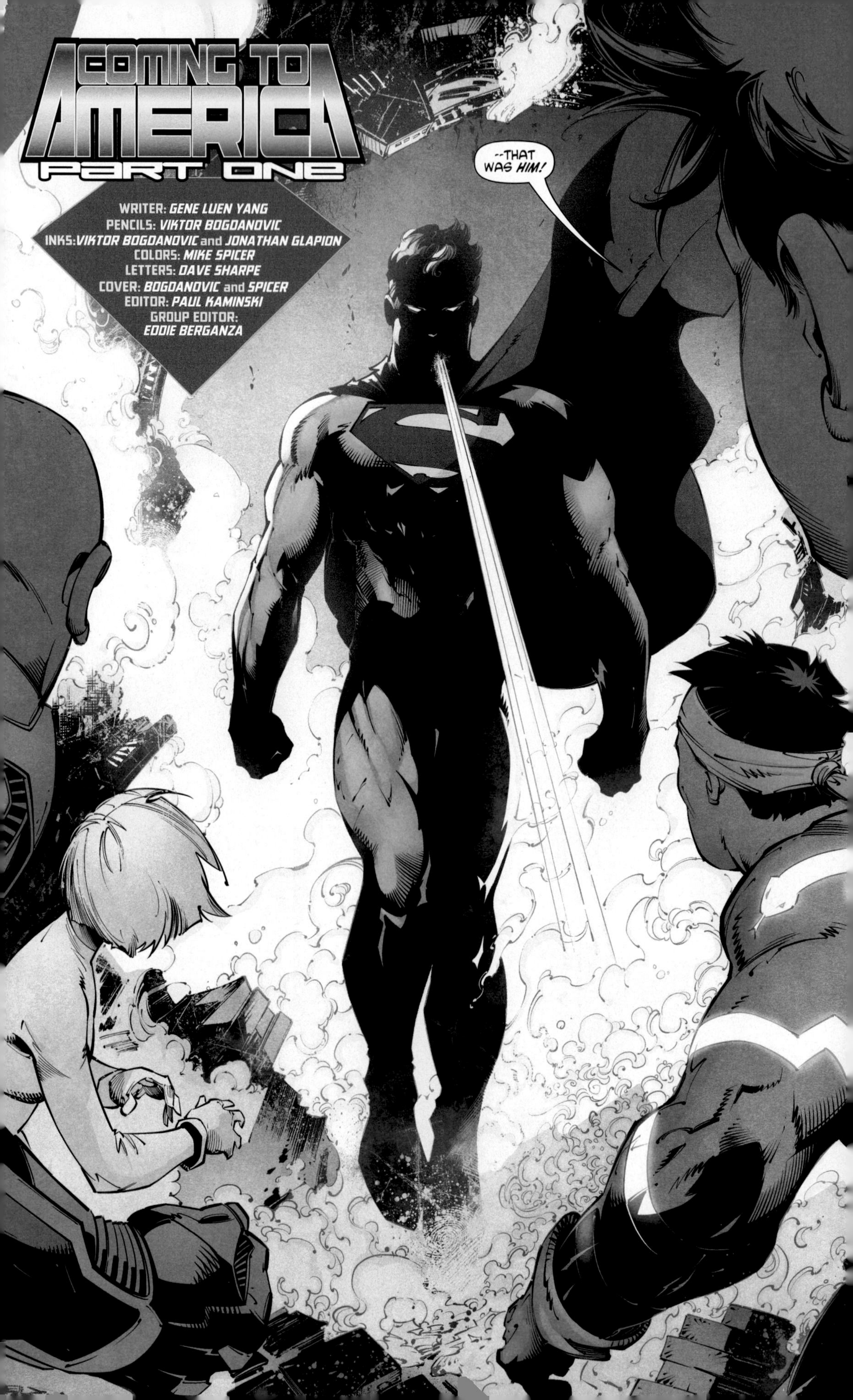
COMING TO AMERICA
PART ONE
WRITER: GENE LUEN YANG
PENCILS: VIKTOR BOGDANOVIC
INKS: VIKTOR BOGDANOVIC and JONATHAN GLAPION
COLORS: MIKE SPICER
LETTERS: DAVE SHARPE
COVER: BOGDANOVIC and SPICER
EDITOR: PAUL KAMINSKI
GROUP EDITOR: EDDIE BERGANZA
--THAT WAS HIM!

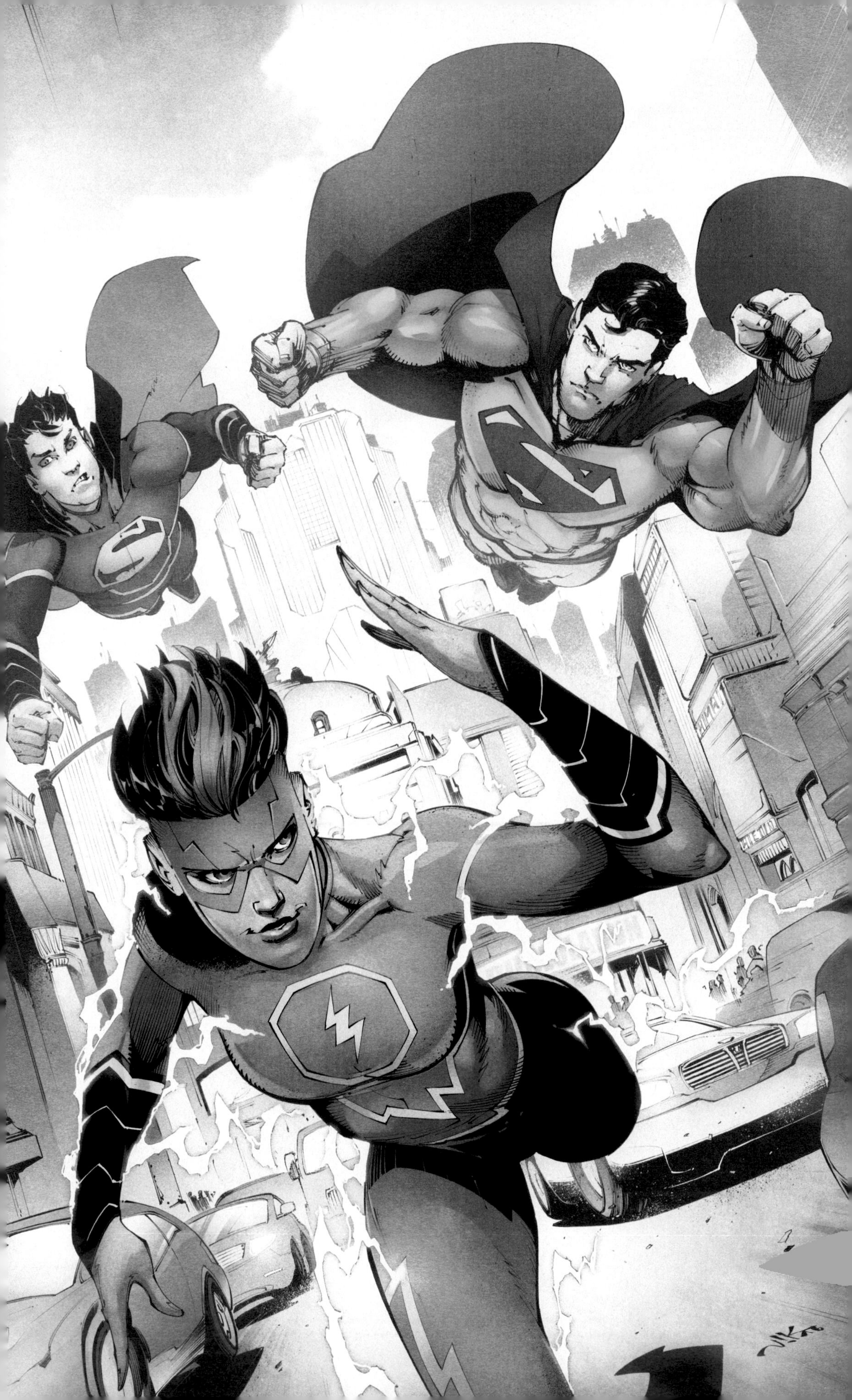

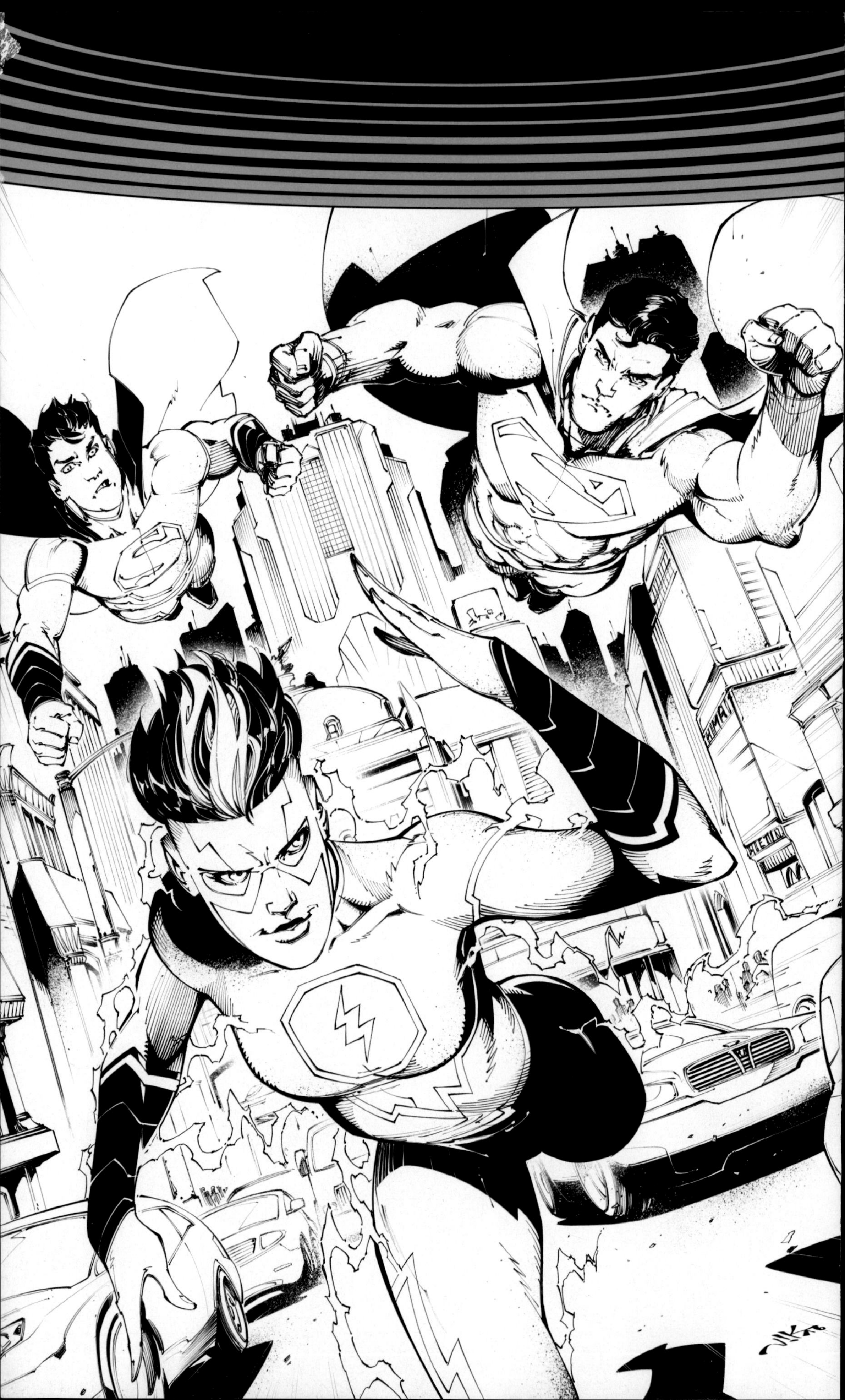

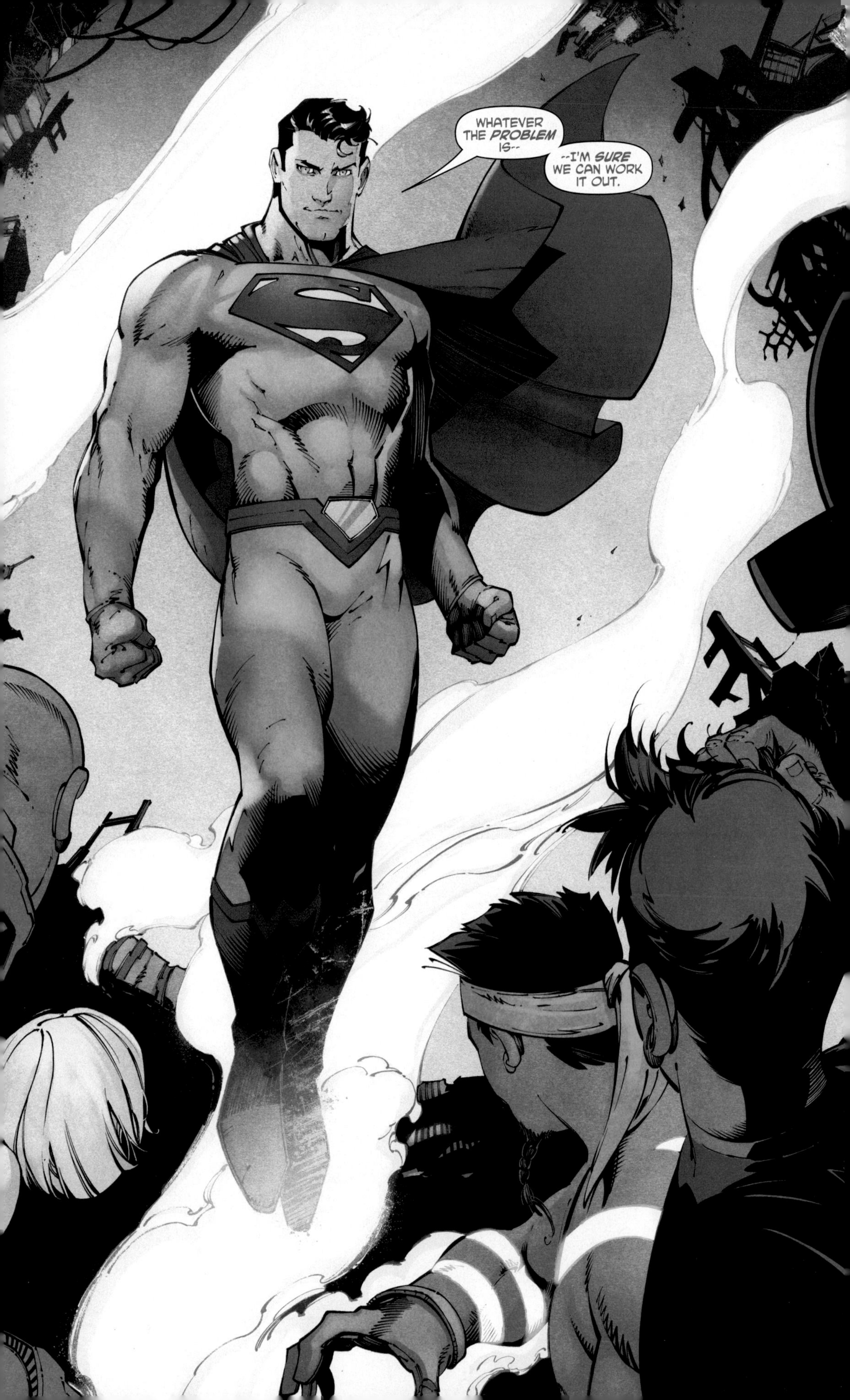
WHATEVER THE PROBLEM IS--
--I'M SURE WE CAN WORK IT OUT.

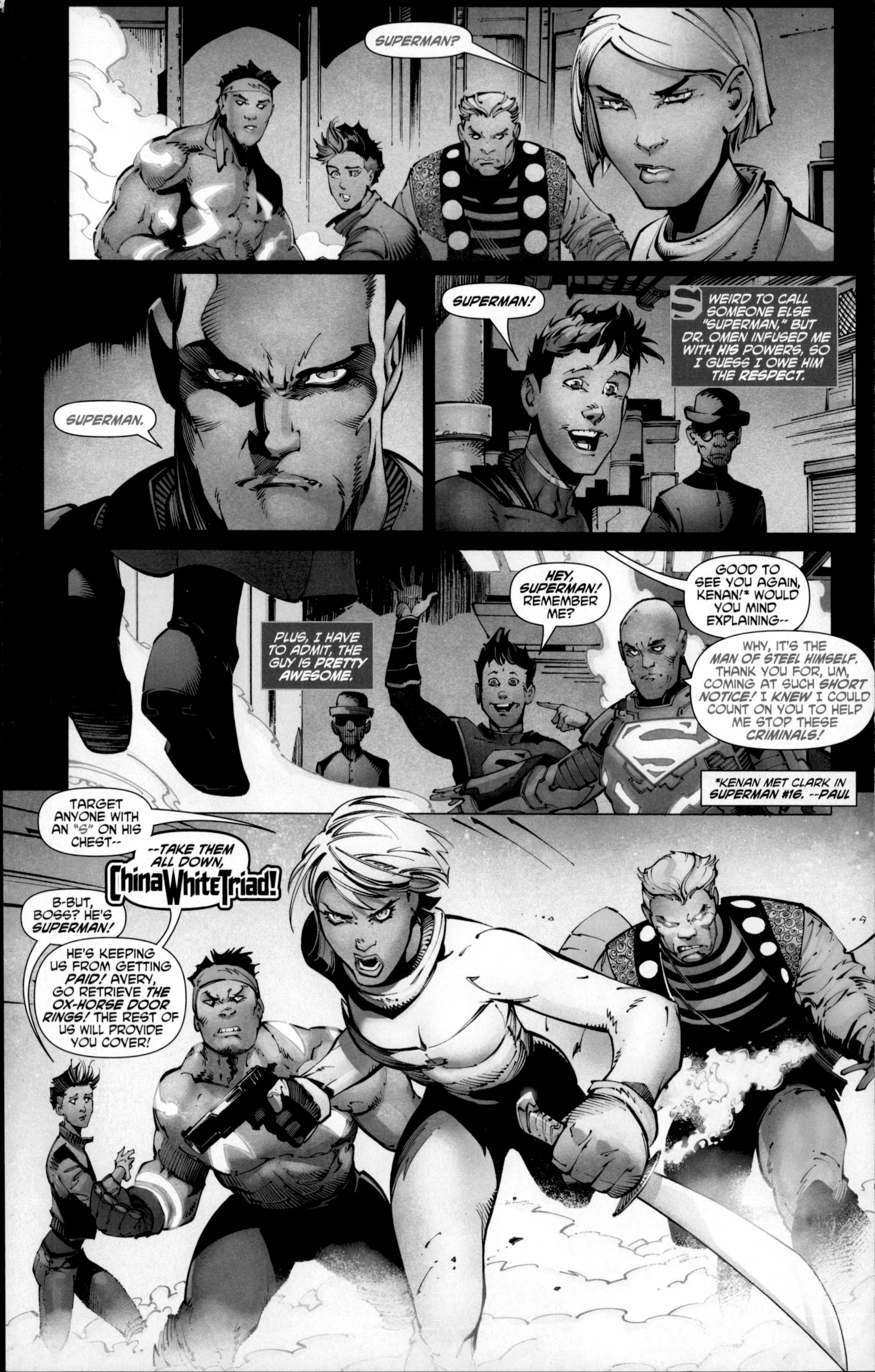
SUPERMAN?
SUPERMAN.
SUPERMAN!
WEIRD TO CALL SOMEONE ELSE "SUPERMAN," BUT DR. OMEN INFUSED ME WITH HIS POWERS, SO I GUESS I OWE HIM THE RESPECT.
PLUS, I HAVE TO ADMIT, THE GUY IS PRETTY AWESOME.
HEY, SUPERMAN! REMEMBER ME?
GOOD TO SEE YOU AGAIN, KENAN!* WOULD YOU MIND EXPLAINING--
WHY, IT'S THE MAN OF STEEL HIMSELF. THANK YOU FOR, UM, COMING AT SUCH SHORT NOTICE! I KNEW I COULD COUNT ON YOU TO HELP ME STOP THESE CRIMINALS!
*KENAN MET CLARK IN SUPERMAN #16. --PAUL
TARGET ANYONE WITH AN "S" ON HIS CHEST--
--TAKE THEM ALL DOWN, China White Triad!
B-BUT, BOSS? HE'S SUPERMAN!
HE'S KEEPING US FROM GETTING PAID! AVERY, GO RETRIEVE THE OX-HORSE DOOR RINGS! THE REST OF US WILL PROVIDE YOU COVER!

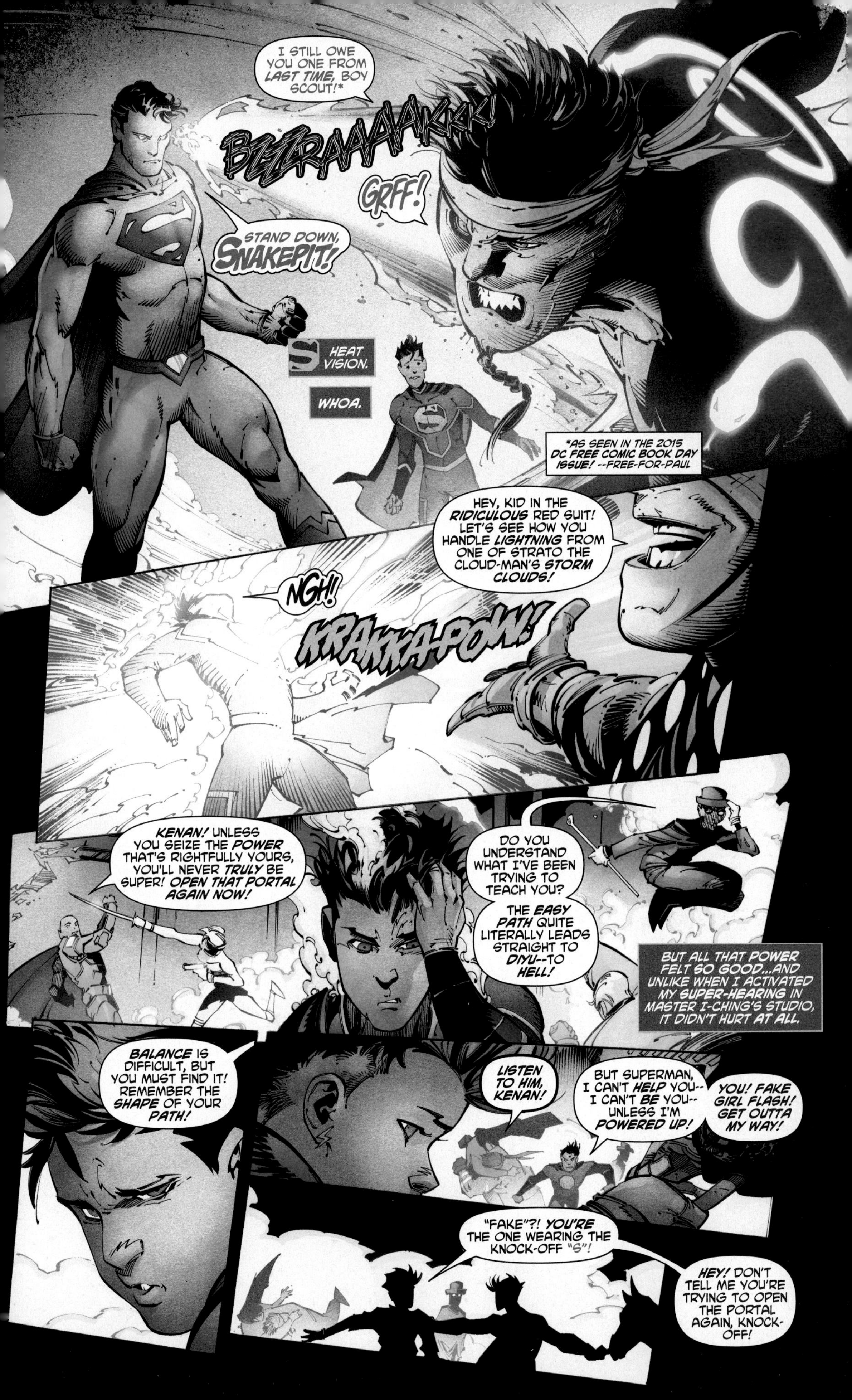
I STILL OWE YOU ONE FROM LAST TIME, BOY SCOUT!*
BZZRAAAAAKKK!
GRFF!
STAND DOWN, SNAKEPIT!
HEAT VISION.
WHOA.
*AS SEEN IN THE 2015 DC FREE COMIC BOOK DAY ISSUE! --FREE-FOR-PAUL
HEY, KID IN THE RIDICULOUS RED SUIT! LET'S SEE HOW YOU HANDLE LIGHTNING FROM ONE OF STRATO THE CLOUD-MAN'S STORM CLOUDS!
NGH!
KRAKKA-POW!
KENAN! UNLESS YOU SEIZE THE POWER THAT'S RIGHTFULLY YOURS, YOU'LL NEVER TRULY BE SUPER! OPEN THAT PORTAL AGAIN NOW!
DO YOU UNDERSTAND WHAT I'VE BEEN TRYING TO TEACH YOU?
THE EASY PATH QUITE LITERALLY LEADS STRAIGHT TO DIYU--TO HELL!
BUT ALL THAT POWER FELT SO GOOD...AND UNLIKE WHEN I ACTIVATED MY SUPER-HEARING IN MASTER I-CHING'S STUDIO, IT DIDN'T HURT AT ALL.
BALANCE IS DIFFICULT, BUT YOU MUST FIND IT! REMEMBER THE SHAPE OF YOUR PATH!
LISTEN TO HIM, KENAN!
BUT SUPERMAN, I CAN'T HELP YOU-- I CAN'T BE YOU-- UNLESS I'M POWERED UP!
YOU! FAKE GIRL FLASH! GET OUTTA MY WAY!
"FAKE"?! YOU'RE THE ONE WEARING THE KNOCK-OFF "S"!
HEY! DON'T TELL ME YOU'RE TRYING TO OPEN THE PORTAL AGAIN, KNOCK-OFF!

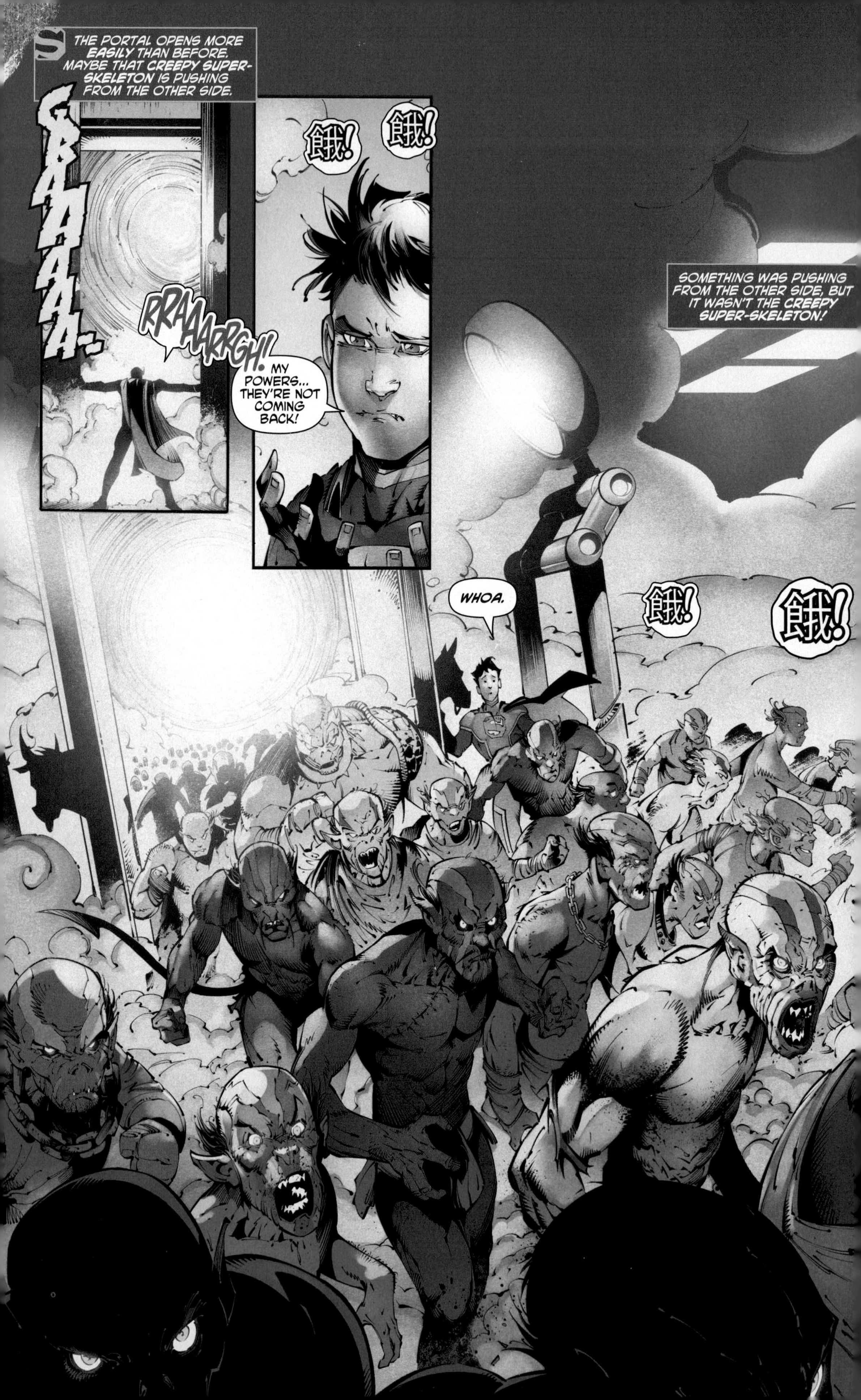
THE PORTAL OPENS MORE EASILY THAN BEFORE. MAYBE THAT CREEPY SUPER-SKELETON IS PUSHING FROM THE OTHER SIDE.
SHAAAAA-
RRAAAARRGH!
餓!
餓!
MY POWERS... THEY'RE NOT COMING BACK!
SOMETHING WAS PUSHING FROM THE OTHER SIDE, BUT IT WASN'T THE CREEPY SUPER-SKELETON!
WHOA.
餓!
餓!

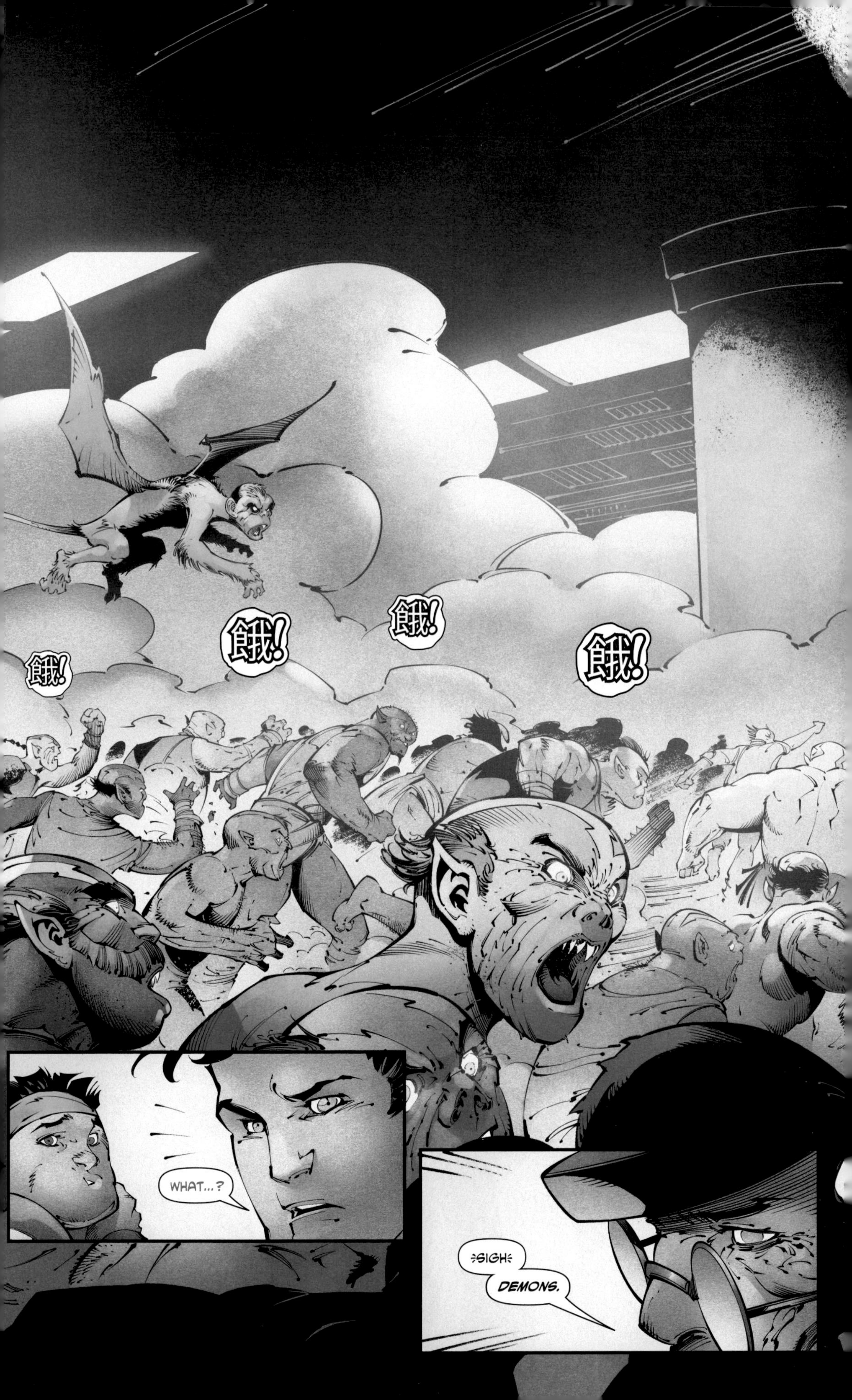
餓!
餓!
餓!
餓!
WHAT...?
SIGH
DEMONS.

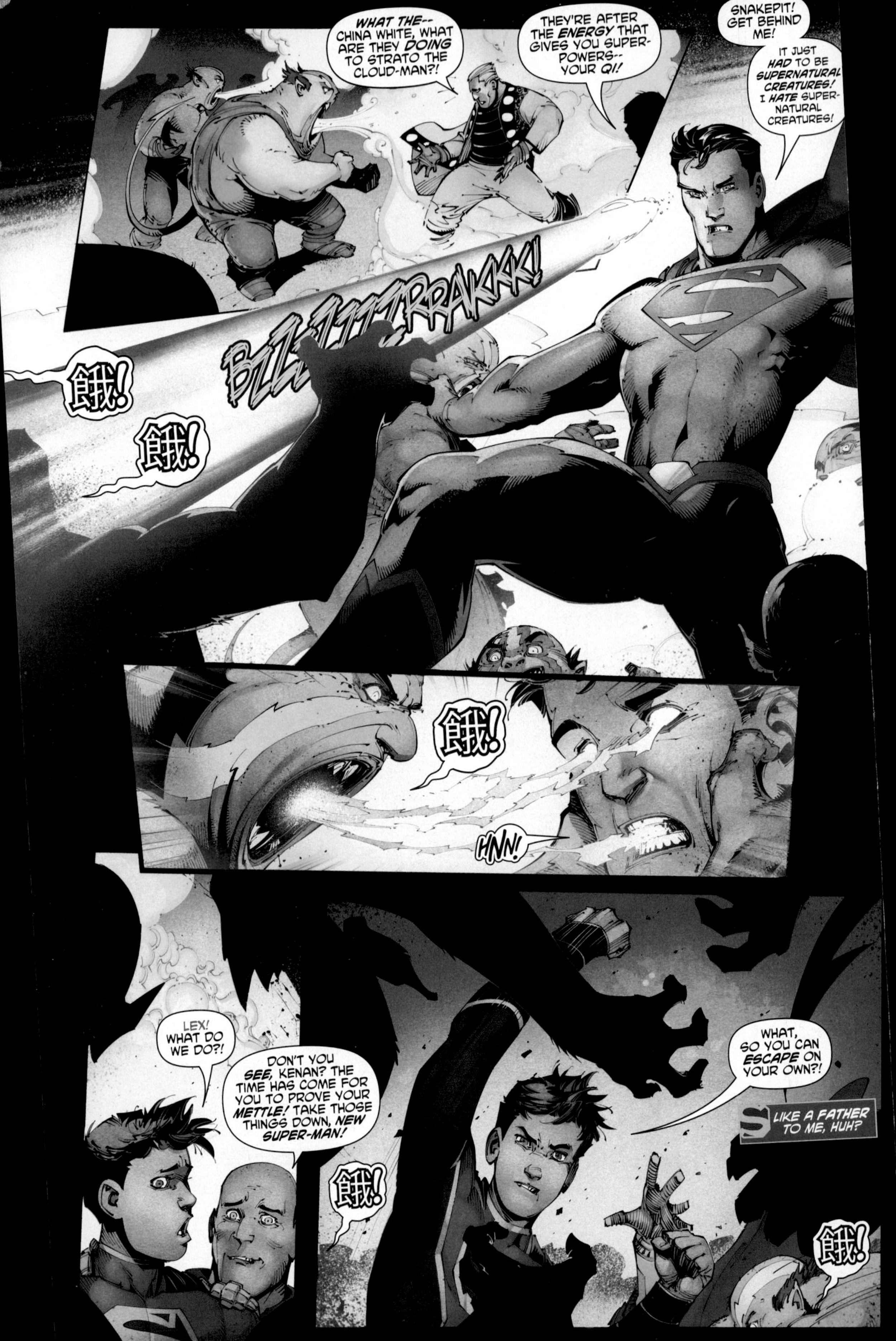

WHAT THE-- CHINA WHITE, WHAT ARE THEY DOING TO STRATO THE CLOUD-MAN?!
THEY'RE AFTER THE ENERGY THAT GIVES YOU SUPER-POWERS-- YOUR QI!
SNAKEPIT! GET BEHIND ME!
IT JUST HAD TO BE SUPERNATURAL CREATURES! I HATE SUPER-NATURAL CREATURES!
BZZZZZZZRRAKKK!
餓!
餓!
餓!
HNN!
LEX! WHAT DO WE DO?!
DON'T YOU SEE, KENAN? THE TIME HAS COME FOR YOU TO PROVE YOUR METTLE! TAKE THOSE THINGS DOWN, NEW SUPER-MAN!
餓!
WHAT, SO YOU CAN ESCAPE ON YOUR OWN?!
LIKE A FATHER TO ME, HUH?
餓!

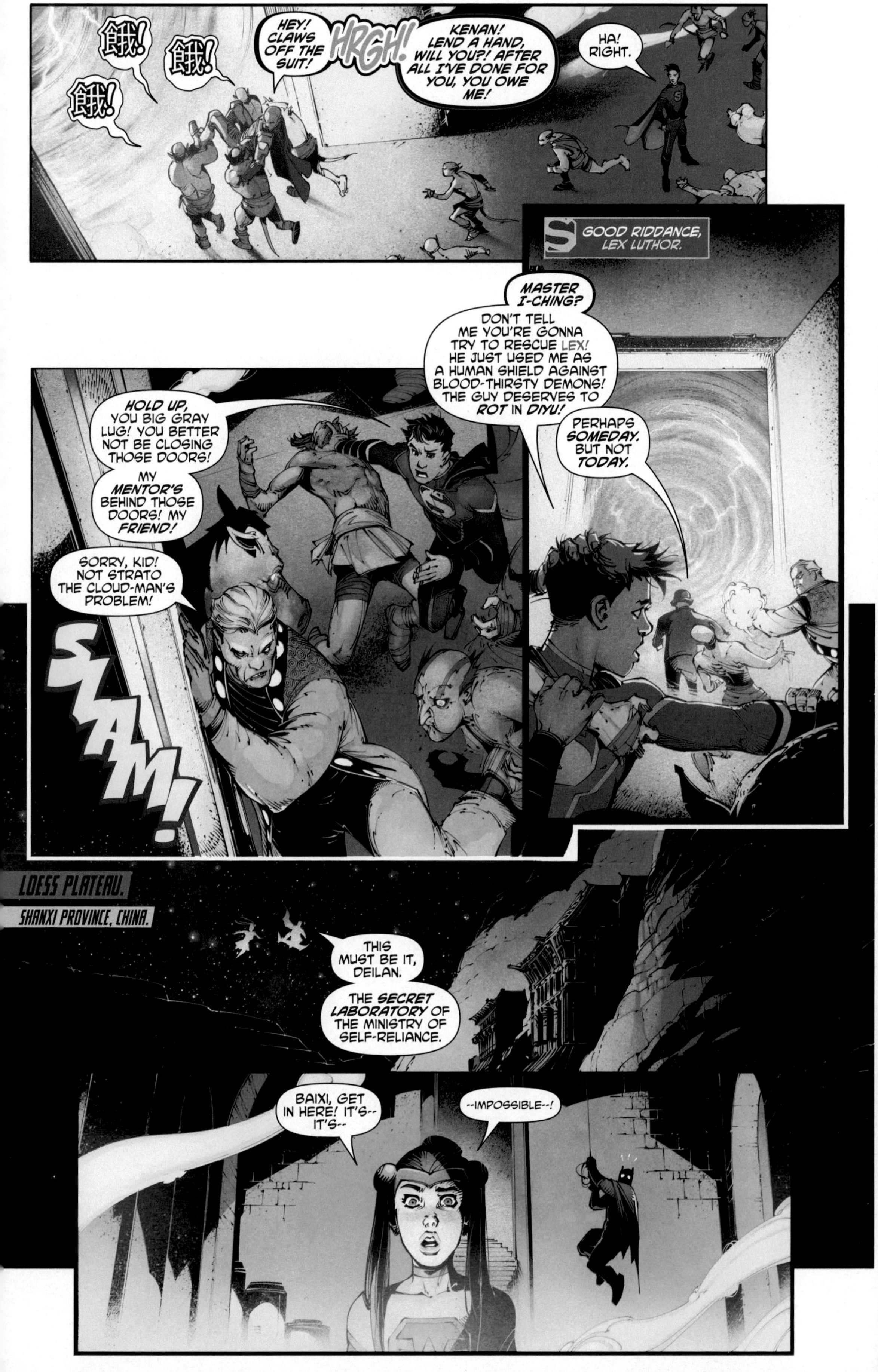

餓!
餓!
餓!
HEY! CLAWS OFF THE SUIT!
HRGH!
KENAN! LEND A HAND, WILL YOU?! AFTER ALL I'VE DONE FOR YOU, YOU OWE ME!
HA! RIGHT.
GOOD RIDDANCE, LEX LUTHOR.
HOLD UP, YOU BIG GRAY LUG! YOU BETTER NOT BE CLOSING THOSE DOORS!
MY MENTOR'S BEHIND THOSE DOORS! MY FRIEND!
SORRY, KID! NOT STRATO THE CLOUD-MAN'S PROBLEM!
SLAM!
MASTER I-CHING?
DON'T TELL ME YOU'RE GONNA TRY TO RESCUE LEX! HE JUST USED ME AS A HUMAN SHIELD AGAINST BLOOD-THIRSTY DEMONS! THE GUY DESERVES TO ROT IN DIYU!
PERHAPS SOMEDAY. BUT NOT TODAY.
LOESS PLATEAU.
SHANXI PROVINCE, CHINA.
THIS MUST BE IT, DEILAN.
THE SECRET LABORATORY OF THE MINISTRY OF SELF-RELIANCE.
BAIXI, GET IN HERE! IT'S-- IT'S--
--IMPOSSIBLE--!

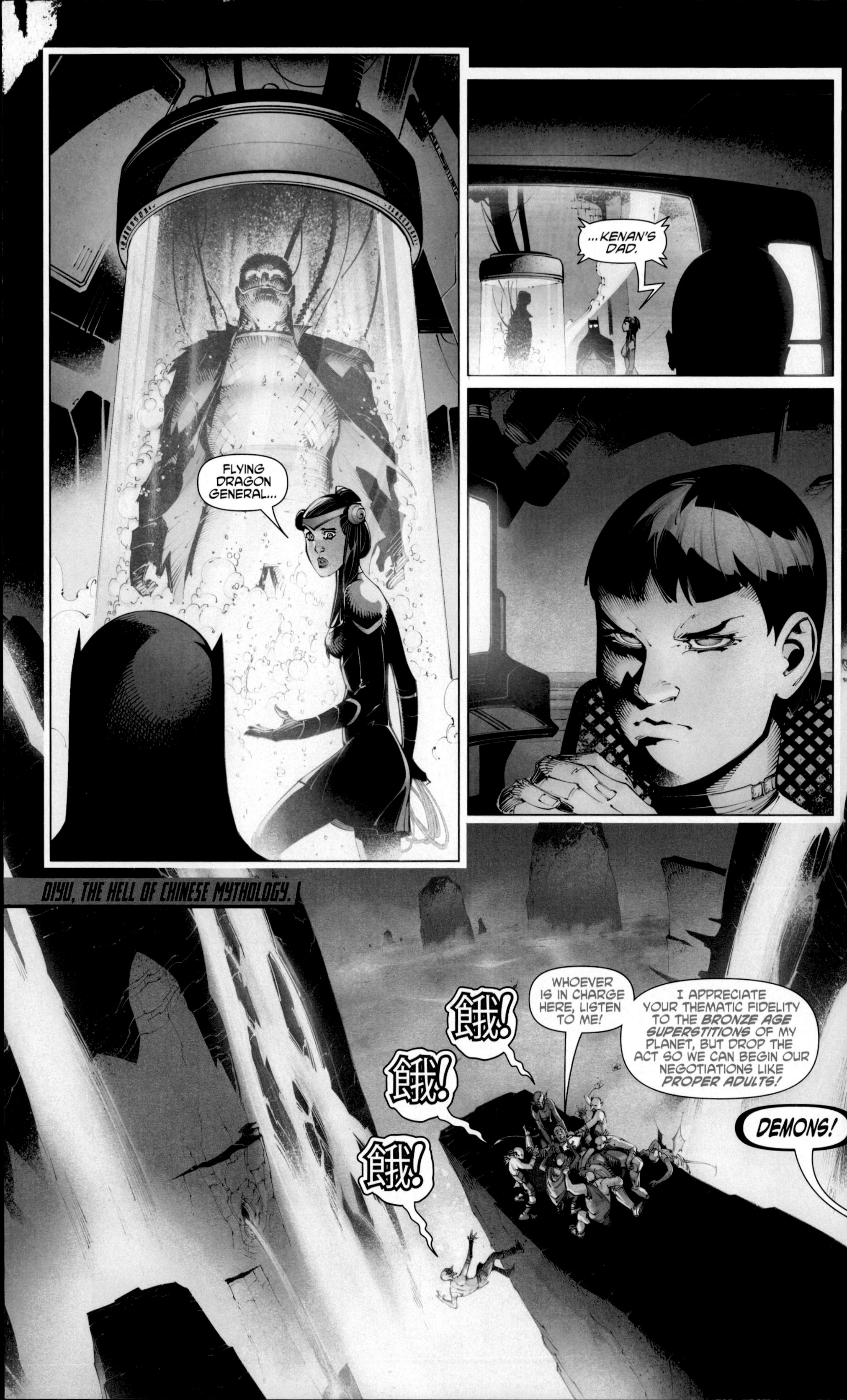
FLYING DRAGON GENERAL...
...KENAN'S DAD.
DIYU, THE HELL OF CHINESE MYTHOLOGY.
餓!
餓!
餓!
WHOEVER IS IN CHARGE HERE, LISTEN TO ME!
I APPRECIATE YOUR THEMATIC FIDELITY TO THE BRONZE AGE SUPERSTITIONS OF MY PLANET, BUT DROP THE ACT SO WE CAN BEGIN OUR NEGOTIATIONS LIKE PROPER ADULTS!
DEMONS!

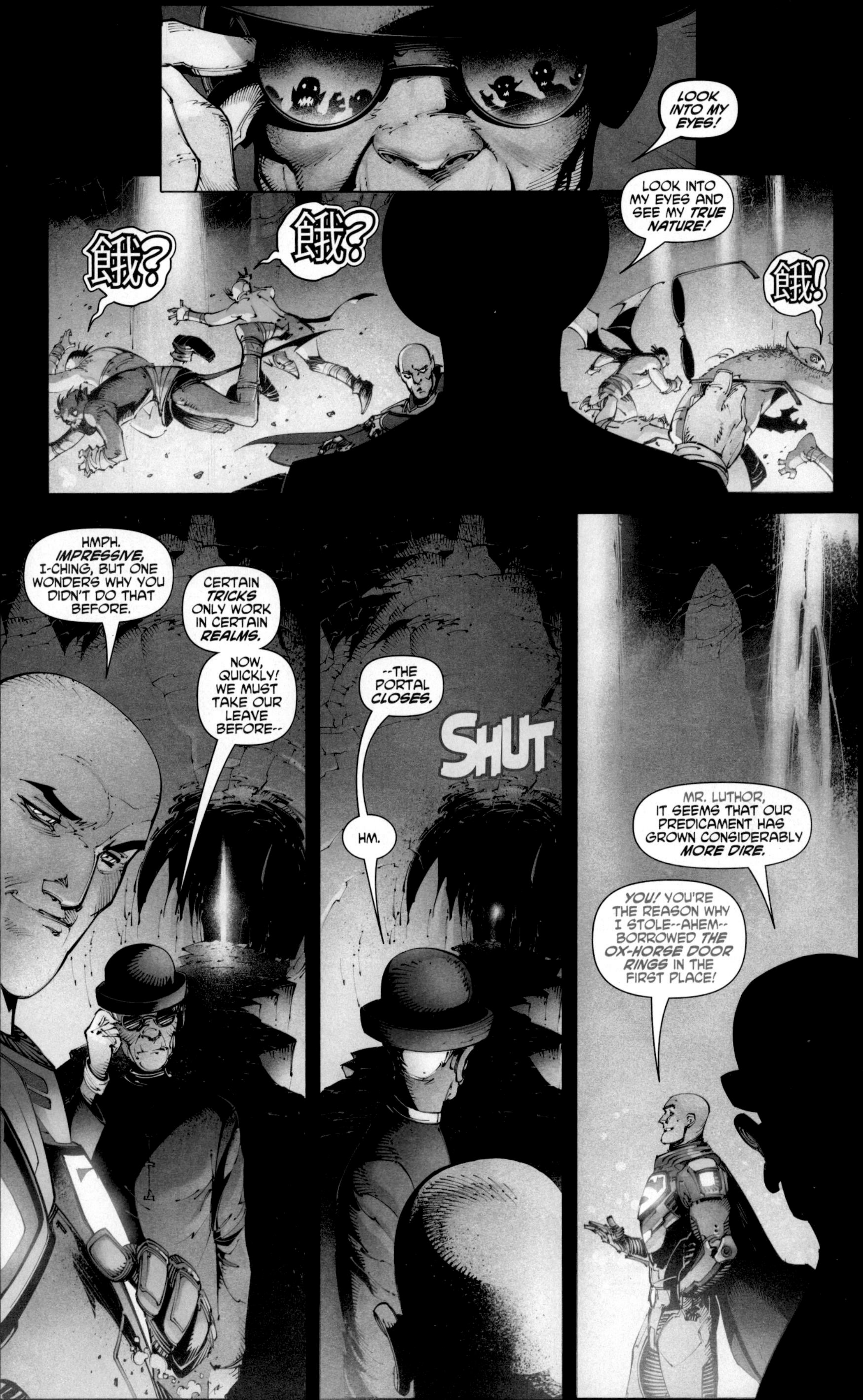
LOOK INTO MY EYES!
LOOK INTO MY EYES AND SEE MY TRUE NATURE!
餓?
餓?
餓!
HMPH. IMPRESSIVE, I-CHING, BUT ONE WONDERS WHY YOU DIDN'T DO THAT BEFORE.
CERTAIN TRICKS ONLY WORK IN CERTAIN REALMS.
NOW, QUICKLY! WE MUST TAKE OUR LEAVE BEFORE--
--THE PORTAL CLOSES.
SHUT
HM.
MR. LUTHOR, IT SEEMS THAT OUR PREDICAMENT HAS GROWN CONSIDERABLY MORE DIRE.
YOU! YOU'RE THE REASON WHY I STOLE--AHEM--BORROWED THE OX-HORSE DOOR RINGS IN THE FIRST PLACE!

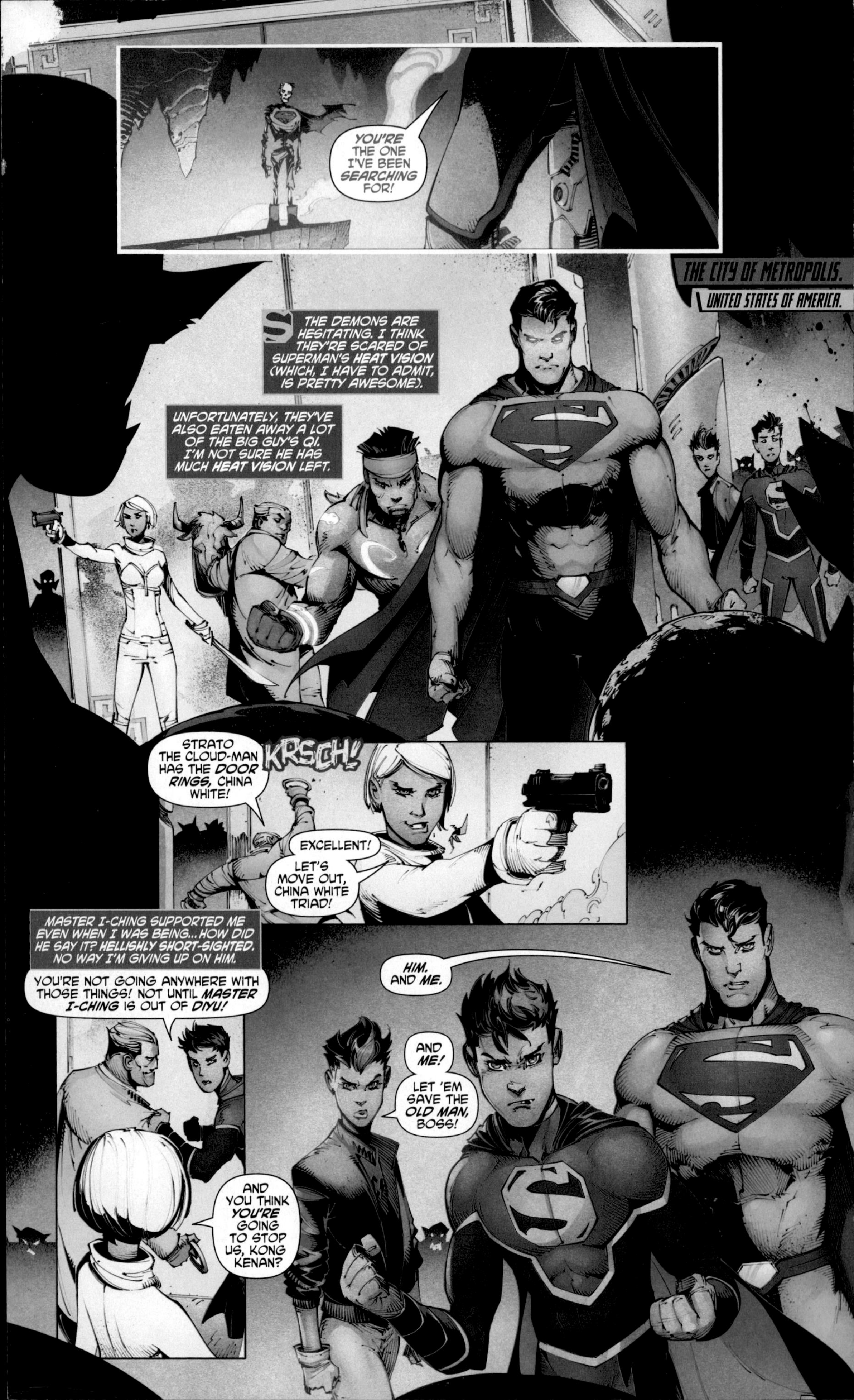
YOU'RE THE ONE I'VE BEEN SEARCHING FOR!
THE CITY OF METROPOLIS.
UNITED STATES OF AMERICA.
THE DEMONS ARE HESITATING. I THINK THEY'RE SCARED OF SUPERMAN'S HEAT VISION (WHICH, I HAVE TO ADMIT, IS PRETTY AWESOME).
UNFORTUNATELY, THEY'VE ALSO EATEN AWAY A LOT OF THE BIG GUY'S QI. I'M NOT SURE HE HAS MUCH HEAT VISION LEFT.
STRATO THE CLOUD-MAN HAS THE DOOR RINGS, CHINA WHITE!
KRSCH!
EXCELLENT!
LET'S MOVE OUT, CHINA WHITE TRIAD!
MASTER I-CHING SUPPORTED ME EVEN WHEN I WAS BEING...HOW DID HE SAY IT? HELLISHLY SHORT-SIGHTED. NO WAY I'M GIVING UP ON HIM.
YOU'RE NOT GOING ANYWHERE WITH THOSE THINGS! NOT UNTIL MASTER I-CHING IS OUT OF DIYU!
AND YOU THINK YOU'RE GOING TO STOP US, KONG KENAN?
HIM. AND ME.
AND ME!
LET 'EM SAVE THE OLD MAN, BOSS!

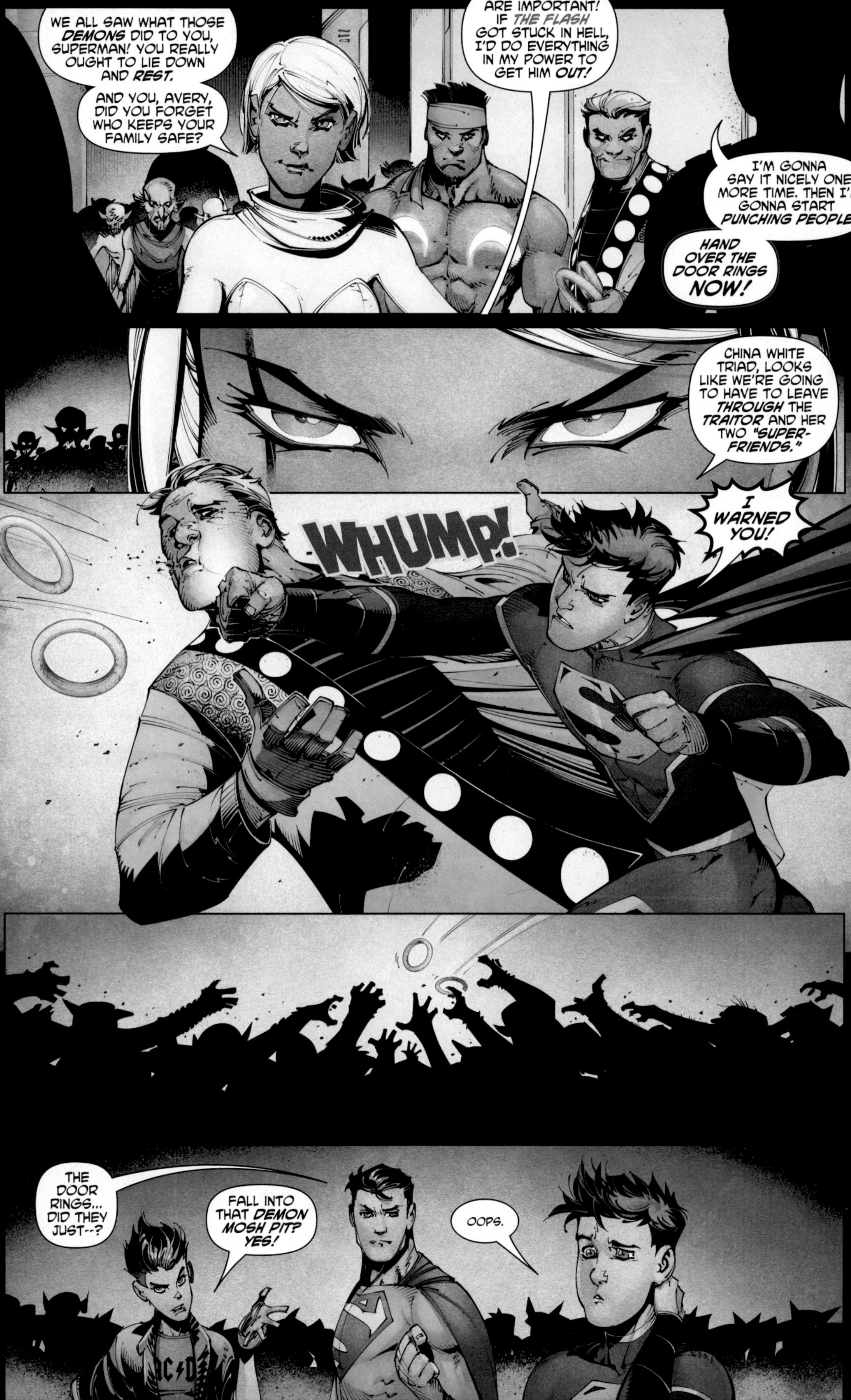
WE ALL SAW WHAT THOSE DEMONS DID TO YOU, SUPERMAN! YOU REALLY OUGHT TO LIE DOWN AND REST.
AND YOU, AVERY, DID YOU FORGET WHO KEEPS YOUR FAMILY SAFE?
MENTORS ARE IMPORTANT! IF THE FLASH GOT STUCK IN HELL, I'D DO EVERYTHING IN MY POWER TO GET HIM OUT!
I'M GONNA SAY IT NICELY ONE MORE TIME. THEN I'M GONNA START PUNCHING PEOPLE.
HAND OVER THE DOOR RINGS NOW!
CHINA WHITE TRIAD, LOOKS LIKE WE'RE GOING TO HAVE TO LEAVE THROUGH THE TRAITOR AND HER TWO "SUPER-FRIENDS."
WHUMP!
I WARNED YOU!
THE DOOR RINGS... DID THEY JUST--?
FALL INTO THAT DEMON MOSH PIT? YES!
OOPS.

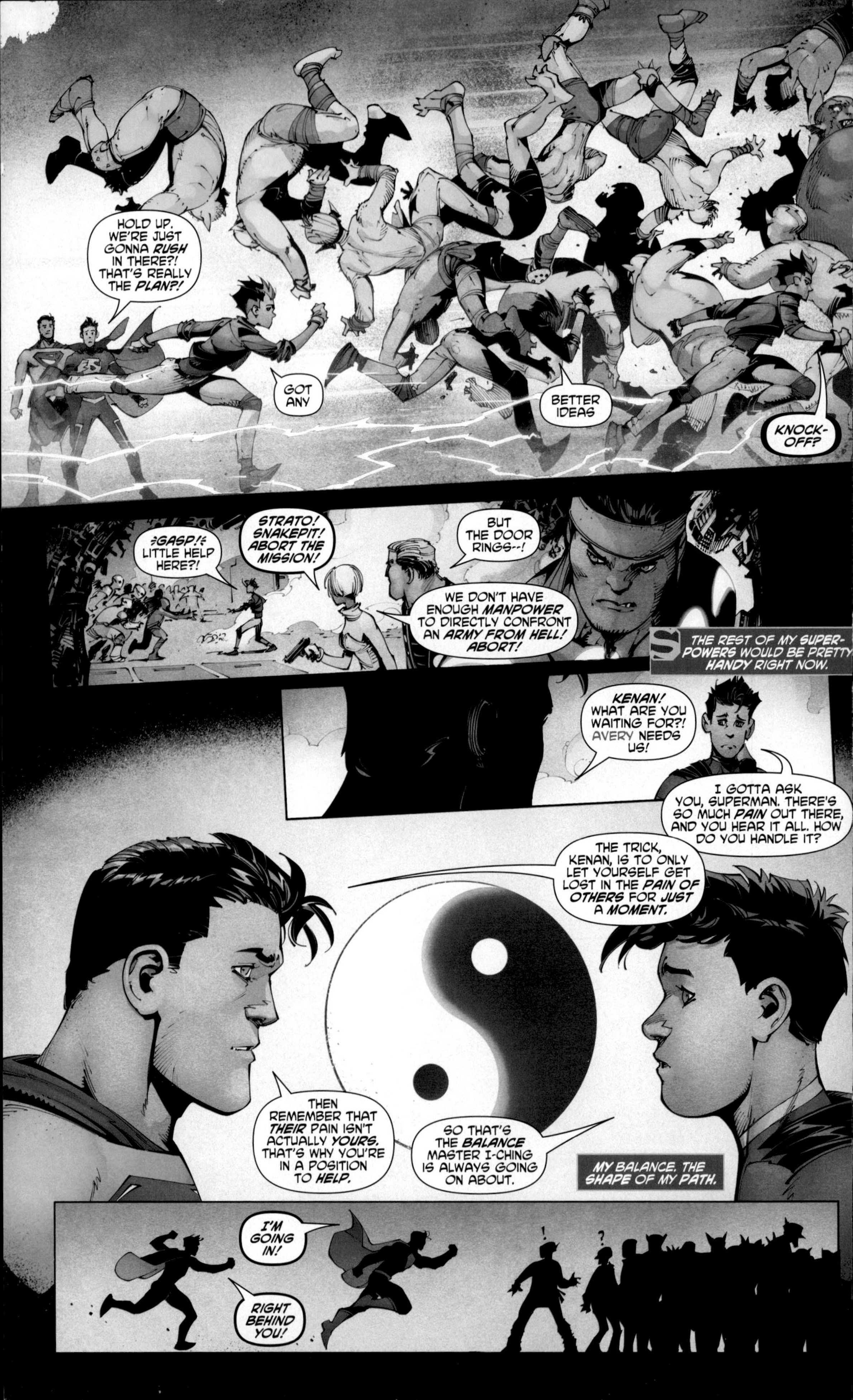
HOLD UP. WE'RE JUST GONNA RUSH IN THERE?! THAT'S REALLY THE PLAN?!
GOT ANY
BETTER IDEAS
KNOCK-OFF?
≶GASP!≶ LITTLE HELP HERE?!
STRATO! SNAKEPIT! ABORT THE MISSION!
BUT THE DOOR RINGS--!
WE DON'T HAVE ENOUGH MANPOWER TO DIRECTLY CONFRONT AN ARMY FROM HELL! ABORT!
THE REST OF MY SUPER-POWERS WOULD BE PRETTY HANDY RIGHT NOW.
KENAN! WHAT ARE YOU WAITING FOR?! AVERY NEEDS US!
I GOTTA ASK YOU, SUPERMAN. THERE'S SO MUCH PAIN OUT THERE, AND YOU HEAR IT ALL. HOW DO YOU HANDLE IT?
THE TRICK, KENAN, IS TO ONLY LET YOURSELF GET LOST IN THE PAIN OF OTHERS FOR JUST A MOMENT.
THEN REMEMBER THAT THEIR PAIN ISN'T ACTUALLY YOURS. THAT'S WHY YOU'RE IN A POSITION TO HELP.
SO THAT'S THE BALANCE MASTER I-CHING IS ALWAYS GOING ON ABOUT.
MY BALANCE. THE SHAPE OF MY PATH.
I'M GOING IN!
RIGHT BEHIND YOU!
!
?

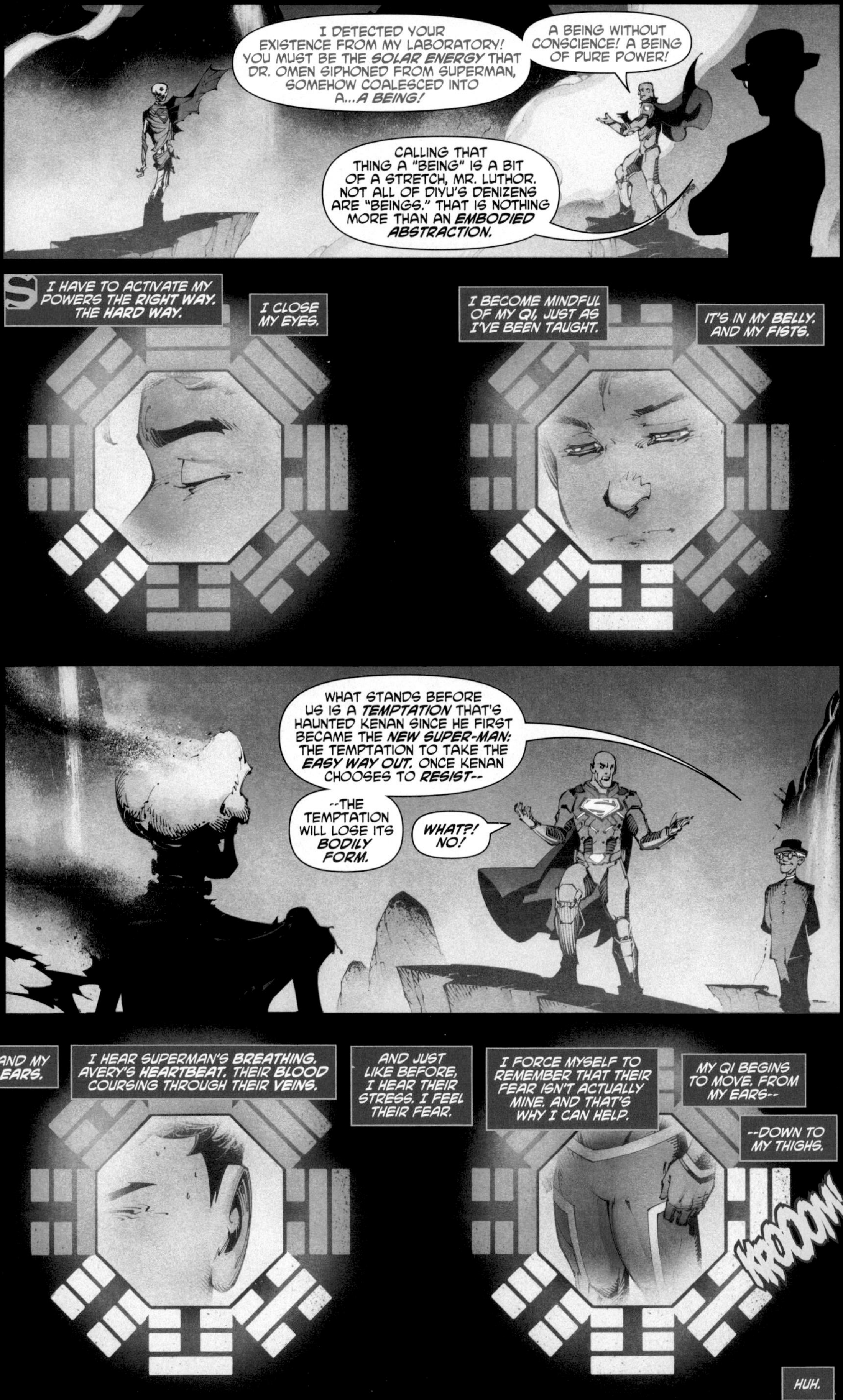
I DETECTED YOUR EXISTENCE FROM MY LABORATORY! YOU MUST BE THE SOLAR ENERGY THAT DR. OMEN SIPHONED FROM SUPERMAN, SOMEHOW COALESCED INTO A...A BEING!
A BEING WITHOUT CONSCIENCE! A BEING OF PURE POWER!
CALLING THAT THING A "BEING" IS A BIT OF A STRETCH, MR. LUTHOR. NOT ALL OF DIYU'S DENIZENS ARE "BEINGS." THAT IS NOTHING MORE THAN AN EMBODIED ABSTRACTION.
I HAVE TO ACTIVATE MY POWERS THE RIGHT WAY. THE HARD WAY.
I CLOSE MY EYES.
I BECOME MINDFUL OF MY QI, JUST AS I'VE BEEN TAUGHT.
IT'S IN MY BELLY. AND MY FISTS.
WHAT STANDS BEFORE US IS A TEMPTATION THAT'S HAUNTED KENAN SINCE HE FIRST BECAME THE NEW SUPER-MAN: THE TEMPTATION TO TAKE THE EASY WAY OUT. ONCE KENAN CHOOSES TO RESIST--
--THE TEMPTATION WILL LOSE ITS BODILY FORM.
WHAT?! NO!
AND MY EARS.
I HEAR SUPERMAN'S BREATHING. AVERY'S HEARTBEAT. THEIR BLOOD COURSING THROUGH THEIR VEINS.
AND JUST LIKE BEFORE, I HEAR THEIR STRESS. I FEEL THEIR FEAR.
I FORCE MYSELF TO REMEMBER THAT THEIR FEAR ISN'T ACTUALLY MINE. AND THAT'S WHY I CAN HELP.
MY QI BEGINS TO MOVE. FROM MY EARS--
--DOWN TO MY THIGHS.
KROOOM!
HUH.

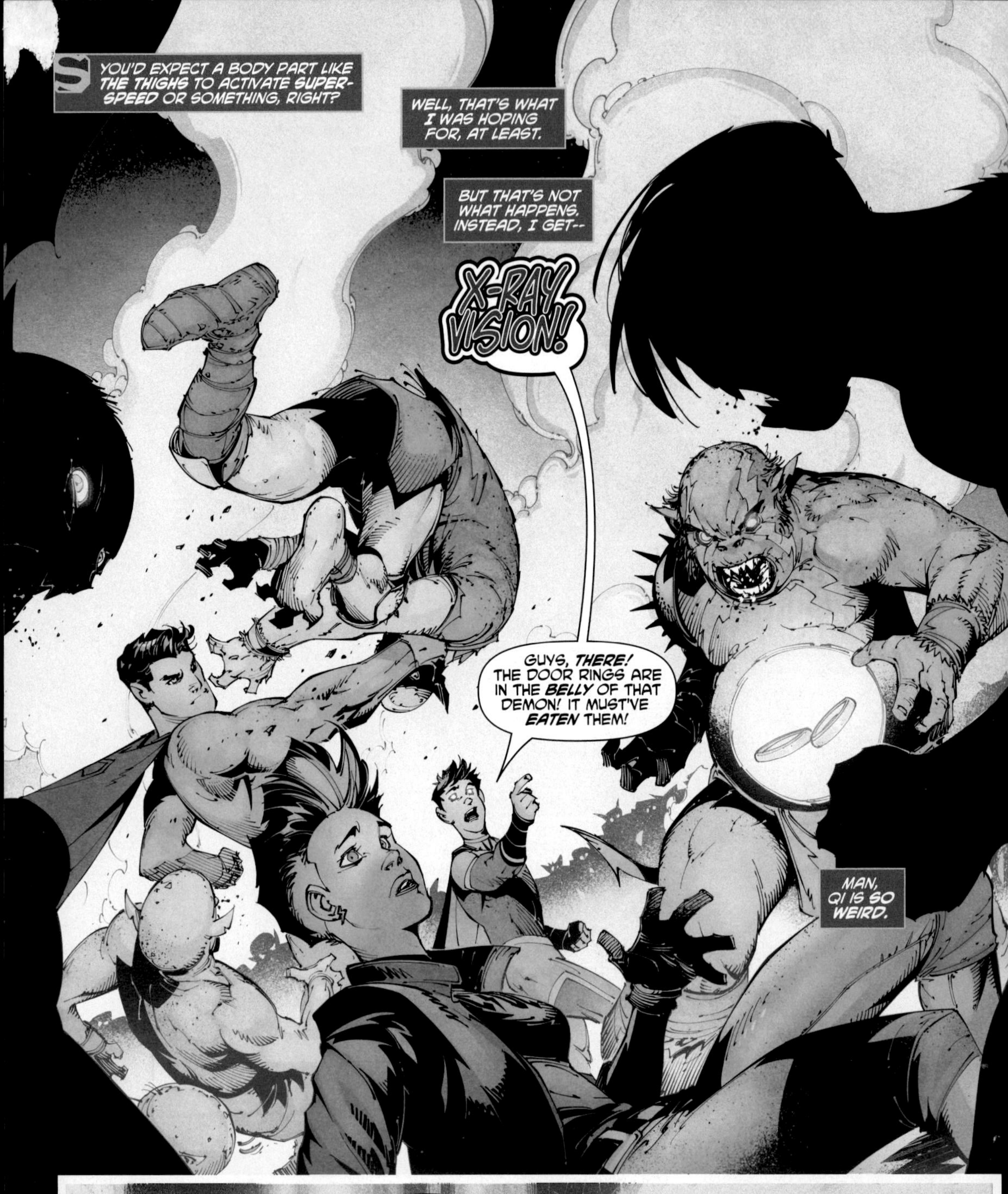
YOU'D EXPECT A BODY PART LIKE THE THIGHS TO ACTIVATE SUPER-SPEED OR SOMETHING, RIGHT?
WELL, THAT'S WHAT I WAS HOPING FOR, AT LEAST.
BUT THAT'S NOT WHAT HAPPENS. INSTEAD, I GET--
X-RAY VISION!
GUYS, THERE! THE DOOR RINGS ARE IN THE BELLY OF THAT DEMON! IT MUST'VE EATEN THEM!
MAN, QI IS SO WEIRD.

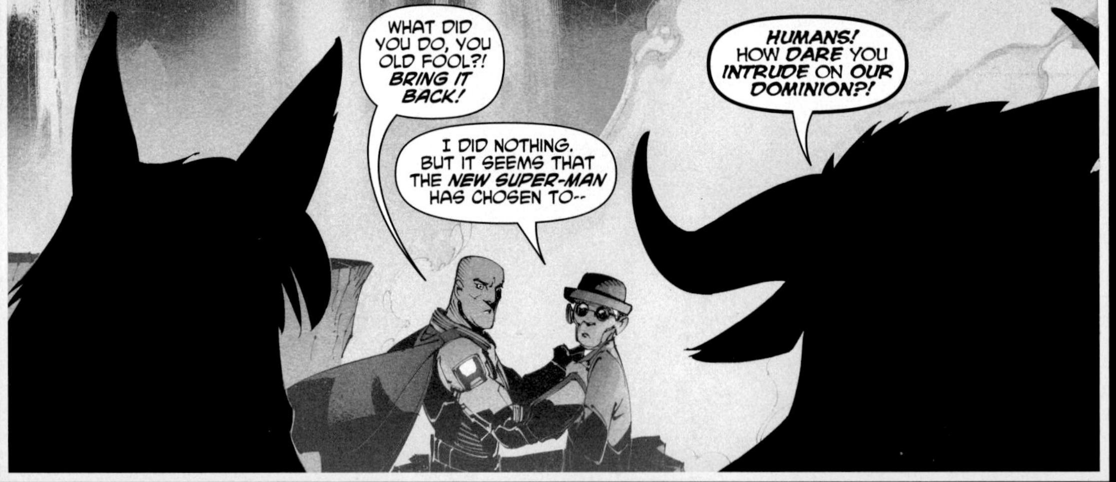
WHAT DID YOU DO, YOU OLD FOOL?! BRING IT BACK!
I DID NOTHING. BUT IT SEEMS THAT THE NEW SUPER-MAN HAS CHOSEN TO--
HUMANS! HOW DARE YOU INTRUDE ON OUR DOMINION?!

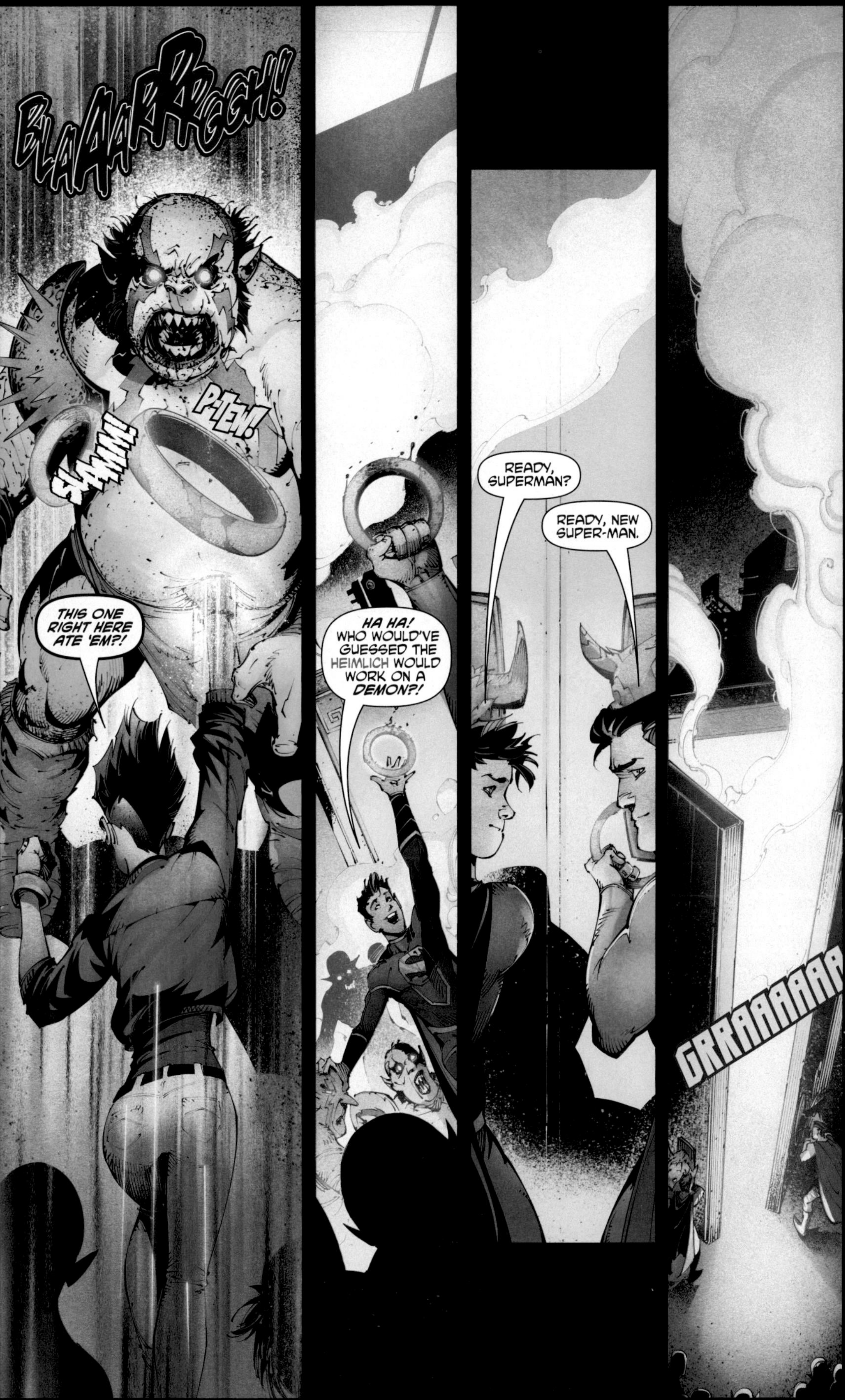
BLAAARRRGGH!!
SHAMM!
P-TEW!
THIS ONE RIGHT HERE ATE 'EM?!
HA HA! WHO WOULD'VE GUESSED THE HEIMLICH WOULD WORK ON A DEMON?!
READY, SUPERMAN?
READY, NEW SUPER-MAN.
GRAAAAAAR

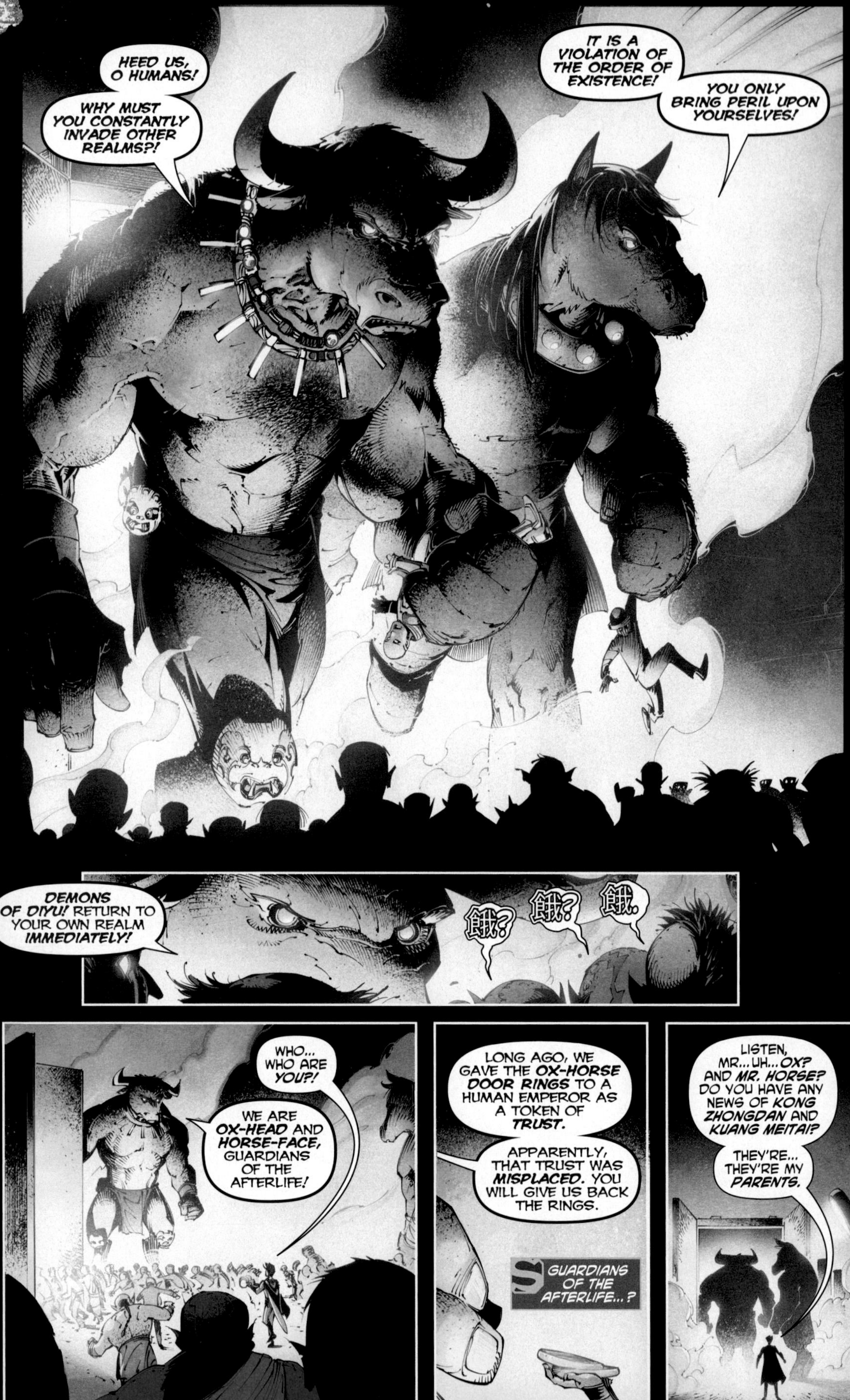
HEED US, O HUMANS!
WHY MUST YOU CONSTANTLY INVADE OTHER REALMS?!
IT IS A VIOLATION OF THE ORDER OF EXISTENCE!
YOU ONLY BRING PERIL UPON YOURSELVES!
DEMONS OF DIYU! RETURN TO YOUR OWN REALM IMMEDIATELY!
餓?
餓?
餓.
WHO... WHO ARE YOU?!
WE ARE OX-HEAD AND HORSE-FACE, GUARDIANS OF THE AFTERLIFE!
LONG AGO, WE GAVE THE OX-HORSE DOOR RINGS TO A HUMAN EMPEROR AS A TOKEN OF TRUST.
APPARENTLY, THAT TRUST WAS MISPLACED. YOU WILL GIVE US BACK THE RINGS.
GUARDIANS OF THE AFTERLIFE...?
LISTEN, MR... UH... OX? AND MR. HORSE? DO YOU HAVE ANY NEWS OF KONG ZHONGDAN AND KUANG MEITAI?
THEY'RE... THEY'RE MY PARENTS.

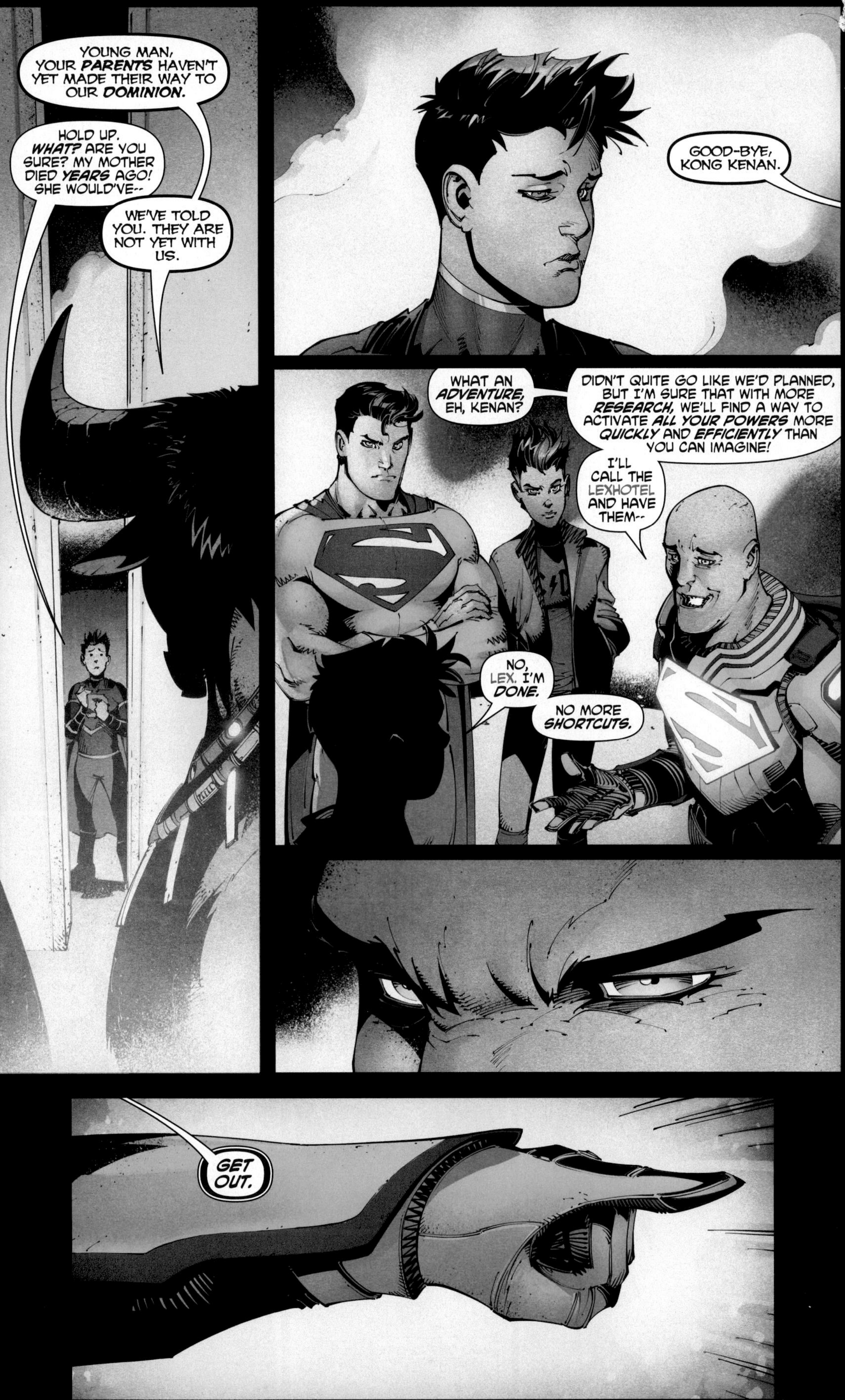
YOUNG MAN, YOUR PARENTS HAVEN'T YET MADE THEIR WAY TO OUR DOMINION.
HOLD UP. WHAT? ARE YOU SURE? MY MOTHER DIED YEARS AGO! SHE WOULD'VE--
WE'VE TOLD YOU. THEY ARE NOT YET WITH US.
GOOD-BYE, KONG KENAN.
WHAT AN ADVENTURE, EH, KENAN?
DIDN'T QUITE GO LIKE WE'D PLANNED, BUT I'M SURE THAT WITH MORE RESEARCH, WE'LL FIND A WAY TO ACTIVATE ALL YOUR POWERS MORE QUICKLY AND EFFICIENTLY THAN YOU CAN IMAGINE!
I'LL CALL THE LEXHOTEL AND HAVE THEM--
NO, LEX. I'M DONE.
NO MORE SHORTCUTS.
GET OUT.

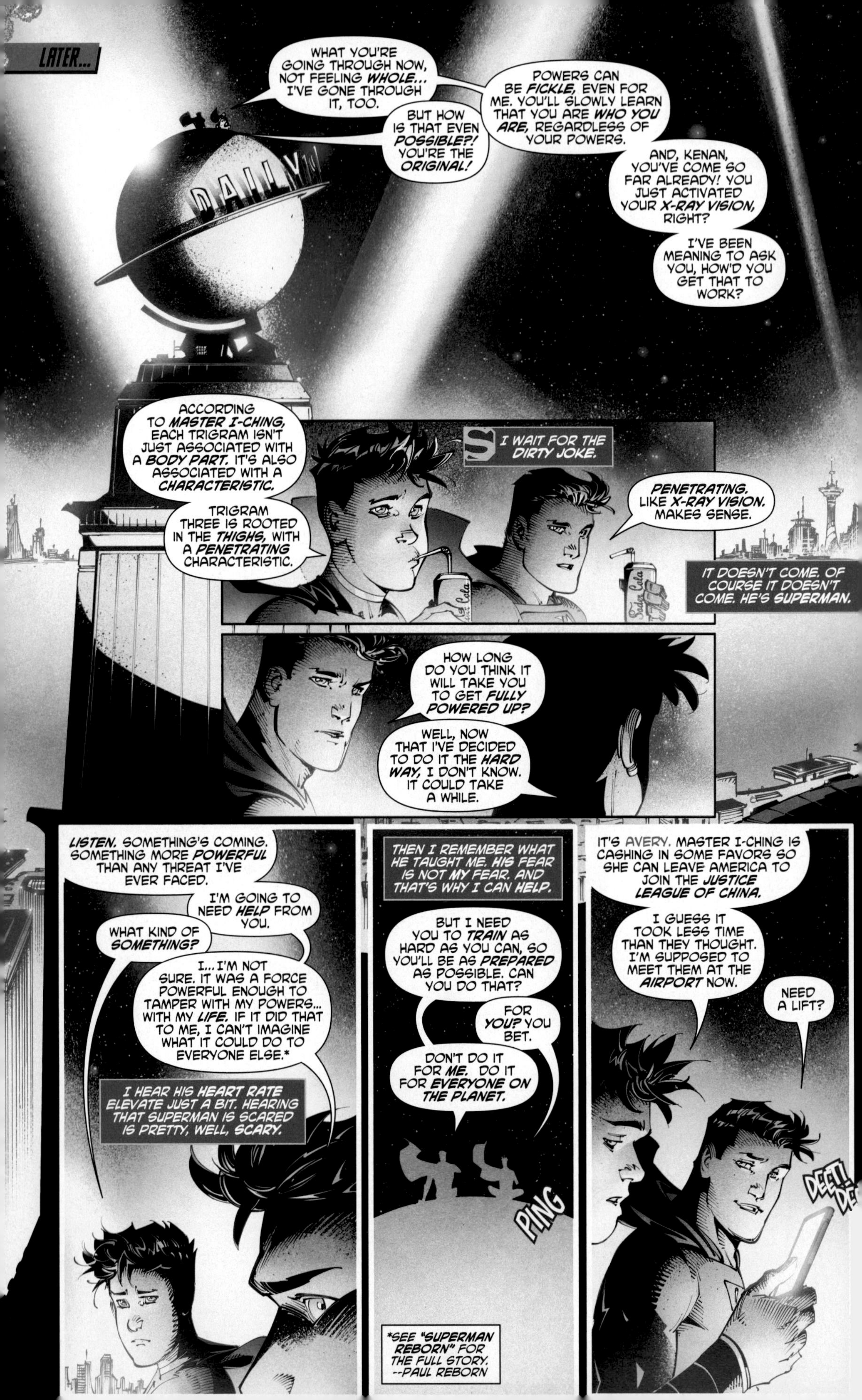
LATER...
WHAT YOU'RE GOING THROUGH NOW, NOT FEELING WHOLE... I'VE GONE THROUGH IT, TOO.
BUT HOW IS THAT EVEN POSSIBLE?! YOU'RE THE ORIGINAL!
POWERS CAN BE FICKLE, EVEN FOR ME. YOU'LL SLOWLY LEARN THAT YOU ARE WHO YOU ARE, REGARDLESS OF YOUR POWERS.
AND, KENAN, YOU'VE COME SO FAR ALREADY! YOU JUST ACTIVATED YOUR X-RAY VISION, RIGHT?
I'VE BEEN MEANING TO ASK YOU, HOW'D YOU GET THAT TO WORK?
ACCORDING TO MASTER I-CHING, EACH TRIGRAM ISN'T JUST ASSOCIATED WITH A BODY PART. IT'S ALSO ASSOCIATED WITH A CHARACTERISTIC.
TRIGRAM THREE IS ROOTED IN THE THIGHS, WITH A PENETRATING CHARACTERISTIC.
I WAIT FOR THE DIRTY JOKE.
PENETRATING. LIKE X-RAY VISION. MAKES SENSE.
IT DOESN'T COME. OF COURSE IT DOESN'T COME. HE'S SUPERMAN.
HOW LONG DO YOU THINK IT WILL TAKE YOU TO GET FULLY POWERED UP?
WELL, NOW THAT I'VE DECIDED TO DO IT THE HARD WAY, I DON'T KNOW. IT COULD TAKE A WHILE.
LISTEN. SOMETHING'S COMING. SOMETHING MORE POWERFUL THAN ANY THREAT I'VE EVER FACED.
I'M GOING TO NEED HELP FROM YOU.
WHAT KIND OF SOMETHING?
I... I'M NOT SURE. IT WAS A FORCE POWERFUL ENOUGH TO TAMPER WITH MY POWERS... WITH MY LIFE. IF IT DID THAT TO ME, I CAN'T IMAGINE WHAT IT COULD DO TO EVERYONE ELSE.*
I HEAR HIS HEART RATE ELEVATE JUST A BIT. HEARING THAT SUPERMAN IS SCARED IS PRETTY, WELL, SCARY.
THEN I REMEMBER WHAT HE TAUGHT ME. HIS FEAR IS NOT MY FEAR. AND THAT'S WHY I CAN HELP.
BUT I NEED YOU TO TRAIN AS HARD AS YOU CAN, SO YOU'LL BE AS PREPARED AS POSSIBLE. CAN YOU DO THAT?
FOR YOU? YOU BET.
DON'T DO IT FOR ME. DO IT FOR EVERYONE ON THE PLANET.
PING
*SEE "SUPERMAN REBORN" FOR THE FULL STORY. --PAUL REBORN
IT'S AVERY. MASTER I-CHING IS CASHING IN SOME FAVORS SO SHE CAN LEAVE AMERICA TO JOIN THE JUSTICE LEAGUE OF CHINA.
I GUESS IT TOOK LESS TIME THAN THEY THOUGHT. I'M SUPPOSED TO MEET THEM AT THE AIRPORT NOW.
NEED A LIFT?
DEE!!

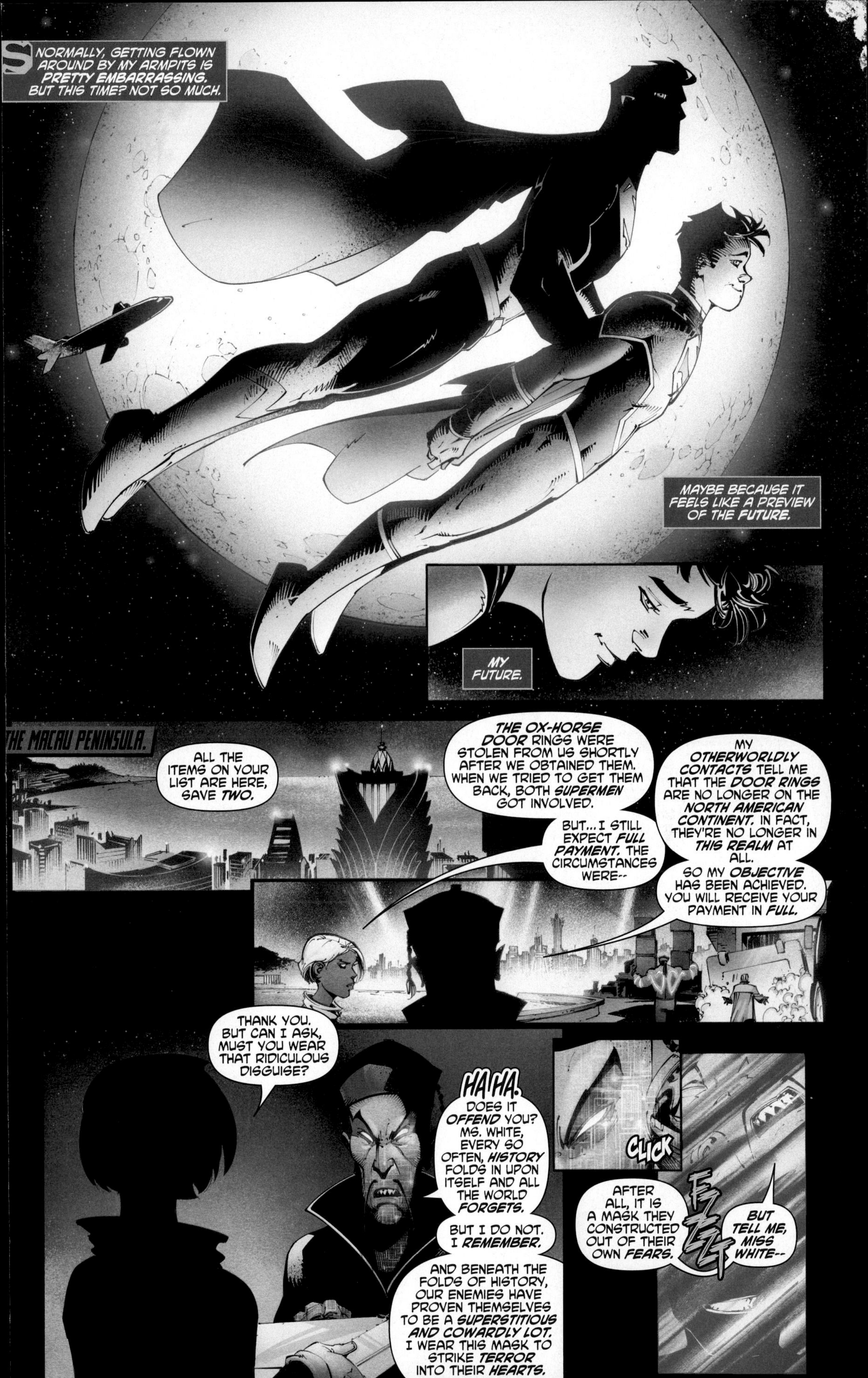
NORMALLY, GETTING FLOWN AROUND BY MY ARMPITS IS PRETTY EMBARRASSING. BUT THIS TIME? NOT SO MUCH.
MAYBE BECAUSE IT FEELS LIKE A PREVIEW OF THE FUTURE.
MY FUTURE.
THE MACAU PENINSULA.
ALL THE ITEMS ON YOUR LIST ARE HERE, SAVE TWO.
THE OX-HORSE DOOR RINGS WERE STOLEN FROM US SHORTLY AFTER WE OBTAINED THEM. WHEN WE TRIED TO GET THEM BACK, BOTH SUPERMEN GOT INVOLVED.
BUT... I STILL EXPECT FULL PAYMENT. THE CIRCUMSTANCES WERE--
MY OTHERWORLDLY CONTACTS TELL ME THAT THE DOOR RINGS ARE NO LONGER ON THE NORTH AMERICAN CONTINENT. IN FACT, THEY'RE NO LONGER IN THIS REALM AT ALL.
SO MY OBJECTIVE HAS BEEN ACHIEVED. YOU WILL RECEIVE YOUR PAYMENT IN FULL.
THANK YOU. BUT CAN I ASK, MUST YOU WEAR THAT RIDICULOUS DISGUISE?
HA HA.
DOES IT OFFEND YOU? MS. WHITE, EVERY SO OFTEN, HISTORY FOLDS IN UPON ITSELF AND ALL THE WORLD FORGETS.
BUT I DO NOT. I REMEMBER.
AND BENEATH THE FOLDS OF HISTORY, OUR ENEMIES HAVE PROVEN THEMSELVES TO BE A SUPERSTITIOUS AND COWARDLY LOT. I WEAR THIS MASK TO STRIKE TERROR INTO THEIR HEARTS.
CLICK
AFTER ALL, IT IS A MASK THEY CONSTRUCTED OUT OF THEIR OWN FEARS.
FZZZT
BUT TELL ME, MISS WHITE--

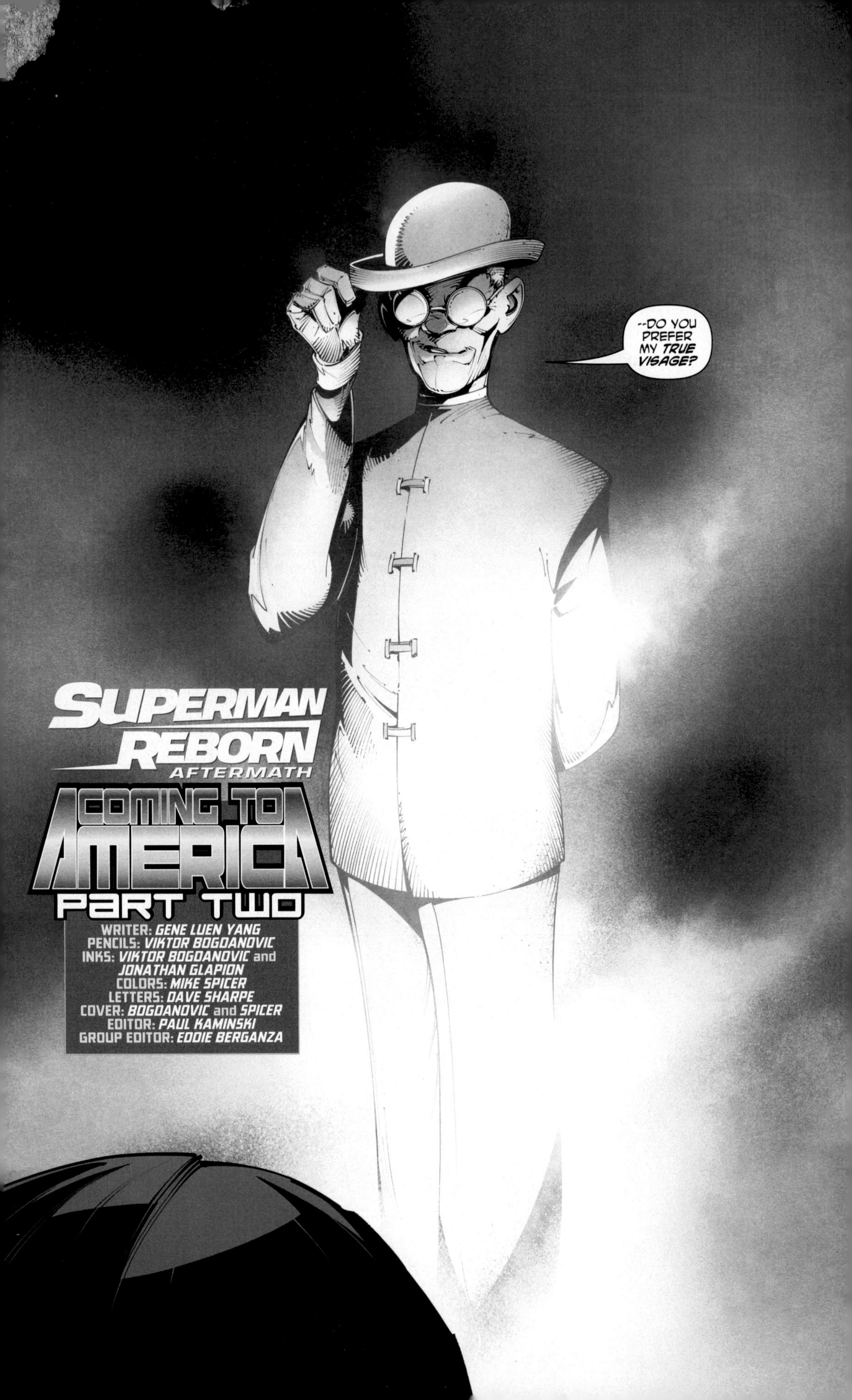
--DO YOU PREFER MY *TRUE VISAGE?*
SUPERMAN REBORN
AFTERMATH
COMING TO AMERICA
PART TWO
WRITER: GENE LUEN YANG
PENCILS: VIKTOR BOGDANOVIC
INKS: VIKTOR BOGDANOVIC and JONATHAN GLAPION
COLORS: MIKE SPICER
LETTERS: DAVE SHARPE
COVER: BOGDANOVIC and SPICER
EDITOR: PAUL KAMINSKI
GROUP EDITOR: EDDIE BERGANZA

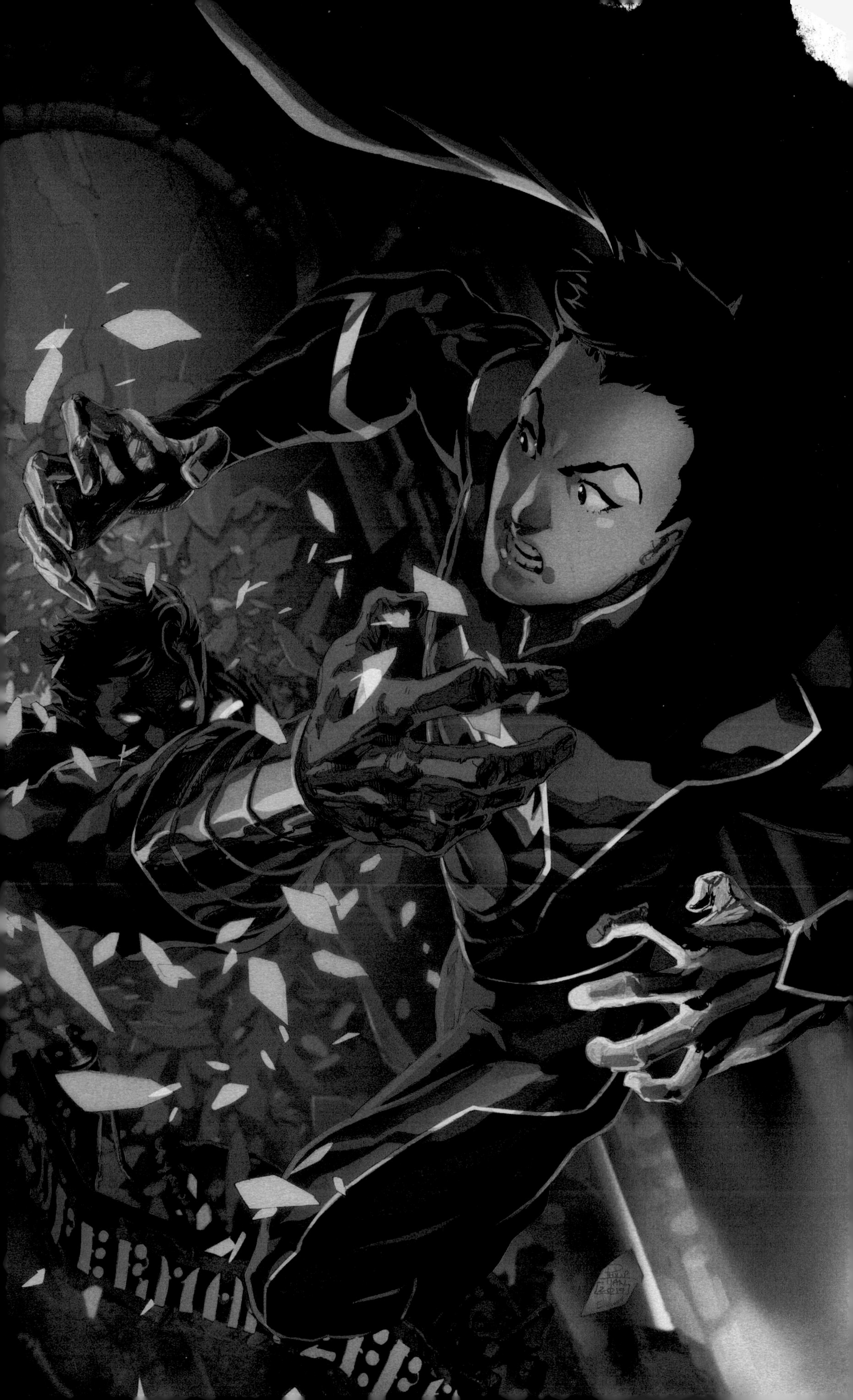

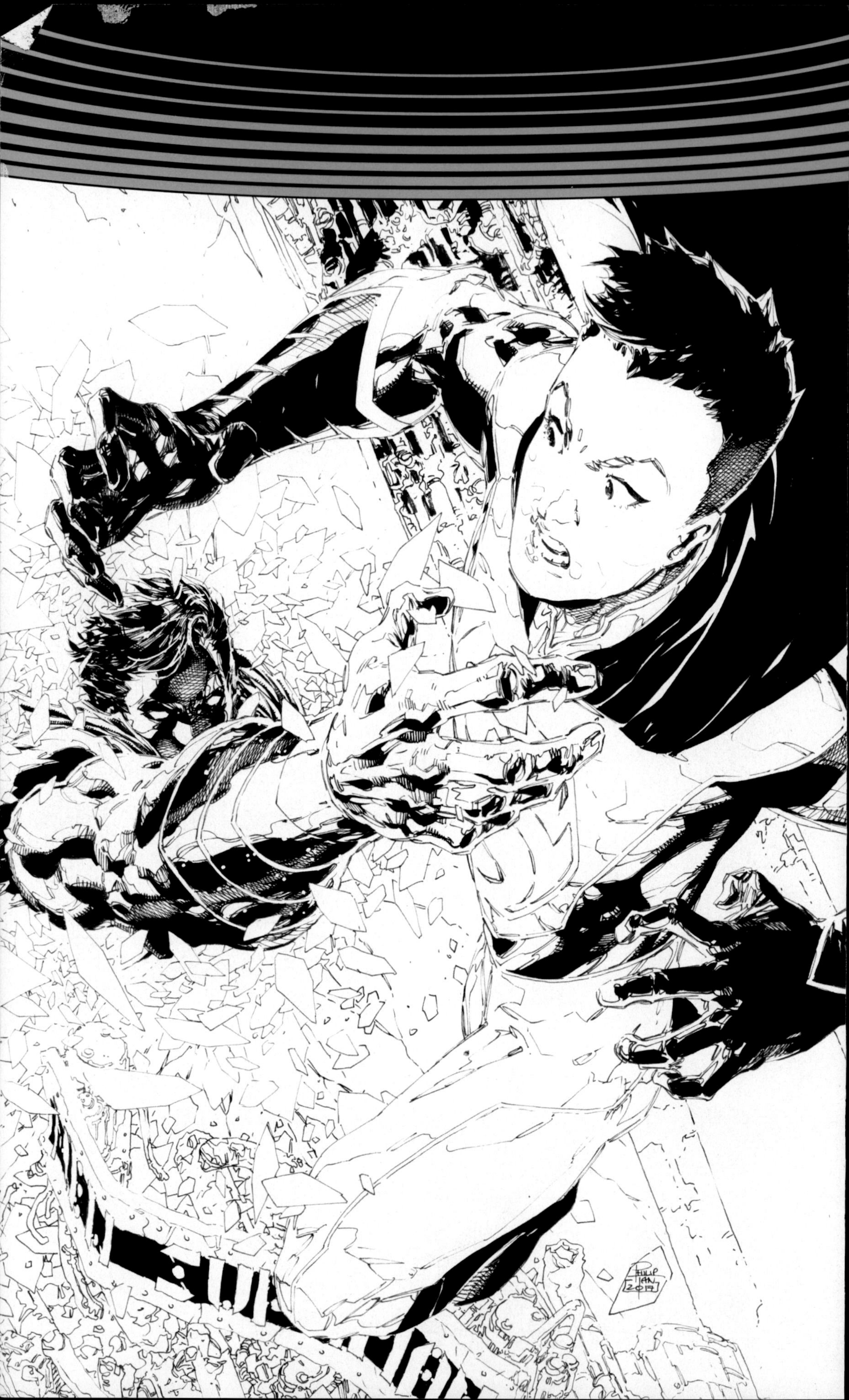

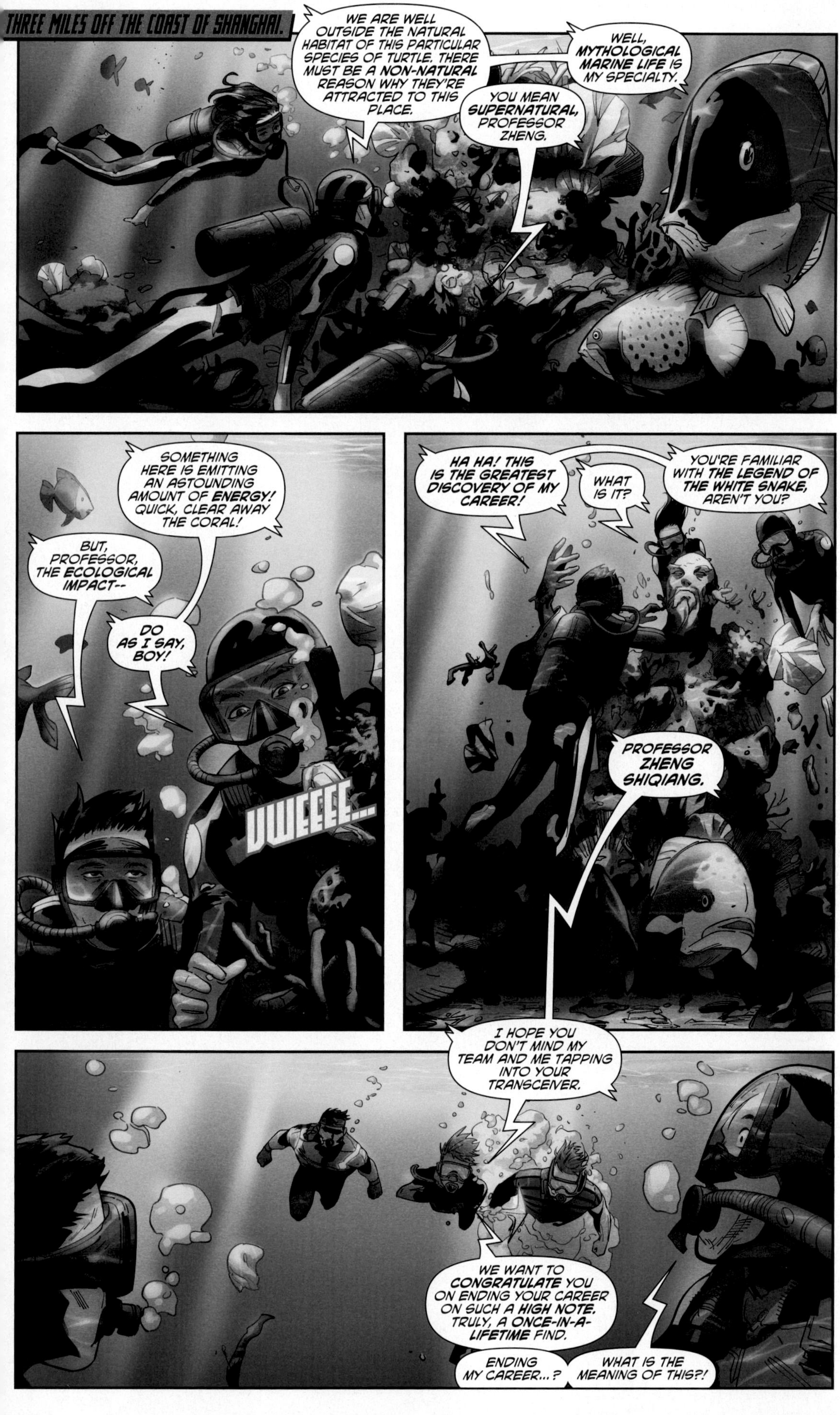
THREE MILES OFF THE COAST OF SHANGHAI.
WE ARE WELL OUTSIDE THE NATURAL HABITAT OF THIS PARTICULAR SPECIES OF TURTLE. THERE MUST BE A NON-NATURAL REASON WHY THEY'RE ATTRACTED TO THIS PLACE.
YOU MEAN SUPERNATURAL, PROFESSOR ZHENG.
WELL, MYTHOLOGICAL MARINE LIFE IS MY SPECIALTY.
SOMETHING HERE IS EMITTING AN ASTOUNDING AMOUNT OF ENERGY! QUICK, CLEAR AWAY THE CORAL!
BUT, PROFESSOR, THE ECOLOGICAL IMPACT--
DO AS I SAY, BOY!
VWEEEE...
HA HA! THIS IS THE GREATEST DISCOVERY OF MY CAREER!
WHAT IS IT?
YOU'RE FAMILIAR WITH THE LEGEND OF THE WHITE SNAKE, AREN'T YOU?
PROFESSOR ZHENG SHIQIANG.
I HOPE YOU DON'T MIND MY TEAM AND ME TAPPING INTO YOUR TRANSCEIVER.
WE WANT TO CONGRATULATE YOU ON ENDING YOUR CAREER ON SUCH A HIGH NOTE. TRULY, A ONCE-IN-A-LIFETIME FIND.
ENDING MY CAREER...?
WHAT IS THE MEANING OF THIS?!

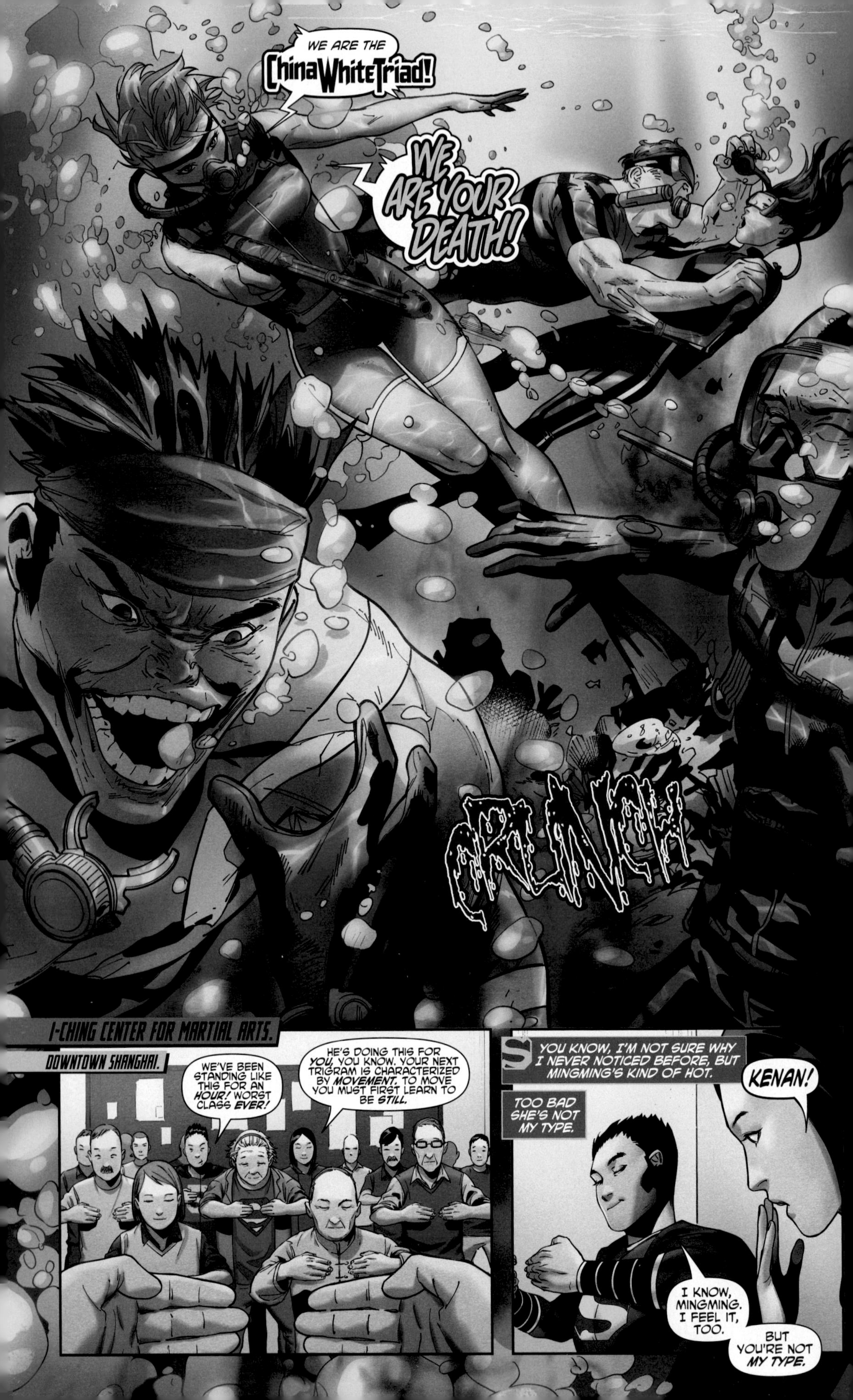
WE ARE THE
China White Triad!
WE ARE YOUR DEATH!
CRUNCH
I-CHING CENTER FOR MARTIAL ARTS.
DOWNTOWN SHANGHAI.
WE'VE BEEN STANDING LIKE THIS FOR AN HOUR! WORST CLASS EVER!
HE'S DOING THIS FOR YOU, YOU KNOW. YOUR NEXT TRIGRAM IS CHARACTERIZED BY MOVEMENT. TO MOVE YOU MUST FIRST LEARN TO BE STILL.
YOU KNOW, I'M NOT SURE WHY I NEVER NOTICED BEFORE, BUT MINGMING'S KIND OF HOT.
TOO BAD SHE'S NOT MY TYPE.
KENAN!
I KNOW, MINGMING. I FEEL IT, TOO.
BUT YOU'RE NOT MY TYPE.

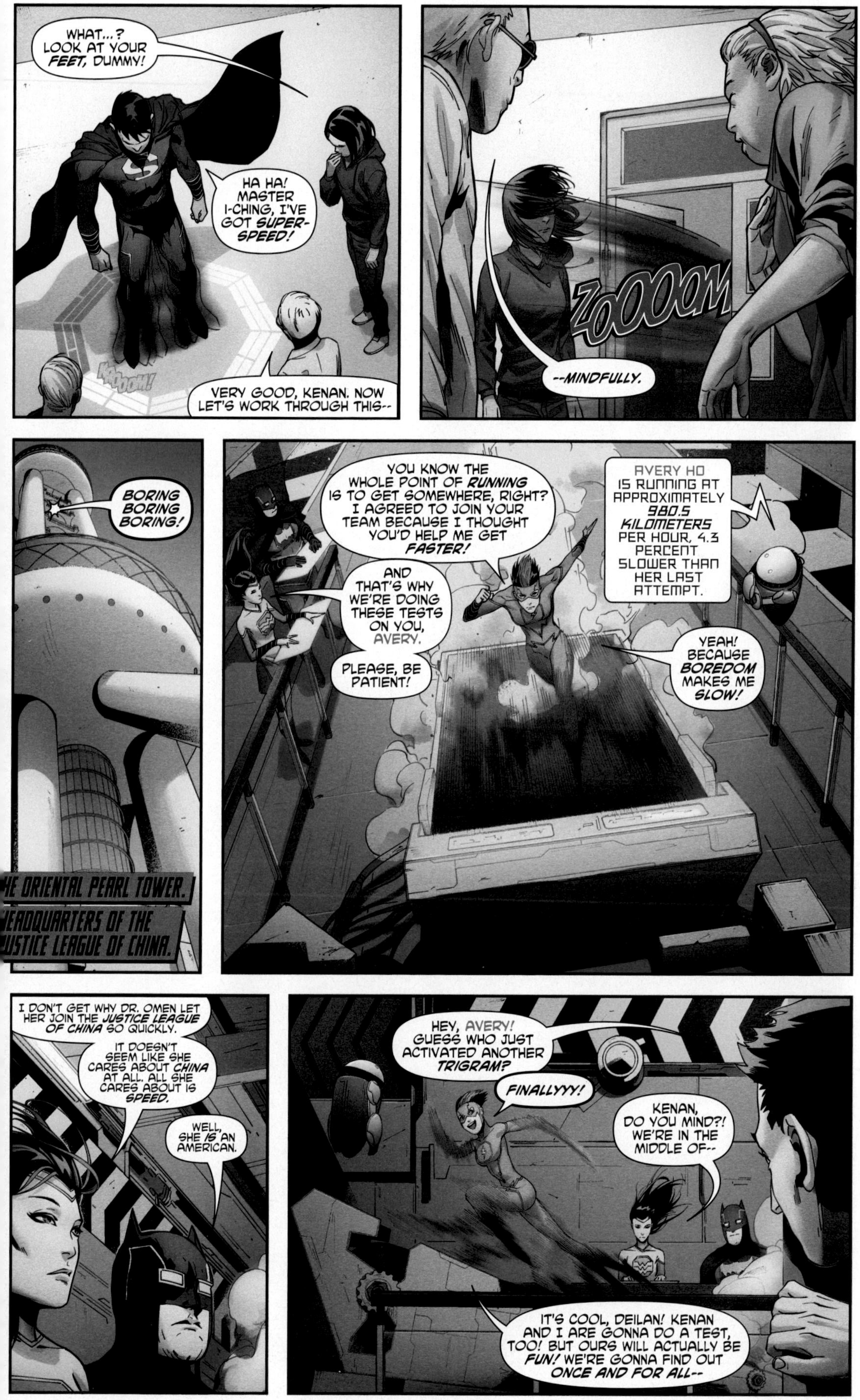
WHAT...? LOOK AT YOUR FEET, DUMMY!
HA HA! MASTER I-CHING, I'VE GOT SUPER-SPEED!
KRAOOOM!
VERY GOOD, KENAN. NOW LET'S WORK THROUGH THIS--
ZOOOOM
--MINDFULLY.
BORING BORING BORING!
HE ORIENTAL PEARL TOWER.
EADQUARTERS OF THE USTICE LEAGUE OF CHINA.
YOU KNOW THE WHOLE POINT OF RUNNING IS TO GET SOMEWHERE, RIGHT? I AGREED TO JOIN YOUR TEAM BECAUSE I THOUGHT YOU'D HELP ME GET FASTER!
AVERY HO IS RUNNING AT APPROXIMATELY 980.5 KILOMETERS PER HOUR, 4.3 PERCENT SLOWER THAN HER LAST ATTEMPT.
AND THAT'S WHY WE'RE DOING THESE TESTS ON YOU, AVERY.
PLEASE, BE PATIENT!
YEAH! BECAUSE BOREDOM MAKES ME SLOW!
I DON'T GET WHY DR. OMEN LET HER JOIN THE JUSTICE LEAGUE OF CHINA SO QUICKLY.
IT DOESN'T SEEM LIKE SHE CARES ABOUT CHINA AT ALL. ALL SHE CARES ABOUT IS SPEED.
WELL, SHE IS AN AMERICAN.
HEY, AVERY! GUESS WHO JUST ACTIVATED ANOTHER TRIGRAM?
FINALLYYY!
KENAN, DO YOU MIND?! WE'RE IN THE MIDDLE OF--
IT'S COOL, DEILAN! KENAN AND I ARE GONNA DO A TEST, TOO! BUT OURS WILL ACTUALLY BE FUN! WE'RE GONNA FIND OUT ONCE AND FOR ALL--

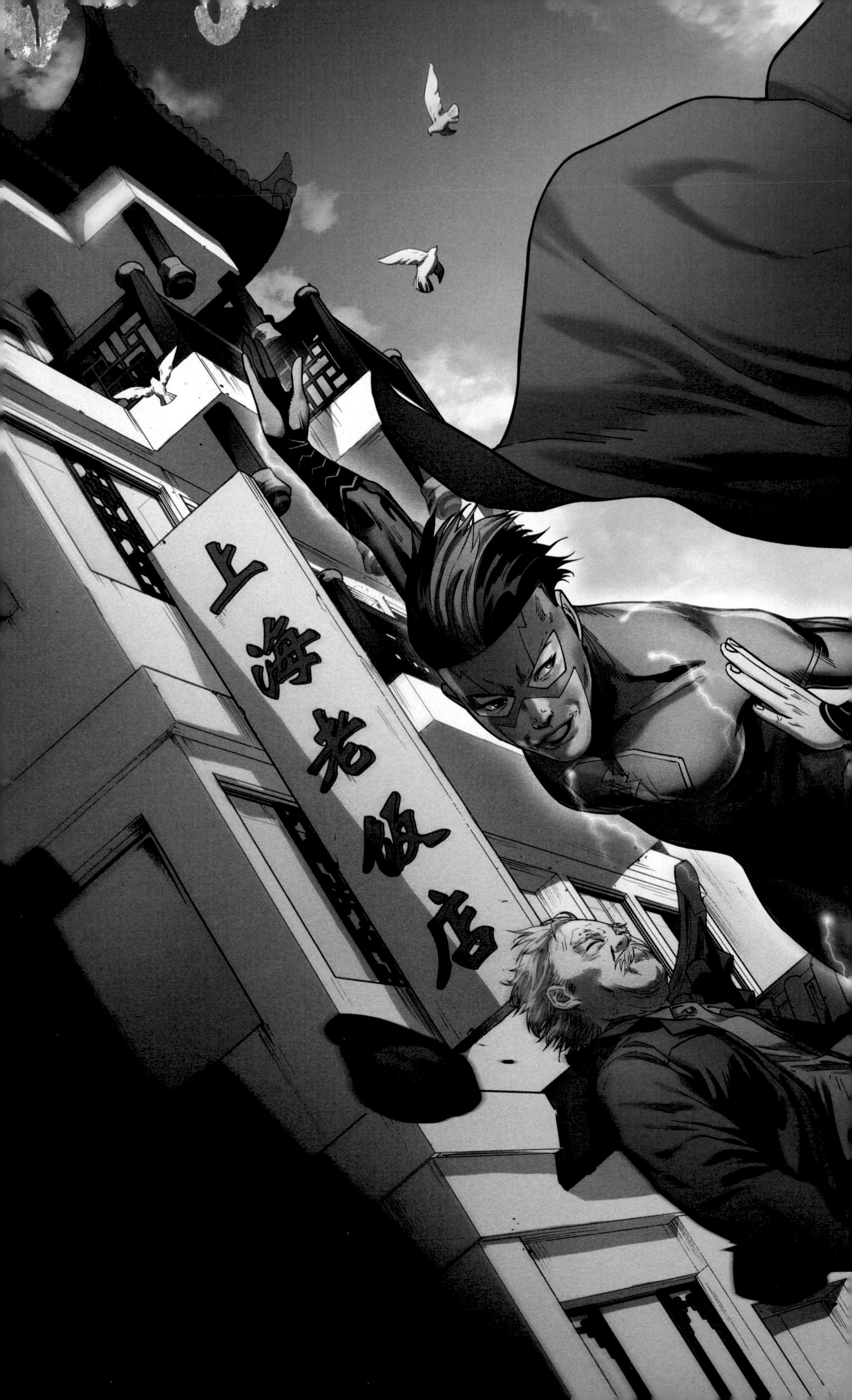
上海老饭店

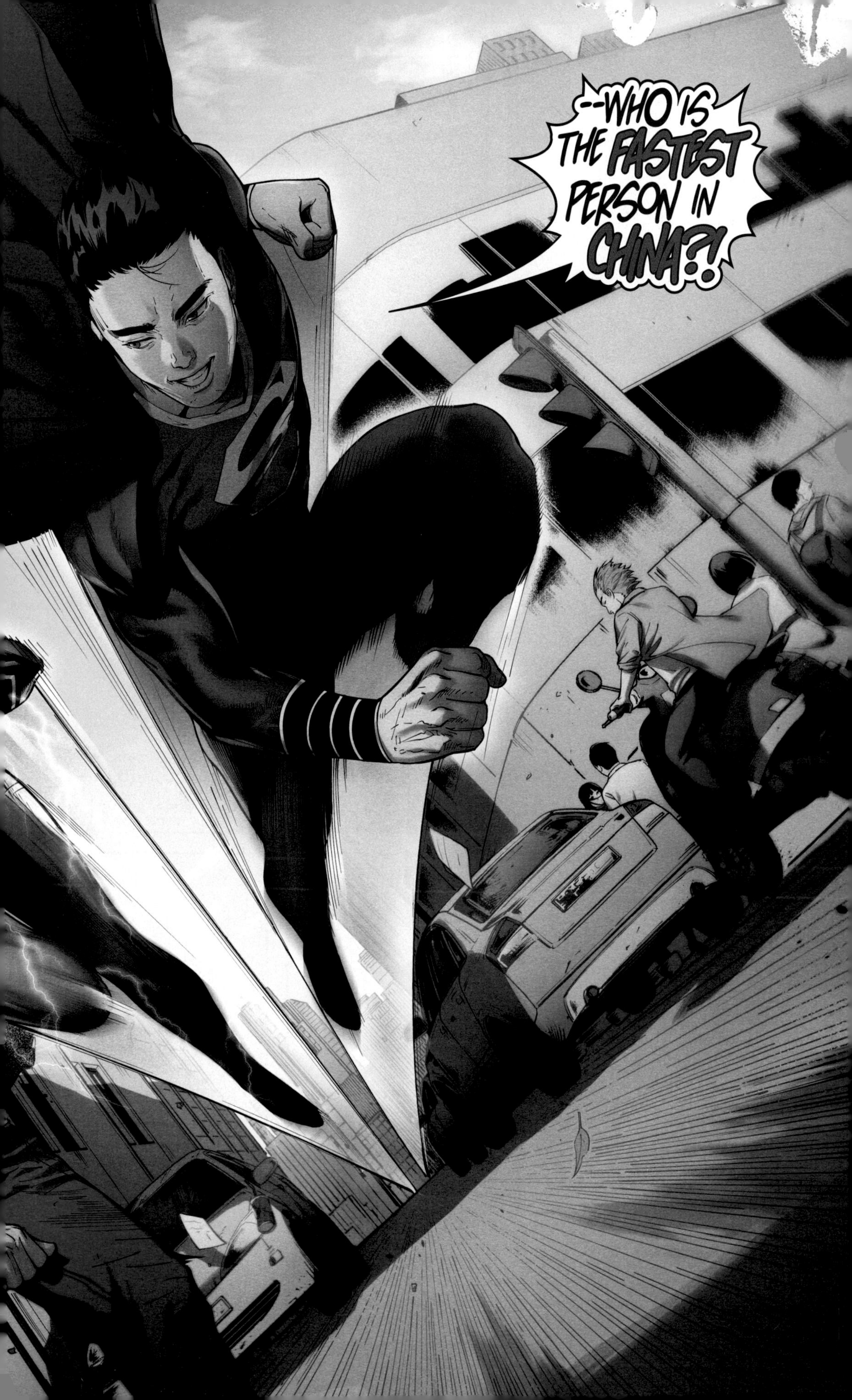
--WHO IS THE FASTEST PERSON IN CHINA?!

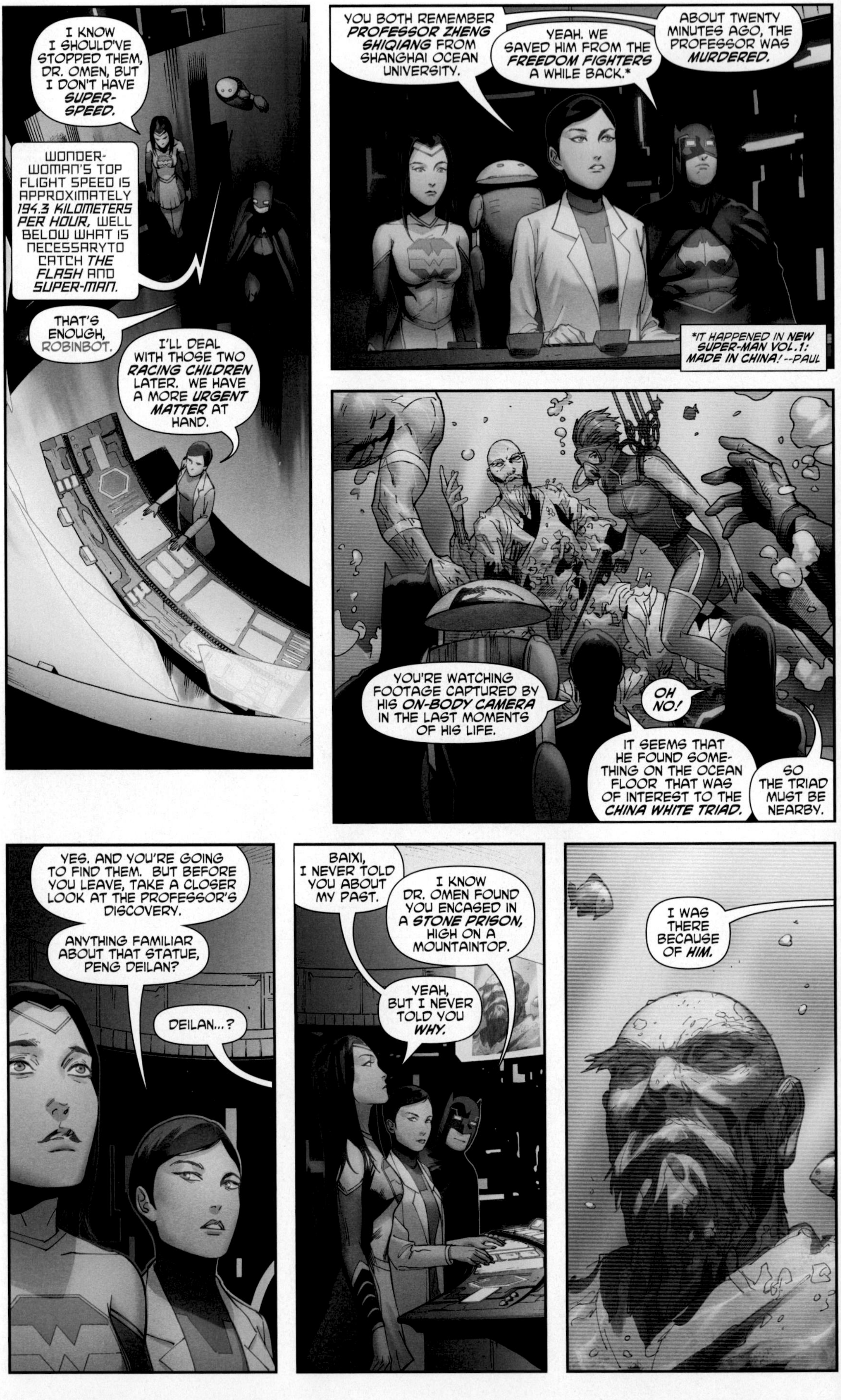
I KNOW I SHOULD'VE STOPPED THEM, DR. OMEN, BUT I DON'T HAVE SUPER-SPEED.
WONDER-WOMAN'S TOP FLIGHT SPEED IS APPROXIMATELY 194.3 KILOMETERS PER HOUR, WELL BELOW WHAT IS NECESSARYTO CATCH THE FLASH AND SUPER-MAN.
THAT'S ENOUGH, ROBINBOT.
I'LL DEAL WITH THOSE TWO RACING CHILDREN LATER. WE HAVE A MORE URGENT MATTER AT HAND.
YOU BOTH REMEMBER PROFESSOR ZHENG SHIQIANG FROM SHANGHAI OCEAN UNIVERSITY.
YEAH. WE SAVED HIM FROM THE FREEDOM FIGHTERS A WHILE BACK.*
ABOUT TWENTY MINUTES AGO, THE PROFESSOR WAS MURDERED.
*IT HAPPENED IN NEW SUPER-MAN VOL.1: MADE IN CHINA! --PAUL
YOU'RE WATCHING FOOTAGE CAPTURED BY HIS ON-BODY CAMERA IN THE LAST MOMENTS OF HIS LIFE.
OH NO!
IT SEEMS THAT HE FOUND SOME-THING ON THE OCEAN FLOOR THAT WAS OF INTEREST TO THE CHINA WHITE TRIAD.
SO THE TRIAD MUST BE NEARBY.
YES. AND YOU'RE GOING TO FIND THEM. BUT BEFORE YOU LEAVE, TAKE A CLOSER LOOK AT THE PROFESSOR'S DISCOVERY.
ANYTHING FAMILIAR ABOUT THAT STATUE, PENG DEILAN?
DEILAN...?
BAIXI, I NEVER TOLD YOU ABOUT MY PAST.
I KNOW DR. OMEN FOUND YOU ENCASED IN A STONE PRISON, HIGH ON A MOUNTAINTOP.
YEAH, BUT I NEVER TOLD YOU WHY.
I WAS THERE BECAUSE OF HIM.

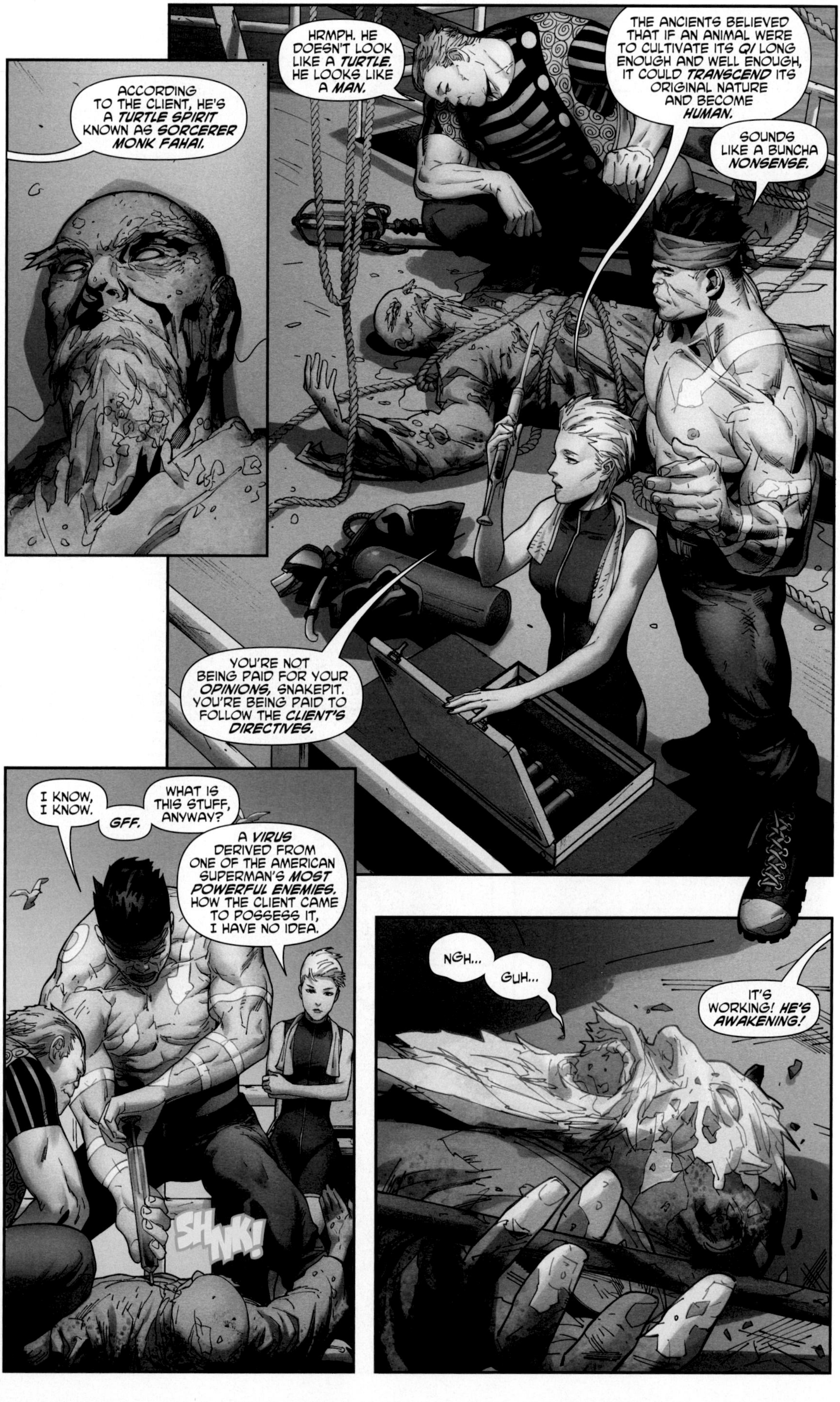
ACCORDING TO THE CLIENT, HE'S A TURTLE SPIRIT KNOWN AS SORCERER MONK FAHAI.
HRMPH. HE DOESN'T LOOK LIKE A TURTLE. HE LOOKS LIKE A MAN.
THE ANCIENTS BELIEVED THAT IF AN ANIMAL WERE TO CULTIVATE ITS QI LONG ENOUGH AND WELL ENOUGH, IT COULD TRANSCEND ITS ORIGINAL NATURE AND BECOME HUMAN.
SOUNDS LIKE A BUNCHA NONSENSE.
YOU'RE NOT BEING PAID FOR YOUR OPINIONS, SNAKEPIT. YOU'RE BEING PAID TO FOLLOW THE CLIENT'S DIRECTIVES.
I KNOW, I KNOW.
GFF.
WHAT IS THIS STUFF, ANYWAY?
A VIRUS DERIVED FROM ONE OF THE AMERICAN SUPERMAN'S MOST POWERFUL ENEMIES. HOW THE CLIENT CAME TO POSSESS IT, I HAVE NO IDEA.
SHNK!
NGH...
GUH...
IT'S WORKING! HE'S AWAKENING!

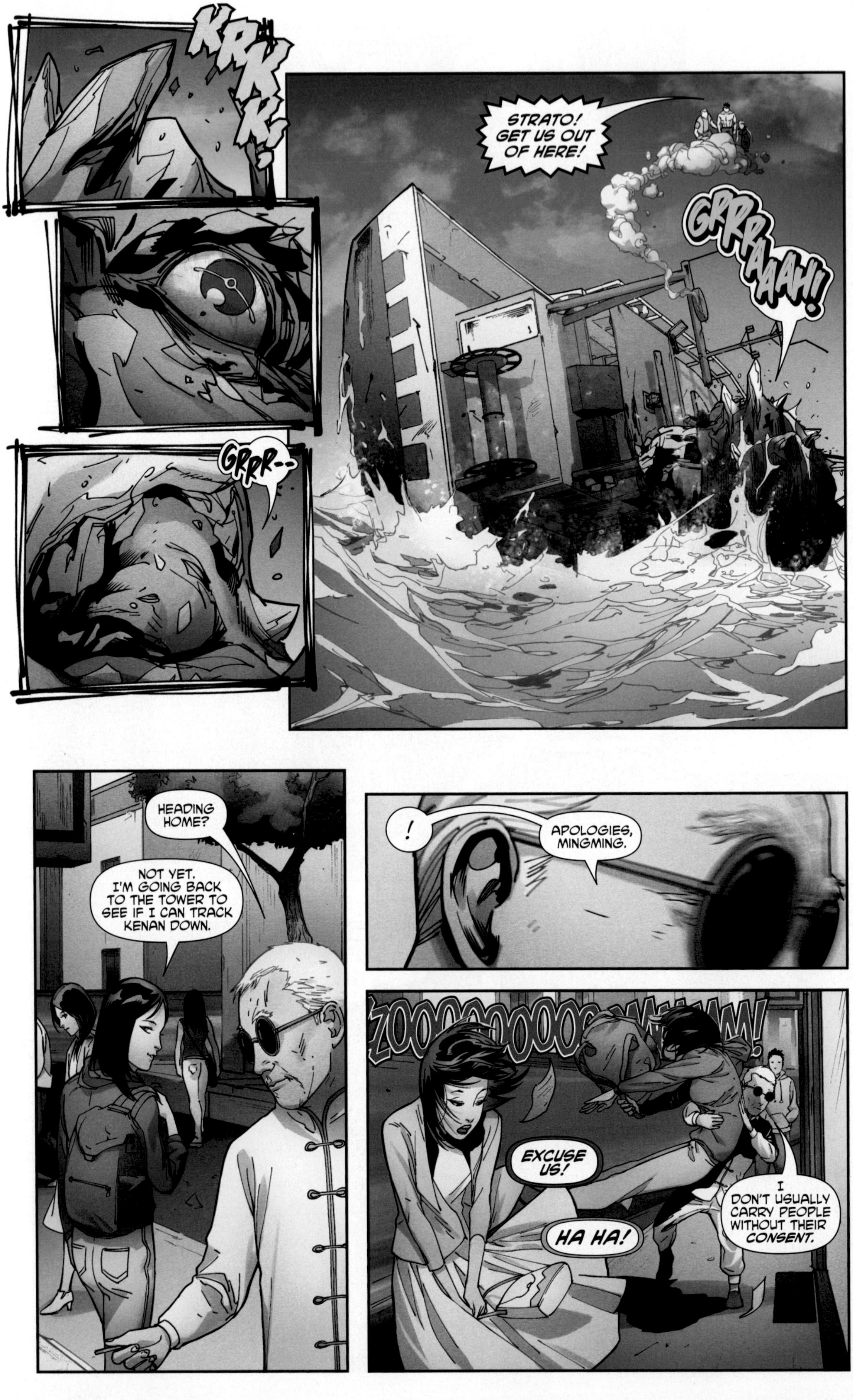
KRKK!
GRRR--
STRATO! GET US OUT OF HERE!
GRRRAAAH!!
HEADING HOME?
NOT YET. I'M GOING BACK TO THE TOWER TO SEE IF I CAN TRACK KENAN DOWN.
!
APOLOGIES, MINGMING.
EXCUSE US!
HA HA!
I DON'T USUALLY CARRY PEOPLE WITHOUT THEIR CONSENT.

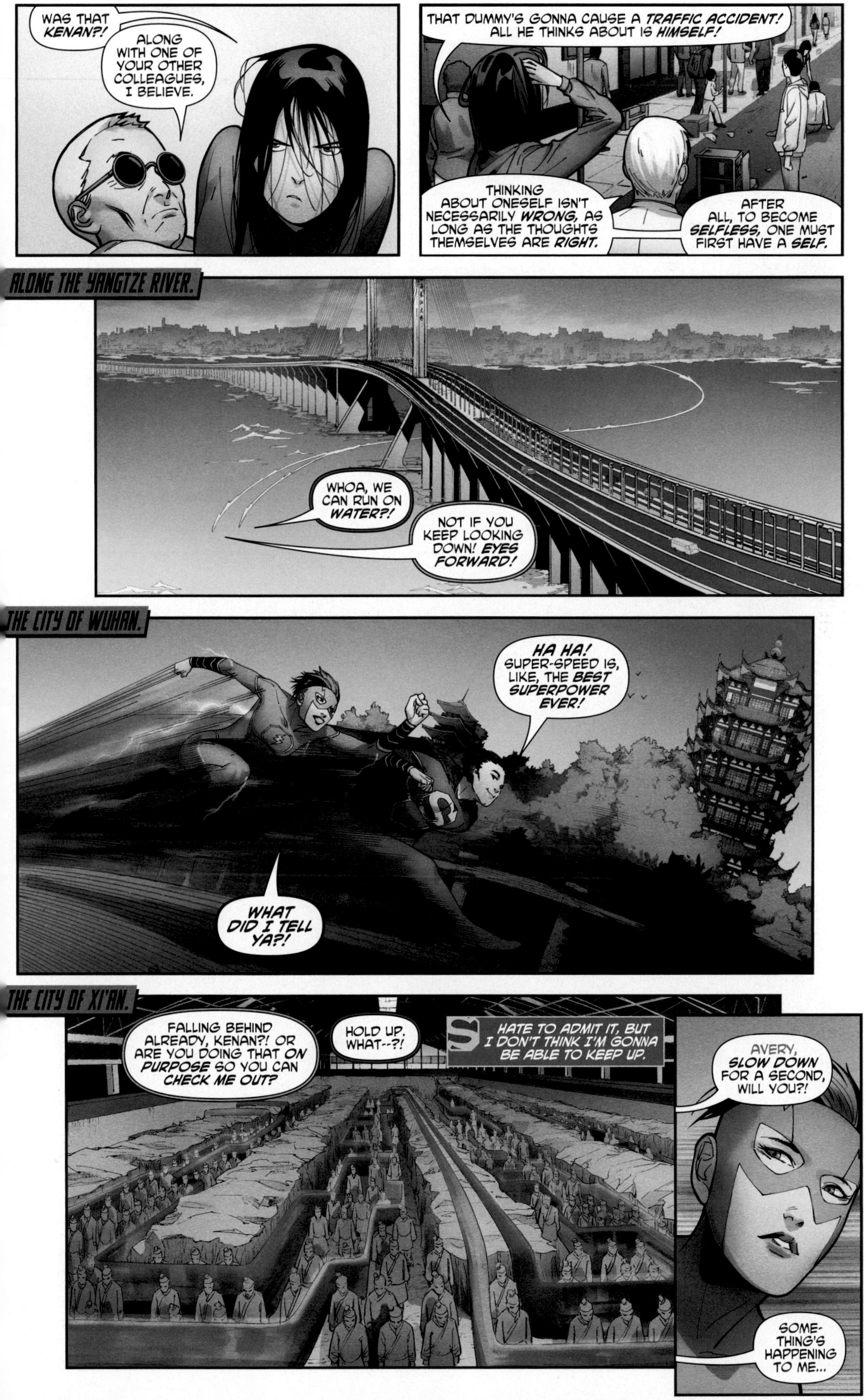
WAS THAT KENAN?!
ALONG WITH ONE OF YOUR OTHER COLLEAGUES, I BELIEVE.
THAT DUMMY'S GONNA CAUSE A TRAFFIC ACCIDENT! ALL HE THINKS ABOUT IS HIMSELF!
THINKING ABOUT ONESELF ISN'T NECESSARILY WRONG, AS LONG AS THE THOUGHTS THEMSELVES ARE RIGHT.
AFTER ALL, TO BECOME SELFLESS, ONE MUST FIRST HAVE A SELF.
ALONG THE YANGTZE RIVER.
WHOA, WE CAN RUN ON WATER?!
NOT IF YOU KEEP LOOKING DOWN! EYES FORWARD!
THE CITY OF WUHAN.
HA HA! SUPER-SPEED IS, LIKE, THE BEST SUPERPOWER EVER!
WHAT DID I TELL YA?!
THE CITY OF XI'AN.
FALLING BEHIND ALREADY, KENAN?! OR ARE YOU DOING THAT ON PURPOSE SO YOU CAN CHECK ME OUT?
HOLD UP. WHAT--?!
HATE TO ADMIT IT, BUT I DON'T THINK I'M GONNA BE ABLE TO KEEP UP.
AVERY, SLOW DOWN FOR A SECOND, WILL YOU?!
SOME-THING'S HAPPENING TO ME...

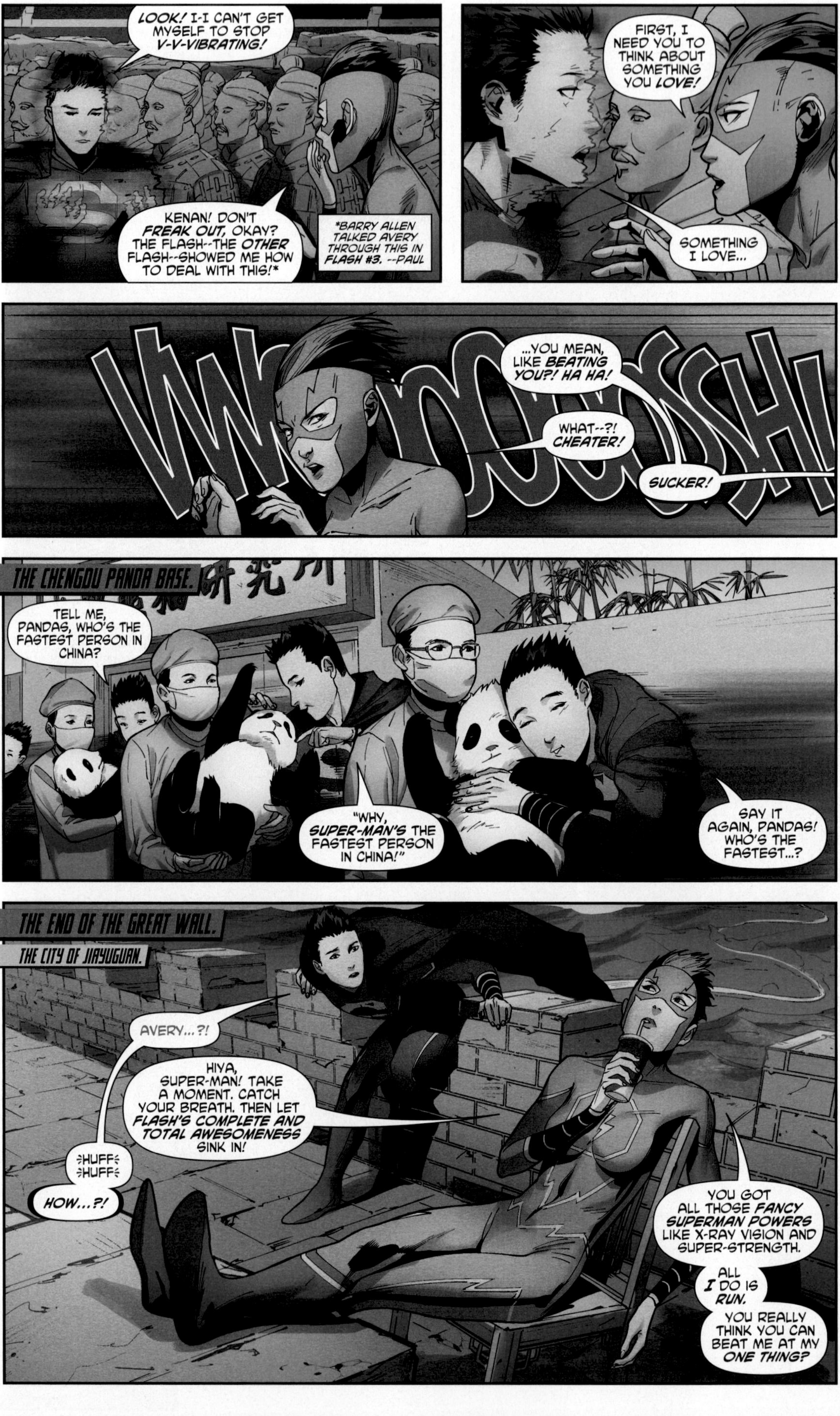
LOOK! I-I CAN'T GET MYSELF TO STOP V-V-VIBRATING!
KENAN! DON'T FREAK OUT, OKAY? THE FLASH--THE OTHER FLASH--SHOWED ME HOW TO DEAL WITH THIS!*
*BARRY ALLEN TALKED AVERY THROUGH THIS IN FLASH #3. --PAUL
FIRST, I NEED YOU TO THINK ABOUT SOMETHING YOU LOVE!
SOMETHING I LOVE...
VWHOOOSSH!
...YOU MEAN, LIKE BEATING YOU?! HA HA!
WHAT--?! CHEATER!
SUCKER!
THE CHENGDU PANDA BASE.
TELL ME, PANDAS, WHO'S THE FASTEST PERSON IN CHINA?
"WHY, SUPER-MAN'S THE FASTEST PERSON IN CHINA!"
SAY IT AGAIN, PANDAS! WHO'S THE FASTEST...?
THE END OF THE GREAT WALL.
THE CITY OF JIAYUGUAN.
AVERY...?!
HIYA, SUPER-MAN! TAKE A MOMENT. CATCH YOUR BREATH. THEN LET FLASH'S COMPLETE AND TOTAL AWESOMENESS SINK IN!
HUFF HUFF
HOW...?!
YOU GOT ALL THOSE FANCY SUPERMAN POWERS LIKE X-RAY VISION AND SUPER-STRENGTH.
ALL I DO IS RUN.
YOU REALLY THINK YOU CAN BEAT ME AT MY ONE THING?

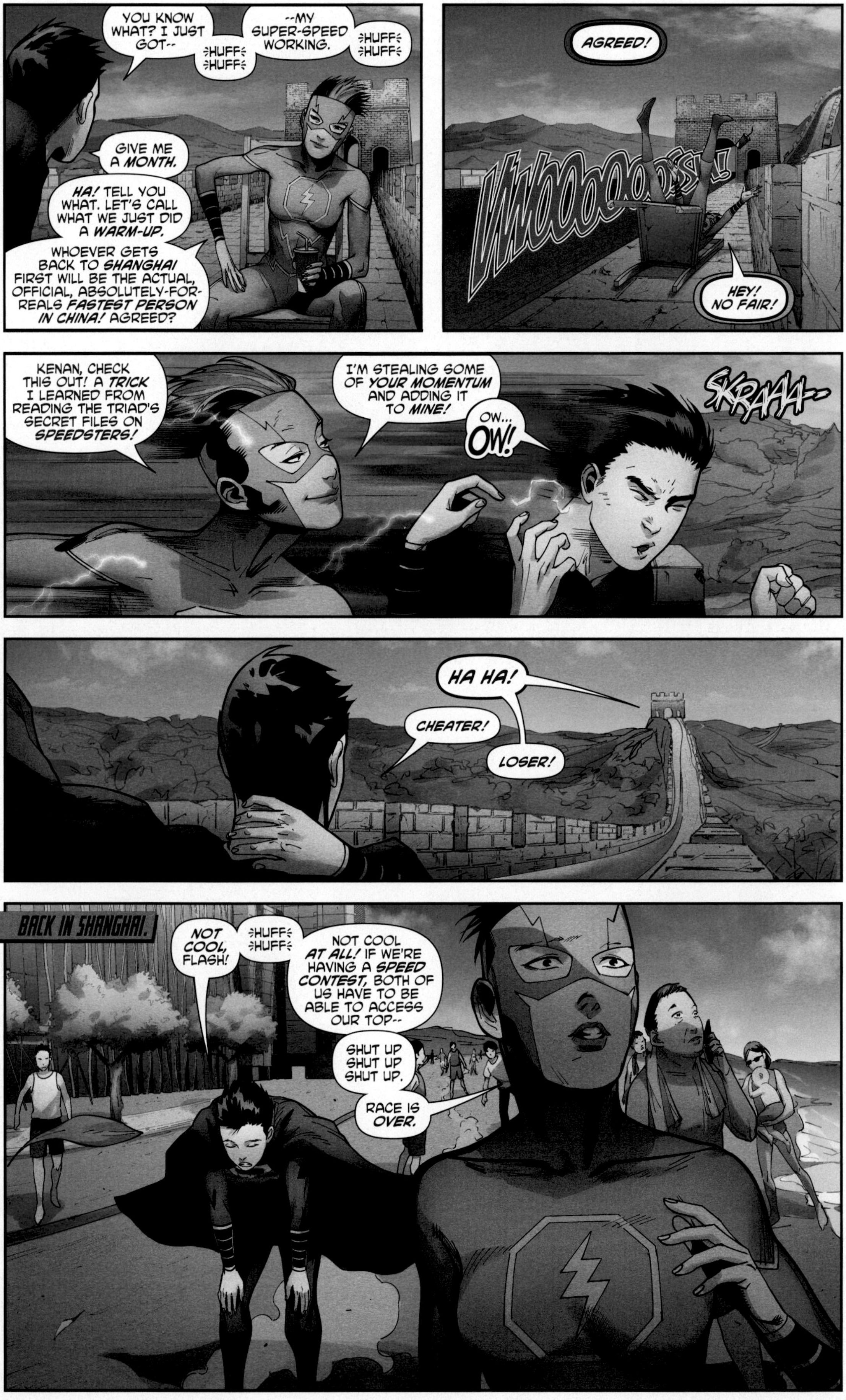
YOU KNOW WHAT? I JUST GOT--
HUFF HUFF
--MY SUPER-SPEED WORKING.
HUFF HUFF
GIVE ME A MONTH.
HA! TELL YOU WHAT. LET'S CALL WHAT WE JUST DID A WARM-UP.
WHOEVER GETS BACK TO SHANGHAI FIRST WILL BE THE ACTUAL, OFFICIAL, ABSOLUTELY-FOR-REALS FASTEST PERSON IN CHINA! AGREED?
AGREED!
HEY! NO FAIR!
KENAN, CHECK THIS OUT! A TRICK I LEARNED FROM READING THE TRIAD'S SECRET FILES ON SPEEDSTERS!
I'M STEALING SOME OF YOUR MOMENTUM AND ADDING IT TO MINE!
OW... OW!
SKRAAA--
HA HA!
CHEATER!
LOSER!
BACK IN SHANGHAI.
NOT COOL, FLASH!
HUFF HUFF
NOT COOL AT ALL! IF WE'RE HAVING A SPEED CONTEST, BOTH OF US HAVE TO BE ABLE TO ACCESS OUR TOP--
SHUT UP SHUT UP SHUT UP.
RACE IS OVER.

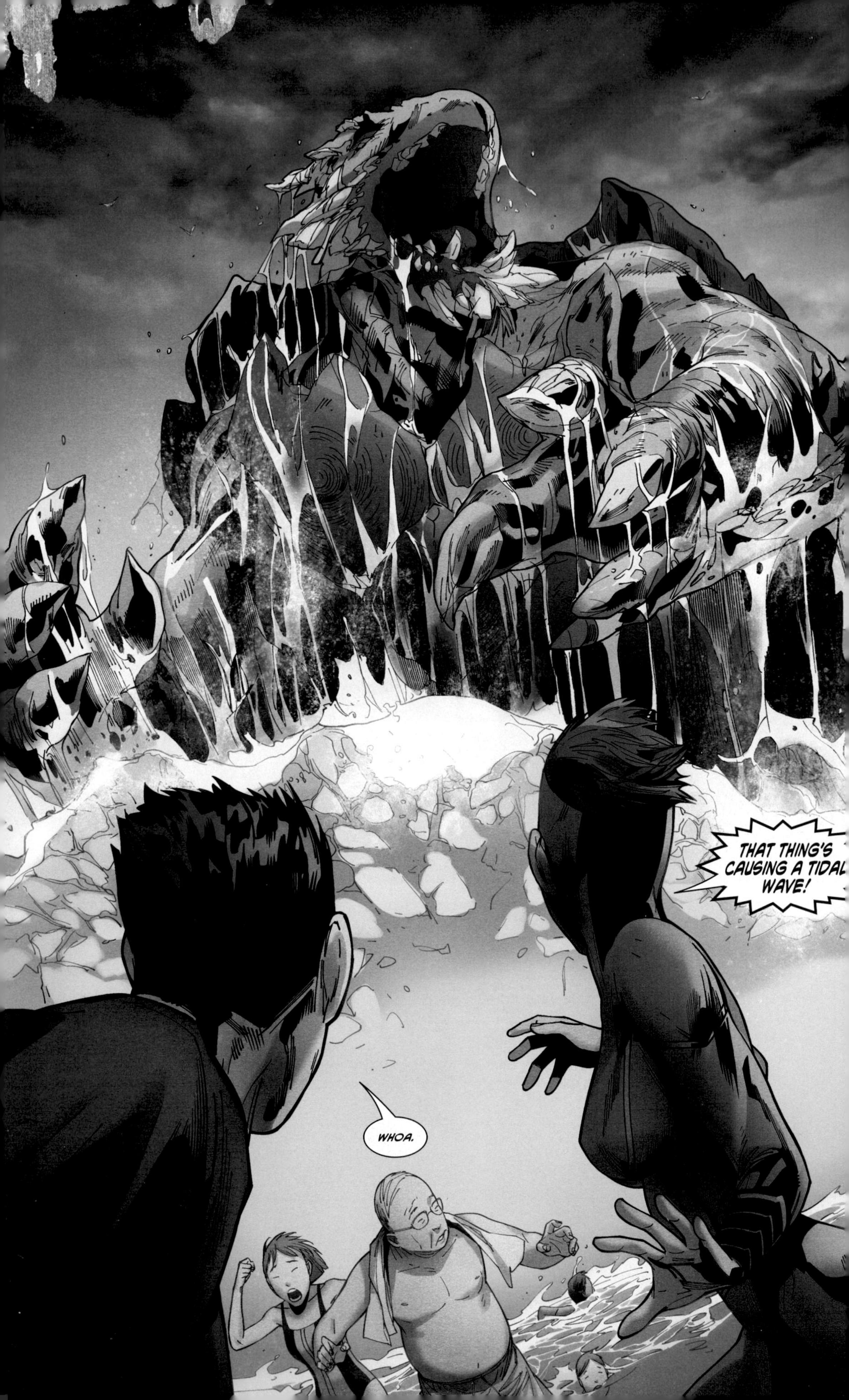
THAT THING'S CAUSING A TIDAL WAVE!
WHOA.

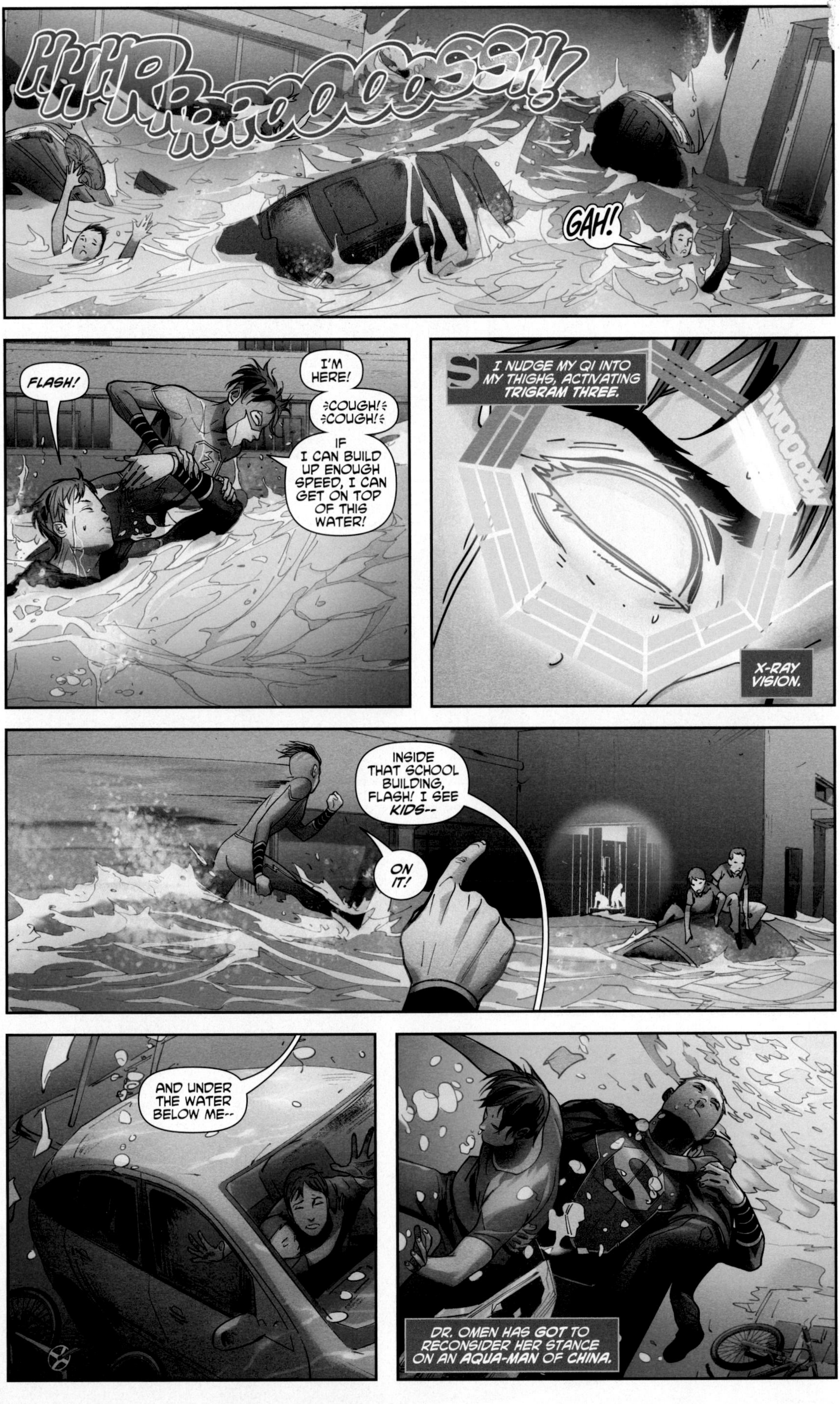
HHHRRRRooooSSH!
GAH!
FLASH!
I'M HERE!
COUGH! COUGH!
IF I CAN BUILD UP ENOUGH SPEED, I CAN GET ON TOP OF THIS WATER!
I NUDGE MY QI INTO MY THIGHS, ACTIVATING TRIGRAM THREE.
X-RAY VISION.
INSIDE THAT SCHOOL BUILDING, FLASH! I SEE KIDS--
ON IT!
AND UNDER THE WATER BELOW ME--
DR. OMEN HAS GOT TO RECONSIDER HER STANCE ON AN AQUA-MAN OF CHINA.

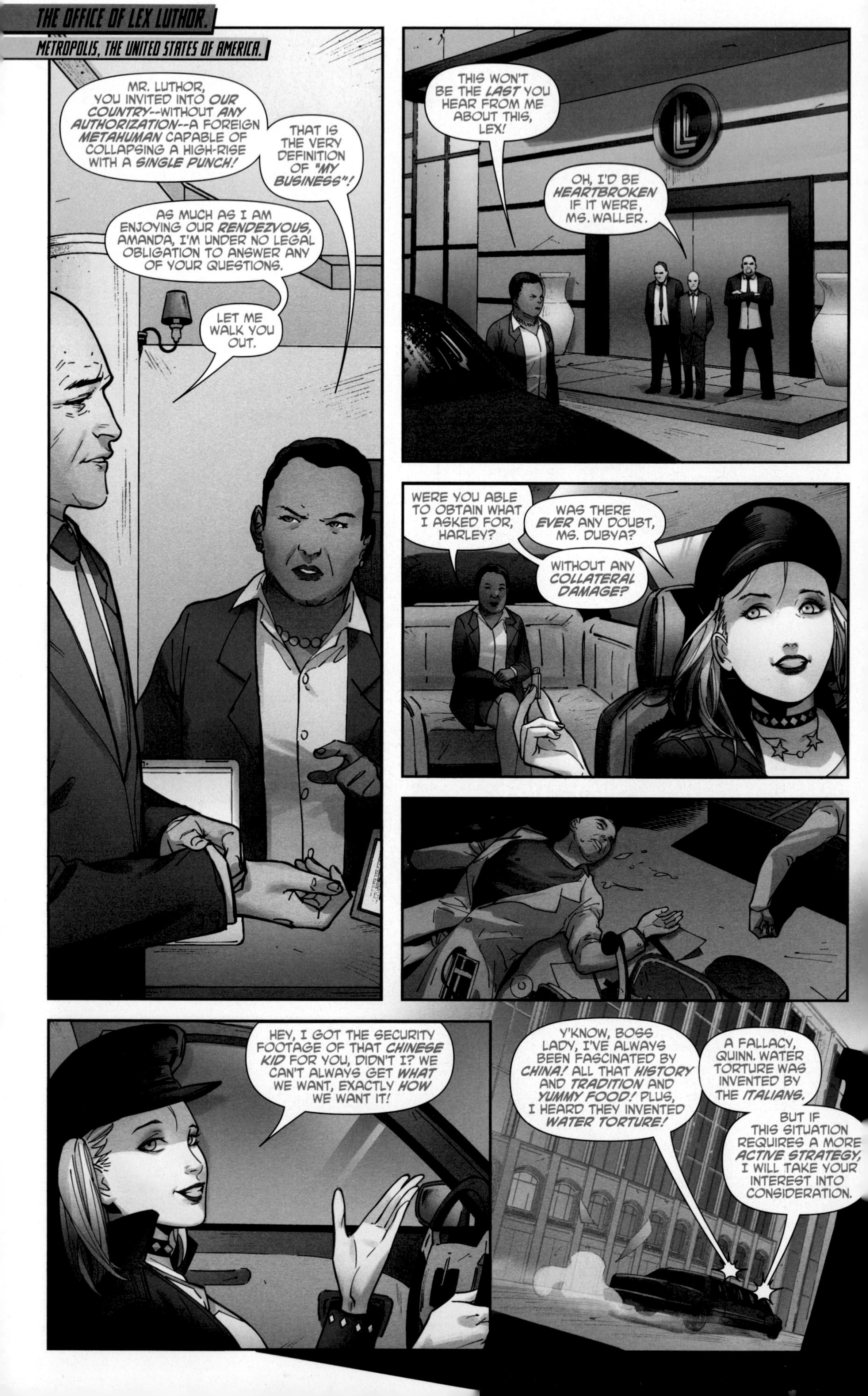
THE OFFICE OF LEX LUTHOR.
METROPOLIS, THE UNITED STATES OF AMERICA.
MR. LUTHOR, YOU INVITED INTO OUR COUNTRY--WITHOUT ANY AUTHORIZATION--A FOREIGN METAHUMAN CAPABLE OF COLLAPSING A HIGH-RISE WITH A SINGLE PUNCH!
THAT IS THE VERY DEFINITION OF "MY BUSINESS"!
AS MUCH AS I AM ENJOYING OUR RENDEZVOUS, AMANDA, I'M UNDER NO LEGAL OBLIGATION TO ANSWER ANY OF YOUR QUESTIONS.
LET ME WALK YOU OUT.
THIS WON'T BE THE LAST YOU HEAR FROM ME ABOUT THIS, LEX!
OH, I'D BE HEARTBROKEN IF IT WERE, MS. WALLER.
WERE YOU ABLE TO OBTAIN WHAT I ASKED FOR, HARLEY?
WAS THERE EVER ANY DOUBT, MS. DUBYA?
WITHOUT ANY COLLATERAL DAMAGE?
HEY, I GOT THE SECURITY FOOTAGE OF THAT CHINESE KID FOR YOU, DIDN'T I? WE CAN'T ALWAYS GET WHAT WE WANT, EXACTLY HOW WE WANT IT!
Y'KNOW, BOSS LADY, I'VE ALWAYS BEEN FASCINATED BY CHINA! ALL THAT HISTORY AND TRADITION AND YUMMY FOOD! PLUS, I HEARD THEY INVENTED WATER TORTURE!
A FALLACY, QUINN. WATER TORTURE WAS INVENTED BY THE ITALIANS.
BUT IF THIS SITUATION REQUIRES A MORE ACTIVE STRATEGY, I WILL TAKE YOUR INTEREST INTO CONSIDERATION.

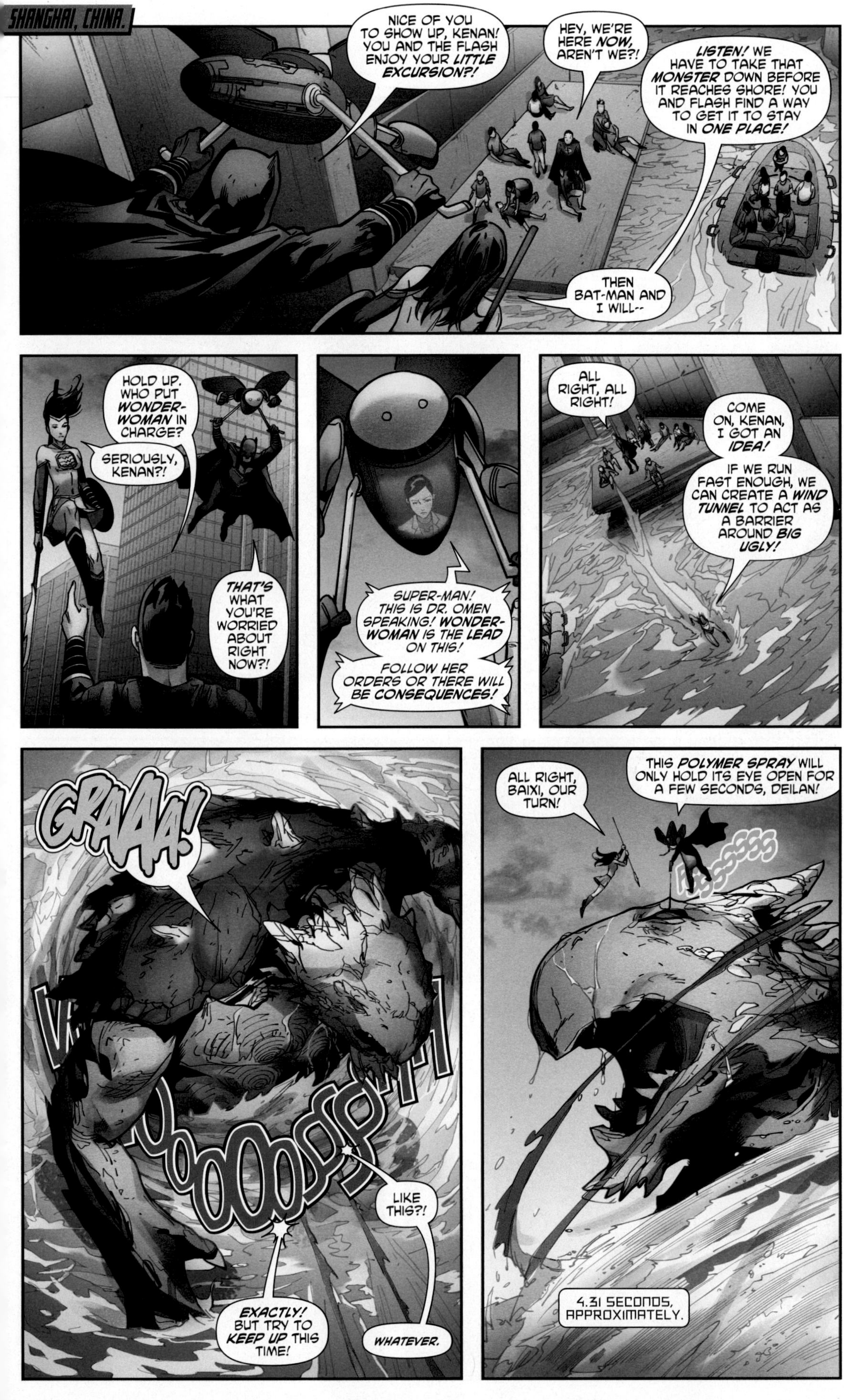
SHANGHAI, CHINA.
NICE OF YOU TO SHOW UP, KENAN! YOU AND THE FLASH ENJOY YOUR LITTLE EXCURSION?!
HEY, WE'RE HERE NOW, AREN'T WE?!
LISTEN! WE HAVE TO TAKE THAT MONSTER DOWN BEFORE IT REACHES SHORE! YOU AND FLASH FIND A WAY TO GET IT TO STAY IN ONE PLACE!
THEN BAT-MAN AND I WILL--
HOLD UP. WHO PUT WONDER-WOMAN IN CHARGE?
SERIOUSLY, KENAN?!
THAT'S WHAT YOU'RE WORRIED ABOUT RIGHT NOW?!
SUPER-MAN! THIS IS DR. OMEN SPEAKING! WONDER-WOMAN IS THE LEAD ON THIS!
FOLLOW HER ORDERS OR THERE WILL BE CONSEQUENCES!
ALL RIGHT, ALL RIGHT!
COME ON, KENAN, I GOT AN IDEA!
IF WE RUN FAST ENOUGH, WE CAN CREATE A WIND TUNNEL TO ACT AS A BARRIER AROUND BIG UGLY!
GRAAAA!
LIKE THIS?!
EXACTLY! BUT TRY TO KEEP UP THIS TIME!
WHATEVER.
ALL RIGHT, BAIXI, OUR TURN!
THIS POLYMER SPRAY WILL ONLY HOLD ITS EYE OPEN FOR A FEW SECONDS, DEILAN!
4.31 SECONDS, APPROXIMATELY.

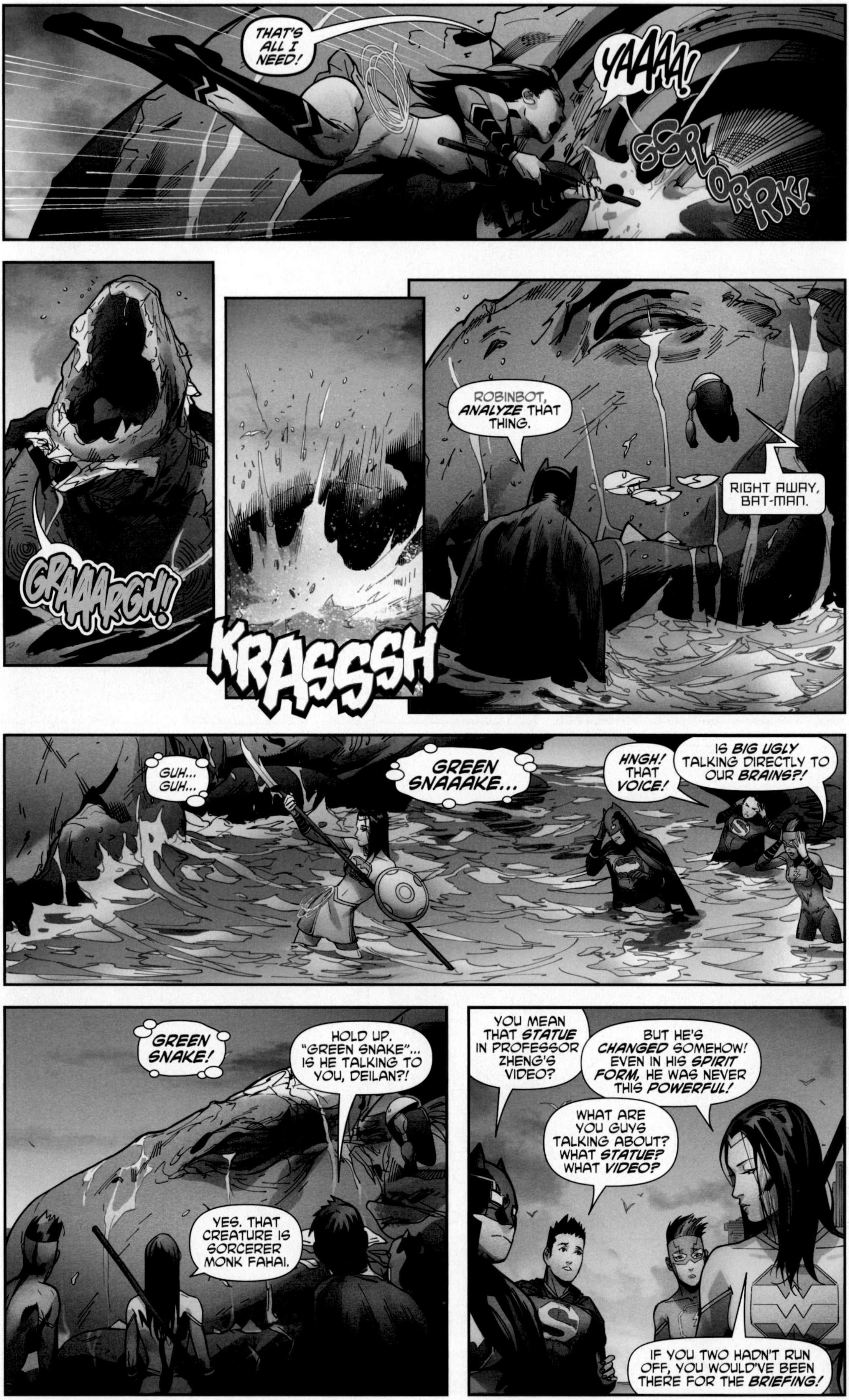
THAT'S ALL I NEED!
YAAAA!
SSRLORRRK!
GRAAARGH!
KRASSSH
ROBINBOT, ANALYZE THAT THING.
RIGHT AWAY, BAT-MAN.
GUH... GUH...
GREEN SNAAAKE...
HNGH! THAT VOICE!
IS BIG UGLY TALKING DIRECTLY TO OUR BRAINS?!
GREEN SNAKE!
HOLD UP. "GREEN SNAKE"... IS HE TALKING TO YOU, DEILAN?!
YES. THAT CREATURE IS SORCERER MONK FAHAI.
YOU MEAN THAT STATUE IN PROFESSOR ZHENG'S VIDEO?
BUT HE'S CHANGED SOMEHOW! EVEN IN HIS SPIRIT FORM, HE WAS NEVER THIS POWERFUL!
WHAT ARE YOU GUYS TALKING ABOUT? WHAT STATUE? WHAT VIDEO?
IF YOU TWO HADN'T RUN OFF, YOU WOULD'VE BEEN THERE FOR THE BRIEFING!

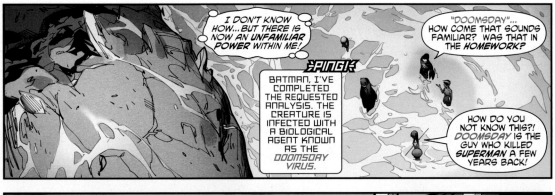

I DON'T KNOW HOW...BUT THERE IS NOW AN *UNFAMILIAR* POWER WITHIN ME!

"DOOMSDAY"... HOW COME THAT SOUNDS *FAMILIAR?* WAS THAT IN THE *HOMEWORK?*

¥PING!

BATMAN, I'VE COMPLETED THE REQUESTED ANALYSIS. THE CREATURE IS INFECTED WITH A BIOLOGICAL AGENT KNOWN AS THE *DOOMSDAY VIRUS.*

HOW DO YOU NOT KNOW THIS?! *DOOMSDAY* IS THE GUY WHO KILLED *SUPERMAN* A FEW YEARS BACK!

AND I CAN HARNESS THAT POWER TO *HEAL.*

TO *GROW!*

THE CREATURE WILL *DOUBLE* IN SIZE IN THREE MINUTES, 24.21 SECONDS.

KRKK!

KRKK!

KRKK!

CREEEEEEEK

GREEN SNAKE, YOU TRAPPED ME AT THE *BOTTOM* OF THE OCEAN FOR CENTURIES! TRAPPED... BUT *AWAKE!* SUCH EXCRUCIATING TORTURE--

--AND YET STILL A BLESSING. FOR DURING THOSE *LONG YEARS,* I MEDITATED UPON ALL THAT TRANSPIRED BETWEEN YOU AND ME. AND NOW, I FINALLY UNDER-STAND *OUR SIN.*

SURRENDER YOURSELF TO ME, GREEN SNAKE! SURRENDER SO THAT WE MAY BOTH *REPENT* AND RESTORE THE *ORDER* OF EXISTENCE!

IF I DO, FAHAI...WILL YOU LEAVE IN *PEACE?*

YOU HAVE MY *WORD.* MY ONLY CONCERN IS *ORDER.*

ALL RIGHT, THEN.

I SURRENDER.

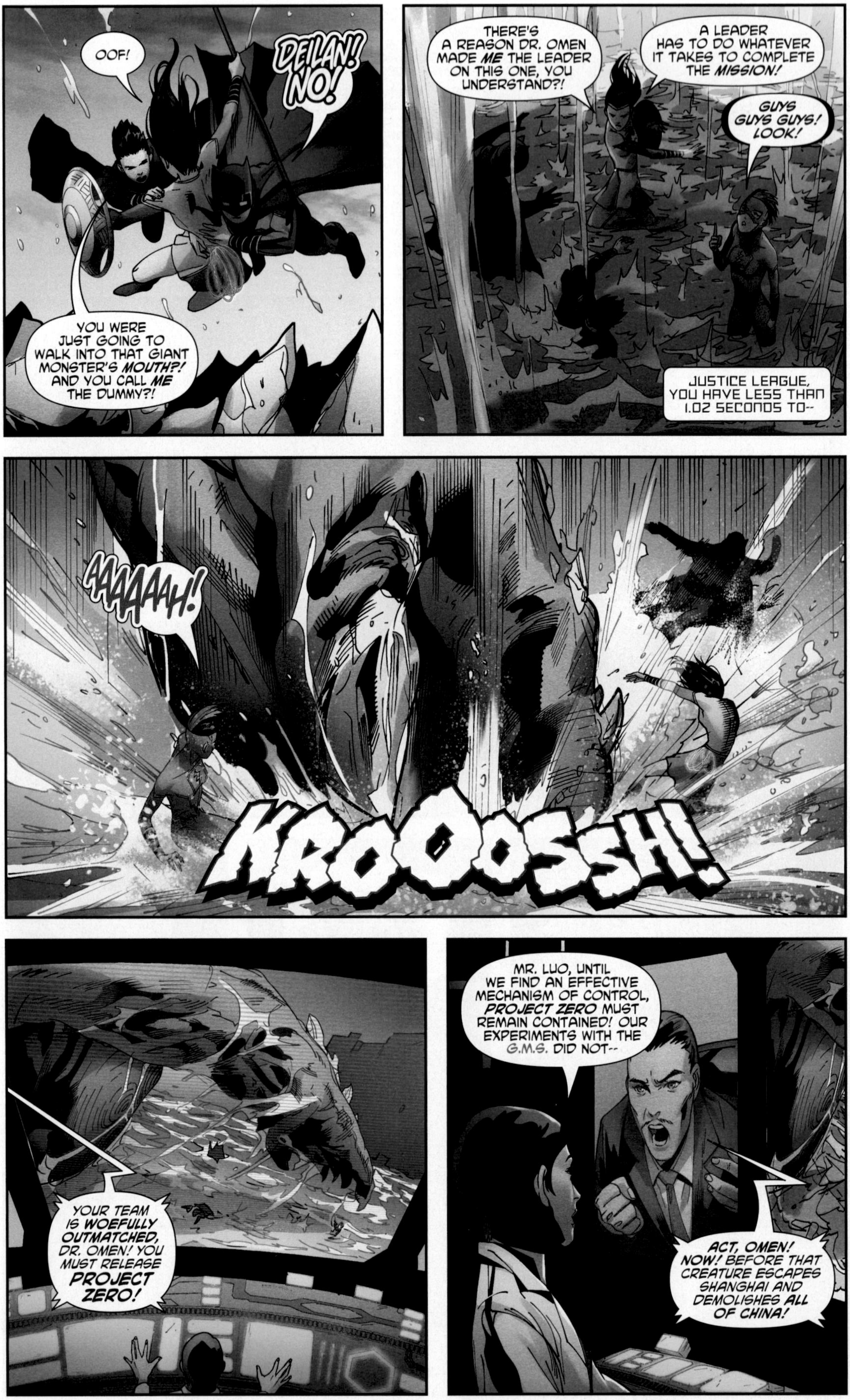
OOF!
DEILAN! NO!
YOU WERE JUST GOING TO WALK INTO THAT GIANT MONSTER'S MOUTH?! AND YOU CALL ME THE DUMMY?!
THERE'S A REASON DR. OMEN MADE ME THE LEADER ON THIS ONE, YOU UNDERSTAND?!
A LEADER HAS TO DO WHATEVER IT TAKES TO COMPLETE THE MISSION!
GUYS GUYS GUYS! LOOK!
JUSTICE LEAGUE, YOU HAVE LESS THAN 1.02 SECONDS TO--
AAAAAAH!
KROOOSSH!
YOUR TEAM IS WOEFULLY OUTMATCHED, DR. OMEN! YOU MUST RELEASE PROJECT ZERO!
MR. LUO, UNTIL WE FIND AN EFFECTIVE MECHANISM OF CONTROL, PROJECT ZERO MUST REMAIN CONTAINED! OUR EXPERIMENTS WITH THE G.M.S. DID NOT--
ACT, OMEN! NOW! BEFORE THAT CREATURE ESCAPES SHANGHAI AND DEMOLISHES ALL OF CHINA!

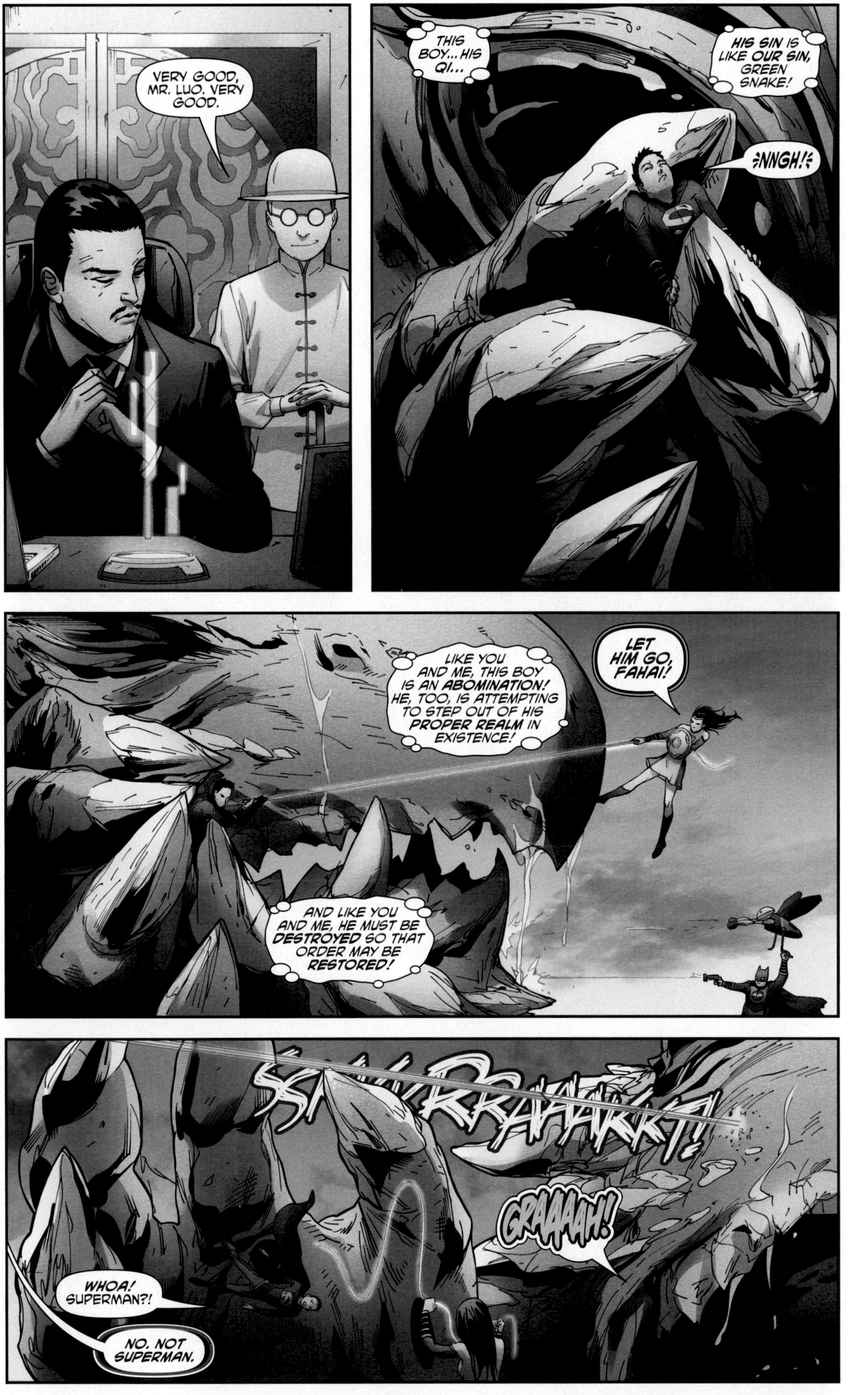
VERY GOOD, MR. LUO. VERY GOOD.
THIS BOY... HIS QI...
HIS SIN IS LIKE OUR SIN, GREEN SNAKE!
NNGH!
LIKE YOU AND ME, THIS BOY IS AN ABOMINATION! HE, TOO, IS ATTEMPTING TO STEP OUT OF HIS PROPER REALM IN EXISTENCE!
LET HIM GO, FAHAI!
AND LIKE YOU AND ME, HE MUST BE DESTROYED SO THAT ORDER MAY BE RESTORED!
GRAAAAH!
WHOA! SUPERMAN?!
NO. NOT SUPERMAN.

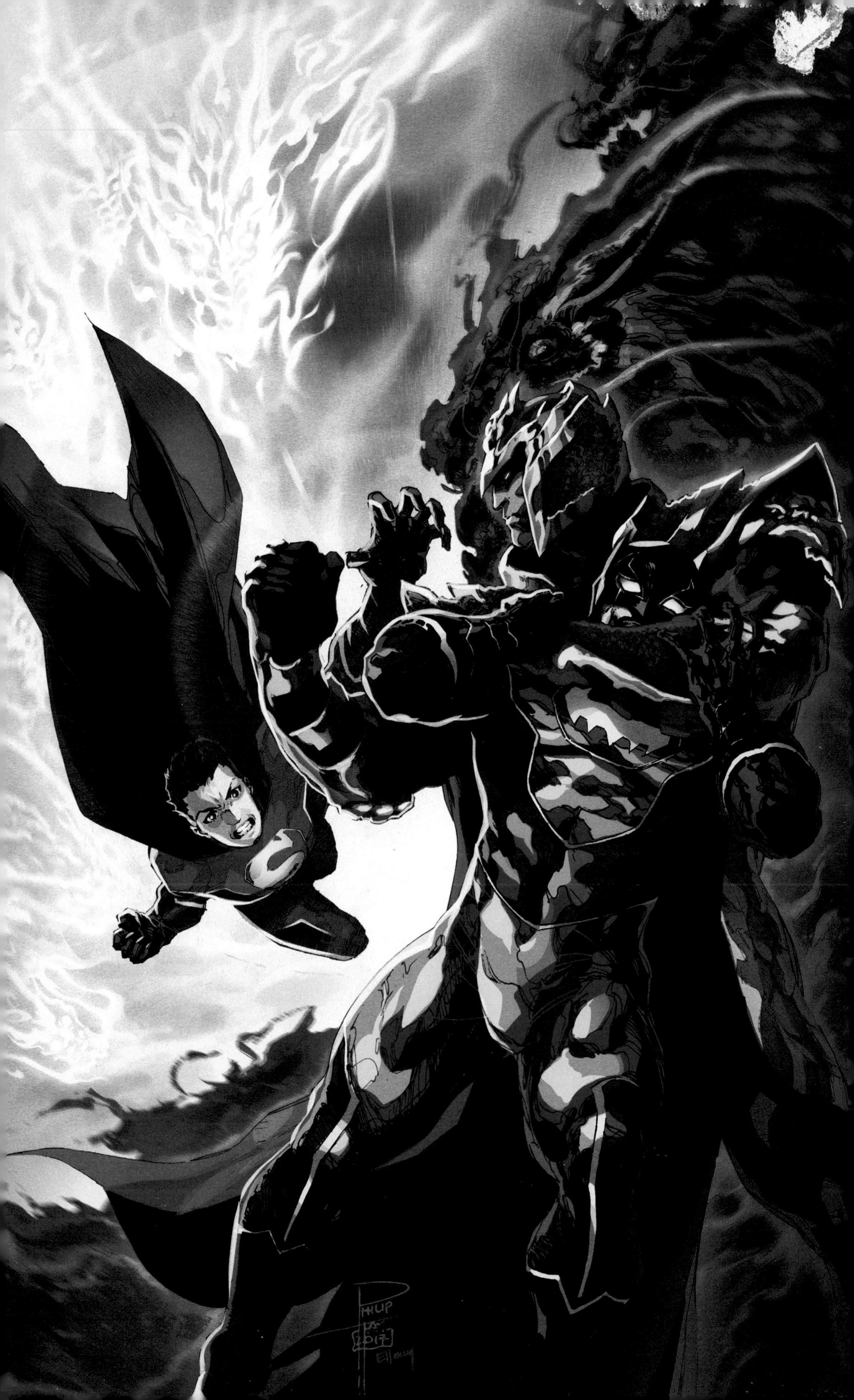

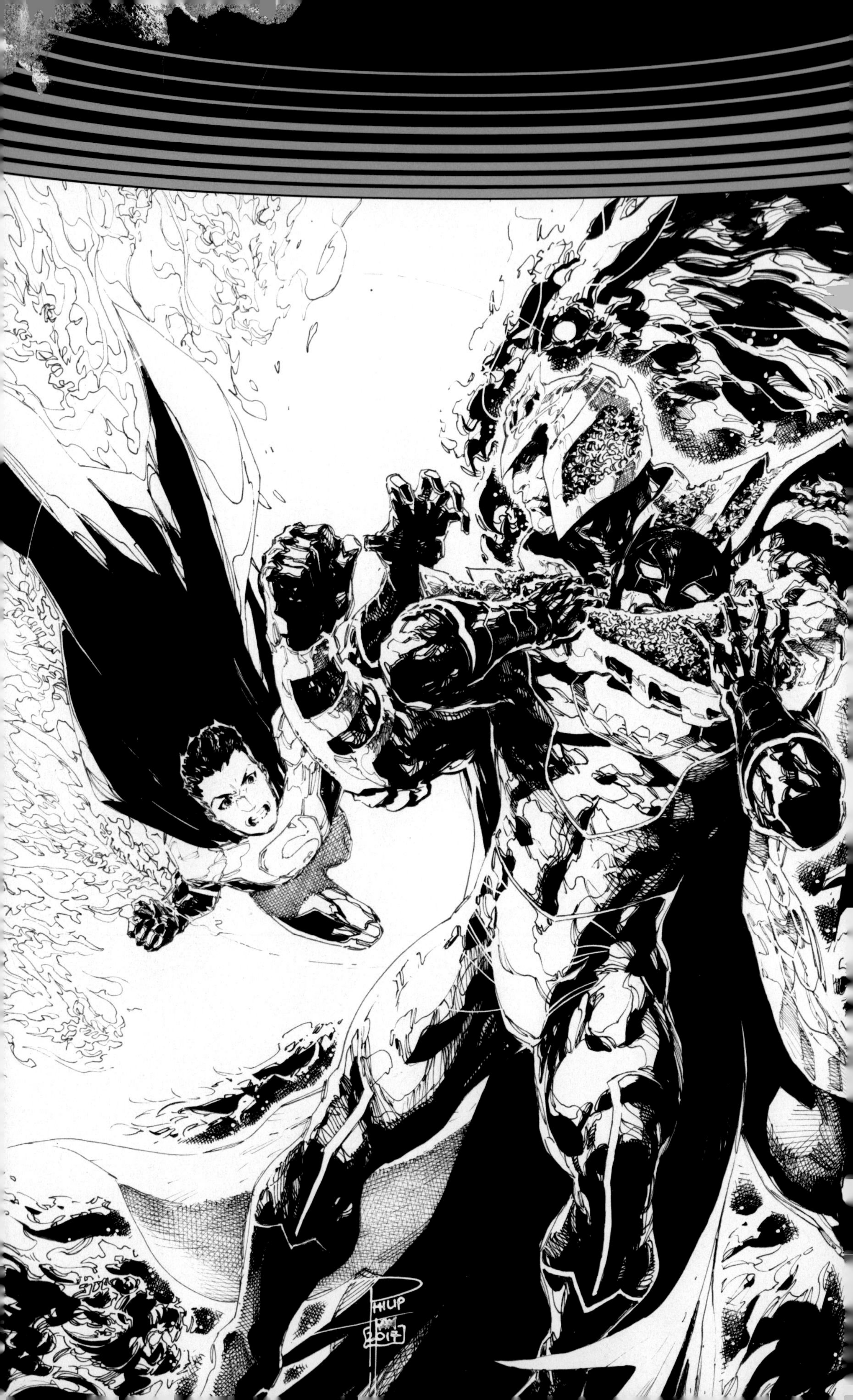

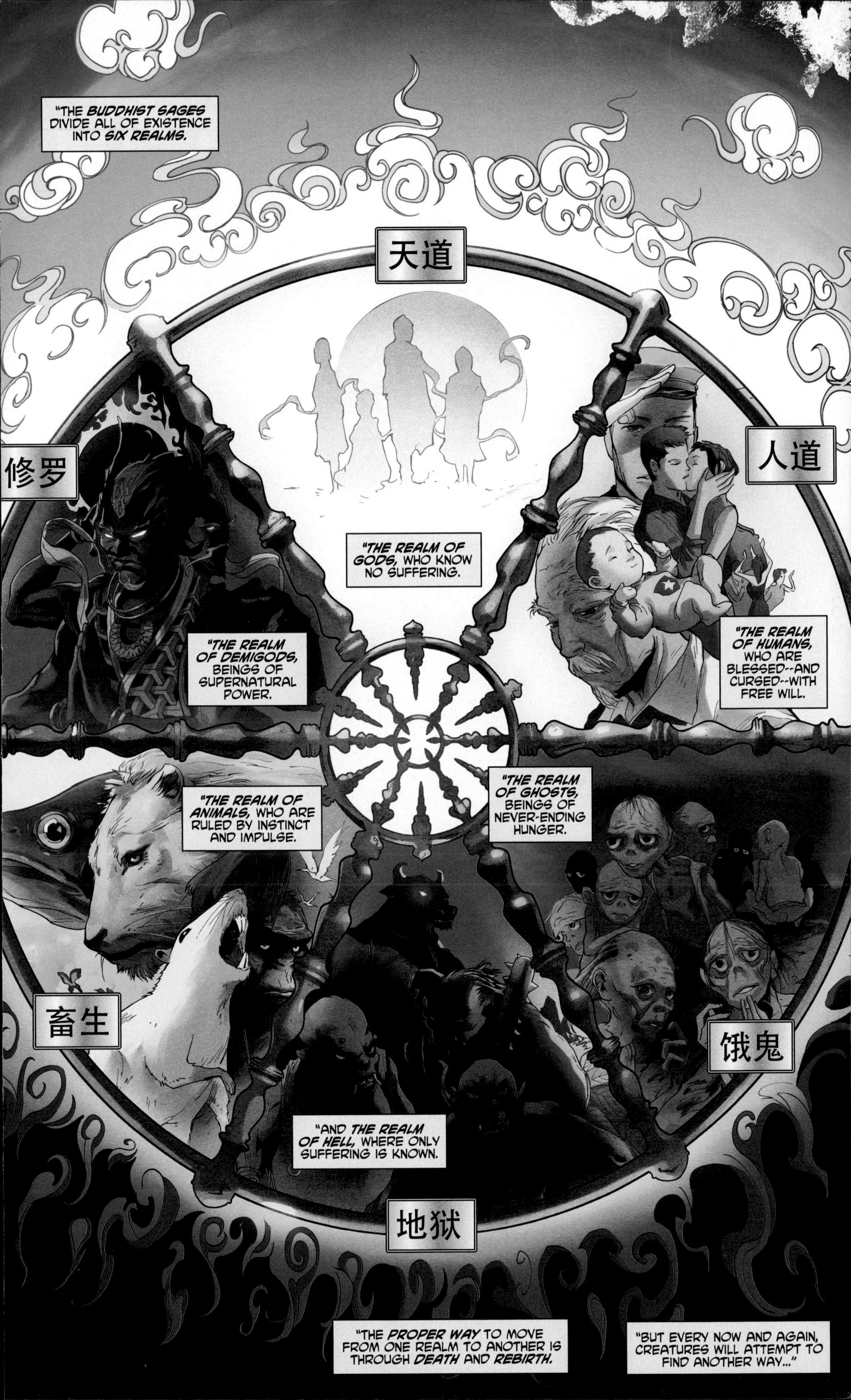
"THE BUDDHIST SAGES DIVIDE ALL OF EXISTENCE INTO SIX REALMS.
天道
"THE REALM OF GODS, WHO KNOW NO SUFFERING.
人道
"THE REALM OF HUMANS, WHO ARE BLESSED--AND CURSED--WITH FREE WILL.
修罗
"THE REALM OF DEMIGODS, BEINGS OF SUPERNATURAL POWER.
畜生
"THE REALM OF ANIMALS, WHO ARE RULED BY INSTINCT AND IMPULSE.
饿鬼
"THE REALM OF GHOSTS, BEINGS OF NEVER-ENDING HUNGER.
地狱
"AND THE REALM OF HELL, WHERE ONLY SUFFERING IS KNOWN.
"THE PROPER WAY TO MOVE FROM ONE REALM TO ANOTHER IS THROUGH DEATH AND REBIRTH.
"BUT EVERY NOW AND AGAIN, CREATURES WILL ATTEMPT TO FIND ANOTHER WAY..."

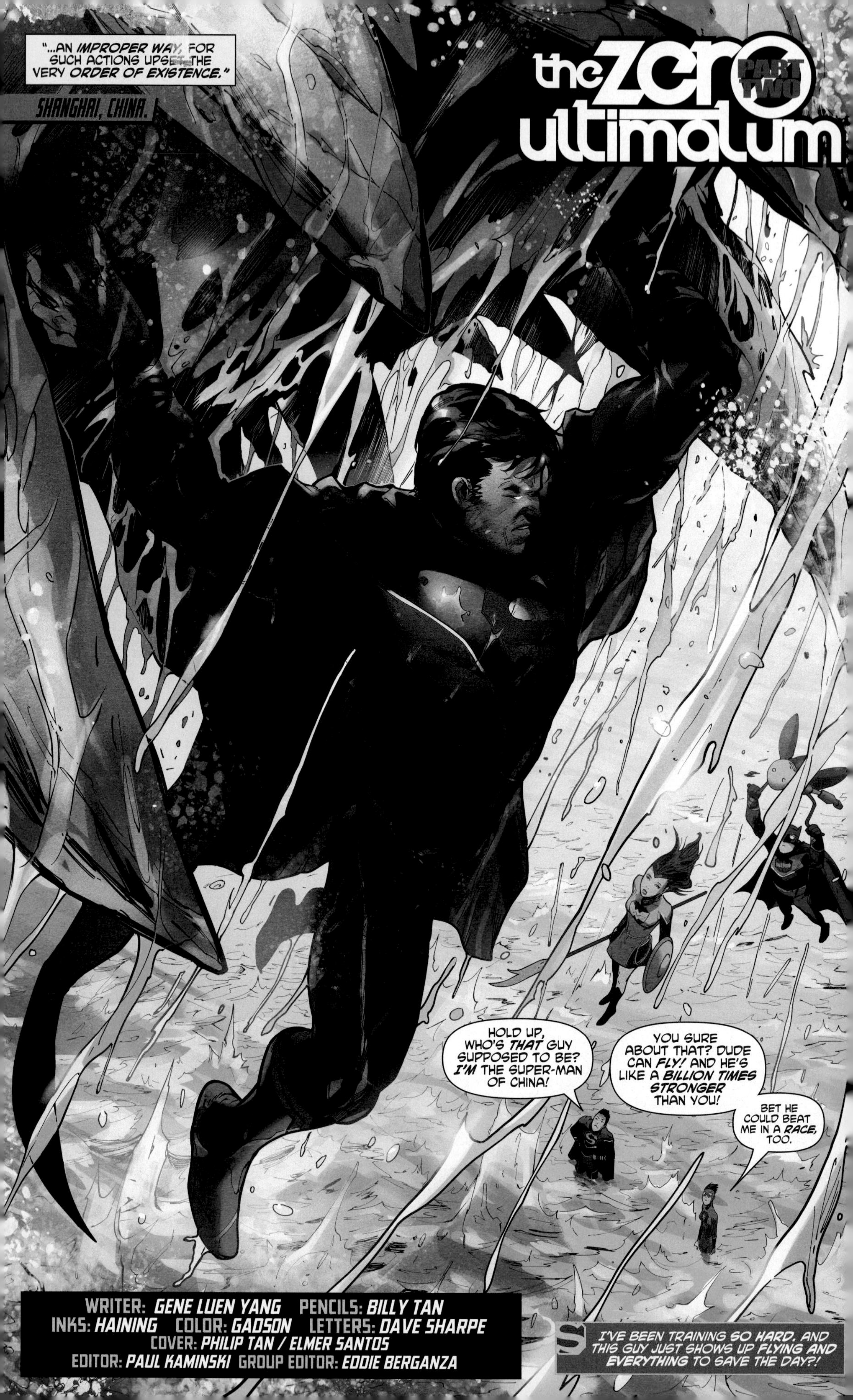
"...AN IMPROPER WAY, FOR SUCH ACTIONS UPSET THE VERY ORDER OF EXISTENCE."
SHANGHAI, CHINA.
the ZERO ultimalum
PART TWO
HOLD UP, WHO'S THAT GUY SUPPOSED TO BE? I'M THE SUPER-MAN OF CHINA!
YOU SURE ABOUT THAT? DUDE CAN FLY! AND HE'S LIKE A BILLION TIMES STRONGER THAN YOU!
BET HE COULD BEAT ME IN A RACE, TOO.
WRITER: GENE LUEN YANG PENCILS: BILLY TAN
INKS: HAINING COLOR: GADSON LETTERS: DAVE SHARPE
COVER: PHILIP TAN / ELMER SANTOS
EDITOR: PAUL KAMINSKI GROUP EDITOR: EDDIE BERGANZA
I'VE BEEN TRAINING SO HARD, AND THIS GUY JUST SHOWS UP FLYING AND EVERYTHING TO SAVE THE DAY?!

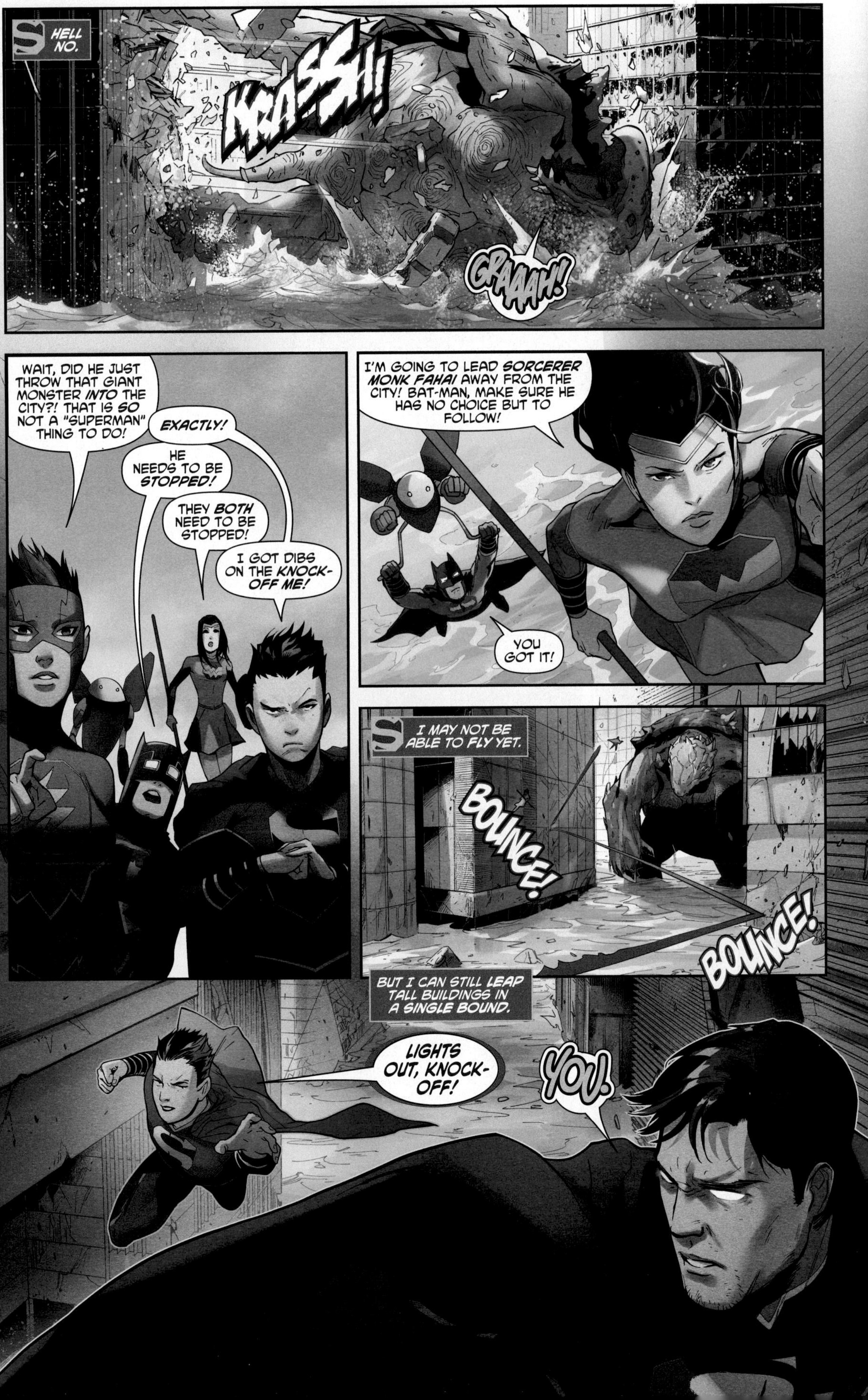
HELL NO.
KRASSH!
GRAAAH!
WAIT, DID HE JUST THROW THAT GIANT MONSTER INTO THE CITY?! THAT IS SO NOT A "SUPERMAN" THING TO DO!
EXACTLY!
HE NEEDS TO BE STOPPED!
THEY BOTH NEED TO BE STOPPED!
I GOT DIBS ON THE KNOCK-OFF ME!
I'M GOING TO LEAD SORCERER MONK FAHAI AWAY FROM THE CITY! BAT-MAN, MAKE SURE HE HAS NO CHOICE BUT TO FOLLOW!
YOU GOT IT!
I MAY NOT BE ABLE TO FLY YET.
BOUNCE!
BOUNCE!
BUT I CAN STILL LEAP TALL BUILDINGS IN A SINGLE BOUND.
LIGHTS OUT, KNOCK-OFF!
YOU.

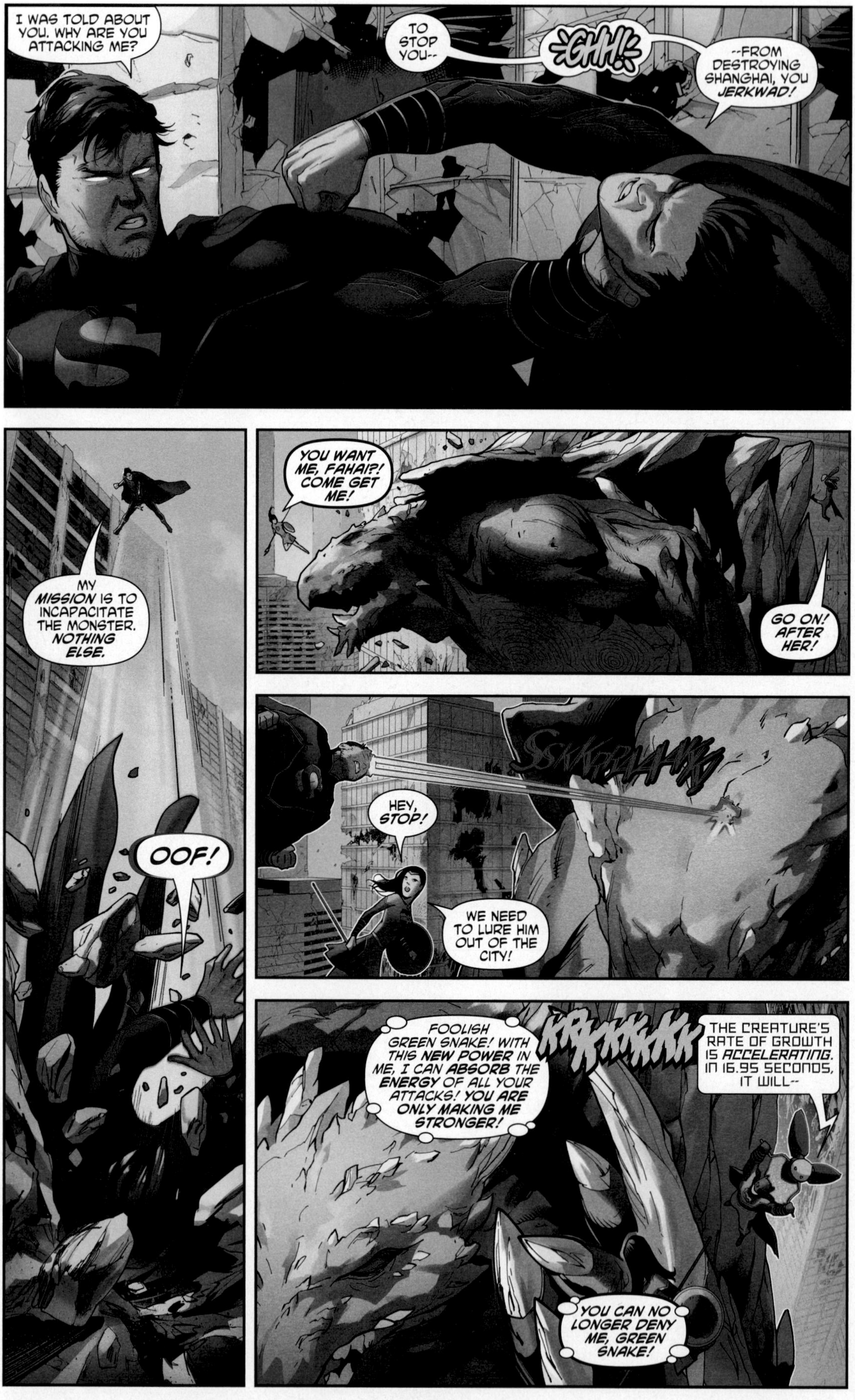
I WAS TOLD ABOUT YOU. WHY ARE YOU ATTACKING ME?
TO STOP YOU--
GHH!
--FROM DESTROYING SHANGHAI, YOU JERKWAD!
MY MISSION IS TO INCAPACITATE THE MONSTER. NOTHING ELSE.
OOF!
YOU WANT ME, FAHAI?! COME GET ME!
GO ON! AFTER HER!
SSKKRRAAAKK
HEY, STOP!
WE NEED TO LURE HIM OUT OF THE CITY!
FOOLISH GREEN SNAKE! WITH THIS NEW POWER IN ME, I CAN ABSORB THE ENERGY OF ALL YOUR ATTACKS! YOU ARE ONLY MAKING ME STRONGER!
KRKKKKK
THE CREATURE'S RATE OF GROWTH IS ACCELERATING. IN 16.95 SECONDS, IT WILL--
YOU CAN NO LONGER DENY ME, GREEN SNAKE!

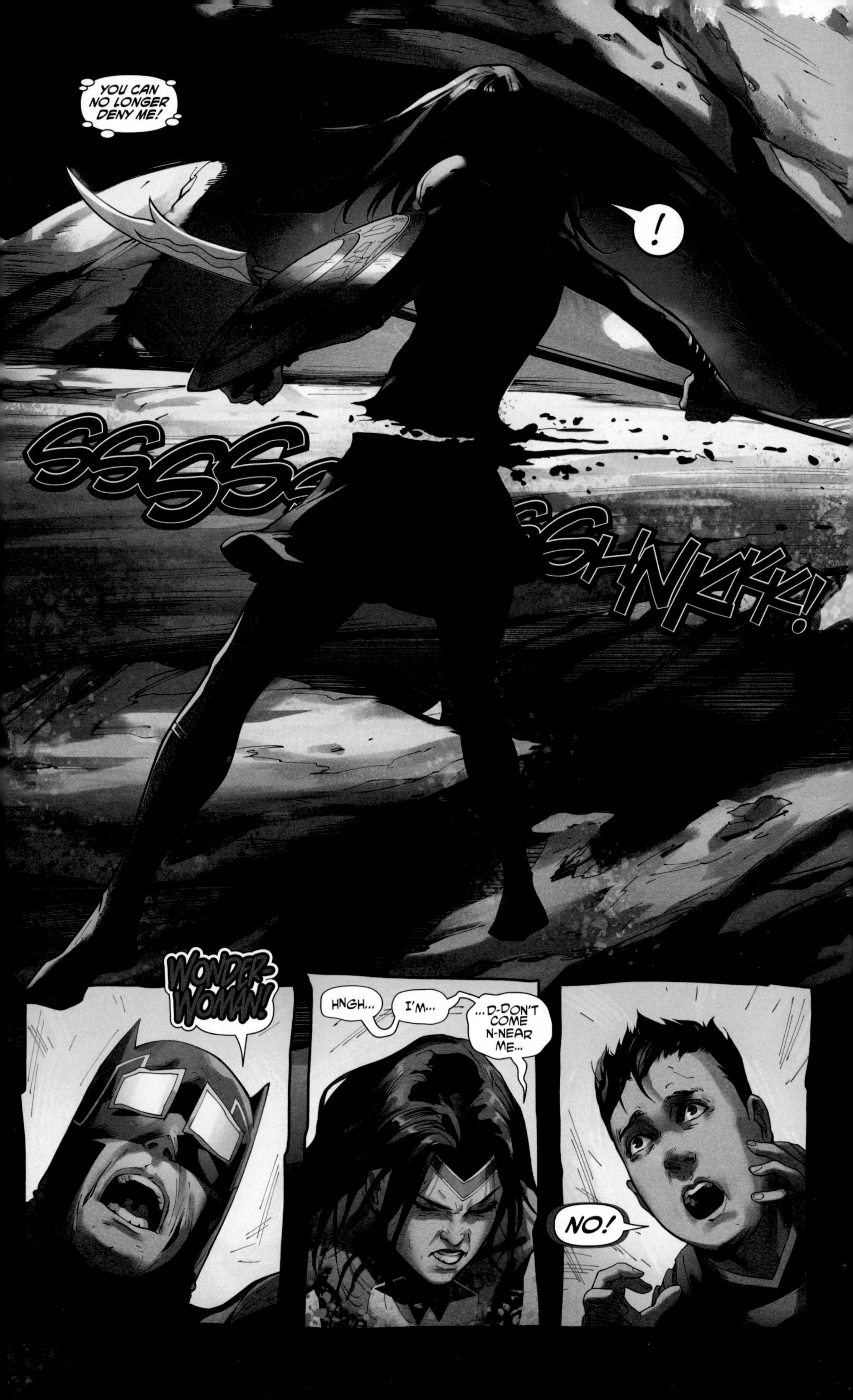
YOU CAN NO LONGER DENY ME!
!
SSSSSSHNKKK!
WONDER-WOMAN!
HNGH...
I'M...
...D-DON'T COME N-NEAR ME...
NO!

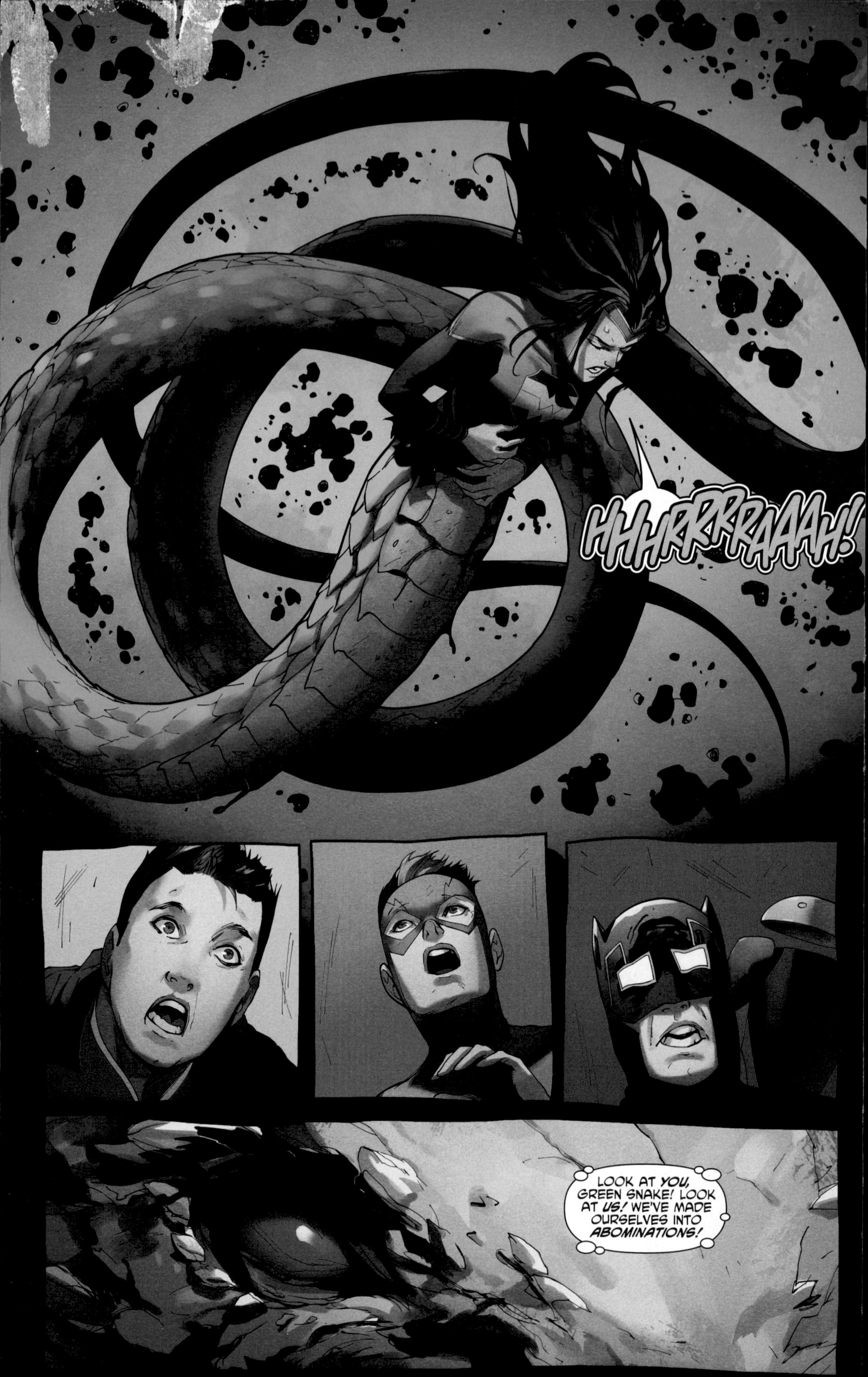

HHHRRRRAAAH!
LOOK AT YOU, GREEN SNAKE! LOOK AT US! WE'VE MADE OURSELVES INTO ABOMINATIONS!

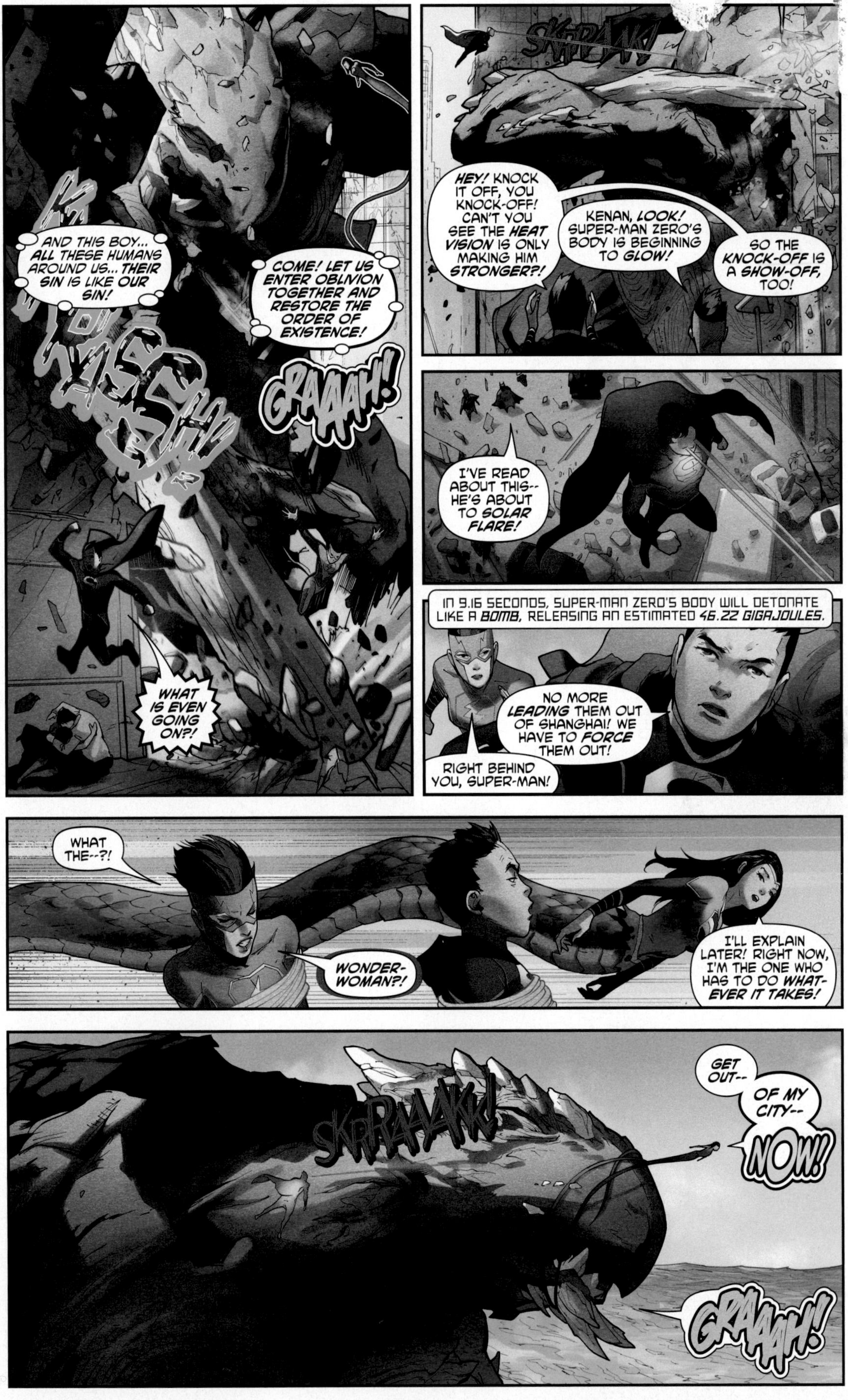
AND THIS BOY... ALL THESE HUMANS AROUND US... THEIR SIN IS LIKE OUR SIN!
COME! LET US ENTER OBLIVION TOGETHER AND RESTORE THE ORDER OF EXISTENCE!
GRAAAH!
WHAT IS EVEN GOING ON?!
SKRRAAK!
HEY! KNOCK IT OFF, YOU KNOCK-OFF! CAN'T YOU SEE THE HEAT VISION IS ONLY MAKING HIM STRONGER?!
KENAN, LOOK! SUPER-MAN ZERO'S BODY IS BEGINNING TO GLOW!
SO THE KNOCK-OFF IS A SHOW-OFF, TOO!
I'VE READ ABOUT THIS-- HE'S ABOUT TO SOLAR FLARE!
IN 9.16 SECONDS, SUPER-MAN ZERO'S BODY WILL DETONATE LIKE A BOMB, RELEASING AN ESTIMATED 46.22 GIGAJOULES.
NO MORE LEADING THEM OUT OF SHANGHAI! WE HAVE TO FORCE THEM OUT!
RIGHT BEHIND YOU, SUPER-MAN!
WHAT THE--?!
WONDER-WOMAN?!
I'LL EXPLAIN LATER! RIGHT NOW, I'M THE ONE WHO HAS TO DO WHAT-EVER IT TAKES!
SKRRAAAKK!
GET OUT--
OF MY CITY--
NOW!
GRAAAH!

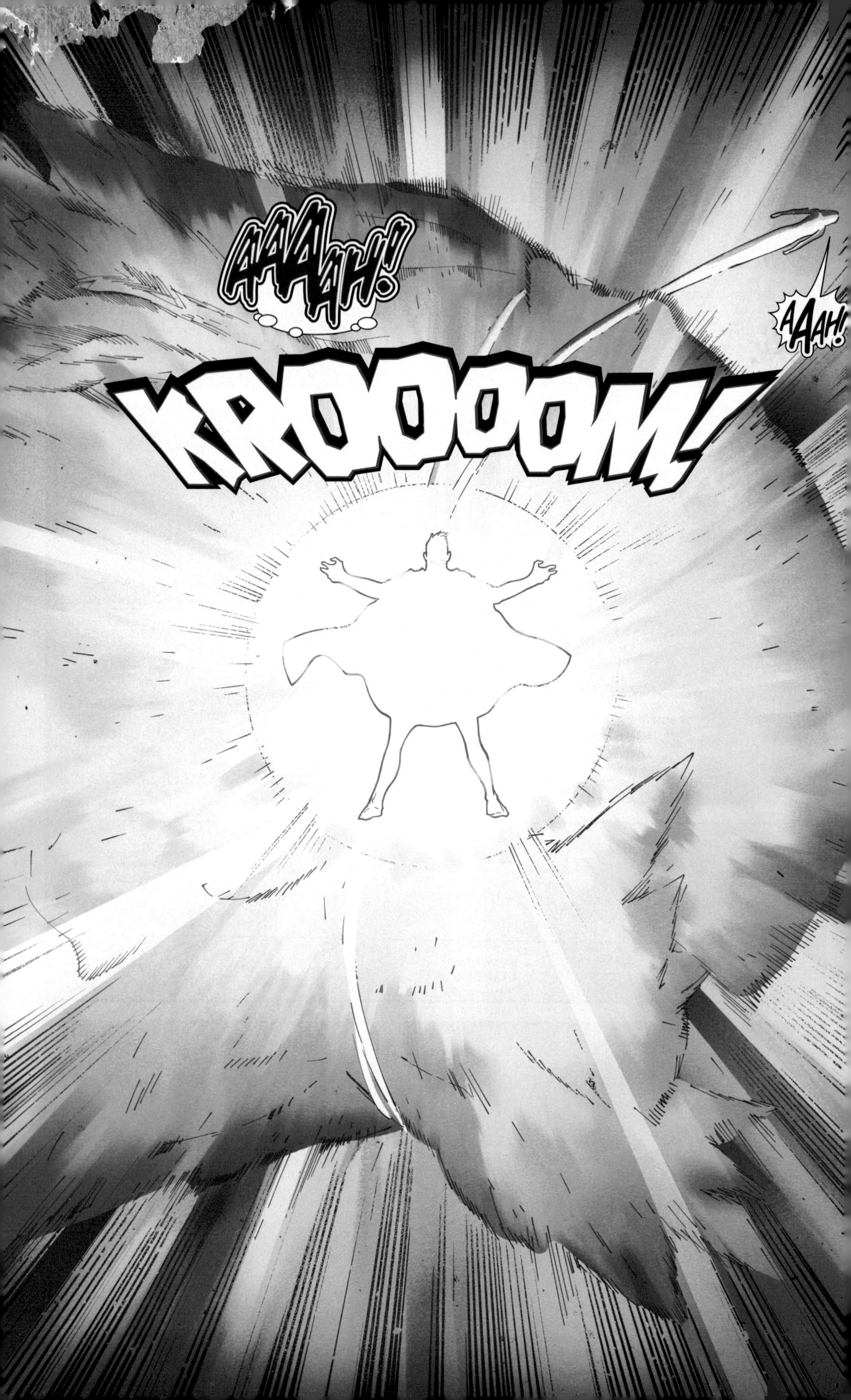
AAAAAAH!
AAAH!
KROOOOOM!

NGH...

GREEN SNAKE... LET US NOT... CLING TO LIFE...

FOR OUR DEATHS... ARE OUR REPENTANCE.

YOU AND WHITE SNAKE... BOTH FELL IN LOVE WITH THAT HUMAN BOY... AND I... I FELL IN LOVE WITH WHITE SNAKE.

BUT WE ARE ANIMALS... THOSE OF OUR REALM ARE... UNWORTHY OF SUCH EMOTIONS.

THAT IS WHY... WE MUST DIE.

THESE HUMANS AROUND US... WEARING SUCH COLORFUL ATTIRE...

EVERY ONE OF THEM... IS TRYING TO... ESCAPE THEIR PROPER REALM... TO BECOME SOMETHING HIGHER.

BUT THOSE OF THEIR REALM ARE... UNWORTHY OF SUCH POWER.

AND THAT IS WHY THEY, TOO...

"...MUST DIE."

WHAT...?

Hnn

YOU KNOW YOU'VE NEVER BEEN A MATCH FOR ME, I-CHING.

WHAT IS IT THAT YOU'RE ALWAYS SO FOND OF SAYING?

"TO BECOME SELFLESS, ONE MUST FIRST HAVE A SELF."

IN BETWEEN WHAT IS AND WHAT IS NOT.

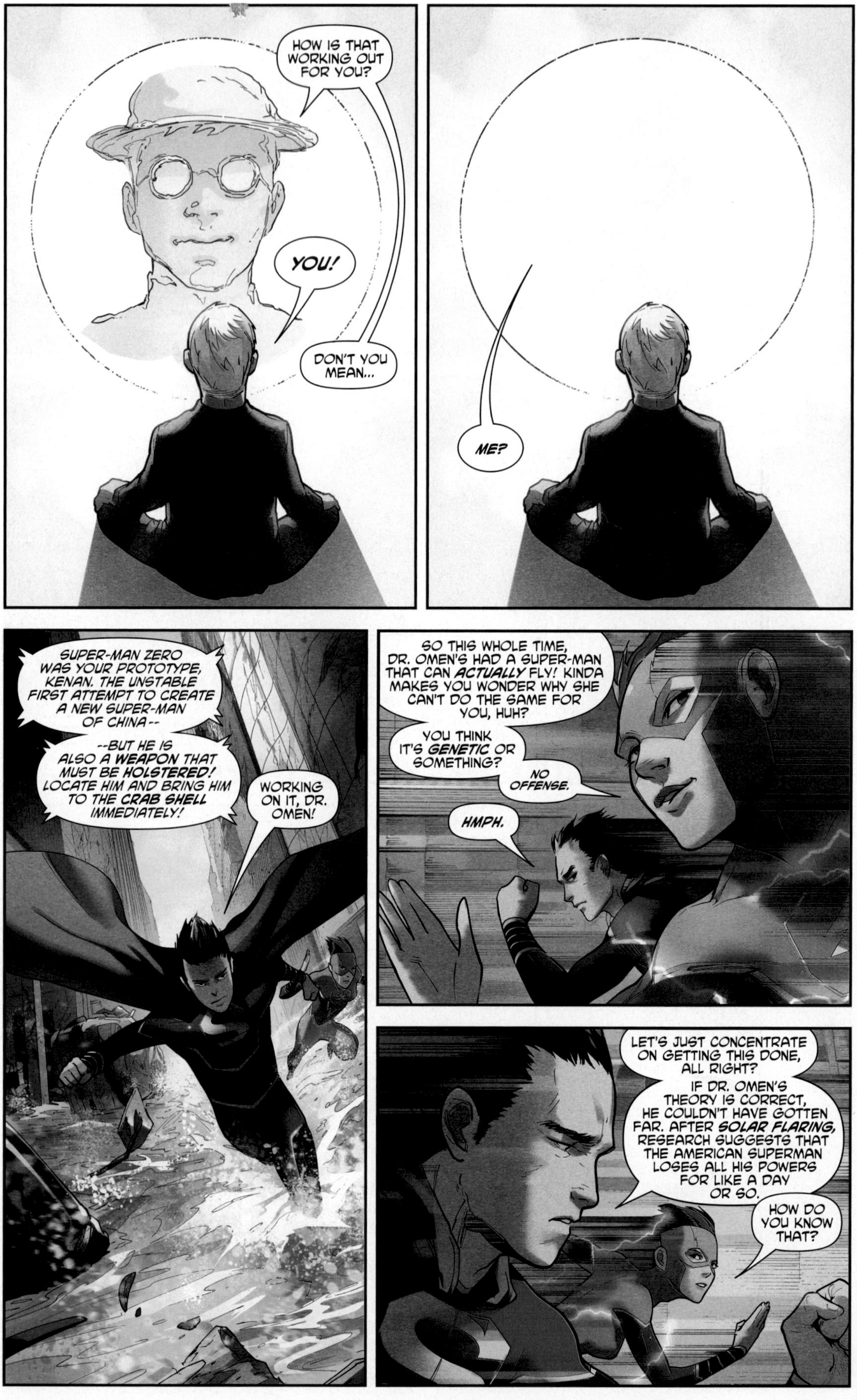
HOW IS THAT WORKING OUT FOR YOU?
YOU!
DON'T YOU MEAN...
ME?
SUPER-MAN ZERO WAS YOUR PROTOTYPE, KENAN. THE UNSTABLE FIRST ATTEMPT TO CREATE A NEW SUPER-MAN OF CHINA--
--BUT HE IS ALSO A WEAPON THAT MUST BE HOLSTERED! LOCATE HIM AND BRING HIM TO THE CRAB SHELL IMMEDIATELY!
WORKING ON IT, DR. OMEN!
SO THIS WHOLE TIME, DR. OMEN'S HAD A SUPER-MAN THAT CAN ACTUALLY FLY! KINDA MAKES YOU WONDER WHY SHE CAN'T DO THE SAME FOR YOU, HUH?
YOU THINK IT'S GENETIC OR SOMETHING?
NO OFFENSE.
HMPH.
LET'S JUST CONCENTRATE ON GETTING THIS DONE, ALL RIGHT?
IF DR. OMEN'S THEORY IS CORRECT, HE COULDN'T HAVE GOTTEN FAR. AFTER SOLAR FLARING, RESEARCH SUGGESTS THAT THE AMERICAN SUPERMAN LOSES ALL HIS POWERS FOR LIKE A DAY OR SO.
HOW DO YOU KNOW THAT?

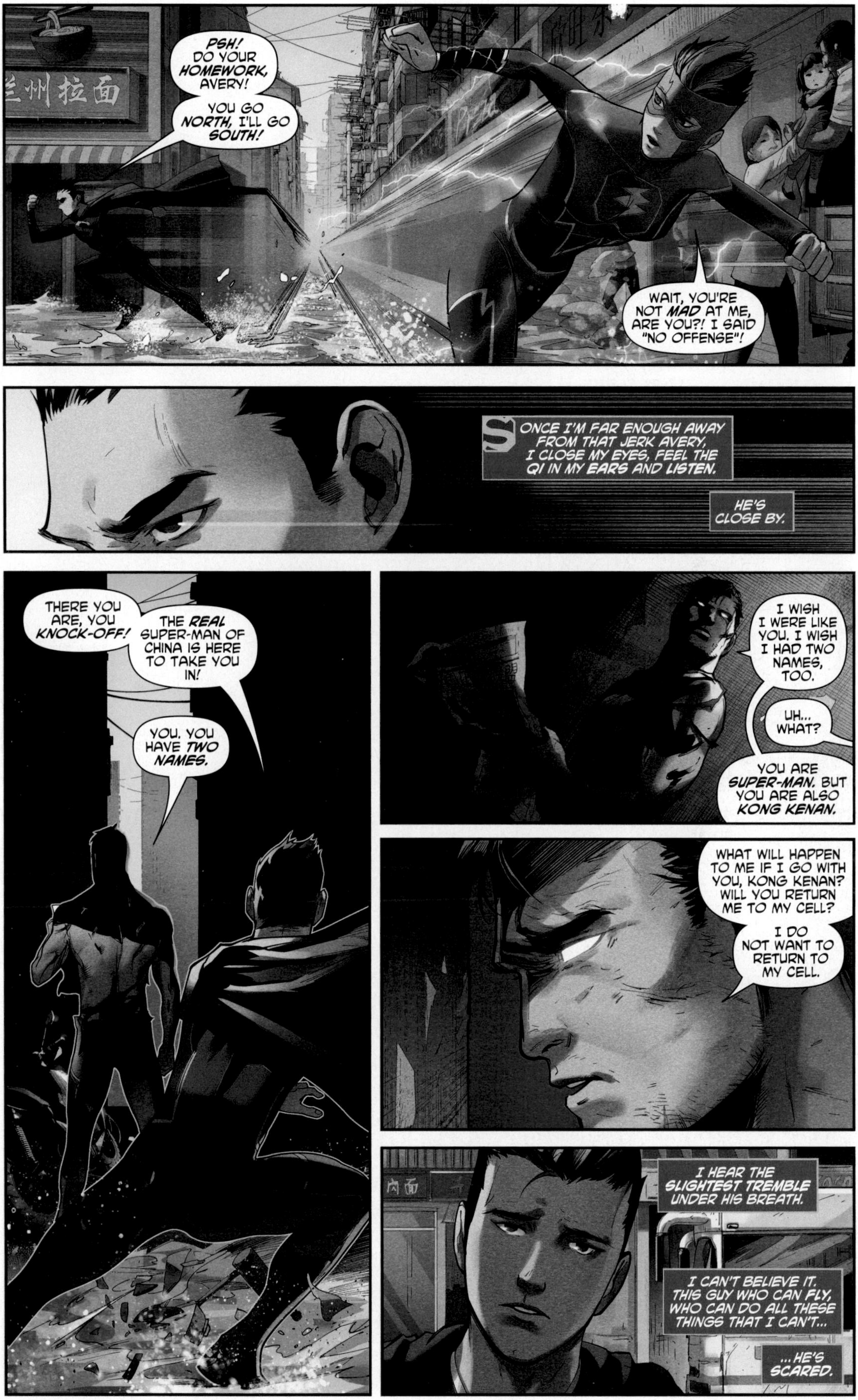
PSH! DO YOUR HOMEWORK, AVERY!
YOU GO NORTH, I'LL GO SOUTH!
兰州拉面
WAIT, YOU'RE NOT MAD AT ME, ARE YOU?! I SAID "NO OFFENSE"!
ONCE I'M FAR ENOUGH AWAY FROM THAT JERK AVERY, I CLOSE MY EYES, FEEL THE QI IN MY EARS AND LISTEN.
HE'S CLOSE BY.
THERE YOU ARE, YOU KNOCK-OFF!
THE REAL SUPER-MAN OF CHINA IS HERE TO TAKE YOU IN!
YOU. YOU HAVE TWO NAMES.
I WISH I WERE LIKE YOU. I WISH I HAD TWO NAMES, TOO.
UH... WHAT?
YOU ARE SUPER-MAN. BUT YOU ARE ALSO KONG KENAN.
WHAT WILL HAPPEN TO ME IF I GO WITH YOU, KONG KENAN? WILL YOU RETURN ME TO MY CELL?
I DO NOT WANT TO RETURN TO MY CELL.
I HEAR THE SLIGHTEST TREMBLE UNDER HIS BREATH.
I CAN'T BELIEVE IT. THIS GUY WHO CAN FLY, WHO CAN DO ALL THESE THINGS THAT I CAN'T...
...HE'S SCARED.

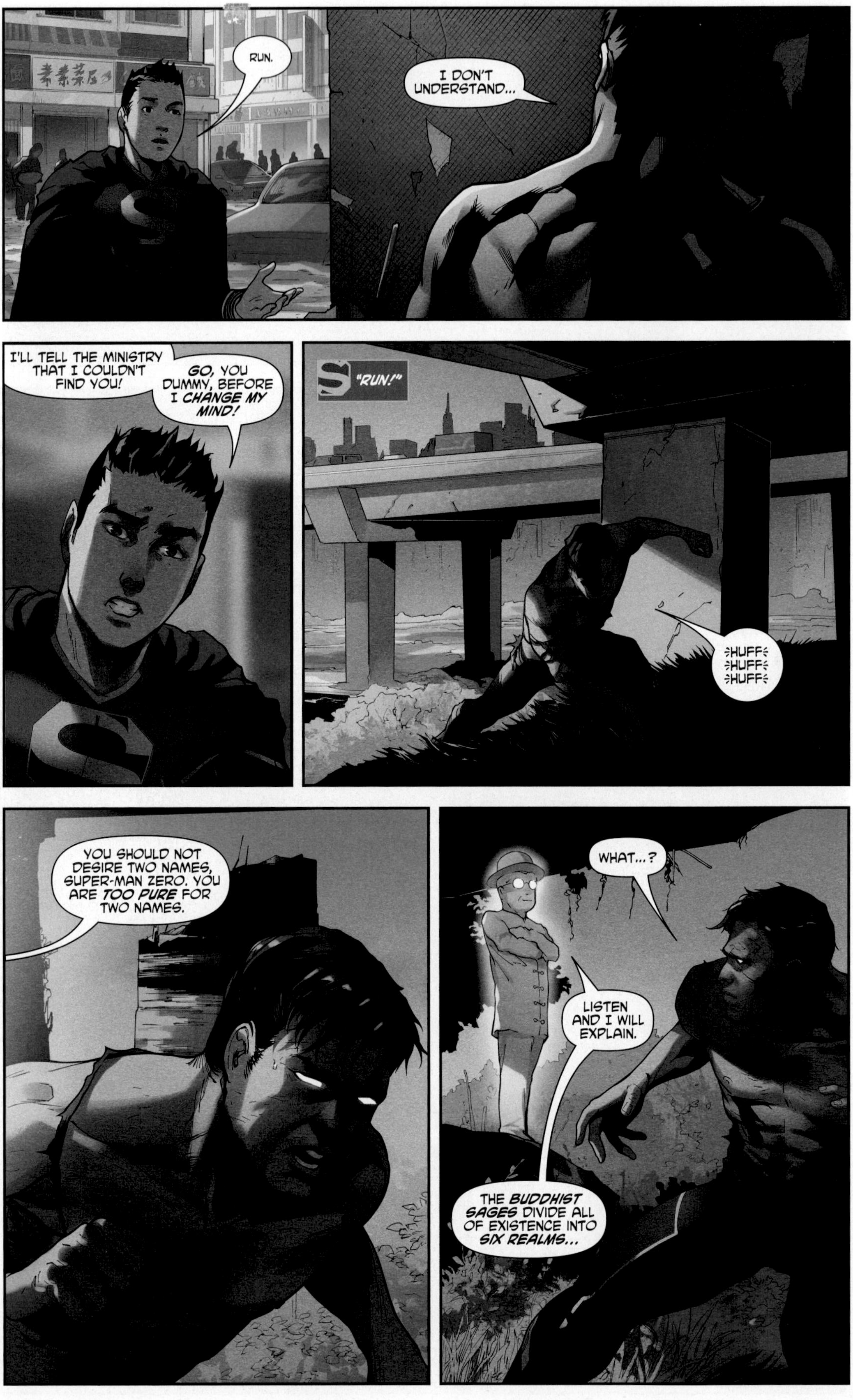
RUN.
I DON'T UNDERSTAND...
I'LL TELL THE MINISTRY THAT I COULDN'T FIND YOU!
GO, YOU DUMMY, BEFORE I CHANGE MY MIND!
"RUN!"
HUFF HUFF HUFF
YOU SHOULD NOT DESIRE TWO NAMES, SUPER-MAN ZERO. YOU ARE TOO PURE FOR TWO NAMES.
WHAT...?
LISTEN AND I WILL EXPLAIN.
THE BUDDHIST SAGES DIVIDE ALL OF EXISTENCE INTO SIX REALMS...

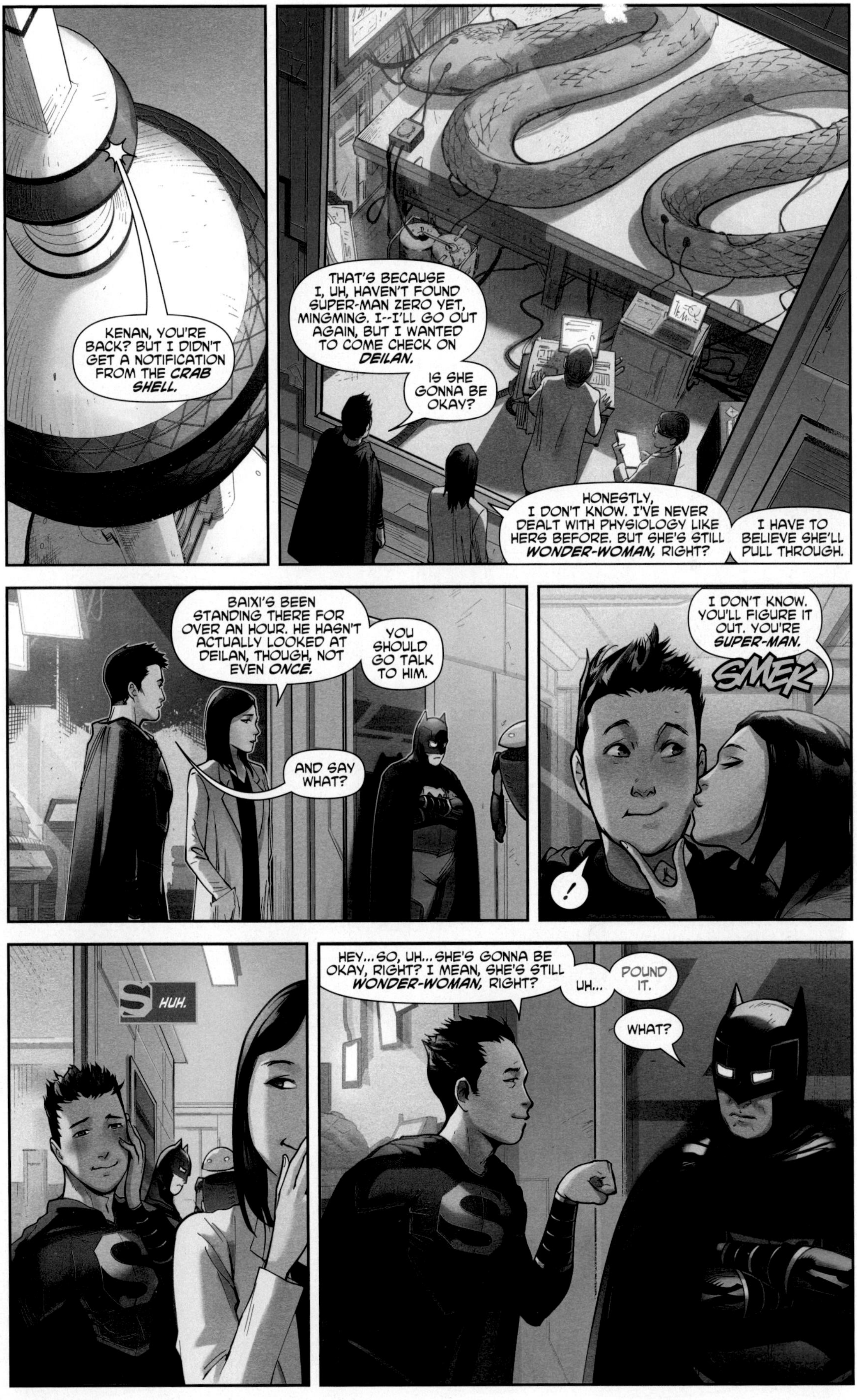
KENAN, YOU'RE BACK? BUT I DIDN'T GET A NOTIFICATION FROM THE CRAB SHELL.
THAT'S BECAUSE I, UH, HAVEN'T FOUND SUPER-MAN ZERO YET, MINGMING. I--I'LL GO OUT AGAIN, BUT I WANTED TO COME CHECK ON DEILAN.
IS SHE GONNA BE OKAY?
HONESTLY, I DON'T KNOW. I'VE NEVER DEALT WITH PHYSIOLOGY LIKE HERS BEFORE. BUT SHE'S STILL WONDER-WOMAN, RIGHT?
I HAVE TO BELIEVE SHE'LL PULL THROUGH.
BAIXI'S BEEN STANDING THERE FOR OVER AN HOUR. HE HASN'T ACTUALLY LOOKED AT DEILAN, THOUGH, NOT EVEN ONCE.
YOU SHOULD GO TALK TO HIM.
AND SAY WHAT?
I DON'T KNOW. YOU'LL FIGURE IT OUT. YOU'RE SUPER-MAN.
SMEK
!
HUH.
HEY...SO, UH...SHE'S GONNA BE OKAY, RIGHT? I MEAN, SHE'S STILL WONDER-WOMAN, RIGHT?
UH...
POUND IT.
WHAT?

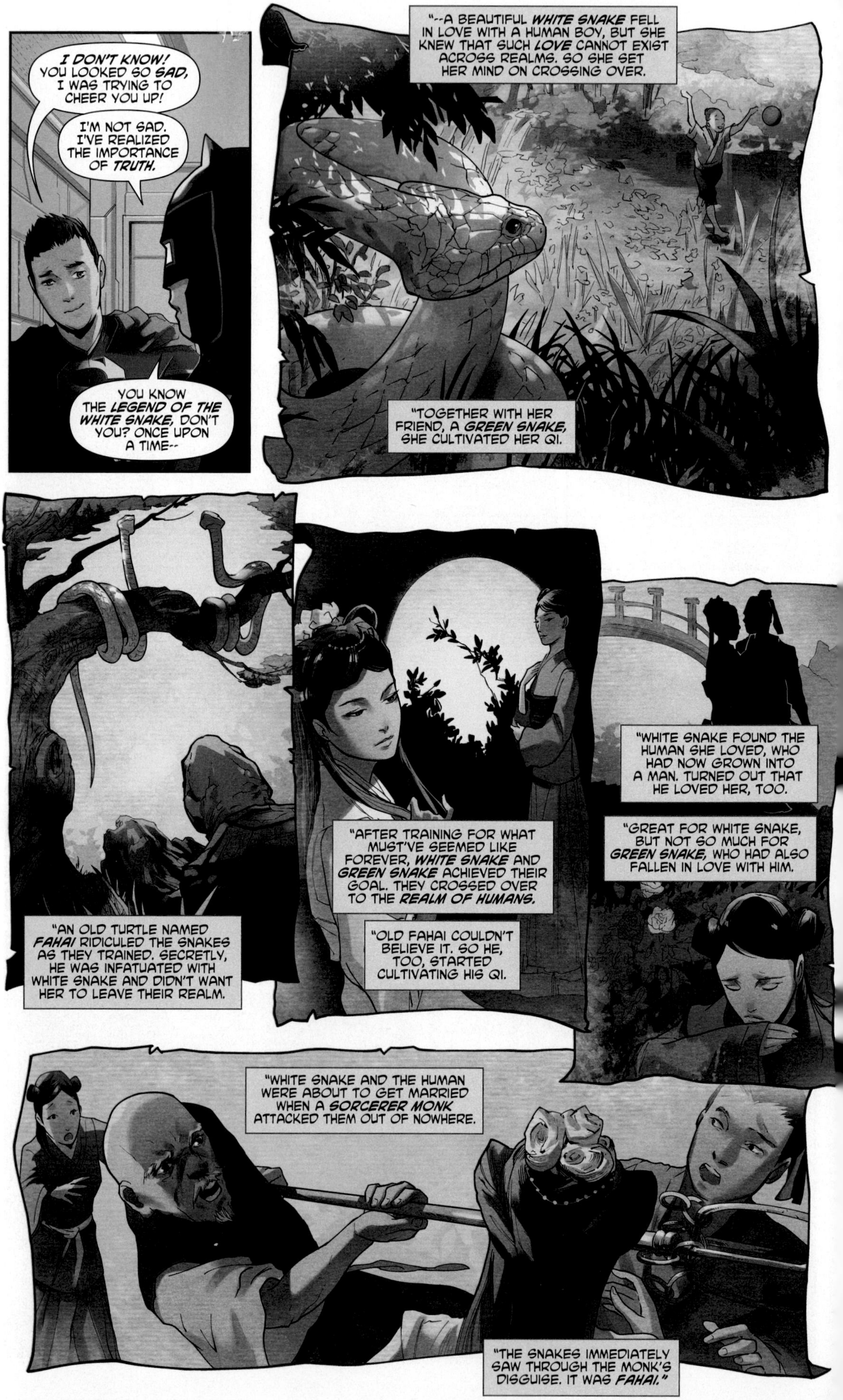
I DON'T KNOW! YOU LOOKED SO SAD, I WAS TRYING TO CHEER YOU UP!
I'M NOT SAD. I'VE REALIZED THE IMPORTANCE OF TRUTH.
YOU KNOW THE LEGEND OF THE WHITE SNAKE, DON'T YOU? ONCE UPON A TIME--
"--A BEAUTIFUL WHITE SNAKE FELL IN LOVE WITH A HUMAN BOY, BUT SHE KNEW THAT SUCH LOVE CANNOT EXIST ACROSS REALMS. SO SHE SET HER MIND ON CROSSING OVER.
"TOGETHER WITH HER FRIEND, A GREEN SNAKE, SHE CULTIVATED HER QI.
"AN OLD TURTLE NAMED FAHAI RIDICULED THE SNAKES AS THEY TRAINED. SECRETLY, HE WAS INFATUATED WITH WHITE SNAKE AND DIDN'T WANT HER TO LEAVE THEIR REALM.
"AFTER TRAINING FOR WHAT MUST'VE SEEMED LIKE FOREVER, WHITE SNAKE AND GREEN SNAKE ACHIEVED THEIR GOAL. THEY CROSSED OVER TO THE REALM OF HUMANS.
"OLD FAHAI COULDN'T BELIEVE IT. SO HE, TOO, STARTED CULTIVATING HIS QI.
"WHITE SNAKE FOUND THE HUMAN SHE LOVED, WHO HAD NOW GROWN INTO A MAN. TURNED OUT THAT HE LOVED HER, TOO.
"GREAT FOR WHITE SNAKE, BUT NOT SO MUCH FOR GREEN SNAKE, WHO HAD ALSO FALLEN IN LOVE WITH HIM.
"WHITE SNAKE AND THE HUMAN WERE ABOUT TO GET MARRIED WHEN A SORCERER MONK ATTACKED THEM OUT OF NOWHERE.
"THE SNAKES IMMEDIATELY SAW THROUGH THE MONK'S DISGUISE. IT WAS FAHAI."

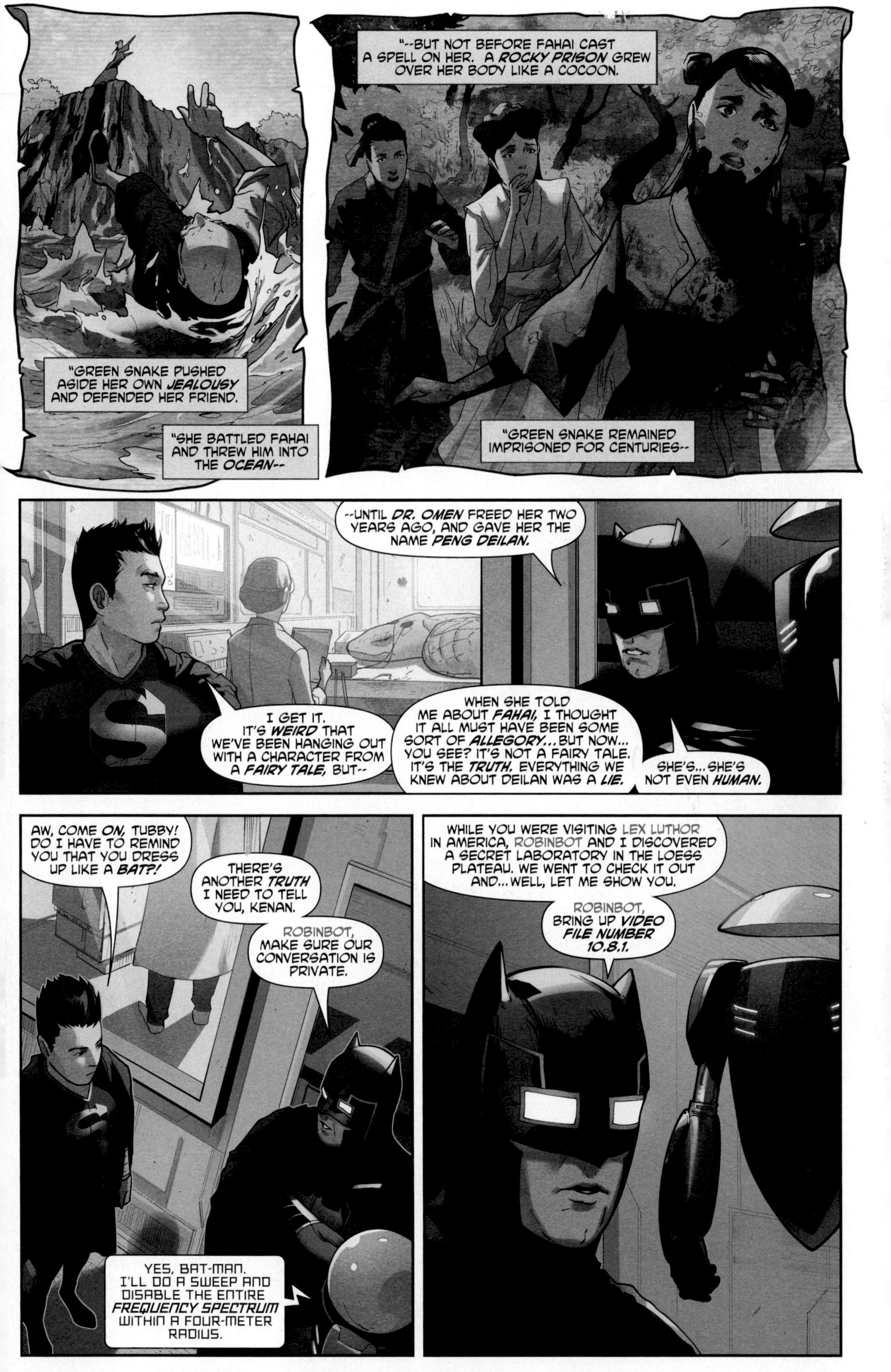
"GREEN SNAKE PUSHED ASIDE HER OWN JEALOUSY AND DEFENDED HER FRIEND.
"SHE BATTLED FAHAI AND THREW HIM INTO THE OCEAN--
"--BUT NOT BEFORE FAHAI CAST A SPELL ON HER. A ROCKY PRISON GREW OVER HER BODY LIKE A COCOON.
"GREEN SNAKE REMAINED IMPRISONED FOR CENTURIES--
--UNTIL DR. OMEN FREED HER TWO YEARS AGO, AND GAVE HER THE NAME PENG DEILAN.
I GET IT. IT'S WEIRD THAT WE'VE BEEN HANGING OUT WITH A CHARACTER FROM A FAIRY TALE, BUT--
WHEN SHE TOLD ME ABOUT FAHAI, I THOUGHT IT ALL MUST HAVE BEEN SOME SORT OF ALLEGORY... BUT NOW... YOU SEE? IT'S NOT A FAIRY TALE. IT'S THE TRUTH. EVERYTHING WE KNEW ABOUT DEILAN WAS A LIE.
SHE'S... SHE'S NOT EVEN HUMAN.
AW, COME ON, TUBBY! DO I HAVE TO REMIND YOU THAT YOU DRESS UP LIKE A BAT?!
THERE'S ANOTHER TRUTH I NEED TO TELL YOU, KENAN.
ROBINBOT, MAKE SURE OUR CONVERSATION IS PRIVATE.
YES, BAT-MAN. I'LL DO A SWEEP AND DISABLE THE ENTIRE FREQUENCY SPECTRUM WITHIN A FOUR-METER RADIUS.
WHILE YOU WERE VISITING LEX LUTHOR IN AMERICA, ROBINBOT AND I DISCOVERED A SECRET LABORATORY IN THE LOESS PLATEAU. WE WENT TO CHECK IT OUT AND... WELL, LET ME SHOW YOU.
ROBINBOT, BRING UP VIDEO FILE NUMBER 10.8.1.

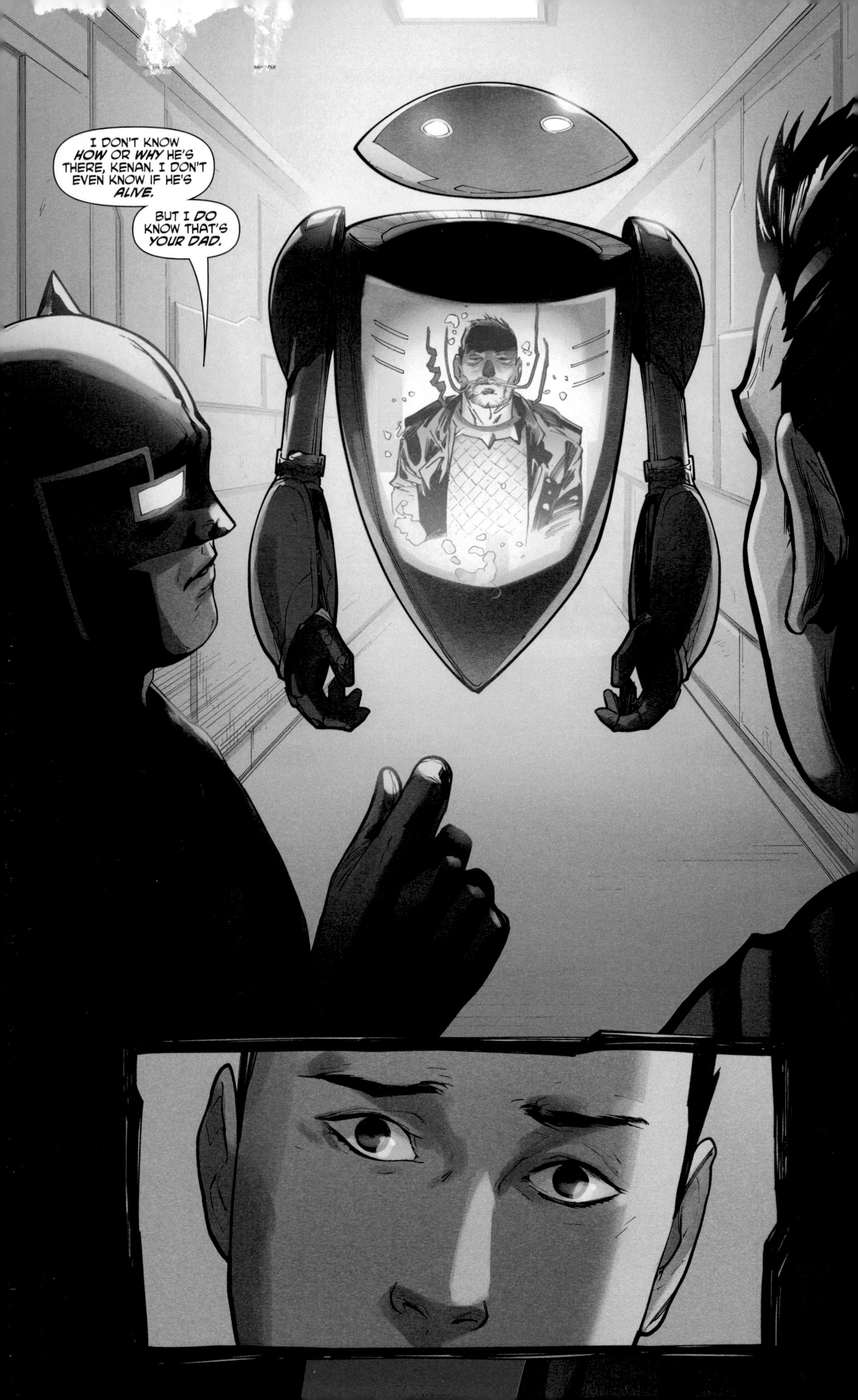
I DON'T KNOW HOW OR WHY HE'S THERE, KENAN. I DON'T EVEN KNOW IF HE'S ALIVE.
BUT I DO KNOW THAT'S YOUR DAD.

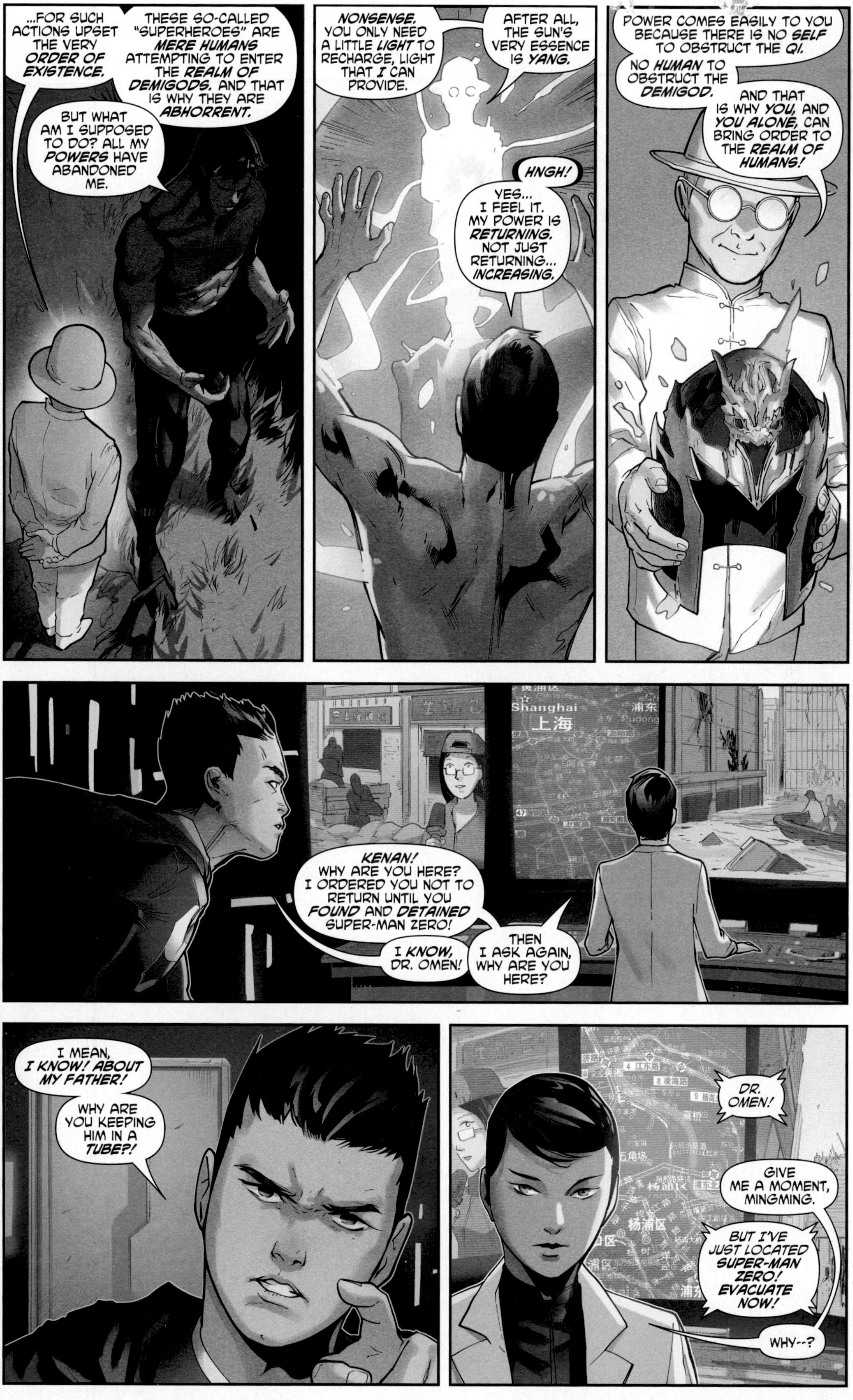

...FOR SUCH ACTIONS UPSET THE VERY ORDER OF EXISTENCE.
THESE SO-CALLED "SUPERHEROES" ARE MERE HUMANS ATTEMPTING TO ENTER THE REALM OF DEMIGODS. AND THAT IS WHY THEY ARE ABHORRENT.
BUT WHAT AM I SUPPOSED TO DO? ALL MY POWERS HAVE ABANDONED ME.
NONSENSE. YOU ONLY NEED A LITTLE LIGHT TO RECHARGE, LIGHT THAT I CAN PROVIDE.
AFTER ALL, THE SUN'S VERY ESSENCE IS YANG.
HNGH!
YES... I FEEL IT. MY POWER IS RETURNING. NOT JUST RETURNING... INCREASING.
POWER COMES EASILY TO YOU BECAUSE THERE IS NO SELF TO OBSTRUCT THE QI.
NO HUMAN TO OBSTRUCT THE DEMIGOD.
AND THAT IS WHY YOU, AND YOU ALONE, CAN BRING ORDER TO THE REALM OF HUMANS!
Shanghai
上海
浦东
Pudong
KENAN! WHY ARE YOU HERE? I ORDERED YOU NOT TO RETURN UNTIL YOU FOUND AND DETAINED SUPER-MAN ZERO!
I KNOW, DR. OMEN!
THEN I ASK AGAIN, WHY ARE YOU HERE?
I MEAN, I KNOW! ABOUT MY FATHER!
WHY ARE YOU KEEPING HIM IN A TUBE?!
DR. OMEN!
GIVE ME A MOMENT, MINGMING.
BUT I'VE JUST LOCATED SUPER-MAN ZERO! EVACUATE NOW!
WHY--?

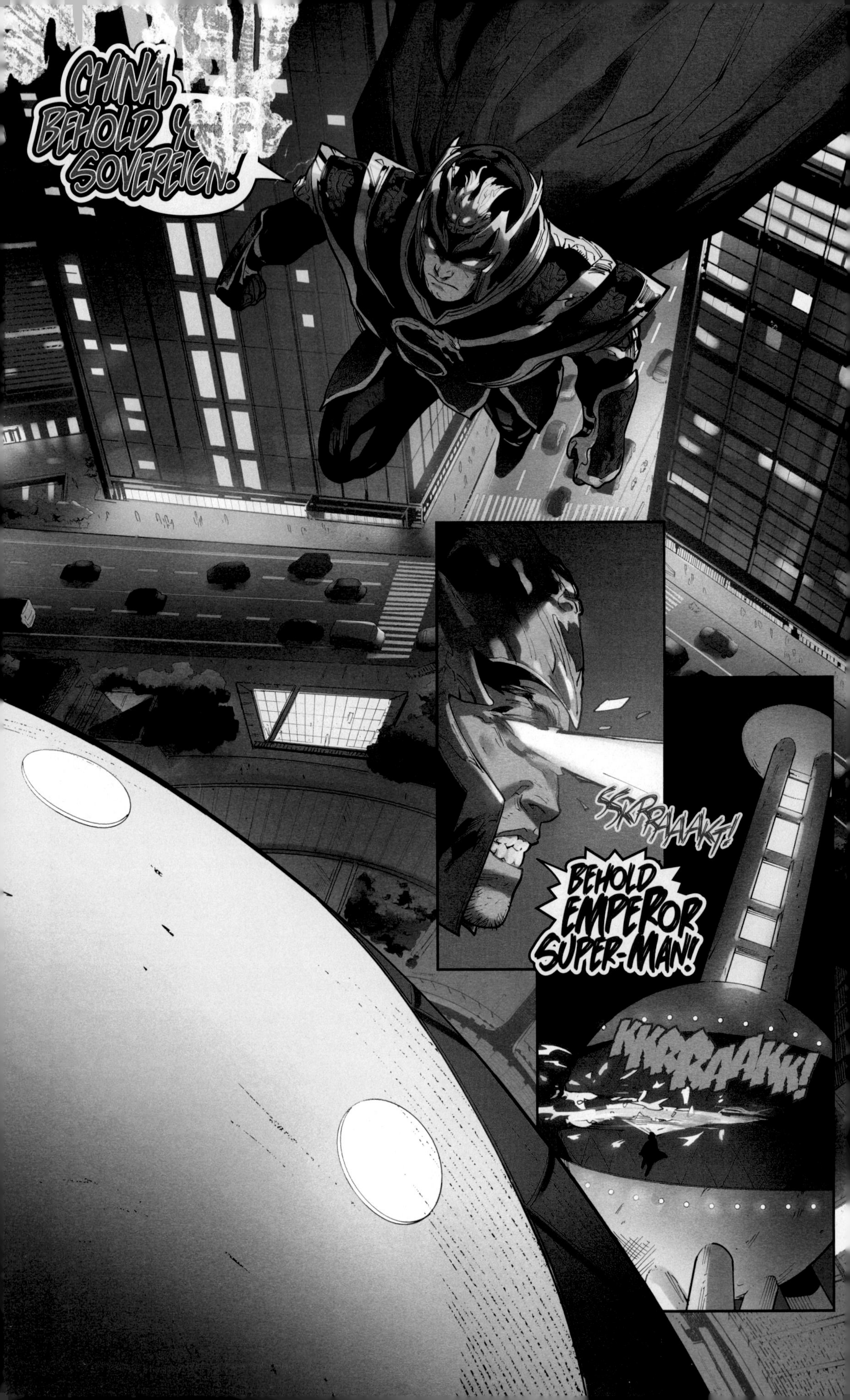
CHINA, BEHOLD YO SOVEREIGN!
SSKRRAAAKT!
BEHOLD EMPEROR SUPER-MAN!!
KKRRAAKK!

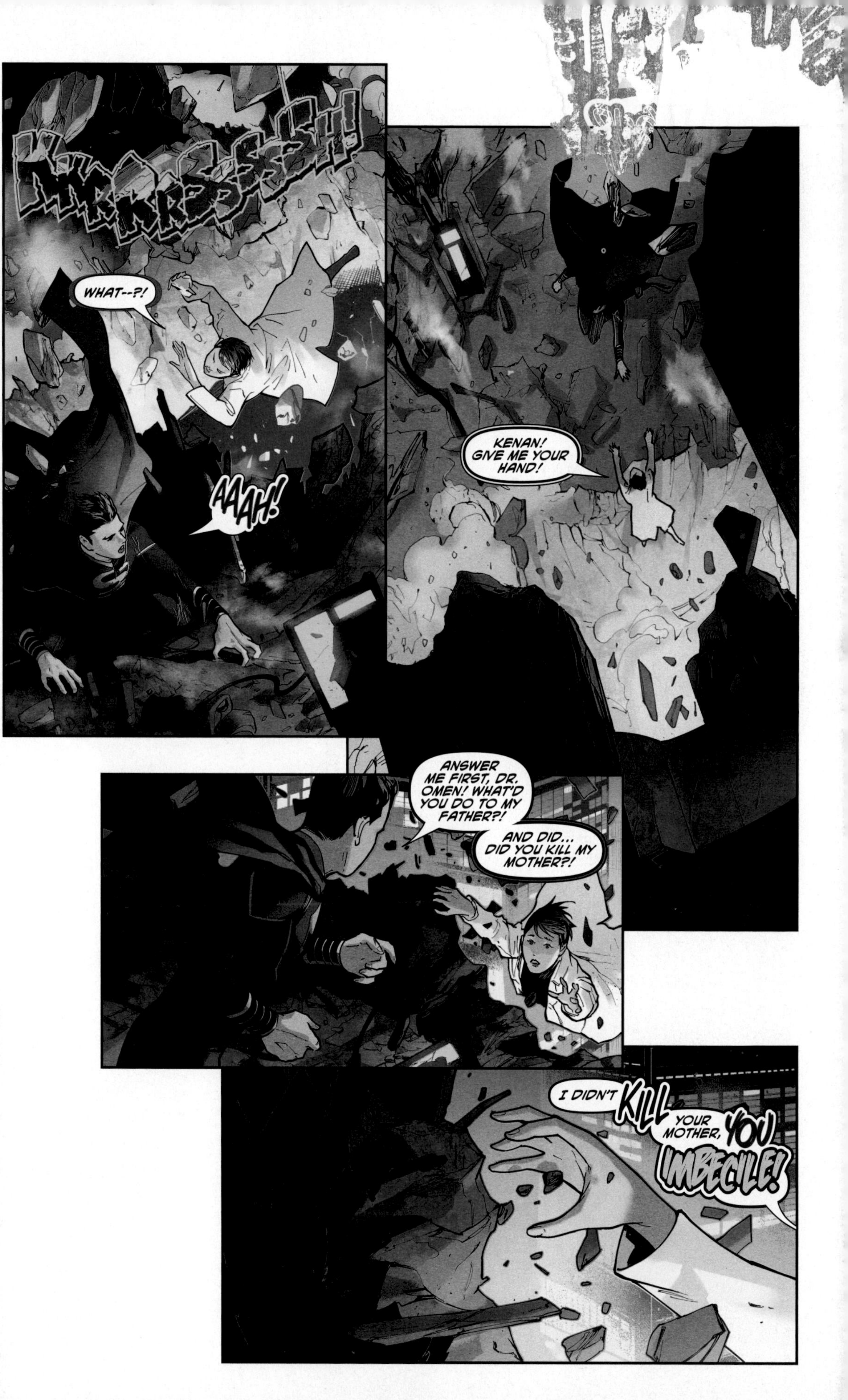
KRRSSSSH!!
WHAT--?!
AAAH!
KENAN! GIVE ME YOUR HAND!
ANSWER ME FIRST, DR. OMEN! WHAT'D YOU DO TO MY FATHER?!
AND DID... DID YOU KILL MY MOTHER?!
I DIDN'T KILL YOUR MOTHER, YOU IMBECILE!

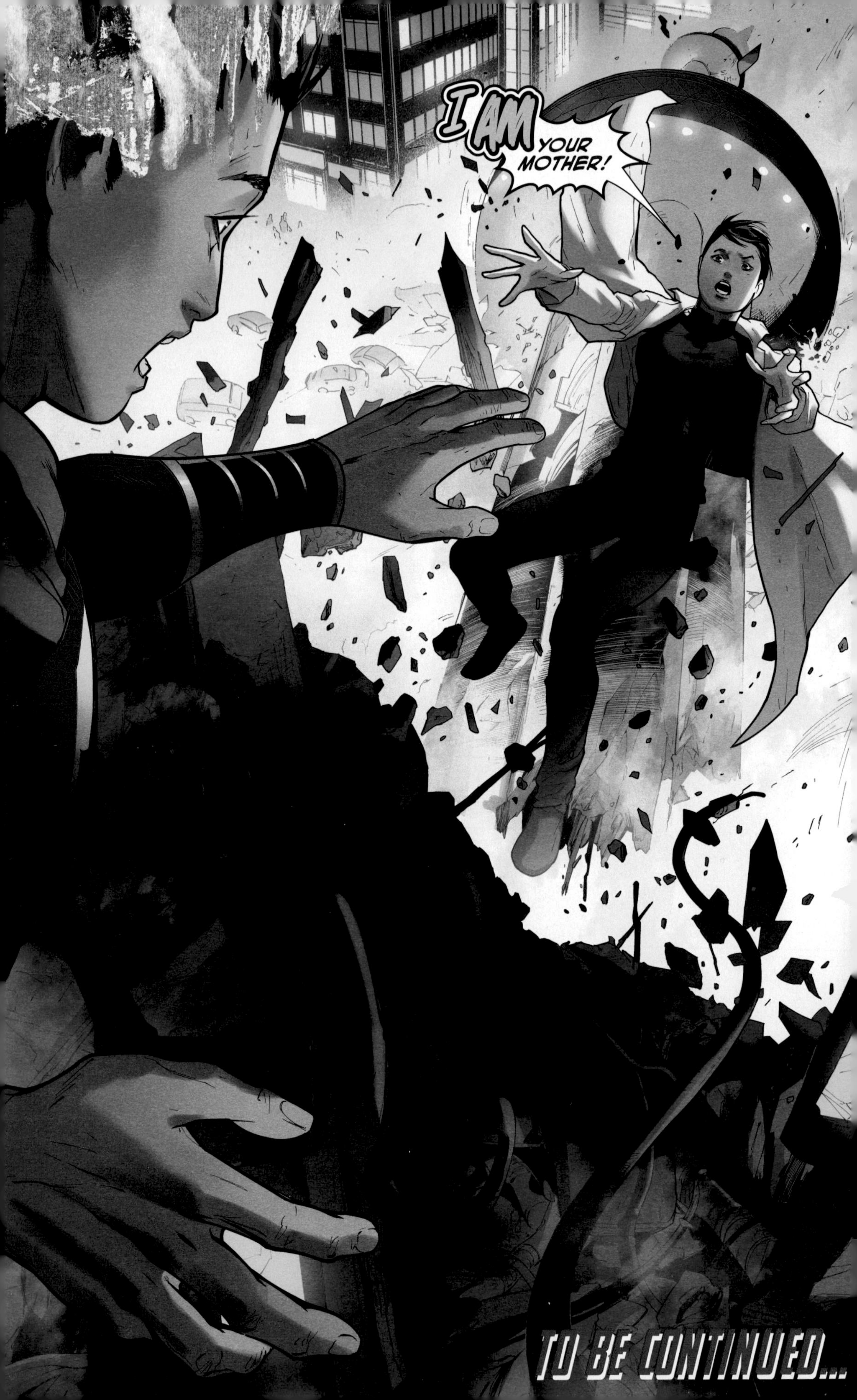
I AM YOUR MOTHER!
TO BE CONTINUED...

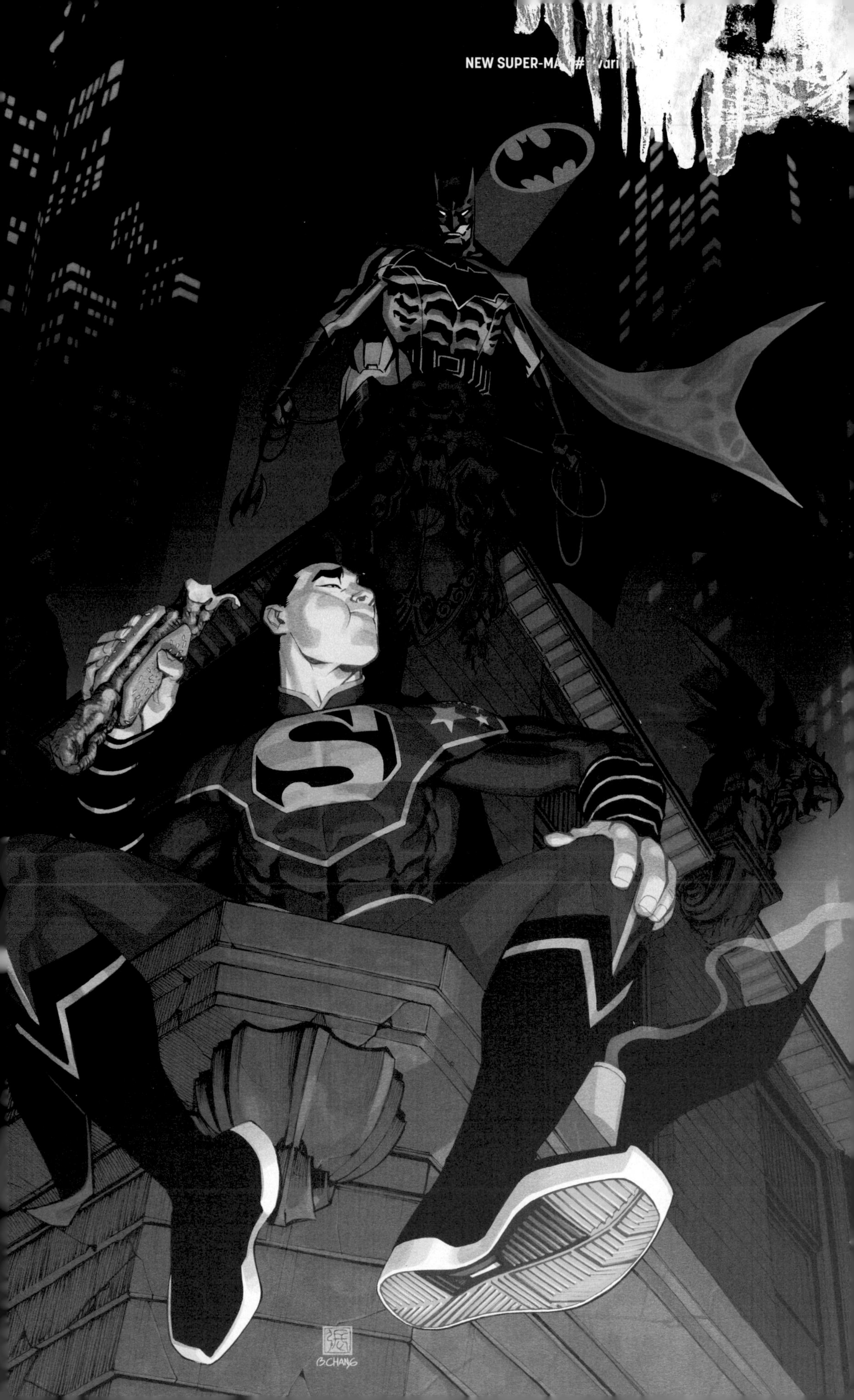
NEW SUPER-MA #   vari
B CHANG

NEW SUPER-MAN #8 variant cover by BERNARD CHANG

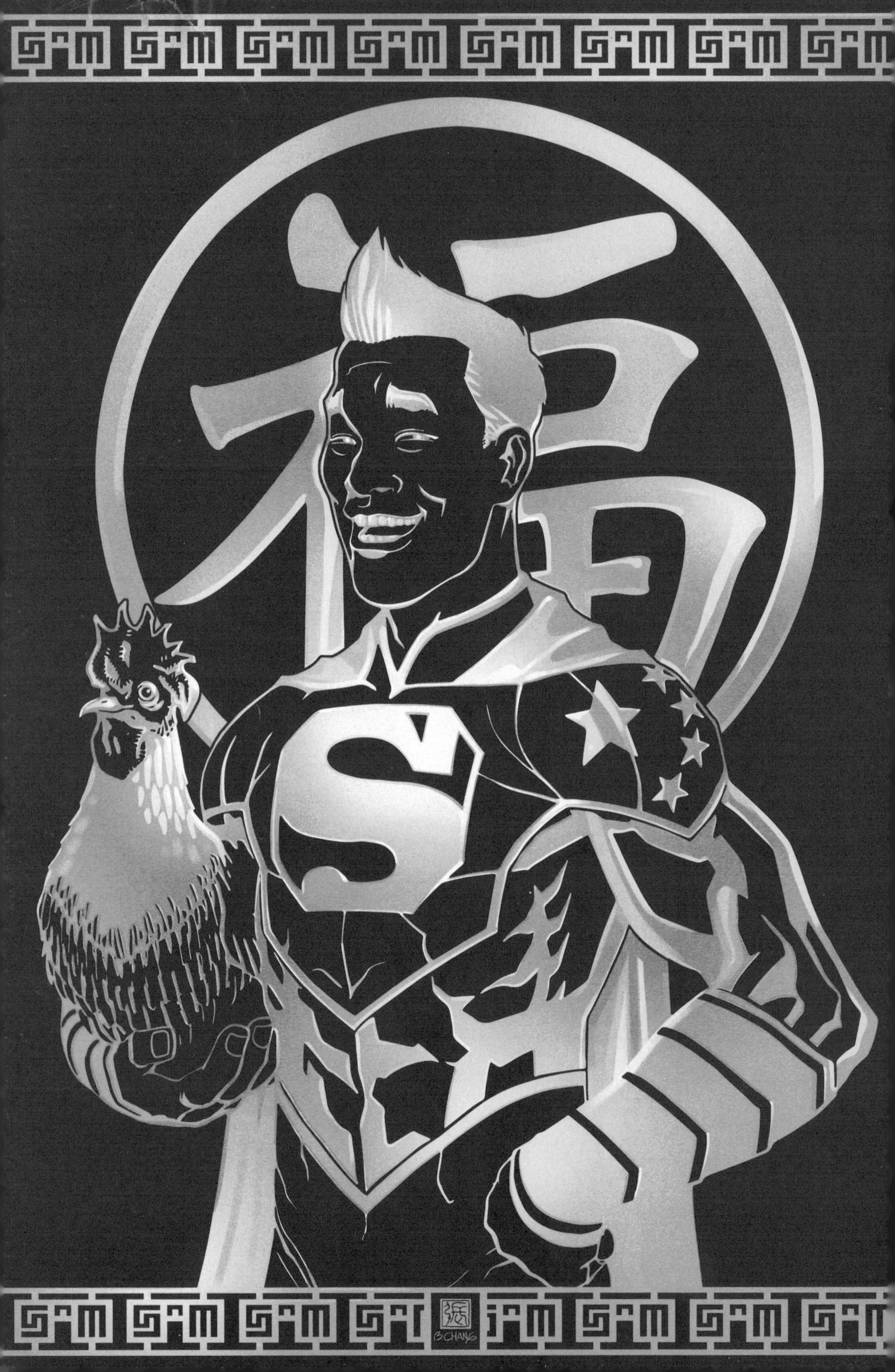
福
B.CHANG

NEW SUPER-MAN #9 variant cover by BERNARD CHANG

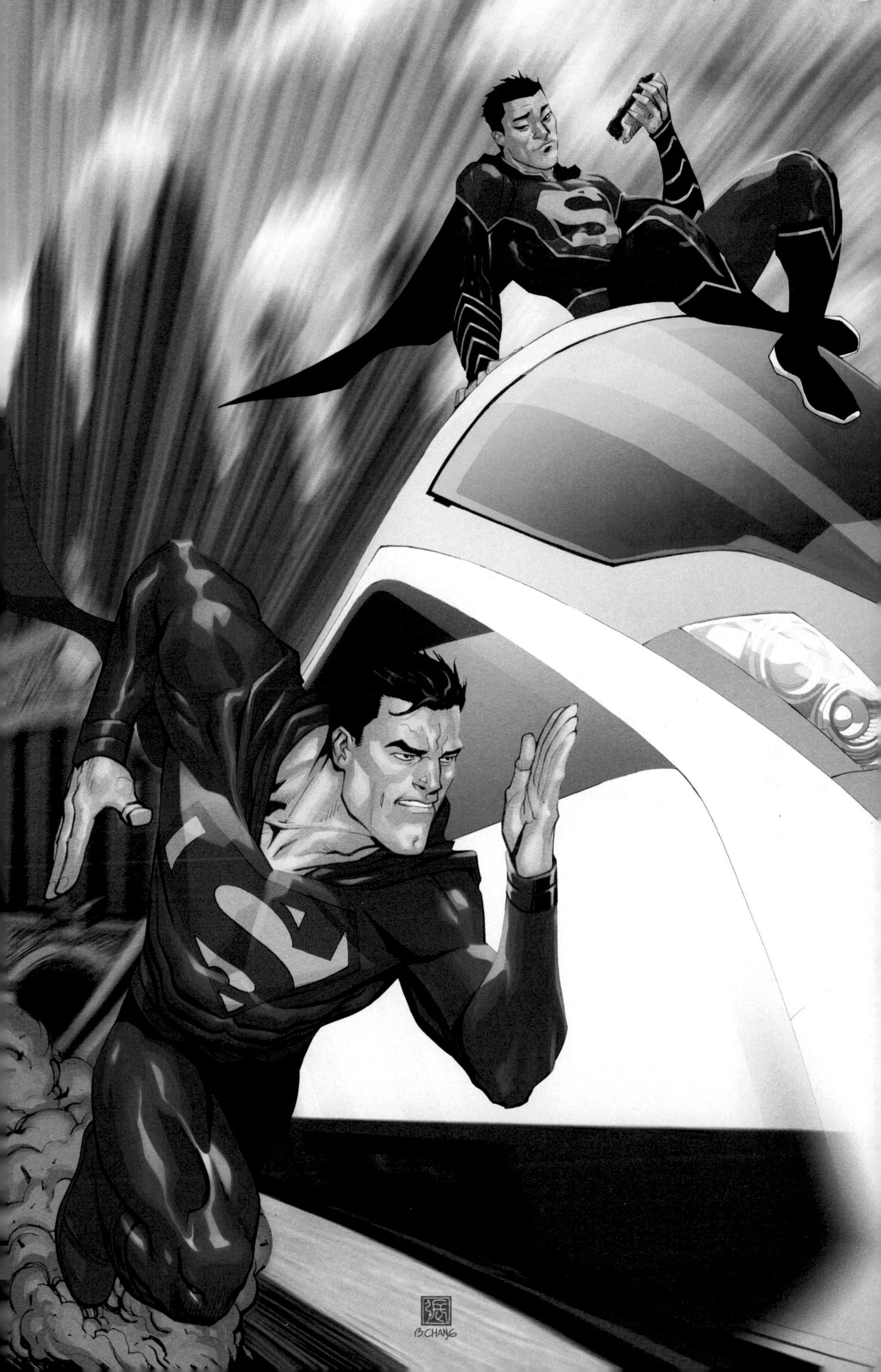
B CHANG

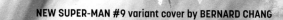

ARD CHANG

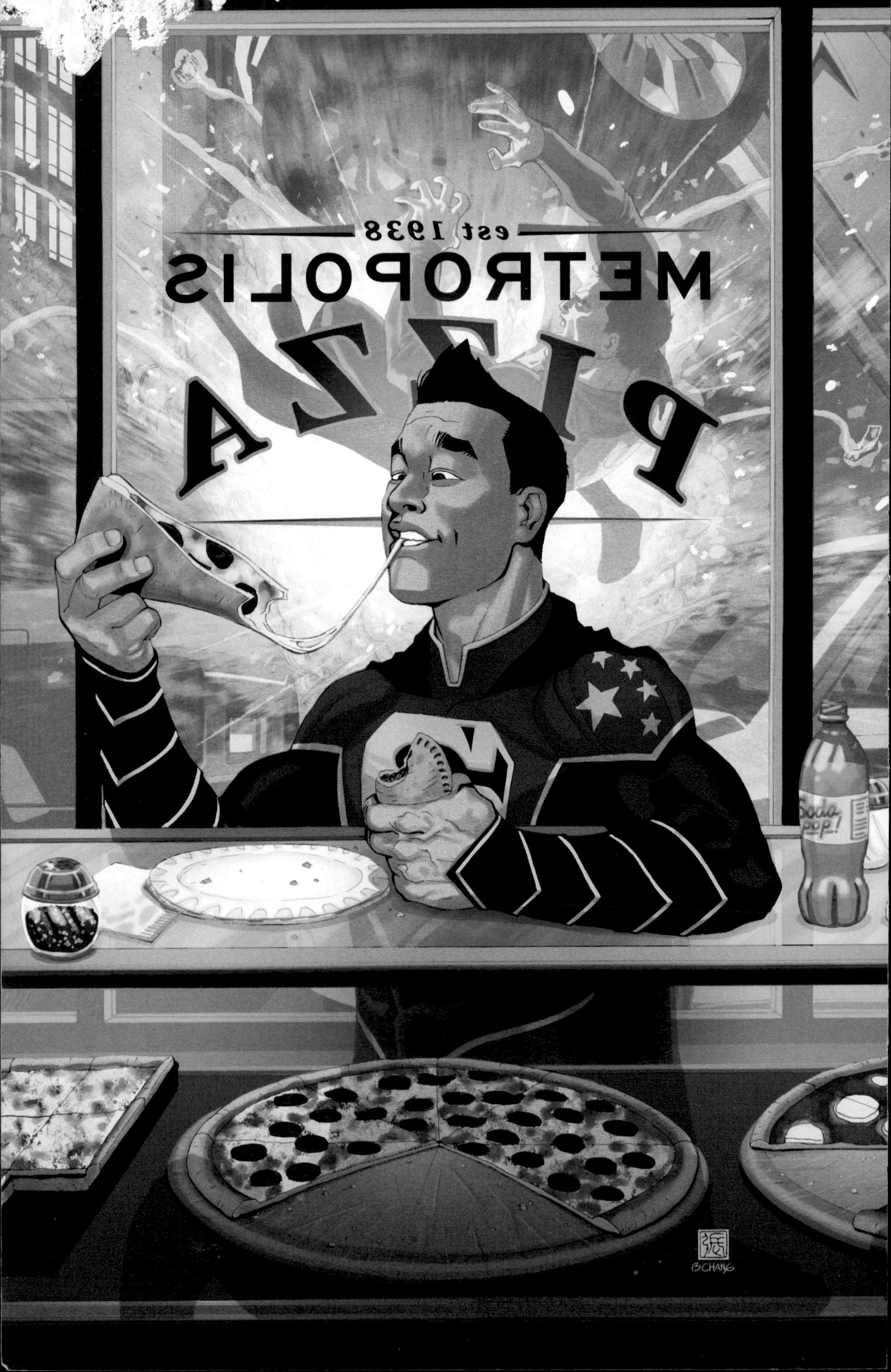

est 1938
METROPOLIS
Soda pop!
BCHANG

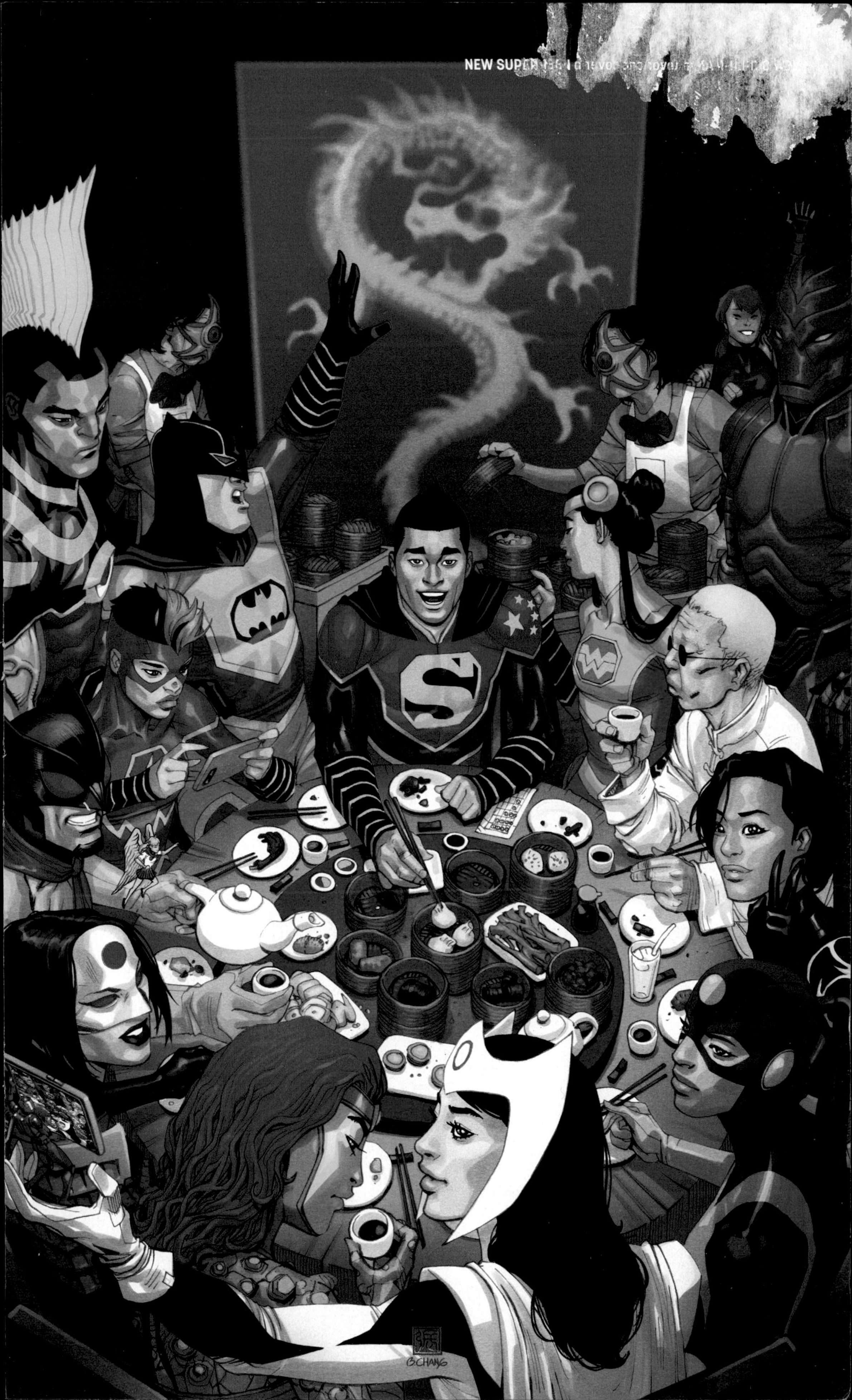
NEW SUPER
B.CHANG

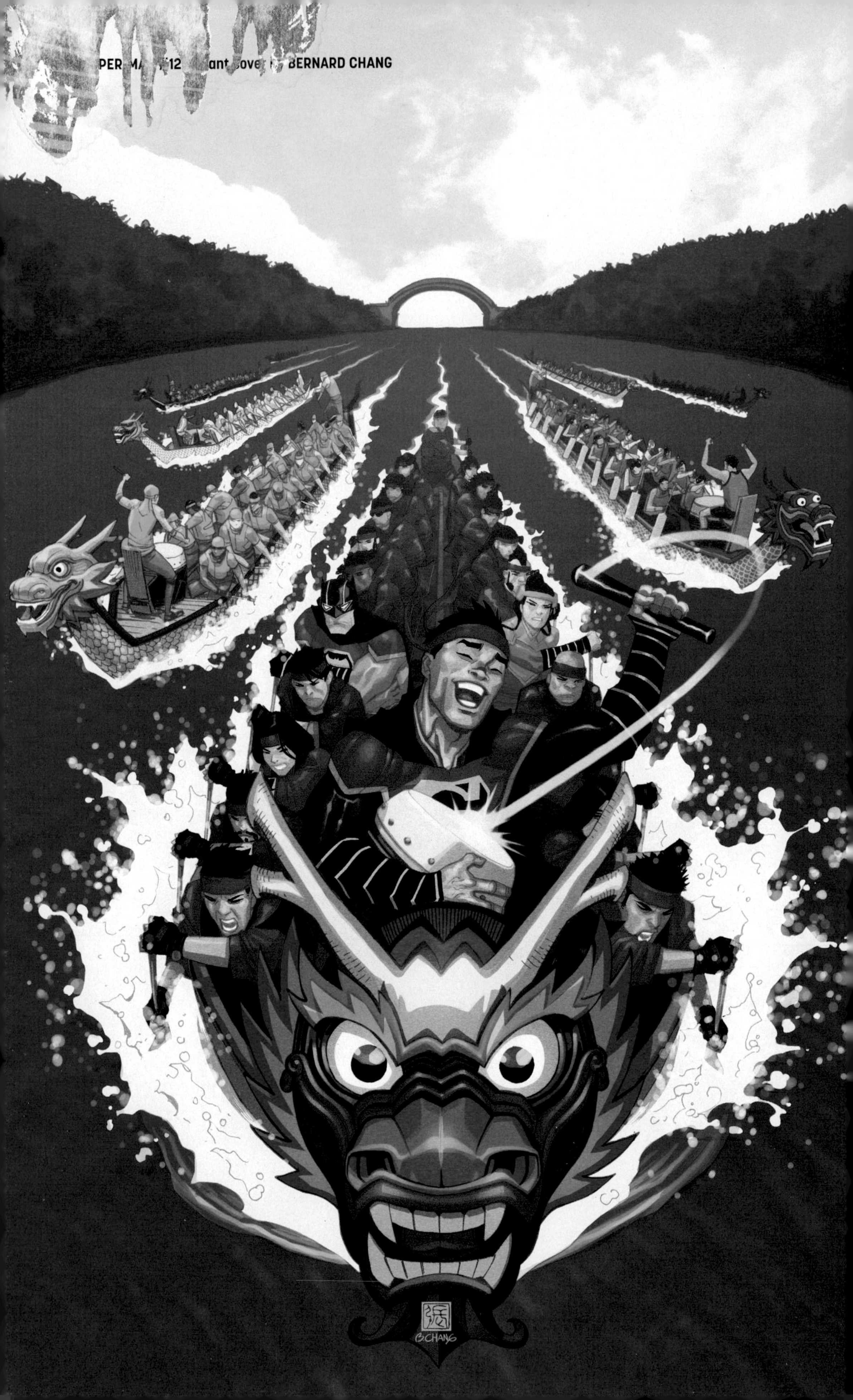
B.CHANG

SUPERMAN #12 variant cover by BERNARD CHANG

CHINESE FLASH CHARACTER DESIGNS
by VIKTOR BOGDANOVIC

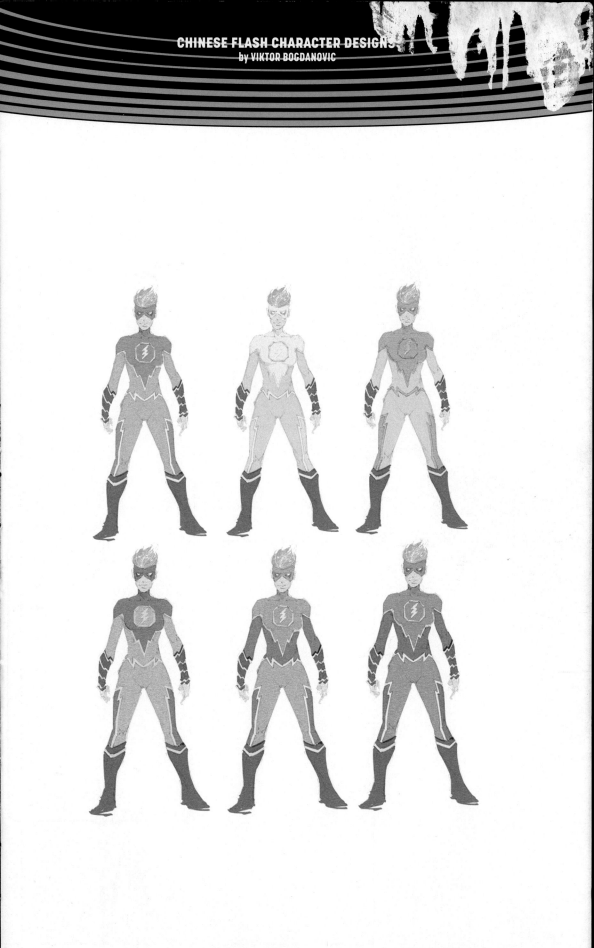

THE ALPACA CHARACTER DESIGNS
by VIKTOR BOGDANOVIC

WONDER-WOMAN HAIR REDESIGN STUDY
by BILLY TAN

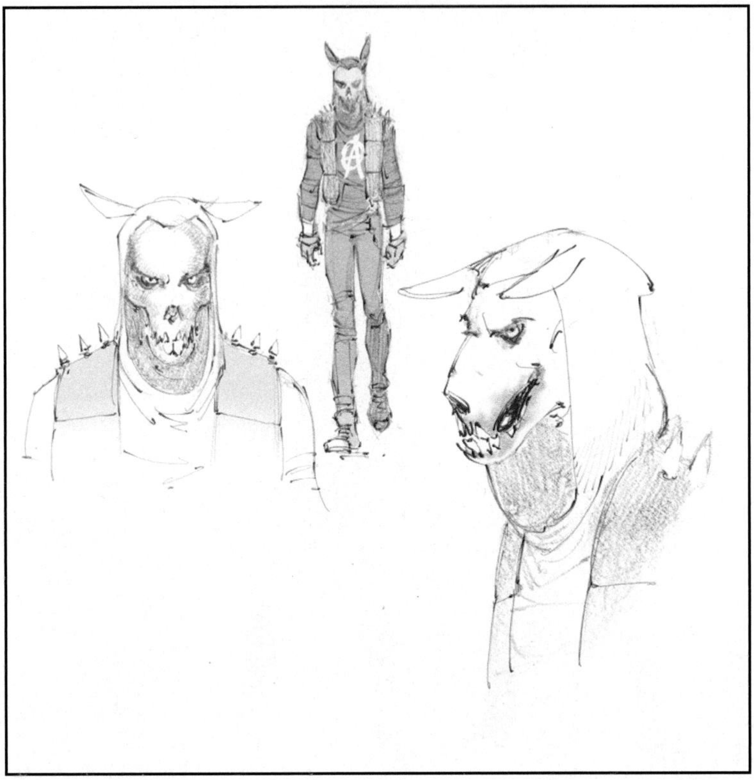

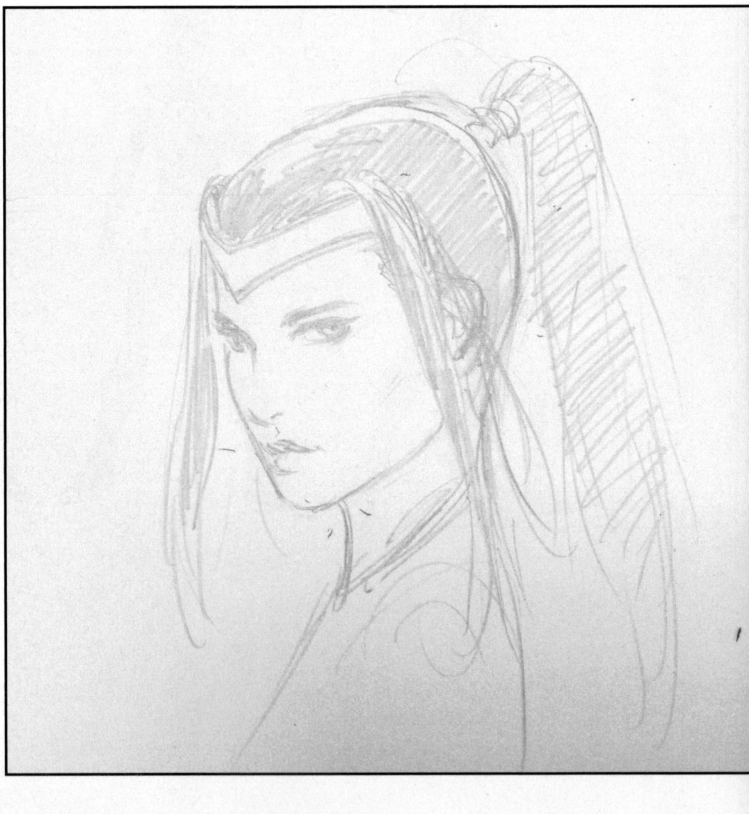